Consciousness and Second Language Learning

SECOND LANGUAGE ACQUISITION

Series Editor: **Professor David Singleton**, *University of Pannonia, Hungary* and Fellow Emeritus, *Trinity College, Dublin, Ireland*

This series brings together titles dealing with a variety of aspects of language acquisition and processing in situations where a language or languages other than the native language is involved. Second language is thus interpreted in its broadest possible sense. The volumes included in the series all offer in their different ways, on the one hand, exposition and discussion of empirical findings and, on the other, some degree of theoretical reflection. In this latter connection, no particular theoretical stance is privileged in the series; nor is any relevant perspective – sociolinguistic, psycholinguistic, neurolinguistic, etc. – deemed out of place. The intended readership of the series includes final-year undergraduates working on second language acquisition projects, postgraduate students involved in second language acquisition research, and researchers and teachers in general whose interests include a second language acquisition component.

Full details of all the books in this series and of all our other publications can be found on http://www.multilingual-matters.com, or by writing to Multilingual Matters, St Nicholas House, 31-34 High Street, Bristol BS1 2AW, UK.

SECOND LANGUAGE ACQUISITION: 83

Consciousness and Second Language Learning

John Truscott

MULTILINGUAL MATTERS
Bristol • Buffalo • Toronto

Library of Congress Cataloging in Publication Data
A catalog record for this book is available from the Library of Congress.
Truscott, John (College teacher)
Consciousness and Second Language Learning/John Truscott.
Second Language Acquisition: 83.
Includes bibliographical references and index.
1. Language acquisition. 2. Language and languages—Study and teaching.
3. Second language acquisition. 4. Psycholinguistics. I. Title.
P118.2.T78 2014
418.0071–dc23 2014021878

British Library Cataloguing in Publication Data
A catalogue entry for this book is available from the British Library.

ISBN-13: 978-1-78309-266-6 (hbk)
ISBN-13: 978-1-78309-265-9 (pbk)

Multilingual Matters
UK: St Nicholas House, 31-34 High Street, Bristol BS1 2AW, UK.
USA: UTP, 2250 Military Road, Tonawanda, NY 14150, USA.
Canada: UTP, 5201 Dufferin Street, North York, Ontario M3H 5T8, Canada.

Website: www.multilingual-matters.com
Twitter: Multi_Ling_Mat
Facebook: https://www.facebook.com/multilingualmatters
Blog: www.channelviewpublications.wordpress.com

Copyright © 2015 John Truscott.

All rights reserved. No part of this work may be reproduced in any form or by any means without permission in writing from the publisher.

The policy of Multilingual Matters/Channel View Publications is to use papers that are natural, renewable and recyclable products, made from wood grown in sustainable forests. In the manufacturing process of our books, and to further support our policy, preference is given to printers that have FSC and PEFC Chain of Custody certification. The FSC and/or PEFC logos will appear on those books where full certification has been granted to the printer concerned.

Typeset by Deanta Global Publishing Services Limited.

Contents

	Acknowledgements	ix
1	Introduction: Setting the Problem	1
	What this Book is About	1
	This Thing Called Consciousness	3
	A Few Preliminaries	9
	Overview of the Book	11

Part 1: Consciousness in Mind: Building a Framework

2	The Mind: Representation and Processing	15
	Perception	16
	Memory and Learning	16
	Emotion	19
	Value	21
	Self	24
	Language	26
	Attention	28
	Modularity	30
	Conclusion	37
3	Theories of Consciousness	38
	Some Early Efforts at a Cognitive Account of Consciousness	38
	Baars' Global Workspace Theory	42
	Dehaene's Global Neuronal Workspace	47
	Cooney and Gazzaniga's Account of Consciousness in Certain Neurological Disorders	48
	Damasio's Body- and Self-oriented Theory	49

	Edelman's Dynamic Core	51
	Tononi's Information Integration Theory	53
	Crick and Koch's Neurobiological Framework	54
	Jackendoff's Intermediate-levels Theory	55
	Baddeley's Working Memory Model	58
	Some Holistic Treatments of Consciousness	59
	Quantum Theories of Consciousness	60
	Towards a Synthesis: Some Common Themes in the Theories	60
	Conclusion	70
4	MOGUL: A Framework for Understanding Consciousness and Learning	71
	MOGUL: Its Nature, Goals and Applications	71
	MOGUL Architecture	72
	MOGUL Processing	83
	Acquisition by Processing Theory (APT)	89
	Conclusion	95
5	Consciousness in the MOGUL Framework	96
	The MOGUL/Activation Account	96
	Informativeness and the Activation Hypothesis	103
	Relations to Some Prominent Theories of Consciousness	111
	Accounting for Some Major Characteristics of Consciousness	118
	Conclusion	125

Part 2: Consciousness in Second Language Learning: Applying the Framework

6	Consciousness in Second Language Learning: A Selective Review	129
	Consciousness and the Language Teaching Tradition(s)	129
	Krashen's Monitor Model	130
	Universal Grammar Approaches	131
	Krashen's Critics	132
	Noticing	142

	Implicit and Explicit Learning	147
	Conclusion	155
7	Perception: Processing Input	156
	Perception: Input and Intake	156
	Consciousness and Perception	159
	The Establishment of New Representations in Perception	168
	Perception and Learning: Implicit, Explicit and Subliminal	181
	Enhancing Input	188
	Conclusion	199
8	Memory Consolidation and Restructuring	201
	Consolidation and Consciousness	202
	Restructuring and Consciousness	218
	Conclusion	229
9	Conclusion: Consciousness in Second Language Learning	231
	Second Language Learning is Primarily an Unconscious Process	232
	Consciously Learned Knowledge can Contribute to Language Use	232
	Conscious Processes Support Unconscious Learning	235
	Some Final Thoughts	238
	References	249
	Author Index	277
	Subject Index	283

Acknowledgements

The writing of this book was supported by a grant (100-2410-H-007-044) from Taiwan's National Science Council. Very different kinds of support came from a variety of other quarters. First, this work is part of a very ambitious ongoing project that I have been carrying out in collaboration with Mike Sharwood Smith for some years. All that is new here is built on the foundation of that collaborative work. Mike was also very helpful in providing feedback on earlier drafts of this book and advice on various aspects of the project. Given its foundations, all those who helped us in previous Modular Online Growth and Use of Language (MOGUL) endeavours have at least indirectly contributed to the work presented here and so deserve thanks as well. For help with materials and grants and the many nuisances that inevitably appear in a project of this sort, many thanks to Pei-yin Chi and Chia-Wen Wu. At Multilingual Matters, Laura Longworth handled the process very professionally and made things relatively easy and pleasant for me. I should also thank National Tsing Hua University (NTHU) and its Center for Teacher Education, as well as a certain dean who led me there, for providing an environment that allowed and encouraged my work and generally made life good. Finally, thanks also to family, colleagues, students, friends and good acquaintances, at NTHU and elsewhere.

1 Introduction: Setting the Problem

What this Book is About

The goal of this book is to explore the place of consciousness in second language (L2) learning. Such an exploration is worthwhile for at least two reasons. First, the subject of consciousness is inherently interesting and important. I would suggest, in fact, that it is the most interesting and most important topic there is, as nothing is more fundamental to human experience than consciousness. It is no exaggeration, to say that consciousness *is* human experience. It would make no sense to talk about what we experience if we were simply unconscious zombies. It would not even make sense to say that we exist at all. Second, issues involving consciousness are of great importance for the field of second language acquisition (SLA), even when they are not recognized as such, because differing ideas about teaching and learning methods are typically based to a very large extent on assumptions about the role of conscious and unconscious processes in learning and in cognition in general.

The goal of exploring consciousness in L2 learning is not a novel one by any means. The topic is in fact quite popular now in SLA. But some of us are profoundly uncomfortable with the way it is being handled. I, for one, have three major concerns. First, this research tends to show insufficient concern with work on consciousness in the source fields, namely cognitive psychology and neuroscience. There is a rich body of research and theoretical development in those fields, but this work has had relatively little impact in SLA, the main exception being the implicit learning literature, which is interesting but has its limitations – limitations that have been imported along with it into SLA (see Chapter 6). Second, SLA work has relied extensively on a very problematic concept: *noticing*. This is a deeply flawed notion (see Chapter 6), but in nearly all the SLA work related to consciousness its validity is uncritically assumed.

The third concern I have about SLA work on consciousness is its reliance on a very debatable assumption about language and its place in the human mind: the assumption that language is nothing very special and so its acquisition is to be explained without appeal to specifically linguistic principles. Language has played a fundamental role in human development, human survival and human success. It spontaneously develops in all people, under a wide assortment of conditions, and has never developed in any member of another species, under any conditions. So it is difficult to escape the conclusion that there is something distinctively natural and distinctively human about language and its development. This conclusion was well expressed by Derek Bickerton, discussing Noam Chomsky's claim that language is innate: 'If what Chomsky said about innate capacities had been said about any species but ours, everyone would have accepted it years ago. The evidence that language is a biologically determined, species-specific, genetically transmitted capacity is simply overwhelming....' (Calvin & Bickerton, 2000: 4).

So, like many others who have looked at this topic, I am profoundly uncomfortable with an approach that assumes that there is nothing special about language, that there is nothing in our evolved nature that got there specifically to make language work. And so I find it difficult to believe that a research programme built on such assumptions is the best way to understand L2 learning or, specifically, the place of consciousness in that learning.

Many have argued that even if language is something special, this specialness does not apply to languages learned after childhood, that learning an L2 at that point is essentially the same process as learning to play chess, for example. The main justification offered for this fundamental divide between first language (L1) and L2 learning is that the latter is typically far less successful than the former. But there is no problem of principle in explaining this difference without assuming that language is special in one case and is not special in the other. In addition to the obvious extraneous differences, such as motivation and learning context, the presence of an entrenched L1 has to be considered a crucial factor in L2 learning, as it inevitably exerts a strong influence on processing of all sorts. This includes the processing of input, which is inseparable from learning, as well as the processing that results in output, which is the usual measure of success and also plays a significant, if smaller role in development.

Of course, saying there is no problem of principle is vastly different from saying there is no problem. Whatever assumptions we make about the specialness of language, the acquisition of an L2 is an immensely complex business, a genuine understanding of which will no doubt require generations of hard work, on the somewhat optimistic assumption that it can really be accomplished at all. The essential point here is that the observed limitations of L2 learning do not indicate, or even weakly suggest, that the specialness of language and its acquisition disappear after childhood. The frequent success of L2 learners in fact suggests the opposite, that the distinctively linguistic processes that guide the acquisition of an L1 remain active in the learning of an L2. This view, I suggest, also represents the most natural and parsimonious assumption *a priori*.

So my exploration of this topic will adopt a rather different perspective from that which is commonly found in discussions of consciousness in L2 learning. Specifically, my assumption will be that knowledge of language, both L1 and L2, is based on a distinct component of the human mind, one that interacts with and shares important features with other components but also has its own distinctive character.

In the following chapters, I will look at the understanding of consciousness that is developing in psychology and neuroscience. This work is quite extensive and often challenging. But I believe that acquiring some grasp of it is a prerequisite for any serious investigation of consciousness in L2 learning, and so I will examine this literature in some depth. A second prerequisite is the adoption of a reasonably clear and explicit view of the cognitive system within which consciousness and L2 learning are to be studied. Any investigation of the place of consciousness inevitably makes assumptions about the nature and functioning of the mind; the more coherent and explicit these assumptions are, the more productive the investigation is likely to be. So in the first half of the book, I will discuss in some depth both the nature of consciousness and the nature of the human mind. These discussions will then serve as background for the exploration of consciousness in L2 learning in the second half of the book.

This Thing Called Consciousness

In a sense, we all know what consciousness is. It is what we have when we are awake, lose when we go to sleep, briefly recover (in an odd sort of way) when we dream and more lastingly recover when we wake up in the morning. But behind this familiar, obvious sort of understanding lie a host of profoundly challenging questions. Why are we aware of one particular thing at this moment instead of the countless other things that we could be aware of? How do we become aware of that one thing? How is the experience of consciousness related to the physical processes of the brain? Can our experience really be the product of electrochemical activity? What exactly does consciousness do for us? Does it really do anything?

For those of us who seriously consider them, such questions can take on great significance and can sometimes arouse great passion – because they are in essence questions of what we are. There is no doubt that we are conscious creatures, in the sense that we are constantly aware of ourselves and our activities (except when asleep, of course). And since the things we directly know about ourselves are exactly the things we are conscious of, it is easy to believe that the conscious me *is* me, that there is nothing else, or that whatever else there is must be relatively minor. If we set aside these intuitions and accept the existence of extensive and important unconscious aspects of 'me', the results can be upsetting – it is easy to feel that we are not the masters of our own minds and bodies, that we are puppets of something we cannot see or control. On the other hand, the idea of an unconscious mind that is wise and powerful can have considerable appeal. It says that

I am much more than I appear to be and maybe I can use this subterranean me to accomplish things that the surface me is not capable of.

Given these natural attitudes toward consciousness and self, it is not surprising that popular discussions often present us with a choice between two relatively simple answers to the question of what we are. One is a common-sense conception in which we are conscious creatures; what we see is what we are. The other holds that an unconscious mind represents our true nature. A natural consequence of the first view is that our decisions and actions should be guided by rational thought; consciousness can be and should be in control. The second prefers to bring consciousness down from this lofty position, suggesting instead that we should go with our intuitions. These two views of consciousness and human nature can be stated, for the sake of argument, in the following rather stark forms.

View 1: We are in essence conscious creatures and should rely on conscious processes in everything we do. Any unconscious aspects of us are unintelligent and unreliable.

View 2: Our conscious selves represent only a limited part of what we are. We have, beneath the surface, a powerful and intelligent unconscious mind that is better equipped than the conscious mind to guide us.

I believe these statements capture, if perhaps in a somewhat exaggerated form, normal untutored ideas about human nature (View 1) and a popular reaction against those ideas (View 2). I will suggest that while each has its roots in genuine features of human nature, each is also flawed in fundamental ways.

However, before critiquing these ideas, I want to reject a common assumption. Discussions of consciousness are commonly framed in terms of contrasts between 'the conscious mind' and 'the unconscious mind'. But these terms are more misleading than helpful, because they turn a complex, fluid reality into a simplistic dichotomy. Many authors have argued, quite reasonably, that each of us has an enormous number of different 'minds' or, more or less equivalently, that we have one mind with a very large number of semi-autonomous components (e.g. Baars, 1988; Gazzaniga, 1985, 2011; Minsky, 1988; Ornstein, 1991; Prince, 1925). This array of minds or mental components does not divide neatly into a conscious mind (or minds) and an unconscious mind (minds). Some components can never be conscious; others are sometimes conscious and sometimes not. Nothing is continually conscious, the sole exception perhaps being the sense of self, which I will consider below. Characterizing these phenomena in terms of two minds, one conscious and the other unconscious, will not help us understand consciousness or human nature.

What's wrong with View 1: Most of what goes on in the mind is unconscious. Unconscious processes are sometimes superior to conscious processes.

Unconscious processes are everywhere. We now know, for example, that an enormous amount of unconscious processing lies behind our conscious perceptual experiences. The most studied case is vision. Light strikes the receptor cells on the retina, which register the presence of light at millions of different points. This primitive display triggers activity in the primary visual area at the back of the brain, which is followed by activity at a number of separate component modules dealing with different aspects of the scene. All of these are then somehow unified to produce a single coherent visual experience. Thus, a very great number of highly sophisticated processes underlie our visual experience. But we are not conscious of any of this rich activity. A similar description could be given for each of the other senses. In each case, the vast majority of what goes on is entirely unconscious. We are conscious only of the outcome of all this activity. And in many cases, we do not even have that much awareness. Subliminal perception, once considered controversial, is now a well-established phenomenon (Greenwald et al., 1995; Kihlstrom, 1996; Merikle et al., 2001).

Language processing is similar. Understanding or producing a typical sentence requires a vast amount of unconscious processing, involving sounds, both as they actually occur and in more abstract forms, plus complex syntactic and morphological processes identifying or establishing the form of the sentence, and of course analysis of meaning. But, again, none of this activity is conscious. And this performance is based on linguistic knowledge that is extremely rich and complex but is also almost entirely unconscious, a point that is nicely demonstrated by the problems that generations of linguists have experienced in determining exactly what this knowledge looks like. The existence of such knowledge also brings out the unconscious nature of language learning: no one seriously believes that three year olds consciously figure out the grammar of their language(s).

We might also ask how a memory gets stored in the brain, and how it is retrieved from memory. What is the capital of Japan? The concept 'Tokyo' is only one of an almost unimaginably large number of concepts that we possess. The process by which this one item is brought up in response to the question has to be quite sophisticated, but we have no awareness of it, nor are we aware of the process by which the information came to be stored. It should be clear as well that skilled performance of all sorts relies very much on the unconscious control of actions: the skilled pianist plays without awareness of individual finger movements; accomplished tennis players hit their strokes without consciously thinking about how to swing the racket or how to place their feet; experienced drivers do not require conscious awareness of the specific hand and foot movements they make. Creativity is another area in which unconscious processes typically play a prominent role, as has been repeatedly shown by reports from the work of artists, scientists and mathematicians (see Hadamard, 1954). To this list of unconscious functions we can add the fine details of muscle control that are essential for ordinary movement, or the processes that maintain our balance or that regulate our body functions.

Research has also identified a great number of more subtle ways in which unconscious processes dominate. There is a wealth of evidence, for example, that our decisions are shaped by factors that we are not aware of (e.g. Bechara *et al.*, 1997; Nisbett & Wilson, 1977; Persaud *et al.*, 2007). Dijksterhuis *et al.* (2006) provided some striking evidence that decisions can be better when they are made without conscious consideration (see also Dijksterhuis & Aarts, 2010; Gigerenzer, 2007; Gilbert, 2005; Lehrer, 2009). In social psychology research, countless examples can be found of unconscious influences on our judgements and actions. One example is Bargh's (1997: 2) finding that dilation of a person's pupils significantly affects how much we like that person. Bargh's review of the literature, including his own very extensive research, led him to the conclusion that 'much of everyday life — thinking, feeling, and doing — is automatic in that it is driven by current features of the environment (i.e., people, objects, behaviors of others, settings, roles, norms, etc.) as mediated by automatic cognitive processing of those features, without any mediation by conscious choice or reflection'. This conclusion does not appear to face any serious opposition now.

There is even extensive evidence that our spontaneous, voluntary actions are initiated by unconscious neural processes before we experience any intention to act (Baumeister *et al.*, 2011; Libet, 1966; Libet *et al.*, 1983; Soon *et al.*, 2008). Wegner (2002) argued at great length against the whole idea of conscious will, maintaining that the feeling of choosing to do an action is something entirely different from the processes that actually produce the action. His claim is a strong one and it might be disputed. But the evidence he presented against conscious will makes it clear that our intuitive ideas are at least in need of some strong qualifications: a substantial gap exists between our actions and our conscious intentions to carry them out.

This is very far from being a complete presentation of the evidence (see also, e.g. Baars, 1988; Baumeister & Masicampo, 2010; Koch, 2012; Lewicki, 1986; Nørretranders, 1998). But the conclusion is inescapable: most of what goes on in our minds is unconscious. And this should not be surprising. In fact, given the limits of consciousness – we can only be aware of one thing at a time – the situation could not possibly be otherwise. There is just far too much going on inside us. If more than a tiny fraction of our mental work had to be done consciously, we simply could not function, and so the great bulk of the work is necessarily done unconsciously. I will explore the implications of this conclusion for L2 learning in later chapters. One preliminary conclusion can be drawn at this point, though: we should not assume that the conscious experiences we have in learning are the essence of the language learning process. We should not assume even that there is any reliable relation between those experiences and the actual process of learning an L2. The issues should be approached without biases of this sort.

What's wrong with View 2: Processes that involve consciousness are very often superior to those that do not.

The second view involves the existence of a superior unconscious mind that we should rely on for guidance. I already rejected the concept of an unconscious mind, but even without such a concept we might still believe that processes which operate without consciousness are superior to those in which awareness is involved, and we might make 'go with your intuitions' a general policy. There is certainly a kernel of truth in the idea of powerful unconscious forces, and it is certainly true that following intuitions is sometimes a good idea. But the limits of unconscious processes must also be recognized, along with the strengths of conscious processes. Research has repeatedly demonstrated an array of unconscious biases and fallacies that we are subject to in our ordinary judgements and decisions. Going with our intuitions makes us easy prey to all these problems; consciously recognizing them and consciously trying to deal with them are the best ways to protect ourselves from them. Here are some examples of these findings (the following discussion owes much to Ariely, 2009; Kahneman, 2011; Lehrer, 2009; Myers, 2002).

Quite generally, our expectations and desires have strong and often irrational effects on our perceptions and judgements, effects that we are usually not aware of. When we hold a questionable belief, we tend to look for evidence that will confirm it and disregard evidence that might tell us it is false. Even when we have clear evidence against a belief, we tend to maintain that belief. When we already know that something happened a certain way, we tend to believe that we could have predicted it in advance (or even that we *did* predict it in advance) when in fact we could not see it coming. When we are in a cool state, we tend to misjudge the way we will act in a more aroused state, believing that we will act more rationally and ethically than we actually will. We tend to see patterns in random events, where no pattern is actually present. We tend to keep our options open even when it is irrationally costly to do so. We tend to overvalue immediate rewards and undervalue delayed rewards. We overreact to unanticipated rewards (in playing slot machines, for instance), leading us to persist in the behaviour that led to them, even when doing so is irrational and destructive. Our responses to questions, as on surveys, are often shaped by subtle features of the way the questions are worded, features of which we may be entirely unaware.

Another downside of a reliance on unconscious processes is the phenomenon of false memory. Research has clearly established that memory is a constructive process (see below), with the construction done primarily unconsciously. A central part of the research findings is that this unconscious construction can result in memories that are distorted or simply false (Loftus, 2005; Frenda *et al.*, 2011). In many cases, the false memories have little or no significance, but in others they can result in inaccurate eyewitness testimony that sends innocent people to prison or in a belief that your parents horribly abused you as a child when in fact nothing of the sort ever occurred. The phenomenon of UFO abduction is interesting in this light. A remarkable number of people appear to have strong, clear memories of being kidnapped by aliens, taken aboard a spaceship and subjected to various unpleasant tests. For most of us, it is extremely difficult to believe that all of these cases (or any of them) are genuine, but there is no doubting the sincerity of vast numbers of people who say they had such experiences, or the emotional impact that these supposed memories have on them. The best way to deal with such a phenomenon is to consciously examine the alleged memories and the contexts in which they were formed in the light of what is known about memory and belief.

Thus, bad things can happen when we trust our intuitions. We can be led by them to any number of false beliefs and counterproductive actions. We can be unknowingly manipulated – by advertisers, by politicians, by people we know and by ourselves. Avoiding or minimizing such problems requires conscious, deliberate evaluation.

This evaluative function is one of the strengths of conscious processes. Another is their role in troubleshooting, a function that has been repeatedly noted by theorists. There is also clear value in consciously planning activities, monitoring progress and evaluating results. Consciousness is also closely associated with novel situations; while familiar tasks can often be handled effectively without awareness, when surprises occur there is often little prospect of success without the involvement of consciousness. Creative thinking uses unconscious processes, as noted above, but they are fed by conscious attention to the problem and to possible solutions, and their output must be evaluated by conscious processes; without this conscious element, creativity is unlikely. In dealing with input from the senses, conscious processing is much more rich and complete than processing that occurs without awareness. Research has demonstrated that subliminal perception is genuine, but there are strong limits on what can be done with the information that is perceived in this way.

Perhaps most interestingly, consciousness has been associated with learning in general. This relation is far from straightforward. Many complexities arise and many arcane debates occur regarding the details. These points will be major concerns throughout this book. But for now the important point is that a strong relation exists between learning and consciousness, which must be carefully explored.

So where does this leave us? First, it leaves us with two partially valid but deeply flawed views of consciousness and human nature. A more viable view would have to recognize the importance of both conscious and unconscious processes, clarify their respective roles and provide a means to judge when a reliance on intuition is or is not appropriate. I will make only limited attempts to address these very large issues in any general way, considering them only to the extent required by my more humble but still quite ambitious purpose: to explore the issues specifically as they apply to L2 learning. The two views of consciousness and human nature can both be found in this area, each pointing to its own distinctive approach to teaching and learning. Much of the history of the field can in fact be characterized in terms of the conflict between them. It will become clear in Part 2 of this book that in the context of L2 learning my sympathies are more with the second view, emphasizing the value of unconscious processes and the limits of conscious processes. However, it will also be clear that conscious processes must be given their due and, even more importantly, that the whole subject is greatly in need of clarification.

To even begin to understand the place of consciousness in L2 learning, we first have to establish a clearer notion of what consciousness is all about. This will necessarily mean asking how it fits into the cognitive system, i.e. the mind, as a whole. This in turn will mean adopting a framework that will constitute an understanding, however provisional, of the mind. The provisional nature of our current explanations should be emphasized. We do not yet have any conclusive account of consciousness or of the mind. But we do have a great deal of relevant knowledge, and the ability to put together coherent frameworks that are reasonably consistent with what is known. Without such a framework, efforts to understand the place of consciousness in the mind and in L2 learning in particular are not likely to amount to much. With a tentative view of the mind and the place of consciousness in it, we can return to the primary question of how it relates to L2 learning, with some hope of obtaining at least provisional answers.

A Few Preliminaries

The word 'consciousness' has been used in many ways. I will use it in its most basic sense, the phenomenal: we are conscious when we are awake but not when we are asleep, except during dreaming. This is also the sense that is commonly assumed in cognitive and neural research, which I take as the foundation for my proposals. The word 'awareness', which has a similar array of uses, will be used here as a synonym of 'consciousness'. The phrase 'conscious awareness' is thus redundant but sometimes has value for the added stress it puts on the subjective experience of the individual.

Hill (2009) described four additional senses of 'consciousness' (along with a variant of his own which I will not consider), reflecting both the philosophy literature and ordinary-language usage. *Agent consciousness* is found in the ideas of gaining and losing consciousness. *Relational consciousness* and *propositional consciousness* are awareness *of* something and awareness *that* something, respectively. *Introspective consciousness* is captured in the sentence 'His affection for me is fully conscious, but his hostility is not'; it seems to crucially involve the potential for phenomenal awareness. To these senses we might add some uses of 'consciousness' based on social and cultural concerns that are distant from the topic of this book. The term also takes on varying meanings in the context of L2 learning, which I will consider in Chapter 6, again taking the phenomenal as basic.

The approach I will take to consciousness and its place in L2 learning is primarily cognitive. In other words, I am concerned with the nature of the mind and will rely, in a broad sense, on the computer metaphor. The mind receives input via the senses. It processes information, including both input and internally generated information. It stores the information, regardless of its source, as mental representations. And it produces output. This system, its origins in particular, is to be understood within the context of natural selection: the system developed as it did because this development served the interests of survival and reproduction. For any effort to obtain a scientific understanding of consciousness and the mind, this assumption is inescapable. We can disagree on the details, but there is no escaping the conclusion that the brain, and therefore the mind, is to a large extent a product of natural selection.

Given this biological orientation, neural research naturally has a place, an important place, in an account of consciousness. Research on the brain has become chic in recent years – and for good reason. Researchers have impressive new tools, large amounts of money are going into their use, and intriguing findings are emerging from this use. In addition to this, it is easy to feel that what we find out about the brain is 'real' in a sense that psychological research might not be. This positive view of neural research is not entirely misguided (see Marcus, 2013, for interesting discussion). But it would be a mistake to see this work as an alternative to cognitive research and theory. There is no contradiction in trying to explain consciousness in both neural and cognitive terms. In fact, it is difficult to imagine any satisfactory account that does not do both. The brain and its activity are the inescapable facts underlying cognition and experience, and they must have a prominent place in any adequate theory. But patterns of electrochemical activity cannot in themselves provide a satisfying account of *us*. We also need to speak of beliefs and feelings and goals and experiences and self and all the other things that we are. In other words, we need two (or more) levels of explanation, and, of course, we have to understand how the two relate to each other.

This point, that multiple levels of explanation are possible and necessary, has been made by a number of authors. Thagard (2006) offered an especially good version of the argument. The book by Shallice and Cooper (2011) is to a large extent a detailed presentation of the position that we need both neural concepts and cognitive concepts if we are to understand the mind/brain. Similarly, Gallistel and King (2009) set out in their book to show that cognitive, computer-based concepts are essential for neuroscience. A great many similar arguments can be found.

The idea of 'representation', which I will use throughout this book, illustrates the point. The concept is appropriate, and probably essential, at the mental level. But at the neural level, its meaning, or meaningfulness, is far from clear. The brain obviously does not literally contain pictures or logical formulas or anything of the sort. Nor does it literally contain knowledge or beliefs or goals or feelings. But it is difficult to see how we can ever understand ourselves without these concepts, or suitable replacements at the mental level. Consideration of the ways that knowledge is represented in our heads is essential for such an understanding, regardless of whether the notion of representation makes sense at the neural level. Mental concepts should be compatible with what is known about the brain, but we should not expect to have a neat translation of mental terms into neural terms, and there is no need for such a translation.

Overview of the Book

The book is divided into two parts. Part 1 develops a framework within which questions about consciousness in L2 learning can be productively addressed. The background information presented here is quite extensive, because the very complex issue of consciousness in L2 learning cannot be adequately addressed without a fairly detailed consideration of both the nature of consciousness and the cognitive context in which it appears. Chapter 2 offers an overview of fundamental aspects of the human mind. Chapter 3 will review a number of past and current efforts to understand consciousness from a cognitive and/or neural perspective and will consider what can be learned from the various theories. In Chapter 4, I introduce the general cognitive framework that will be used throughout the book: Modular Online Growth and Use of Language (MOGUL). Chapter 5 will then develop the place of consciousness within that framework. The remainder of the book, Part 2, addresses SLA and the place of consciousness in it. Chapter 6 critically reviews the ideas on the role of consciousness that have so far characterized the field of SLA. Chapter 7 focuses on the processing of input, specifically awareness of input and the relation between that awareness and successful learning. Chapter 8 looks at what happens after the input is processed, i.e. at the way that memories are established, strengthened and altered. Chapter 9 puts the pieces together to form general conclusions about the place of consciousness in L2 learning and offers some final thoughts on the subject.

Part 1

Consciousness in Mind: Building a Framework

2 The Mind: Representation and Processing

Consciousness must be understood in the context of a coherent picture of the mind, which is a very large project in itself. Jackendoff (1996) noted that a prominent philosopher had questioned whether his book, *Consciousness and the Computational Mind* (Jackendoff, 1987), was really about consciousness, because the subject was not mentioned until Chapter 14, all the previous chapters being devoted to the development of a cognitive architecture within which consciousness was to be examined. The ground laying here will not be nearly so extensive, because much of it has been done elsewhere. But it will be extensive.

For this cognitive background, the view I want to suggest is that the mind consists of representations and processors that manipulate those representations. Manipulate here means establishing new, and possibly lasting, representations by combining existing ones, as well as establishing relations among existing representations of different types, such as the concept of an apple and the visual image of an apple. This is information processing.

The information in 'information processing' requires some clarification, though. The biological perspective, in particular, points to the limits of the idea. Organisms do not seek generic information, but rather information that means something to them, information that has value for them (see Freeman, 2003). Once obtained, it is stored in terms of this value. In other words, representations are *valued*, in the sense that each is marked with an indication of its significance, positive or negative. This addition of value to the picture is not a weakening of the simple processor-representation view of the mind, as value itself can be and should be seen as a representation, not differing from others at the most fundamental level. To say that a representation has a certain value is to say that it is linked to a value representation.

I suggest then that we should seek to understand all cognition as simply this: processors manipulating representations. In the remainder of this chapter, I will offer a sketch of the human mind and its workings along these lines, focusing on aspects that will be especially important for an understanding of consciousness and second language (L2) learning. This sketch will then be further developed in Chapter 4.

Perception

Perception is constructing representations for input from the senses. From another perspective, it is deciding what the senses are experiencing at the time, meaning both what each modality (sense) is experiencing and how information from the various modalities fits together. In the context of language acquisition, perception amounts to the processing of input (or the *construction* of input – see below), clearly an essential aspect of acquisition.

Information from the various senses is of course processed by distinct systems. There is some degree of interaction (how much interaction and of what sort remains an unsettled question), but distinct systems clearly exist for each modality. This description can be extended to processing within a modality – it also consists of a set of distinct though interacting subsystems. In the words of Mather (2011: 52): 'Functional specialization is a key feature at all levels of every sensory system'. The most studied and best understood example is the visual system, in which a substantial number of components have been identified with a reasonable degree of confidence. The work of the various components has to be brought together of course. The colour, shape and motion of an object, for example, are not experienced separately but are integrated into a single experience. Similarly, all the information from the various senses must be brought together. The sight of a dog, its bark, its smell and the feel of its fur are not separate experiences for us but rather a unified whole. So the output of the various modalities somehow becomes unified. I will consider the question of how this occurs in subsequent chapters.

The *constructive* character of the process should be emphasized in any discussion of perception. The representations that are the products of perception are by no means simple copies of the external world. They are constructions resulting from a number of extremely complex multistage processes. The input that is used in learning, of an L2 or of anything else, thus consists not of what is objectively present in the world but rather of the ultimate output of the perceptual processes. If we are to understand learning, that understanding must be in terms of these 'perceptual output representations'.

Memory and Learning

Memory is about representation, i.e. it is the information side of information processing. Our memories have various components and take various forms, including at least the perceptual, the conceptual, the affective and the linguistic; and some or all of these can be broken down into subtypes. An adequate understanding of memory must take all of them into account.

To understand memory, it is essential to recognize that there is no single system or location that is memory. This point has been made especially in regard to the organization of the brain. Memories are found in many locations, reflecting the character of the particular memory (see Fuster, 2009; Gottfried *et al.*, 2004; Jonides *et al.*, 2008; Just *et al.*, 2010; Martin, 2007; Martin & Chao, 2001; McClelland & Rogers, 2003; Rissman & Wagner, 2012). Visual features of a memory are found in visual areas, auditory features in auditory areas, action features in motor areas and so on. Such findings have even been extended to associations of 'run' with brain areas involved in processing biological motion and of 'eat' with areas that appear to process taste (Mitchell *et al.*, 2008). LeDoux (2002), noting that memory is found all through the many systems that make up the brain, concluded that it is best seen simply as changes in those systems, changes that allow them to become better at their functions as a result of experience. This is long-term memory (LTM).

The functional split in the types of memory extends to short-term memory (STM) as well. STM is commonly seen now as an active, functioning memory, and so the term *working memory* (WM) is now popular. The idea of WM, as it is currently understood, was proposed by Baddeley and Hitch (1974) and has since been extensively developed and tested (see Baddeley, 1986, 2000, 2007, 2012). The leading idea is that appropriate information must be made temporarily available to cognitive processes, as it is needed. In the original formulation, WM was divided into phonological and visuospatial components plus a central executive managing their functions, but Baddeley (2000) subsequently added an *episodic buffer*, which puts together information from various sources.

In more recent applications, a great many varieties of WM have been assumed, particularly in neural work, where we commonly see reference to *somatosensory* WM (Haegens *et al.*, 2010), *tactile* WM (Hannula *et al.*, 2010; Harris *et al.*, 2001; Savolainen *et al.*, 2011), *gustatory* WM (Lara *et al.*, 2009), *olfactory* WM (Dade *et al.*, 2001; T. White, 1998) and *visual* WM (e.g. Hyun *et al.*, 2009; Pasternak & Greenlee, 2005), in addition to the *auditory* component realized in Baddeley's phonological loop. What this suggests is what was no doubt the most plausible conclusion *a priori*, that a distinct WM exists for each sensory modality. The visuospatial and the phonological (acoustic) components have enjoyed a privileged status not because they are in any way unique, but because they are considered especially interesting and important in humans.

But the fragmentation of WM appears to go well beyond sensory modalities. Baddeley has long held that his visuospatial component contains distinct visual and spatial subcomponents, and in research practice this separation has occurred, with frequent reference being made to *spatial* WM as a component in itself (Courtney *et al.*, 1998; Ricciardi *et al.*, 2006). In the research literature, we also find *motor* WM (Grossberg & Pearson, 2008; Tong *et al.*, 2002; Wigmore *et al.*, 2002), *emotional/affective* WM (Davidson & Irwin, 1999; Mikels *et al.*, 2008) and *musical* or *pitch* WM (Peretz & Zatorre,

2005). For each of these (and probably more), there is reason to believe that a distinct WM exists. A reasonable hypothesis is that every major component of the mind has its own WM. This is probably what should be expected, given that the function of WM is to provide necessary information to cognitive processes: distinct cognitive systems require distinct types of information.

Another important issue for WM is the nature of its relation to LTM. The traditional view is that WM is a special store (or stores), a location in the mind/brain where things are temporarily placed while they are being used. An alternative view that has become quite popular sees this as a metaphor; a more accurate characterization of WM is that it is simply the set of LTM items (representations) that are currently active (Cowan, 1993, 2001, 2005; Fuster, 2008; Miyake & Shah, 1999; Nairne, 2002; Ruchkin et al., 2003; see Norman, 1968, for an early version of the idea).

Putting the findings about LTM together with these two points – the extensive fragmentation of WM and its status as activated LTM items – we obtain a natural conclusion about the nature of memory. The representations that constitute memory are found in various locations in the brain, reflecting the function of those locations. Activation of the memory in one of them is local WM. Coactivation of related representations in different WMs allows them to be bound together as a single memory.

This process of coactivating and binding together the various components of a memory is a major research topic, called *memory (re)consolidation* (Hardt et al., 2010; Hupbach et al., 2007; Walker & Stickgold, 2006). When a representation is activated, it becomes somewhat stronger as a result. When a set of representations is activated together as a unit, they become more strongly tied together. But activation of one representation or a set of representations does not normally occur in isolation from activation of others. Whenever two related representations are active at the same time, the possibility exists of them influencing and altering each other, or of one being incorporated into the other. This phenomenon can be called *restructuring*. In its typical, positive form, it serves the essential function of integrating new information with old. In its more negative form, it can alter memories in ways that they should not be altered. This is the well-studied phenomenon of false memory (e.g. Frenda et al., 2011; Loftus, 1997, 2005; Roediger & McDermott, 1995; for a discussion in the context of neural reconsolidation, see Hupbach et al., 2007).

From a system-internal perspective, this is learning. Processing of input leads to the creation of new memories (representations) in the appropriate locations in the brain. Repeated coactivation of the various representations that are the components of the new memory will strengthen these representations and the connections among them. Activation of other representations, possibly of new input, can alter these existing representations, hopefully in desired ways.

Of course, this is a very focused view of learning. A fuller treatment requires attention to a number of other internal and external factors, and I will consider these factors below. But this brief, focused treatment does establish the basic framework that is needed for a cognitive understanding of learning. This has also been a focused account of memory. Researchers have proposed a number of interesting distinctions among types of memory, including semantic vs. episodic (including autobiographical), declarative vs. procedural and implicit vs. explicit. I will consider these sometimes controversial distinctions later on, particularly the implicit–explicit distinction, but I will not go into them in any detail at this point.

Emotion

Emotion and cognition were traditionally treated as separate domains, making emotion a questionable or at least peripheral area of research for cognitively oriented researchers. But this separation has gradually yielded in recent years to an increasing recognition that the two cannot be so easily separated and that a cognitive theory that does not incorporate emotion can never be satisfactory. And so there is an increasing tendency to integrate the two (e.g. Barrett *et al.*, 2005; Evans & Cruse, 2004; Izard, 2009; Lane & Nadel, 2000; Moore & Oaksford, 2002; Phelps, 2006; Storbeck & Clore, 2007). The importance of emotion in conscious experience is also clear, simply from everyone's ordinary experience. One case which demands integration of the emotional and the cognitive is L2 learning. Learners' feelings towards the language and the process of learning it are an integral part of how they learn and how well they learn.

Emotions are best understood as biological adaptations (see Damasio, 1994, 1999, 2003, 2010; Evans, 2001; Evans & Cruse, 2004; LeDoux, 1996; Lundqvist & Öhman, 2005; Seager, 2002; Tooby & Cosmides, 1992; Turner, 2000). They have been called states of 'action readiness' by Frijda (1986, 1988/1998), and similar descriptions appear throughout the literature (see especially Panksepp, 2003a, 2005). Disgust keeps us from eating things that are likely to be harmful. Fear saves us from dangers by encouraging us to flee, hide or freeze. Anger encourages strong action against someone or something blocking the achievement of our goals. Happiness serves as a goal encouraging us to try to achieve or sustain a positive situation. (Fredrickson [1998] suggests additional possible benefits of happiness.) Sadness has the complementary function of leading us to try to avoid negative situations and to abandon efforts that are failing.

Emotion in the brain is associated with what has traditionally been called the limbic system, located beneath the cortex, though some cortical areas are now commonly considered part of the system. The concept of the limbic system, at least as it was originally formulated (MacLean, 1949, 1952, 1990), does not receive a great deal of respect anymore (see

Calder et al., 2001; Lawrence & Calder, 2004; LeDoux, 1996; Reiner, 1990), because it implies a much neater organization of emotional systems than actually exists. But the term is still frequently used to refer to brain regions associated with emotion. Regarding emotion and memory, neural research suggests an interesting parallel with findings described in the previous section: brain activity associated with the emotional aspects of a memory is found in the same locations in which it was originally found during the experience that is being remembered (Buchanan, 2007; Kosslyn et al., 2001). Thus, the intimate association between perception and memory (learning) can probably be extended to include emotion.

A common, if not universally accepted way of analyzing emotions divides them into basic and secondary (or social) emotions (see Demoulin et al., 2004; Evans, 2001; LeDoux, 1996; Power & Dalgleish, 1997; for a critical view see Ortony et al., 1988). The facts are complex and the criteria used for the classification have varied considerably, so it is perhaps unsurprising that the proposed set of basic emotions varies with the person who is proposing it, but there is a considerable amount of agreement nonetheless. The best candidates for the status of basic emotions are fear, disgust, anger, happiness (or joy) and sadness, and maybe surprise. Secondary emotions, including for example pride, awe and jealousy, are sometimes analyzed as combinations of basic emotions (see especially Plutchik, 1970, 1980; also Du et al., 2014), though we can question how far such an analysis can be taken without bringing in additional factors. Basic emotions are also applied to social situations beyond their original function. Disgust at another person's behaviour does not save us from ingesting toxic substances. Fear of failing a test or of being criticized is far removed from the basic survival function of fear. In each case, the primeval survival mechanisms have been co-opted for more sophisticated social purposes.

Bodily arousal is clearly a prominent feature of emotion. But the body, minus the brain, does not distinguish different emotions, since it takes a brain to decide if a situation is cause for flight or attack or investigation or just contentment. This more cognitive process of identifying the emotion that is appropriate in a given situation has been referred to as *cognitive appraisal, stimulus appraisal* or *evaluation* (see Frijda, 1986, 1988/1998; Lazarus, 1991/1998; Oatley, 2004; Ortony et al., 1988; Schachter & Singer, 1962; Scherer et al., 2006). The brain has two appraisal circuits. The older one, starring the amygdala, is very basic and very fast. Its influence appears when we quickly, unthinkingly react to something that gives an immediate appearance of danger, real or otherwise. The newer circuit includes the cortex. It provides a more informed, reasoned assessment of the situation, which has the downside of requiring more time. In both cases, though, the appraisal is, by intuitive standards, quite fast and primarily unconscious. Conscious feeling is in fact the tip of the iceberg – a finished product of extensive processing that occurs largely unconsciously (see especially LeDoux,

1996). Partly for this reason, researchers commonly distinguish between emotion – the biological adaptation – and feeling – the conscious experience of emotion. Berridge and Winkielman (2003) provided evidence that the unconscious processing that constitutes an emotion can occur without any accompanying conscious experience (feeling).

Thus, a useful way to think of emotion is in terms of a combination of bodily arousal and appraisal. The appraisal establishes the nature of the situation and what should be done. The arousal gives that assessment the force to dominate mental activity and bring about the required action. The conscious feeling that goes with the process is thus a product of the arousal shaped by the appraisal (for related discussion, see Bechara & Naqvi, 2004; Critchley *et al.*, 2004; Damasio, 2010).

Value

The 'basic' emotions described in the previous section are probably decomposable, though exactly how this decomposition is to be done is far from clear. One point that *is* reasonably clear is that all emotional experiences share the features of positive–negative and intensity (which can be associated with arousal). In other words, they all express whether something is considered good or bad to the person and to what extent. This is what is commonly called *value*. In its most basic sense, it is about what matters to us, what we care about; in other words, what value we assign to the things that make up our experience. Since things can matter to us in good or bad ways, value can be either positive or negative. Since we care about some things more than others, each valuation has a degree; value can, at least in principle, be quantified.

In this section, I will first consider value in its natural biological context – as a product of natural selection, that is. This includes its place in the complex array of emotions and related aspects of the psyche and the brain. One conclusion that will emerge is that value has a crucial role in decision-making and in learning, with important implications for the acquisition and use of an L2, which I will consider in later chapters.

Value in the context of evolution

For any living organism, the most essential, fundamental principles for relating to its environment are 'seek x' and 'avoid y', where x represents things that will nourish and sustain it and will help to pass on its genes, while y represents things that will harm it or reduce its chances of passing on its genes. The most basic x's are food and drink and opportunities for mating. An organism that does not value mating is not likely to have its genes passed on. One that does not value food is not likely to survive long enough to do so. The y's can include predators, substances that are toxic to the organism and situations of natural danger. An organism that is not interested in avoiding such things is not likely to survive and reproduce.

Given their importance for survival, mechanisms for seeking valuable things and avoiding harmful things are necessarily built into living beings and so are part of the inheritance of every human. In other words, they are fundamental features of the human brain. Value in the brain is associated with projections that originate in the limbic system and lower areas and extend very generally throughout the cortex. These projections give it very broad influence on neural activity. Positive value, or reward, is especially associated with a circuit (the 'reward circuit') that includes subcortical emotion centres, especially the amygdala, and parts of the prefrontal cortex involved in rational cognitive functions (see, for example, Damasio, 2010; Edelman, 1992, 2006; Montague, 2006; Morrison & Salzman, 2010). This circuit is intimately associated with learning, a subject to which I will return below.

These survival mechanisms rely on internal representations of the x's and y's that are important for the species. Each representation of a thing in the environment is valued in terms of its positive or negative relation to the organism. This also applies to representations of potential actions. These values are necessarily quantitative, not just yes or no, good or bad, because some good things are more valuable than others and some bad things are more harmful than others. Adaptive behaviour is thus a matching of active perceptual representations with representations of seeking and avoidance actions, based on the value assigned to the perceptual respresentation. In simple organisms this matching can be quite simple, restricted to basic innate functions such as seeking food, drink and mates or avoiding toxins, predators and dangerous situations, while in more complex creatures, humans for example, it can get extremely complex, going far beyond its innate base.

Value and emotion

Value, in the sense in which I am using it here, is inseparable from affect. Underlying all emotions, the central features are positive/negative and intensity/activation/arousal, i.e. the heart of emotion is valuation. In emotion research, there is a fairly broad, though probably not universal, recognition of the centrality of value. Smith and Ellsworth (1985), reviewing extensive previous research, concluded that the once-popular effort to analyze emotions into a number of dimensions had produced inconsistency and relatively limited success – with the striking exception of the dimensions of pleasantness and activation, which appeared over and over in the various studies. For Ortony *et al.* (1988: 6), based on past research, 'any dimensional characterization of emotions is likely to include at least the two dimensions of *activation* and *valence*'. For Frijda (1986, 1988/1998), pleasure and pain are the core of all emotion. Barrett and Russell (1999; Barrett, 2005) reviewed research in detail and concluded that affective states can be characterized by the dimensions of pleasure and intensity, an idea they attributed initially to Wundt. For similar statements on the centrality of value, see, among others, Anderson et al. (2003), Hamann (2003) and Lang (1995).

The intimate relation between value and emotion should, in fact, be clear. The basic function of emotions is to guide an organism towards actions that are beneficial for it and away from actions that are harmful to it. Positive value provides the definition of beneficial, along with a measure of its degree. Its negative counterpart defines and quantifies potential negative effects.

Beyond emotion

Seen in this light, emotions are part of a larger set of adaptations, all based on valuation, that serve to manage the body and its relations with the external world. This is to say that they serve to maximize positive value and respond to conditions that are associated with negative value. Because of this general shared function, these adaptations can all be called 'regulatory mechanisms' (Damasio, 2003, 2010). In addition to emotion, they include pain, pleasure, motivation, drives and a number of other phenomena. The prototypical positive state is pleasure (see Linden [2011] for a good overview from a largely neural perspective). It represents, in a variety of forms, the conscious expression of value. The prototypical experience associated with avoidance and negative value is pain, which serves as an indicator of damage to the organism.

While value started out as a tool for biological survival, its role now extends far beyond the basic biological functions for which it developed. Positive value can be attached to an unlimited variety of more sophisticated objects and activities, yielding experiences of social, intellectual and artistic pleasure. Similar comments apply to negative value. In addition to its basic biological functions, it is also found in social emotions such as guilt and shame. It can readily become attached to an activity, of any sort, discouraging us from engaging in that activity. In both forms, positive and negative, value is very much part of conscious experience and so should be accommodated in a theory of consciousness.

Value and emotion in decision-making and learning

According to an increasingly prominent line of thinking, decisions are based, largely or entirely, on the emotional value that is associated with the possible choices (see Barrett, 2005; Charland, 2005; Dolan, 2002; Evans, 2004; Gray et al., 2005; Mameli, 2004; Thagard, 2006). Value is therefore fundamental in decision-making, and the role it plays must be a central concern of any adequate model. The best known account of this sort is Damasio's neurally based theory of *somatic markers* (Damasio, 1994, 2003; Damasio *et al.*, 1998). In this theory, somatic markers are the emotional value, positive or negative, that has become associated with specific past experiences. The relative appeal of the various options to be considered in a decision is determined by their associations with these markers. Specifically, those options that are negatively valued are eliminated from consideration, leaving at most a relatively narrow set of options to be considered.

This neural work ties in with economic thinking on decision-making, particularly in the overlapping fields of neuroeconomics and behavioural economics (see Ariely, 2009; Glimcher *et al.*, 2009; Kahneman, 2011). Ideas on value are also intertwined with ongoing neural research on reward (e.g. Montague, 2006; Montague *et al.*, 2006; Morrison & Salzman, 2010; Wallis, 2007). Researchers have long known that the brain contains a reward circuit, closely associated with the experience of pleasure, that is active when the organism undergoes some positive experience, particularly one that is more positive than expected. A positive experience is defined by the value that is associated with it. This work commonly focuses on the neurotransmitter, dopamine, that is at the heart of the system's functioning. Information and ideas coming from research on reward naturally have important implications for how we learn, including how we learn an L2, and how we subsequently use or fail to use the knowledge and ability that we have acquired.

More generally, extensive research has established what was probably clear in advance, that value and emotion strongly affect learning and memory (Edelman, 1992, 2006; Linden, 2011; McGaugh, 2004, 2006; Montague, 2006; Phelps, 2006; Thompson & Madigan, 2005; Uttl *et al.*, 2006). First, they are crucial parts of the mental set that determines attention (e.g. Buchanan & Adolphs, 2002; Evans, 2001; Gray *et al.*, 2005; Lundqvist & Öhman, 2005). We pay attention to the things that we care about, the things that arouse feelings in us – and we remember the things that we pay attention to. Beyond the attentional factor, the involvement of value and emotion helps to strengthen and consolidate the memory. Finally, when we positively value something that we have learned, we are more likely to put it into practice in our lives; when we negatively value something we have learned, we are more likely to avoid such application. And this use or non-use then exerts a continuing influence on the memories. All these points will play a role in the discussion of L2 learning in later chapters.

Self

The concept of self as such has not played a large role in cognitive theory. Reading cognitive works on the major components of the mind, we do not usually come across in-depth discussions of it. Not surprisingly, it does not often enter into cognitive accounts of L2 learning either. But it does come into cognitive theorizing under various guises, including motivation, self-regulation, willpower, executive control and autobiographical memory. It also plays a large role in some prominent ideas about consciousness, a role that I will consider in Chapter 3 and beyond, and in studies of L2 acquisition.

One place where self does explicitly appear in cognitive theory is especially important for considerations of consciousness. This is Baars' theory of consciousness, which I will discuss in some detail in Chapter 3. In this theory, a central role is played by the very large set of unconscious *contexts*, which influence the current contents of consciousness while themselves remaining in the background. In this scheme, self is a stable and exceptionally important context, strongly affecting mental activity (Baars, 1988; Baars *et al.*, 2003). It is identified with regions of parietal and especially prefrontal cortex (see also Vogeley & Fink, 2003). Also worth noting is Neisser's notion of the conceptual self, which he treats as a mental representation (Neisser & Jopling, 1997: 3; see also Kihlstrom & Klein, 2006).

The idea of self naturally appears in discussions of motivation as well (see Feather, 1990; Kuhl, 1986; Leary, 2007; Raynor & McFarlin, 1986). Not surprisingly, value has played a substantial role in such discussions, sometimes a central role. Raynor and McFarlin (1986: 316), for example, wrote that 'Our primary assumption is that there are two basic functions of personality: to maximize positive value and to minimize negative value'. While this may be stronger than the usual view, it does bring out the importance of value in motivation. People care about things and are motivated to seek those they like and avoid those they dislike. It is quite natural to suppose that at some level such considerations are at the heart of personality and behaviour. Motivation, value and self are all intimately connected.

Another area in which self figures prominently is work on self-regulation, often in the context of executive function. Baumeister *et al.* (2007), reviewing the literature on self-regulation, presented it as one of the self's two major executive functions, choice being the other. As such, it plays a large role in defining the self. Social psychologists have explained a wide range of personal and social problems, directly or indirectly, in terms of failure in self-regulation (e.g. Muraven & Baumeister, 2000; Wills & Stoolmiller, 2002). A central point for Baumeister and colleagues is that self-control and decision-making draw on the same resources and that these resources can be temporarily depleted through use (see Baumeister *et al.*, 1998, 2007; Baumeister & Tierney, 2011). A meta-analysis of research has largely supported these claims (Hagger *et al.*, 2010). Baumeister and colleagues explain the findings in terms of a limited supply of the glucose that is used to produce neurotransmitters crucial for mental action (see especially Gailliot & Baumeister, 2007; Gailliot *et al.*, 2007, 2009). Effortful actions draw down this stockpile, a process called 'ego depletion', making further such actions difficult. These authors offer extensive discussion of ways that people can improve their willpower and their ability to exercise it. In such ideas there is a largely implicit notion of the self exercising willpower and learning to use it. The ideas of willpower, self-regulation and self-control are difficult to separate from the more cognitive notion of executive control (see Aron, 2008; Smith, 2009). Self might in fact be seen as the highest-level executive controller.

The discussion to this point has been concerned largely with self as actor or controller. The other major aspect is found in work on autobiographical memory (e.g. Conway, 2005; Conway et al., 2004). This aspect is particularly important because the self is defined to a large extent by its memories; a self without memories would not be much of a self. These memories interact with goals and motives and the thoughts and actions that spring from them. They thus greatly influence cognition. They are also strongly influenced by the self, in the form of self-image. In other words, memories tend to be shaped to some extent by the needs of the self – a major source of the false memories briefly described above (see Greenwald, 1980; Loftus, 2005; Ross, 1989).

The idea of self is somewhat awkward in scientific psychology because of the danger of it becoming a kind of homunculus. When we do not have a good understanding of a mental process or phenomenon, it is tempting to simply attribute it to the self, creating the illusion of an explanation where none exists and so doing more to impede understanding than to facilitate it. Baddeley has repeatedly acknowledged this concern in regard to his central executive (e.g. Baddeley, 1996a, 1996b, 2000, 2012). His long-term solution is to gradually identify the distinct mechanisms for which the central executive is now given responsibility and so 'retire' the executive. This analysis of the central executive into explicit components and functions should be the goal for any homunculus-like entity, including self. It is doubtful, though, that self must be or should be retired. It might instead be kept on as a genuine part of a theory but with well-defined functions, abilities and limitations.

Language

Language can be understood from a wide variety of perspectives, including social, cultural, psychological, neurological, developmental, functional and aesthetic. My interest is in the cognitive perspective, that is, in the nature of mental representations of language and the use and development of those representations. From such a perspective, spoken language is commonly seen as the most fundamental and is therefore the focus of investigation. This is not to deny the importance of written language, or sign language or Braille, just to say that they are best understood on the basis of an understanding of spoken language.

The first step in achieving this understanding is to see language as sounds and meanings and the complex connections between the two. Language is primarily about expressing concepts and feelings through sound and understanding the expressions of other people by relating their speech to concepts. The central concern of linguistics can thus be seen as the nature of the sounds, the nature of the meanings and the nature of the relations between them.

The study of linguistic sound includes phonetics, which is concerned with the sounds as they are produced in the vocal tract of a person or as the systematic disturbances in the air that result from speech. But language sounds are represented in the mind not just in this relatively straightforward way but also in a more abstract form, in terms of the role they play in the computational system of a particular language. The t in *tea*, for instance, is quite different from the t in *steep*, if it is considered in terms of the way the sounds are produced or the disturbances in the air that they represent. But for the language system of English, they are a single entity, a phoneme, appearing in different contexts. This is phonology, the study of these abstract phonemes and the complex ways that they function.

Turning to the meaning side of language, meanings of words are conceptual representations associated with the forms of the words. Neural research has found that these concepts are not specifically linguistic; it seems instead to be a matter of connecting language forms with representations that are distributed throughout the brain in terms of the kinds of concepts they represent: visual features are in visual areas, action features in motor areas and so on. These concepts are influenced by language but are not inherently linguistic. Thus, their connections to language forms are an inherent part of the language system in the mind, but the conceptual representations themselves have a more peripheral status in this system. These basic concepts can be combined in complex ways to produce the meanings of phrases and sentences. The study of word meanings and the higher-level meanings found in sentences is called semantics. Linguists often distinguish semantics and pragmatics, the former dealing with meaning specifically as it is inherently tied to sentences and other linguistic units, the latter focusing on meaning as it is affected by the broader context in which language is used. This distinction is quite fuzzy. It has been useful as a means of focusing research but probably should not be seen as a genuine distinction within the cognitive system.

The other fundamental part of mental language is the system of connections between sounds and meanings. It is necessary because the number of concepts that we have in our heads is vast; the number that we potentially have is in fact unlimited, since those that we already possess can always be combined to make ever more complex concepts. A system that sought to express each of these concepts with a distinct sound of its own would very quickly run out of sounds and would make impossible demands on memory. The solution to this problem is to have a system that relates sounds to meanings in principled ways. This system is commonly divided into two parts: syntax, which is concerned with the structure of sentences, and morphology, which focuses on word structure. Many different theories have been proposed regarding the nature of this system, and fundamental differences remain the norm among linguists. But it is clear that some such system must (and does) exist.

These separate branches – phonetics, phonology, semantics (pragmatics), syntax and morphology – together cover the basic language system of the mind. A simple cognitive view of language learning could see learning as simply the proper development of these components. But language is actually much more than this. This is to say that the language system is, crucially, connected to other systems of the mind. Knowledge, use and acquisition of language are, especially, inseparable from the personal identity of the individual, i.e. the self. This is hardly a novel or controversial point, but it is one that has typically not had a place in cognitive accounts of language. In a cognitive framework, self is to be understood as another mental system, or perhaps a representation or set of representations within the system. It crucially involves goals and values, as described above, and so the language system must make contact with the mental representations that constitute those goals and values.

A final aspect of language that must be recognized is knowledge that is *about* language but is not a part of the mental language system itself, or is only a peripheral element of that system. People can treat essentially any topic as an object of study, about which they are capable of developing extensive knowledge. Someone who speaks a particular language has an integrated system of specialized knowledge underlying that ability, but is quite capable of acquiring linguistic knowledge that is separate from this system. This *metalinguistic knowledge* is an important and often confusing topic in the study of L2 acquisition, and I will discuss it in some detail in later chapters.

Attention

The intuitive idea of attention is that it is a focusing on one thing rather than others. Researchers have sought, since the beginnings of cognitive psychology, to understand this common-sense phenomenon in scientific terms, with very mixed results. I will not go into the many ways that attention has been conceptualized in cognitive theory or the many ways that the various notions of attention have been studied. My interest is in the way the idea has been used in theories of consciousness, in the limitations of the concept and the way it is applied, and in how we should respond to those limitations.

Attention has played a prominent role in theories of consciousness. Baars, like many others, treats attention as the gateway to consciousness. Unlike many others, he prefers (at least at times) to see it 'not as a separate system but rather as the name for the process of gaining access to global workspace [i.e. to consciousness] by reference to long-term or current goals' (McGovern & Baars, 2007: 200; but see also Baars, 1997b).

This reluctance to treat attention as a genuine entity is appropriate, I suggest, and considerable caution is required with the concept. Discussions of this topic routinely begin with a quote from William James (1890/1950: 403–404): 'Every one knows what attention is. It is the taking possession by the mind, in clear and vivid form, of one out of what seem several simultaneously possible objects or trains of thought'. This description nicely captures our intuitive idea of attention, and James was certainly right that the ordinary-language concept is clear and widely shared. But in efforts to obtain a scientific understanding of the mind, this clarity and the easy consensus that follows can become a liability. The cognitive literature contains a great many differing conceptualizations of attention, with very uncertain relations among them, and a great many different processes are subsumed under the term (see Allport, 1993; Johnston & Dark, 1986; Mack & Rock, 1998; Meyer & Kieras, 1997; Moray, 1969; Parasuraman, 1998; Pashler, 1995). Reviewing the literature on the neurobiology of attention, Schuchert (2004) concluded that the concept of attention does not correspond in any neat way to anything in the brain (but see Posner & Fan, 2008). Few, in fact, would now say that there is any one thing to which the term *attention* refers. It is best seen as an 'umbrella-term for a general topic, subsuming a host of questions about selective processing' (Driver *et al.*, 2001: 64). But most discussions do not recognize this diversity, instead using the term as if it had one clear, well-established meaning – as if everyone knows what attention is, when in fact we do not. This problem extends to the second language acquisition (SLA) literature, which I will discuss in Chapter 6.

Another potential danger involved in the use of 'attention' is the homunculus problem (see Johnston & Dark, 1986). Discussions of attention routinely speak of allocating, shifting or focusing attention, implying an intelligent agent controlling it. As long as this controller remains unanalyzed, as it too often does, these cannot be genuine explanations. This situation is quite similar to the problem that Baddeley (1996a, 1996b, 2000) and others (e.g. Jarrold, 2001; Lehto, 1996; May, 2001; Miyake *et al.*, 2000; Towse & Houston-Price, 2001) have found with his central executive idea.

These concerns have important implications for theories of consciousness, which routinely appeal to attention to explain how a particular representation is selected for consciousness. Given the diversity and the confusion in the cognitive and neural concepts of attention, this appeal to attention has a magical quality to it. We feel that we know what attention is, as in the James quote, so the statement that it is responsible for picking out the object of awareness has the appearance of a genuine explanation. But in the context of research and theory in cognitive psychology, a simple appeal to attention hides a host of important issues. It might be the beginnings of an explanation, pointing out directions in which a genuine explanation may be found, but it cannot be anything more than that.

Perhaps the best approach then is to see attention as shorthand for the complex processes and circumstances that somehow result in a particular representation receiving extensive, sustained processing. This non-reification of attention is similar to the position of Baars described above. A useful analogy can be drawn, again with Baddeley's (1996a, 1996b, 2000) treatment of his own homunculus, the central executive. The approach that Baddeley has taken is, again, to gradually retire the executive by assigning its functions to various clearer processes, as this change becomes feasible. The two homunculi, the central executive and attention, are in fact difficult to separate from one another. Both operate within the context provided by current processing and the lingering effects of previous processing. Both are guided by the person's values and goals, immediate and long term. These are, to a very large extent, about the self, which has been the focus of some prominent research on consciousness (Damasio, 2010; Kihlstrom, 1987, 1997), and can to some extent be equated with the central executive. Explicating the self and its relations to processing throughout the system is a likely way to bring about the retirement of both the executive homunculus and the attention homunculus.

Modularity

In this discussion, I have assumed that the mind can be broken down into a number of component parts based on their functions and the nature of the knowledge they use. Linguistic knowledge and processing, for example, is distinct from perceptual knowledge and processing and from conceptual knowledge and processing, and linguistic knowledge itself consists of two primary components, phonology and morphosyntax. This sort of functional splitting of the mind goes under the name *modularity* and is the subject of considerable controversy. Theorists have strongly disagreed on the extent to which the mind is modular, the extent to which the modularity is innately based, what modules exist and even what it means for something to be a module (see Barrett & Kurzban, 2006; Carruthers, 2006; Fodor, 1983, 2000; Jackendoff, 1987, 1997; Karmiloff-Smith, 1992; Kurzban, 2010; Pinker, 1994, 1997; Sharwood Smith & Truscott, 2014; Truscott, 2013a). The cognitive framework I will present in Chapter 4 and apply throughout the remainder of the book adopts a particular modular view of the mind, based in large part on the work of Ray Jackendoff (1987, 1997, 1999, 2002). This sort of view receives wide support, but any particular position taken on modularity will inevitably provoke controversy; some openness to alternatives is necessary.

Modularity and its critics

The general idea of the modular mind has received considerable criticism. A surprising amount of this criticism rests on the naïve idea that modularity means complete isolation of functions (see discussion by Barrett & Kurzban, 2006). Critics point out, often through elaborate experimentation, that interaction occurs between processes that have been attributed to distinct modules and then conclude that there are no such modules. But this could only be a refutation of a truly extreme version of modularity. On any serious version, significant interaction occurs between the modules; a system in which modules carry out their tasks with no influence of any sort from other modules is a system that could not possibly work; it could not even be called a system.

A more serious argument against modularity claims that a highly modular mind could not have the flexibility and creativity that the human mind clearly does possess. One response to this objection is that these properties can result from interactions among modules, particularly through cycles of processing activity involving a number of distinct modules. This is the position of Carruthers (2006), who appeals to the *global workspace* idea of Baars (which I will discuss in Chapter 3) as a means of coordinating activity across the system. The other major response is that individual modules inherently possess a degree of flexibility. This idea is expressed in Sperber's (1994) distinction between a module's *proper domain* – the input it was designed by natural selection to process – and its *actual domain* – the broader class of input that it is capable of processing. A system that evolved to process faces, for instance, must have considerable flexibility if it is to handle its function, since every new face we see is novel. In fact, the face recognition module is receiving different visual input every time we see a familiar face from a different angle or in different lighting or with a different motion or a different expression. The flexibility required to deal with this range of variation in the visual input should allow a face recognition module some ability to process non-facial input as well, as long as that input shares some sorts of formal properties with faces. Underlying this flexibility is the compositional nature of modules: each consists of various components that can be combined in a variety of ways. It should also be noted that the flexibility criticism is only relevant to relatively strong versions of modularity. Those that see the mind as containing both a number of modules and a non-modular portion, as in Fodor's (1983) original proposal, can attribute the flexibility to the latter.

Another common criticism of modularity is that the human genome does not contain enough genes to specify the structure of a large number of sophisticated modules. The problem with this argument is that it rests on a 'blueprint' view of the relation between genes and modules, a view which is not necessary and is generally disavowed (see Barrett & Kurzban, 2006; Carruthers, 2006; Marcus, 2004). On the blueprint view, a one-to-one correspondence exists between genes and the characteristics of individual modules, implying that a vast number of genes is required. A more realistic view, based on the way that the body in general develops, is that the development of the modules involves a complex interaction of genes with the wealth of other factors that influence the developing brain, and that considerable overlap exists in the genes that underlie the various modules. Given this more realistic view, the size of the genome does not pose any principled problem for modularity, even in very strong versions (see the previous references for discussion).

A neural version of the flexibility argument is that the brain is capable of considerable change based on circumstances and that this *plasticity* is inconsistent with a high degree of modularity. But this argument would only be valid if the brain were *completely* plastic, a claim that no one to my knowledge would make (and see Gazzaniga [2011] on the limits of plasticity). The initial requirements for the language module, for instance, are the processors and the primitives they work with, which together should represent only a tiny fraction of the space taken by the module in its developed form, after language acquisition has occurred. Ultimately, a vastly greater portion of the module's neural space is devoted to the combinations of the primitives that develop on the basis of linguistic input, to say nothing of the rich connections these combinations form with other modules. The proportion of the brain taken up by the language module, in its earliest form, would be minute. This area should greatly expand if conditions are right (i.e. if sufficient natural language input occurs). If conditions are not right, most of the space that would otherwise be claimed by the language module is likely to be taken by other modules. Furthermore, nothing in the idea of modularity implies that the module could only be in one precise location. Modularity is thus consistent with a high degree of neural plasticity.

Some neural criticisms of modularity have focused on word meanings, an example of a practice that Paradis (2004) strongly criticized. Goldberg (2009), for example, rejected the idea of a language module on the basis of findings that word meanings are distributed throughout the brain, in various sensory and motor areas. This might be a problem for a view of modularity on which word meanings are part of the language module, but this is by no means a necessary or universal view. Jackendoff, in particular, sees word meanings as connected to the language module but not included in it. Within an account of this sort (which I adopt), the facts that Goldberg pointed out are exactly what should be expected.

Standard arguments against modularity are thus far from convincing. Arguments in favour of it are, I suggest, much stronger. The general logic of modularity is that it allows more effective and efficient computation. A subsystem that is designed to deal with one specific type of information should be able to handle that information more quickly and accurately than a general, undifferentiated system. This point might be made more strongly:

it may be impossible for a general-purpose system to accurately process its input in any reasonable amount of time, given the virtually unlimited number of possible analyses it must consider. This is the *computational tractability* problem. Carruthers (2006: 13) argued that the modular mind is logical in design terms and evolutionary terms: it makes sense for a complex system 'to be constructed hierarchically out of dissociable sub-systems...in such a way that the whole assembly can be built up gradually, adding sub-system to sub-system; where the properties of sub-systems can be varied independently of one another; and in such a way that the functionality of the whole is buffered, to some extent, from changes or damage occurring to the parts'. He suggested that this modular design characterizes biological systems very generally.

Focusing on language, the traditional logic behind the hypothesis of an innate module is the poverty of the stimulus argument. The grammar of every natural language is extremely complex – so complex that generations of linguists have struggled to make sense of it, with only limited success. And yet every small child masters the grammar of at least one language (often more than one) simply by being around people who are using that language, even though the speakers use it in ways that are not always clear or consistent and at times violate the principles of the underlying grammar. This remarkable situation becomes perfectly explicable if we assume that the core of the grammar is innately present and that acquisition is the development of this core through exposure. The innate core is commonly referred to as *universal grammar* (UG).

The UG hypothesis is greatly strengthened by a broader look at the conditions under which language acquisition occurs. First, these conditions vary tremendously across cultures, but these variations do not seem to have any effect on the process. Language develops in any more or less normal child under any more or less normal conditions. Even more strikingly, it develops under conditions that are far from normal, including a wide variety of adverse conditions that should be expected to hinder or prevent it. Bishop and Mogford (1988: 255) concluded from a broad look at such cases that 'language development is...remarkably robust'. It also develops in children whose general learning ability is exceptionally weak (e.g. Flavell *et al.*, 1993; Smith & Tsimpli, 1995), an extreme illustration of the fact that success in language learning is not related to the learner's intelligence.

Research on deaf children's development of sign language further strengthens the case for an innate, specifically linguistic capacity (e.g. Goldin-Meadow, 2003; Lust, 2006; Morgan, 2005). First, it is well established that sign languages are genuine languages, with all the complex grammar of their spoken counterparts. Deaf children acquire them, through input, in essentially the same way that hearing children acquire spoken language. Most strikingly, deaf children who are exposed only to an impoverished version of a sign language (their parents have only limited ability) go beyond this input and end up with a fully developed grammar, paralleling the development of creoles from pidgins in the case of hearing children. When they are not exposed to any sign language at all, they tend to create one. The systems created by different children in different parts of the world tend to resemble each other, pointing again to the conclusion that they are expressing an innate capacity for language.

These seemingly remarkable success stories can be set alongside cases in which children have difficulty acquiring language even when there is no apparent problem with their non-linguistic abilities or with the conditions in which the learning occurs. Importantly, these failures show a clear genetic basis (Bishop, 2006). The inevitable conclusion of all these observations, I suggest, is that language acquisition *is* something special. It is the development, through linguistic experience, of a specifically linguistic component of the mind on the basis of innate features that are themselves specifically linguistic. These are the features that make up UG. More generally, there is very good reason to believe that the human mind has a highly modular character.

Specialized and non-specialized processes

One aspect of a modular approach will be especially important later on and so requires some discussion here. This is the distinction between the specialized workings of a module and the ability to carry out related functions in a non-specialist manner. Examples can be found in a variety of domains.

In first language, we have the ability to spontaneously use our language based on naturally acquired knowledge; we can also have knowledge of theories of language, obtained in the same deliberate ways that we obtain knowledge on any other subject. Each type of knowledge and ability can exist without the other. Our naturally acquired knowledge can be used to make intuitive judgements of whether a sentence is grammatically acceptable or not, with little or no conscious understanding of the reasons behind them. We can also use consciously acquired rules of how language *should* be used to make those judgements. And, again, the two can be quite independent of one another. Knowledge of the prescriptive rule that infinitives should not be split does not make 'to boldly go where no one has gone before' intuitively unacceptable or 'to go boldly where no one has gone before' intuitively acceptable. Nor do intuitive judgements prevent us from establishing and applying prescriptive rules that contradict them.

Good, non-linguistic analogies can be found in visual judgements. Consider the two blocks shown in Figure 2.1, which is based on Shepard (1990). The intuition, a product of our visual system, is that one block is much longer and narrower than the other. But if we appeal to conscious processes operating outside the visual system, i.e. we measure the two

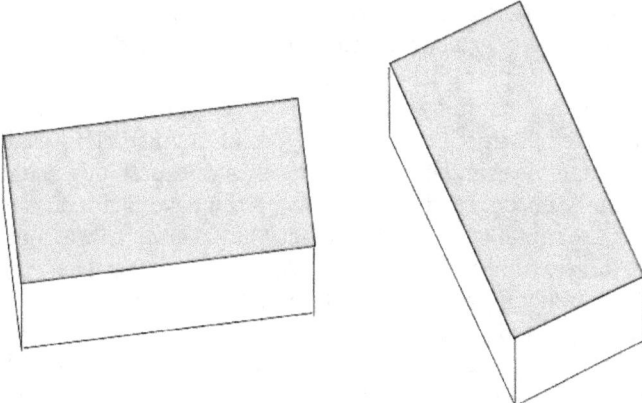

Figure 2.1 An example of the specialist visual system operating without awareness

images, we find that they are in fact identical (try it). Interestingly, the firm, indisputable knowledge obtained in this way does not in the least alter our intuitive feeling that they are *not* the same. In such cases, the visual system produces its own assessment of relative sizes while processes that are not specifically visual make a separate and very different assessment. In the case of the automatic, specialized system, the output of the system is conscious but its operations are not. In contrast, consciousness plays a much more prominent role in the non-specialized analysis.

The same phenomenon can be seen in perceptions of motion. We have little difficulty consciously understanding that what we see when we are watching a movie is not actually continuous but rather a series of still images, one quickly succeeding another. But this knowledge does not alter our experience – the output of the visual system – that it *is* continuous.

We also have an expert system for recognizing faces, operating in a largely unconscious manner, and a much weaker ability to carry out this function more consciously, without the expert system. This can be seen in people who have damage to the portion of the brain that instantiates the system and therefore have great difficulty recognizing other people by their faces. Oliver Sacks (2010) provides an interesting description of his own difficulties of this sort and of the conscious strategies he uses to get around them, explicitly noting and focusing on particular features of particular faces (such as his own large ears, which help him realize when he is seeing his face in a mirror rather than looking at another person).

Another example of a largely unconscious expert system is *theory of mind*: our ability to recognize that other people have minds like ours, and to make judgements about their knowledge, beliefs, intentions etc. For almost everyone, a particular portion of the prefrontal cortex is crucially involved in this ability, presumably representing the system that is specialized for theory of mind. But in Asperger's patients this area does not seem to be functional. Judgements about other people's mental states are made, with greater difficulty, in a separate part of the prefrontal cortex, one that is normally associated with impersonal judgements. This appears, then, to be analogous to the hypothesized distinction between types of linguistic knowledge.

Further examples can be found in the area of moral judgements (Haidt, 2012). When we encounter a situation, we often have clear and strong intuitions about the morality of particular actions taken in that situation, coming from a largely unconscious system. We can also consciously analyze the situation and make moral judgements based on such analysis. And, again, the two types of judgement can be entirely independent of one another. A good example is the case of two siblings deciding to have sex. When people are presented with an invented story in which this occurs (Haidt, 2001), they typically have a clear and strong intuition that the behaviour is wrong. They can also consciously produce a variety of rational arguments for that belief. Even when all these arguments are shown to be irrelevant (the story was carefully constructed to rule them out), the intuitive judgement remains clear and strong: the behaviour is wrong, whether or not we can come up with reasons for saying it is wrong. Such cases show a clear parallel with judgements of visual illusions.

Cases of this sort are very much the norm in regard to higher cognitive processes, including social judgements, leading to the widespread popularity of a *dual-process* view of the mind (see Evans, 2008; Kahneman, 2011). Researchers have identified a number of characteristics that cluster together to establish two distinct types of processes, commonly called S1 and S2, corresponding to the specialist and non-specialist distinction I have drawn here. One of the characteristics routinely associated with S2 (non-specialist) systems is consciousness.

Consider one final case: our responses to danger, as when we suddenly encounter a snake (LeDoux, 1996). The amygdala specializes in judging danger and initiating responses to it. It carries out this function very quickly, operating on its own in an automatic, unconscious manner, largely beyond voluntary control. The cortex is capable of carrying out this same function, but it does so by bringing to bear any available knowledge and ability. Not surprisingly, it works much more slowly, in a conscious, controlled manner. Phobias provide an illustration of the specialized system operating on its own, largely outside the control of its non-specialist counterpart.

This duality is a ubiquitous feature of cognition. We repeatedly encounter distinctions between a specialist system, operating largely without consciousness, and a non-specialized process that can carry out similar functions but typically not as well and typically in a more conscious manner. The specialist systems are modules. It is not clear if the non-specialist processes are best seen as representing non-modular systems in the mind or as interactions among the various modules (for related discussion, see Carruthers, 2006; Eraña, 2012; Evans & Over, 2008). In either case, I suggest that this distinction must be recognized and taken as a central concern in any serious exploration of consciousness in L2 learning. We cannot understand this topic without a clear recognition that two very different kinds of processes are at work.

Conclusion

In this chapter, I have offered a sketch of what a useful framework for studying the mind may look like. The cognitive system (mind) consists of the basic architecture of processors and memory stores with the processing principles of the former and the representations of the latter. Within this sketch, all the traditional topics of psychology are to be understood in these terms. One implication is that these topics do not represent inherently distinct parts of the mind or its functioning. In an important sense they do not exist at all. They are best seen as useful ways to break up and understand the complex web that is the mind and its workings. The same can be said of the various topics that make up the study of L2 acquisition from a cognitive perspective.

This is only a preliminary sketch, though. In Chapter 4, I will describe a more specific framework, instantiating these ideas. For a study of consciousness, the fundamental issues are how consciousness fits into such a framework. What representations do we become conscious of? Under what conditions? How does this state affect processing? How does it affect learning? With a basic framework in place to provide provisional answers to such questions, we can then go on to ask how consciousness fits into the specific topics that we are interested in, namely those involving the acquisition of an L2.

3 Theories of Consciousness

Considering the importance of consciousness and its inherent interest, it is not surprising to find that a great many efforts have been made to explain it. Nor is it surprising to find that there is great diversity in the perspectives adopted and the specific proposals offered. In this review, I will focus on the rich set of cognitively oriented theories, which have become increasingly neurally oriented as well. I will generally stay clear of strictly philosophical proposals – however interesting such proposals may be in their own right, they have relatively little to contribute to my project. Given the cognitive orientation, I will only briefly mention the intriguing ideas regarding the application of quantum theory to consciousness, as well as holistic views of consciousness and the brain. All of these are difficult to connect to second language acquisition (SLA), at least as I conceive it, and in some cases are either highly controversial or largely ignored in current cognitive and neural discussions of consciousness. Even with this narrowing of the field, we are left with a rich set of ideas to consider.

I will start with a brief look at a few early theories that play only a limited role in current discussions of consciousness but have helped make the topic scientifically respectable and still have insights to offer. Within this set of early theories, I will seek to identify a few important themes, especially ones that carry through into current theories. With these themes in mind, I will then discuss in more detail a few theories that play a particularly important role in current discussions of consciousness, while also making reference to several additional theories and approaches. I will conclude the chapter by returning to examine in more depth the themes that I find most important in these theories, themes that will be incorporated in the approach that I will develop in Chapter 5 and will then apply to second language learning in the remainder of the book.

Some Early Efforts at a Cognitive Account of Consciousness

The theories that I will consider here share the cognitive, information-processing perspective, treating the mind as a collection of distinct but interacting functional components and exploring the place of consciousness in such a system. Although they play little role in current discussions of consciousness, they still have things to say to those of us who wish to explore the subject.

Shallice's models

Shallice (1972) proposed an information-processing model in which conscious experience is associated with control of action. He was quite cautious in the claims he made for this model, and later moved away from it. But he deserves considerable credit for his effort to show that an information-processing theory can and should have a place for consciousness, at a time (1972) when consciousness was still widely considered a topic unsuitable for scientific investigation. Shallice (1988b) further explored the possibilities of connecting conscious experience to the workings of an information-processing system, concluding the discussion with another tentative account of his own. The architecture assumed in this account includes four control systems: language, episodic memory processing, a supervisory system and contention scheduling. They often come together in their operations, working on related representations and information and establishing coherence in their control operations. The contents of consciousness correspond to the information flowing through the system during these episodes of 'coherent shared control' (Shallice, 1988b: 327). This idea, of consciousness as the product or corollary of different processing elements operating together in a coherent way, is one of the more important insights in the study of consciousness. It has echoes in the idea of *synchronization* that is at the heart of various contemporary models, and in the account that I will develop in later chapters.

Shallice's view of consciousness was further expressed and developed, in limited ways, by Jack and Shallice (2001). Shallice and Cooper (2011) placed this view in the context of a more thoroughly developed account of the mind/brain, especially looking at neural implications and making connections to the neuronal global workspace (GW) theory of Dehaene (see below).

Johnson-Laird and executive control

Johnson-Laird (1988) emphasized that consciousness is to be explained in terms of computation, rather than the physical characteristics of the brain. Within this perspective, he hypothesized a modular system consisting of many independent processors operating in parallel but communicating with one another. The system is hierarchically organized in the sense that a processor is monitored by a processor above it and it monitors the ones below it. The lowest levels are sensory and motor processors and the topmost is the operating system, which exercises substantial but incomplete executive control over the system as a whole. It is the operating system that is associated with consciousness, and this relation is intimately associated with its ability to model its own operations in its current situation. Johnson-Laird thus gave the notion of self a central place in efforts to understand consciousness.

Mandler and the construction of the contents of consciousness

Mandler (1975, 1984, 1992, 1997, 2002) was less concerned with the architecture in which consciousness is realized, focusing instead on its general characteristics, its adaptive functions and especially the way that conscious contents are produced. He stressed that consciousness is *constructed* from unconscious mental contents. Simplifying somewhat, these contents are *schemas*, which are very close to the idea of representations as I use the term in this book. Schemas can be activated by sensory input, by spreading activation from other schemas and from top-down influences. Conscious structures are constructed from a selection of some of the currently active schemas, especially those that are most successful in making sense of sensory input. Interestingly, Mandler treats emotional experience as constructed, like other types of consciousness, but specifically from the combination of autonomic arousal, which establishes the intensity of the experience, and cognitive evaluation, which he eventually decided to describe in terms of 'value'. Examples of value as used by Mandler include hostility, desire and uncertainty, along with the most basic values of good/bad and approach/avoid. Mandler's theory is especially interesting here because it is similar in several respects to the approach that I will offer in Chapter 5.

Kihlstrom and the self

Kihlstrom (1987, 1997) developed a theory in terms of Anderson's (1983a, 1993) ACT*/ACT-R model, which has also played a role in SLA (e.g. DeKeyser & Sokalski, 1996; Towell & Hawkins, 1994). His idea, which he attributed to William James, was that self is the essential element in consciousness. In his approach, self is a representation within a semantic network, a piece of declarative knowledge that is distinguished by the uniquely important role that it plays. It is a representation of personality and is connected to visual images of the person and to autobiographical information. This representation is in working memory, apparently because it is highly active; other representations thus become associated with it when they also come into working memory. It is this association that yields consciousness: 'Whatever is concurrently or retrospectively linked to the self is represented in awareness' (Kihlstrom, 1997: 456). Experiences that never enter working memory and therefore do not become connected to self become implicit memories. Kihlstrom argued that this approach can explain a variety of interesting phenomena: dissociative fugue, multiple-personality disorder, hysteria and some hypnosis-induced phenomena.

Schacter's DICE model

A final example of an information-processing theory in this group is Schacter's (1990) Dissociable Interactions and Conscious Experience (DICE) model. The components of the model are (a) a set of functionally specified modules, including lexical, conceptual, facial, spatial and self; (b) two memory systems, declarative/episodic and procedural/habit; and (c) a conscious awareness system (CAS) that interacts with the other components. He describes CAS as shorthand for the idea that awareness requires processing beyond the modular level, focusing his interest on its relations to the other components and disavowing any claim that it provides an account of awareness itself. Modular activity that activates CAS becomes conscious, though it can affect performance even without any involvement by CAS. His primary concern was to make progress towards an explanation of the way that mental functions are selectively lost to consciousness in various cases of brain damage.

Recurring themes in the early theories

Some important recurring themes can be identified in these models, themes that often reappear in later models. First, they nearly all share the idea that consciousness should be understood in terms of its place in a modular system, consisting of a number of relatively independent subsystems, or modules. Within the modularity assumption, consciousness is commonly treated in terms of information flow, activation, executive control, attention and short-term memory (STM).

The idea that consciousness is the product of (or at least associated with) the flow of information through the cognitive system is widely shared among these theories, and the association of consciousness with information has been carried on into more recent theorizing. It is difficult to separate from the idea that the (or at least a) function of consciousness is to deal with novelty. This idea shows especially in the recurring contrast between tasks that can be handled by well-established routines, which tend not to be conscious, and tasks for which such routines either do not exist or are not firmly established, which are typically conscious. Note that this distinction parallels that between unconscious, specialized, S1 processes and conscious, non-specialized, S2 processes (see Chapter 2).

The theme that will be most important for my purposes is the role of activation in a theory of consciousness. For Shallice (1972), activation level was crucial. For Mandler (1975, 1984, 1992, 1997, 2002), conscious representations are selected from and constructed from unconscious representations that are active and they in turn activate other unconscious representations that are not yet active. Schacter (1990: 174) did not stress activation, but the input to his CAS is 'the highly activated outputs of various modules; weakly activated outputs do not gain access to the awareness system'. In other words, activation is a necessary condition for consciousness.

Also common in the information-processing literature is the notion that executive control, in the form of a central processor or operating system, is important for consciousness, Johnson-Laird (1988) being the best example. The controller can be either the seat of consciousness or just an important element in its occurrence. Kihlstrom's (1987, 1997) use of the self can reasonably be seen as a variant on this idea. Closely related is the theme of attention, commonly treated either as a means of control or as a controller itself. The theories considered in this section did not emphasize the role of attention, though Mandler (1975, 1984, 1992, 1997, 2002) tied consciousness to *focal attention* and suggested that in much previous writing on the subject the latter term frequently could (and perhaps should) be replaced by consciousness. This close connection between consciousness and attention has appeared repeatedly in information-processing theories that are not directly about consciousness but nonetheless find a place for it (e.g. Posner, 1994; Posner & Boies, 1971; Umiltà, 1988).

A final noteworthy theme is the connection between consciousness and the contents of a STM store. This idea was suggested more explicitly by theorists who were not directly concerned with consciousness but focused instead on the cognitive architecture (Atkinson & Shiffrin, 1968; Baddeley, 1986; Broadbent, 1958). These authors saw the short-term store as the location of the current contents of consciousness. Among the theories of consciousness considered so far, Kihlstrom's (1987, 1997) is the most concerned with this aspect, treating awareness of a representation as a consequence of its being connected with self in working memory.

Consciousness has thus been seen, within modular views of the mind, as information flow, as activation, as an executive controller or the process of executive control, as a product of attention and as the contents of a STM store. All of these ideas have some validity. Each is associated with consciousness and each is associated with all the others. The problem is that the nature of these associations is not clear. It is easy to feel that all of these ideas are getting at some common underlying entity or process and that some reconceptualization is needed to bring it out. I will return to these points at the end of the chapter and again in later chapters. But first it is necessary to consider some more recent theories, which have considerable current influence, in greater depth.

Baars' Global Workspace Theory

Bernard Baars' GW theory can reasonably be seen as the beginning of the current interest in consciousness as a part of a cognitive system. It owes much to previous work, including some of that considered in the previous section, but Baars put these ideas together in novel and insightful ways and developed his theory with an extensive review of the relevant psychological literature, later placing it in the context of the nature and functioning of the brain as well. Because of its importance for current thinking, its occasional appearance in SLA theory (e.g. Ellis, 2005; Schmidt, 1990) and its influence on the Modular Online Growth and Use of Language (MOGUL) framework, I will describe GW theory in some detail.

Processors

This theory continues the theme of earlier information-processing theories in treating the mind as composed primarily of a very large number of functionally specialized processors, each working independently in its own domain. Baars (1988: 384) defined a processor as 'a relatively unitary, organized collection of processes that work together in the service of a particular function', where a *process* is 'a set of transformations of a representation'. In other words, a processor is dedicated to a specialized function, which it serves by manipulating representations. In this theory, the mind includes a very large number of these processors, operating for the most part independently and unconsciously. They are structured componentially (or 'recursively' in Baars' terms): one processor can be composed of others, which are in turn composed of others and so on. The system is dynamic, with processors that serve related functions continuously forming new coalitions to serve more general functions, or breaking old ones.

One example of a large-scale processor is the visual system. The two eyes act as subprocessors, usually cooperating to form a visual experience. Their independence is shown when two incompatible images are presented, one to each eye, in which case one will take control of conscious experience at the expense of the other. Many other, more specialized processors can also be identified in the visual system, ranging from a large-scale colour processor to basic feature detectors. Other examples, outside of vision, are standard action sequences, such as answering the telephone. This process consists of the separate actions of picking up the telephone, placing it in the appropriate position against the head and saying 'Hello.' Each of these actions is handled by its own processor. Together, they make up the larger, telephone-answering processor.

Consciousness as global broadcasting of information

The function of consciousness in GW theory is to allow the system to cope with novelty. It does this by facilitating information sharing, thereby allowing a variety of otherwise independent elements to work cooperatively on the novel situation. Processors normally work independently, in their own domains, but when some of them produce coherent information that is of more general relevance, that information occupies the GW and is thereby broadcast to all the others. The information being globally broadcast makes up the current contents of consciousness.

Coalitions of processors constantly compete with one another for access to the GW. Winners are determined by the characteristics of the representations they produce as candidates for consciousness. Basic requirements are that the representation must be coherent and must be active. But Baars has been more concerned with the requirement of *informativeness*: the information that becomes conscious must be such that other processors (other than those that produced it) must adapt to it. Only representations that meet this requirement can become conscious.

Global broadcasting is a slow process, slow in cognitive or neural terms, that is. It begins with a subliminal message, giving processors a preliminary taste of what is on offer. If the potentially conscious representation is sufficiently informative, it receives additional support from these processors, which gradually builds until it reaches a level at which the message becomes conscious and a full broadcast occurs. The relevant processors then make their adaptations to it, after which the informativeness of the message quickly declines, as it has nothing more to offer to those processors. Due to this loss of informativeness, it loses its place in the GW and therefore disappears from awareness, its place being taken by another informative representation.

A representation that has been displaced from the GW becomes part of the unconscious *context*. Baars discussed contexts in some detail, especially in terms of goals and their relation to attention. They are not themselves conscious – i.e. they do not occupy the GW – but they exercise a constant influence on the competition for the GW and therefore help determine the contents of consciousness. The most important context is self, which Baars treats as a relatively stable representation that plays a central background role in shaping consciousness. Thus, self is accommodated in the theory, not as a direct part of conscious experience but rather as a strong and continuous influence on what does become a direct part of it.

As an example of how the theory works, consider what might happen when a person hears his/her name called. All the processors normally involved in recognizing and interpreting speech together produce a representation of the utterance. This representation, because it could lead to adjustments by many other processors, is a good candidate for the GW. The adjustments will include processing for voice recognition, activation of reasoning processes to determine the reason for the call (which will include activation of potentially useful memories), activation of other processes developing and evaluating possible responses and preparation for any oral and/or motor response that might be selected.

The system's efforts to deal with the input produce constant shifts in the contents of the GW. Once the interested processors have made their adjustments, the initial representation (of the person's name being called) ceases to be informative and therefore loses its claim to consciousness, becoming instead part of the unconscious context that shapes subsequent conscious experiences. It is replaced in the GW by whatever new representation best meets the requirements. This could be a representation of the significance of the call, of one or more potential responses or of the actual response itself.

The perceptual bias of consciousness

Baars (1988, 1997a) discussed the *perceptual bias* of consciousness at some length. The things we are normally aware of are things we are seeing and hearing and otherwise sensing, along with internally generated experiences that are inseparable from the senses, especially mental imagery and the 'voice inside the head'. Non-perceptual information, conceptual information in particular, does not seem to play any direct role in this experience, appearing in awareness only to the extent that it evokes related images or corresponds to perceived words, either coming from the senses or uttered by the inner voice. Concepts in themselves lack reportable qualities and seem to be very much a secondary part of phenomenal consciousness. One might speculate (as Baars appears to do) that this perceptual bias is a product of the phylogenetic development of the GW. The GW came into being before the abstract conceptual systems and therefore developed as a means of making sensory information widely available, without any provisions for broadcasting more abstract representations lacking sensory features. Whatever the validity of this idea, it is clear that perceptual representations dominate awareness while concepts remain just offstage.

Novel tasks vs. established routines

A useful way to think of the role of consciousness in GW theory is to distinguish between the type of task that can be carried out by an already existing processor and the type for which no suitable processor yet exists. If a person wants to perform a particular dance step, for example, the awareness that goes with the action will depend to a very large extent on this distinction. If the dance step is not well established – i.e. there is no single processor that can carry it out effectively – the system must activate and coordinate all of the various independent processors that are needed for the action. This is done by means of a series of globally broadcast messages. In other words, awareness of individual subgoals is required, the subgoals being those actions for which suitable processors *do* already exist. This awareness necessarily occurs in the order in which the subgoals are to be carried out, because the processors must be activated in this order.

In contrast, if the system already contains a single processor that can carry out the dance step (which is to say that the step has already been learned), there is no need to recruit independent processors. The GW can simply send out a message that this step is to be carried out; the appropriate processor can take it from there. The phenomenal correlates of this message could be vague and perhaps fleeting, if the processor is well established. It is important to note also that activation of a large-scale processor, such as the visual system, can trigger a very extensive and complex chain of actions, all occurring without any additional involvement by the GW.

Strengths and limitations of GW theory

GW theory has much to recommend it. Baars has been extremely concerned about dealing with evidence that can be connected to his theory (see especially Baars, 1988), and the theory generally does well in this regard. These strengths have been discussed at length in many other places, so I will focus instead on a few points that I see as limitations.

First, the place of emotion in the theory is unclear (but for some discussion, see Schutter & van Honk, 2004). Does emotional awareness involve the GW, just as perceptual awareness does? If so, do the same conditions apply in the determination of which emotion dominates the GW at a given point? Something should also be said in the theory about the simultaneous broadcast of emotional and perceptual elements, a challenge for coherence and seriality in the simple form in which they are commonly presented (I will develop this point in more detail in Chapter 5). Nor is it clear, within GW theory, why conscious experience is so dominated by perceptual elements. Baars' comments on the source of the perceptual bias have been quite limited and tentative.

Another limitation of GW theory is that the concept of a 'representation' has received little development. Baars (1988) defined processors in part as entities that transform representations, and it is representations that occupy the GW and are broadcast to all the processors of the system. But beyond a brief mention of 'memories' and the notion of the GW as a 'blackboard' on which they are written, there was little concern with the questions of what exactly representations are, where exactly they are found in the cognitive system and how they are related to learning. Some additional explication is therefore needed.

GW theory handles the informativeness of consciousness in the most straightforward way, making it an explicit principle: a representation cannot occupy the GW unless it is informative. This approach does the job but has a brute force flavour to it. It would be preferable to derive informativeness from the characteristics of the cognitive system rather than to stipulate it as a principle in itself.

Overall, GW theory is a very impressive effort to put together what is known about consciousness in a coherent and plausible cognitive framework. Not surprisingly, it has inspired a great deal of subsequent experimentation and theorizing, from both cognitive and neural perspectives. Baars' ideas are not universally accepted – little or nothing related to consciousness is – but the extent to which they are accepted is in a sense remarkable, a point that is developed by McGovern and Baars (2007) in their review of current theories. The widespread influence of this approach will be seen repeatedly in the other theories that I will consider in the remainder of this chapter.

Dehaene's Global Neuronal Workspace

One approach that explicitly embraces the GW idea is that of Dehaene and colleagues (Dehaene & Changeux, 2005, 2011; Dehaene et al., 1998, 2003; Dehaene & Naccache, 2001; Gaillard et al., 2009). They have developed an account of consciousness that instantiates the GW idea in neural terms, an account that Shallice and Cooper (2011: 452) describe as the 'first real cognitive neuroscience theory of consciousness'.

Like Baars and many others, Dehaene and colleagues place consciousness in the context of a highly modular system, neural in this case. The individual modules normally act without any involvement of consciousness. The information represented by a given network of neurons becomes conscious as a result of attentional amplification, which connects it to a much broader network, the GW, primarily involving neurons in prefrontal and anterior cingulate cortex along with various associative areas, with thalamocortical connections playing a crucial role. When the activity of the workspace network and the local representation becomes coherent and self-sustaining (they sometimes use the term 'ignition' here), the information is then widely available through the brain, and this availability is the conscious experience. Establishment of this coherent state depends on the local representation of the information achieving sufficiently intense and enduring activation (Condition 2 of Gaillard et al., 2009). The idea of an 'active representation' plays a large role in this account.

These researchers emphasize that no executive controller is involved in any part of this process (see also Dehaene & Changeux, 1997). Instead, other processors constantly exert a strong influence on the activity, especially those that 'encode the behavioral context, goals, and rewards of the organism' (Dehaene & Naccache, 2001: 15). This idea looks a great deal like Baars' notion of *contexts*, described above. The interplay of these various processors with the workspace network and with each other results in a dynamic process of one active representation replacing another as the content of consciousness. It also implies a dynamic, shifting workspace, highly reminiscent of Edelman's (1992, 2003; Edelman & Tononi, 2000) *dynamic core* (see below). This process is also strongly influenced by reward signals, which allow representations in the workspace to be associated with a positive or negative value (Dehaene & Changeux, 2000; Dehaene et al., 1998).

The neuronal GW model has been applied to a number of interesting phenomena, including the Stroop effect (Dehaene et al., 1998), the attentional blink (Dehaene et al., 2003) and inattentional blindness (Dehaene & Changeux, 2005). Using simple simulations of the phenomena based on the model, the authors were able to provide reasonable, if tentative accounts.

This neural theory is of course closely associated with Baars' GW idea, but Dehaene and his colleagues also tie it to various other proposals, including the central executive of Baddeley (1986), the supervisory attentional system of Shallice (1988a), the anterior attention system of Posner (1994) and the dynamic core of Tononi and Edelman (1998), each of which captures the idea of a central system that takes processing beyond the individual modules and is necessary for consciousness, working memory and executive control (see Sigman & Dehaene, 2006). The model thus shows important affinities to other work that has approached the problem of consciousness from a variety of directions. I will return to these shared points at the end of this survey.

Cooney and Gazzaniga's Account of Consciousness in Certain Neurological Disorders

The approach to consciousness offered by Cooney and Gazzaniga (2003) is an application of Gazzaniga's more general ideas on the brain and the mind, developed over a great many years (e.g. Gazzaniga, 1989, 1992, 1998, 2011). He has consistently argued, very forcefully, for a highly modular view of the brain, in which it is made up of an enormous number of independent controllers. The basic modular structure reflects genetic guidelines. One important module is the *interpreter*, a left-brain module that seeks to make sense of the world and of the mind itself, constructing a mythical self that provides a coherent and satisfying account of the workings and products of the vast ensemble of separate processes, over which it actually has no control and little understanding. This concept was based primarily on Gazzaniga's extensive work with split-brain patients, but his various books have offered an array of additional evidence for it.

Cooney and Gazzaniga's (2003) treatment of consciousness has much in common with various other accounts, especially Baars and Dehaene. The contents of consciousness come from particular modules currently involved in processing, but consciousness requires the participation of a global neuronal workspace, which integrates the activity of the various modules and makes locally produced information widely available. They associated the workspace, somewhat tentatively, with prefrontal cortex, anterior cingulate cortex and thalamocortical interactions. Activation appears to play a central, if usually implicit role in this account. The information that can make up the conscious experience is that which is active at the time, and it actually becomes conscious when it is 'sufficiently amplified within the system to generate a coherent network state' (Cooney & Gazzaniga, 2003: 162). Also worth noting is the focus on perceptual representations as the contents of consciousness.

Cooney and Gazzaniga offered this theory as an account for a variety of often bizarre problems that occur with particular types of brain damage. A person who has lost the ability to perceive the left half of their visual world is completely unaware that anything is wrong. A person who has lost awareness of one hand denies that a problem exists and even denies that the hand belongs to them. Such cases are analyzed as examples of the interpreter making sense of whatever input it receives. If the input lacks the information that would indicate the existence of a hand, it will accept that the hand does not exist and seek to construct a story in which observed facts are compatible with this idea. These disorders thus represent the normal functioning of the interpreter module, the problem being that it is dealing with odd, impoverished input.

Damasio's Body- and Self-oriented Theory

Antonio Damasio brings to the study of consciousness a perspective based on clinical experience with various forms of breakdowns in consciousness. The emphasis in his thinking has always been on the inseparability of brain and body and the centrality of bodily survival for the development of consciousness and as the foundation for everything that we are (see Damasio, 1994, 1999, 2003, 2010). Recently, the idea of self has come to play an increasingly large role in his work (Damasio, 2010). Damasio's books and papers are a treasure trove of insights, though getting a grasp on them and precisely relating them to one another can be a challenge.

Damasio stresses that brain development is about managing life, i.e. maintaining an appropriate internal body state and handling external concerns – finding food, avoiding danger and reproducing. The basic element underlying this development is *biological value*: everything in the organism's experience is valued in terms of its contribution, positive or negative, to the basic functions of survival and reproduction. Development is thus about managing biological value. At perhaps the most fundamental level, the mechanisms are pleasure and pain, pleasure reflecting body states that contribute to the organism's survival and reproduction and pain reflecting states that are potentially harmful to those goals. Drives and motivations represent somewhat more sophisticated regulatory mechanisms, again pushing the organism towards actions that contribute to survival and reproduction and away from those that do not. Emotions serve the same function in a still more sophisticated manner. Rational decision-making also has its basis in value, which serves to mark available options in terms of their desirability, which in turn is ultimately based on considerations of survival and reproduction, though at this level of sophistication the biological roots can be quite far removed. Finally, the ultimate manager of value, and therefore the ultimate regulator of life, is the conscious self.

Damasio actually distinguishes three selves, representing successive stages of evolutionary development. The *protoself* directly represents the state of the body and serves to maintain homeostasis. It gives rise to *primordial feelings*. From this basis the *core self* developed from interactions between the organism and objects in its environment. It is responsible for *core consciousness*, the immediate experience of a self dealing with the here and now. The latest, most sophisticated and most human version of self is the *autobiographical self*, which gives rise to *extended consciousness*, involving a more developed sense of self, placed in a broader context, with a history and a future.

The requirements for consciousness are, first, a protoself representing the body and its current condition and needs and, second, unified *images* of the surrounding world that allow the organism to act in ways that can maintain or improve that condition and fulfil its needs. Consciousness brings the two together, allowing action guidance that is based on the state of the body and its needs. This combination has great survival value, explaining why consciousness evolved in the first place.

The idea of *image* is crucial in this account. The term is used in a broad sense to include all the senses, plus feelings, and even abstract elements. Damasio originally drew a sharp distinction between the mental – images – and the neural – *maps* or *neural patterns*. But Damasio (2010) largely abandoned this distinction, using the three terms more or less as synonyms. When used in the mental sense, his terms are, as far as I can see, indistinguishable from *representation* as I use it throughout this book. Particularly noteworthy in this regard is that we both include affect under the terms.

A recurring theme in the theories previously discussed is the idea that consciousness is the product of synchronized activity across broad and varying areas of the brain. Damasio's work shares this theme. This synchronized activity relates images to each other in coherent ways. Perhaps the most important and distinctive element of his view, in this respect, is that self appears to be the essential synchronizer.

Many authors give attention a central place in their accounts of synchronization. Damasio, in contrast, does relatively little with the concept. Damasio (2010: 203) refers to attention as a common name for the focus of processing resources on a particular object, suggesting that he is reluctant to treat attention as a genuine cognitive or neural entity, a reluctance that I share (see discussion in Chapter 2). While other theorists treat attention as the mechanism that selects certain images for current consciousness, Damasio seems to rely at least partly on value for this function. Different degrees of value are assigned to images, helping to shape the conscious experience in terms of what images are experienced, in what order, and what parts of the images are most prominent.

The concept of activation is not directly developed in Damasio's work but is clearly present, in the neural sense, as a central background notion, as can be seen in the idea of synchronized neural activity for example. Images can be active or inactive, and it is the pattern of their activity that underlies conscious experience. Damasio (2010: 67) offers electronic billboards as a metaphor for what goes on in the brain in visual experience. The potential experiences are present in the array of light bulbs, and the actual experience at any given moment is defined by the pattern of currently active bulbs, which constantly shifts.

Damasio's emphasis on self as an inherent part of conscious experience distinguishes his thinking, in a fundamental way, from most of the other theorists considered here. Others tend to treat it as a background feature, part of the context that determines the current content of consciousness without actually being part of it. This is, most notably, the position of Baars, who takes self as a context, the ultimate context. Most other authors are closer to Baars than to Damasio in this respect, if they consider the issue at all. It is not hard to understand why differences occur on this point, as it is largely a matter of introspection, which can be quite slippery. I am inclined to go along with Damasio: when I see a sunset, the experience is not just a sunset but rather me seeing a sunset; I am inherently involved in that experience. But it is difficult to entirely dismiss the alternative perspective, that this self is not actually part of the experience but is rather a context that shapes that experience and imposes an interpretation on it.

Edelman's Dynamic Core

Nobel Prize winner Gerald Edelman has offered a complex and challenging account of consciousness, in the context of no less complex and challenging an account of the brain in general. In the past, he collaborated extensively with Giulio Tononi, and so it is not always clear what ideas are to be attributed to one or the other or both. But Edelman appears to have primary responsibility for the ideas considered in this section, while Tononi's important extensions will be presented in the following section. The most accessible presentations of the ideas are Edelman (2004, 2006) and the book he wrote together with Tononi (Edelman & Tononi, 2000; but see also Boitano, 1996; Edelman, 1989, 1992, 2003; Edelman *et al.*, 2011; Tononi & Edelman, 1998).

Scene

A central idea in Edelman's presentation is *scene*, which appears to be comparable to Damasio's image. Edelman describes it as a product of categorization – the brain using memories to categorize perception, i.e. to impose objects and events on what is currently being perceived. But of course sensory input at any given time is compatible with an enormous number of possible experiences. In an ordinary instance of walking down a street, for example, we can be aware at any given moment of the movements of our legs, the tightness of our shoes, the feel of the wind; or the sound of the wind or of people speaking or cars honking or our feet hitting the pavement; or the sight of any of countless objects around us or particular features of any of the things we are hearing or seeing. Or we could be conscious of memories, thoughts, feelings, with little or no relation to what the senses are currently receiving. The selection among the possibilities is based on *value systems*: the things that are important to the organism based on its genes and its life experience. Those candidate scenes that are made especially salient by the organism's values are the contents of consciousness.

The dynamic core

Edelman's theory is very much a neural approach. Its emphasis is on the thalamocortical system, i.e. the system of rich connections between the thalamus and cortical areas in general and also among the various cortical regions. Consciousness was made possible by the development of massive bidirectional fibre systems connecting these different areas of the brain. These connections produce rich, high-speed crosstalk between the different regions, allowing them to synchronize their activity, in the absence of any executive controller. The synchronization is brought about by *re-entrant* connections: most of the rich connections in the thalamocortical system are, crucially, bidirectional, allowing the various areas to constantly talk back and forth to each other, integrating their information.

The synchronized areas and their activity represent the *dynamic core*. The core is constantly shifting (hence 'dynamic'), though it is not always clear if Edelman wants to see it as one core with the activity within it constantly shifting or as an arbitrary number of different cores, defined by current activity; he seems to use the term both ways at different points. The current details of the core depend very much on the value systems. These are based on relatively tiny centres in the brain stem from where neuromodulators are widely distributed across the cortex, greatly affecting neural activity and the potential for local changes (i.e. learning).

The characteristics of the theory are illustrated by the simple example of a person who is exposed to pure blue, with no competing input or internal activity (Edelman & Tononi, 2000: 166, 173). The sensory stimulation leads to activity in neuronal groups in inferotemporal cortex that respond to blue. These groups are part of the dynamic core and so the activation creates a 'perturbation' that quickly spreads throughout the core, leading to sustained re-entrant activity over wide areas of the brain. This activity results in, or entails, the experience of blue. The dynamic core includes neuronal groups representing all the various senses, not just vision. It also includes a variety of additional elements, all those that are needed to establish the necessary information, in the technical sense, i.e. everything needed to distinguish the current state of the system from all other possible states. The active elements that constitute the dynamic core are extremely numerous and diverse.

Edelman's attention in such matters centres on the global activity rather than the local activity that provides the content for the experience – that of the 'blue' neuronal groups in the example just presented. His main interest in discussing such cases seems in fact to be in rejecting the idea that consciousness is about what is going on at a particular location (the 'blue' location, for example) and stressing the broad integration needed for awareness. While the importance of the integration is clear, this approach risks undervaluing the local element. A theory of consciousness must deal with both the general, global activity that makes consciousness possible and the specific, local activity that provides its content, as well as the relation between the two. Edelman and Tononi (2000: 166) do acknowledge that the 'blue' neuronal groups are highly active during an experience of blue and that groups corresponding to other colours are not (and this is presumably what it means to say that a certain possible scene is made salient/selected by the value systems) – but only in passing, and with no development. The point deserves more attention than they are inclined to give it.

Tononi's Information Integration Theory

Giulio Tononi worked extensively with Edelman, and his ideas about consciousness appear to have their roots firmly in this work. Tononi (2004, 2007, 2008, 2012; Tononi & Edelman, 1998) proposed that consciousness results from the integration of large amounts of information. Any system that does this is conscious. A crucial virtue of his approach is that it includes an explicit and quantifiable notion of information, *phi*, beginning with Claude Shannon's traditional account of information but going well beyond it (see especially Tononi & Sporns, 2003). The mathematical details are challenging and have little significance for the discussion in this book, so I will not go into them.

With this background, Tononi was able to show that the greatest information integration, i.e. the highest levels of phi, comes from systems that are made up of distinct modules with strong interconnectivity among them. An extremely modular system is not conducive to consciousness because the information in the various modules is integrated only locally. But nor is a homogeneous, undifferentiated system. This is an important finding. Its implication is that consciousness should be found in the portions of the cognitive system that are modular but with strong interactions among the modules. There is a significant resemblance between this conclusion and the GW idea that the essence of consciousness is the sharing of information among a set of independent modules. The major difference is in the notion of information. For Tononi it is not so much a matter of sharing existing information as it is the creation of information, defined as the reduction of uncertainty. But this difference should not obscure the fundamental agreement between the approaches.

Tononi differs from the other theorists considered here in that he takes the additional step into metaphysics, making the intriguing claim that experience, i.e. integrated information, is comparable to mass and energy; it is one of the basic components of reality. This idea certainly has appeal. But like other metaphysical positions its validity is quite difficult to evaluate, and I will not try to do so here.

Tononi's approach is impressive in the way that it takes a central characteristic of consciousness, namely informativeness and the need for its integration, and develops from it a coherent theory with a quantitative measure of the key variable: information integration. The practical value of the measure is greatly limited by the extreme complexity of the calculations involved, but the relatively successful effort to quantify the factor underlying conscious experience and draw predictions from that measure should not be taken lightly. A possible challenge for the theory is the finding of Mudrik et al. (2011) that a considerable amount of information integration can occur in a visual scene without awareness.

The place of emotional experience is an open question for the work of Edelman and Tononi. They repeatedly say that the thalamocortical system is not necessarily the only system that yields consciousness, but to the best of my knowledge they have not developed this point anywhere. In the context of consciousness, at times they refer to the limbic system, which is closely associated with emotion, suggesting that perhaps it acts in a manner comparable to the thalamocortical system, producing emotional consciousness. Value systems are intimately associated with emotion, but Edelman and Tononi are vague on just what this association amounts to. The place of emotion in their approach needs to be developed more fully and explicitly.

Activation is not a major concept for Edelman and Tononi – not explicitly, that is. It could well be seen as a fundamental, if implicit element in their work. The integration of information is presumably a matter of neural activity. The high levels of integration needed for consciousness presumably involve especially high levels of this activity. Crucially, this activity must be in some sense focused. They stress that homogeneous activity corresponds not to consciousness but rather a lack of consciousness, as in sleep or an epileptic seizure. Nor does isolated local activity yield consciousness. The activity that represents (or is) information integration must be widespread and yet have a focus, the latter presumably being the neural correlates of the current contents of consciousness.

Crick and Koch's Neurobiological Framework

Francis Crick's participation in the study of consciousness did much to make it respectable as a legitimate scientific pursuit (see especially Crick, 1994). He worked extensively with Christof Koch (e.g. Crick & Koch, 1990, 1998, 2000; Koch, 2004), who has continued with the work since Crick's death. They described their joint work as seeking the neural correlates of consciousness. Perhaps the most notable and influential theme in their efforts to identify these correlates was the idea of synchronized firing of neurons across the brain, particularly in the thalamocortical system. This work did not produce a theory as such but rather a variety of insights loosely connected in a 'neurobiological framework' (Crick & Koch, 2003, 2007) that can guide research and theory development.

Koch's current thinking on consciousness is summarized in his recent book (Koch, 2012). One point that he emphasizes is the importance of unconscious processes, what he and Crick referred to as 'zombies' (Crick & Koch, 2000). This is not to minimize the importance of consciousness but rather to clarify its special status. Koch describes *enabling factors* that make consciousness possible. These are subcortical structures that 'tune' general activity up or down by releasing various chemicals – neuromodulators such as dopamine and serotonin – into the thalamocortical system. Consciousness probably requires a threshold level of activity, which is made possible by these enabling factors. Conscious experience is associated with a coalition of neurons in the thalamocortical system. This coalition must become dominant and maintain itself for a relatively long period (long in neural terms). This crucially involves a dialogue between front and back portions of the brain, the word 'dialogue' referring to the activity of re-entrant loops of the sort described above in regard to Edelman's ideas. Local posterior areas provide the content of the conscious experience but cannot in themselves yield consciousness, which requires their participation in a stable coalition including frontal areas. An interesting feature of Koch's more recent writing is his acceptance of Tononi's information integration theory and his joint work with Tononi (Koch & Tononi, 2008, 2011; Tononi & Koch, 2008).

Jackendoff's Intermediate-levels Theory

Ray Jackendoff is a linguist by training, a former student of Noam Chomsky. But his interests are broad, ranging from formal syntax and semantics to culture. He took on the subject of consciousness in one of his early books (Jackendoff, 1987) and has further developed his ideas in a number of subsequent books and papers (e.g. Jackendoff, 1996, 1997, 2007; see also Prinz, 2007). The central point of Jackendoff's (1987) proposal is that consciousness is a characteristic of intermediate levels of the cognitive system. In this view, the lower levels represent early sensory processing while the higher levels are primarily conceptual. Consciousness is found between the two, in representations that are not so abstract as the conceptual and not so specific as the early sensory. Jackendoff (2007) characterized the intermediate level as perceptual, in contrast to the sensory below it and the cognitive above it.

Consciousness of language

For the case of language, Jackendoff (1987) argued that the intermediate level is represented by his *phonological structures* (a central part of his theory of language, to which I will return in the following chapter), but noted that only some aspects of phonological structures can be conscious. We are aware of individual language sounds and of stress, for instance, but not of the formal phonological features which compose the sounds. This partial, and rather loose, association of awareness with a component of his theory must be seen as a weakness in the proposal, a weakness which appears in different forms in later versions. For Jackendoff (1997), the conscious aspect of language is 'phonetic form', which is not an explicit component of his theory and is not explained. The use of 'phonetic' rather than 'phonological' suggests that the representations that become conscious are much closer to the sounds themselves than they are to his more abstract level of phonological structures, an idea that fits well with the general notion of intermediate level. But in the brief comments on consciousness found in Jackendoff (2002), he returned to 'phonological', again hedging with a statement that the linguistic structures we are aware of are 'essentially phonological'. Jackendoff (2007) continued to use 'phonological structure' but added other hedges, at one point referring to awareness of 'phonetic form'.

I suggest that the brief uses of 'phonetic' in place of 'phonological' are on the right track. Awareness of linguistic sound does not in fact appear to be distinguishable in any fundamental way from awareness of meaningful but non-linguistic sounds such as the ringing of a bell. So what we are aware of in speech is probably best characterized not as linguistic sound but simply as sound. Thus, the intermediate level of language processing is not part of language processing itself, but rather a stage that precedes it. This conclusion fits well with the spirit of Jackendoff's hypothesis, defining intermediate levels entirely in terms of perceptual processing: the output of perceptual processing is in all cases the intermediate level. I will return to this point in Chapter 5.

How a representation becomes conscious

To this point, the theory offers an explanation for the kinds of representations that can become conscious but does not specify which of them actually do become conscious at a given time, or how the process occurs. For this, Jackendoff's (1987) first requirement was that the representation must be *active*, meaning in use by the processing system.[1] But he then replaced this with a requirement that it be in STM. His cognitive architecture included a number of distinct STM systems, so this requirement means that a visual representation must be currently in visual STM, a phonological representation must be currently in linguistic STM, etc. In other words, the visual system is currently treating the representation as a possible account of what the person is currently seeing, or the linguistic system is currently treating it as a possible account of what the person is hearing, etc. The relevant STM may contain a number of such structures at a given time, so the next requirement is that a *selection function* picks out the most salient or coherent of them, i.e. the one that offers the best guess at what is currently being perceived. This function is an inherent part of each STM and/or processor. It excludes all the candidates except one and so results in unitary contents of consciousness. After this, attention serves to focus processing on particular portions of the selected representation, producing a more articulated representation and thereby making it more vivid. Jackendoff (2007) also speaks of attention determining which of many potentially conscious objects in the perceptual world actually become conscious.

Valuation

Jackendoff argues that conscious experience includes two types of elements: the usual perceptual elements, or *content features*, and an additional set of features, the *value features*, which become attached to individual content features in experience and give that experience a 'feel'. Conscious experience for Jackendoff thus consists of an intermediate representation along with whatever value features are associated with it. The most important of these value features, for my purposes, is *affective* value. Jackendoff (2007) presented it as a feature that can be either present or absent and, when present, can assume either a positive or negative value (valence) and can have, as a separate element, varying intensities. When an experience is tagged with [+affective], this means it *matters* to the person, positively or negatively. He also raised the possibility that this treatment might be extended to emotion in general but declined to pursue the idea. Thus, it remains unclear how emotions themselves are to be realized in his account or exactly how they are related to the affective value features.

Consciousness and thought

One strength of Jackendoff's approach to consciousness and of his theory in general, I suggest, is the way that it deals with the nature of thought as an interaction between unconscious concepts and conscious percepts. Recall the 'perceptual bias' of consciousness discussed above: we are directly aware of perceptual but not conceptual elements, the latter instead playing a background role in consciousness. This central fact of conscious experience, which any adequate theory must explain, is a natural consequence of Jackendoff's approach. For Jackendoff, concepts are necessarily high-level representations and therefore cannot appear in consciousness, while perceptual representations are the prototypical intermediate-level items and therefore should be a normal part of conscious experience. He developed these ideas in depth in Jackendoff (1996) and to some extent in various other publications (especially Jackendoff, 1997). My own comments on the relation between concepts and consciousness, to be presented in Chapter 5, differ little from those of Jackendoff.

Strengths and limitations of Jackendoff's theory

The Intermediate-Levels Hypothesis is not as clear as one might like but nonetheless represents a valid and important observation, which should be accommodated in a theory of consciousness. I will do so in Chapter 5. Jackendoff's notion of a selection function is also interesting and will also appear there, in a quite different form, as will the idea of valuation and the recurring ideas that attention and STM (activation) are crucial for awareness. Finally, his account of thought and consciousness is, in my judgement, quite insightful and should have a place in a theory of consciousness.

Baddeley's Working Memory Model

The working memory model, briefly described in Chapter 2, was not meant to be a theory of consciousness and has never been presented as one, but its relevance to studies of consciousness is clear. In recent years, Baddeley has suggested a specific connection between the model and consciousness, so some discussion is appropriate here. (For interesting discussion of awareness in the working memory model, see McGovern & Baars, 2007.)

Baddeley's model was based on existing models of STM (see Atkinson & Shiffrin, 1968; Foster, 2009), differing from them mainly in its fractionation of the short-term store into component parts and its emphasis on the active character of the store, as a place in which work is done with its current contents. The model originally consisted of a *phonological loop*, where language sounds are held and can be continually reconstructed (hence 'loop'), a *visuospatial sketchpad* holding visual and spatial information and a *central executive* with rather murky functions commonly considered to centre around allocation of attention. For present purposes, the most interesting aspect of the working memory model is the addition of the *episodic buffer* (see Baddeley, 2000, 2007, 2012, and discussion in Andrade, 2001). The function of the buffer is to integrate information from memory and perception with that in the loop and the sketchpad, to produce a temporary unified representation. Baddeley (2007: 316) said that he was 'inclined to identify the episodic buffer with the representation of events that are currently in conscious awareness'.

Working memory has come to play an increasingly important role in neural research, the focus being on what happens in the brain when information is held in memory for a short period of time, i.e. the information is presented at one time and put to use after a short delay. There has not been much concern with consciousness, no doubt because animal studies have dominated this research, but the intimate connection between working memory and consciousness makes the ideas relevant to theories of consciousness. They might well be seen as implicit theories of consciousness. In these theories once again we find the theme of activity sustained by reciprocal connections across widely separated areas of the brain. Fuster (2009: 2054), for example, wrote that 'the mechanisms of working memory are not yet established, but there is increasing evidence that they include the reverberation in circuits within the neural network, part of long-term memory, that has been activated by the memorandum' (see also Brunel & Wang, 2001).

Some Holistic Treatments of Consciousness

A number of theories have emphasized the more holistic aspects of consciousness. I will briefly review some of them here.

An important example is the *dominant focus* model of Marcel Kinsbourne (1988, 1997, 2006). It differs from GW theory and other approaches in that it does not associate consciousness with any particular system. Consciousness is about general activity in the system as a whole, not about special structures designed to support it. For Kinsbourne, the first requirement for a representation to become part of conscious experience is thus strong activation. The second is duration. But this factor can probably be reduced to activation. A representation's rise to consciousness is, in neural terms, a slow process (cf. Baars, 1988). During this period, its activation level can be said to gradually rise towards the consciousness threshold. If the period is too brief, it will never reach the threshold. Thus, the single factor of activation can probably explain the role of duration. Kinsbourne (1997) discussed a third factor, *congruence*, but this factor does not appear in his more recent work (Kinsbourne, 2006), so I will not consider it here.

The work of Susan Greenfield (e.g. Greenfield, 2002; Greenfield & Collins, 2005; see also Koch & Greenfield, 2007) shares its leading idea with Kinsbourne. Greenfield strongly rejects the idea that conscious experience is associated with any particular locations, in favour of a holistic view in terms of neuronal assemblies varying in size as a function of neuromodulatory activity in the lower parts of the brain. She offers this variation as the basis for differing states of consciousness – normal adult assembly sizes vs. excessive sizes associated with depression and reduced sizes associated with childhood, dreaming, schizophrenia and the use of 'lose-your-mind' drugs such as ecstasy. Her focus is on the presence or absence of consciousness and the broad characteristics of the current state, not in the specific contents of a conscious experience. A view in harmony with that of Greenfield was presented by Goldberg (2009), who strongly rejected modularity, treating the idea with scorn.

A different variety of holistic thinking can be found in the work of Pribram (1971; Pribram & Meade, 1999). He focused on a type of neural processing that has received relatively little attention, that which goes on in the web of fibres formed by the ends of an axon (the *teledendrons*) and the dendrites of the neighbouring neuron to which they indirectly connect. Such activity going on across the cortex produces wave patterns, comparable to holograms. For Pribram, awareness occurs when the novelty of input creates a 'temporal hold' on the formation of a wave pattern.

Quantum Theories of Consciousness

A number of theorists have sought to explain consciousness in terms of quantum theory (e.g. Hameroff & Penrose, 1996; Lockwood, 1989; Penrose, 1989, 1994; Stapp, 2007; Yasue, 1999). A leading idea in this work is that mind and physical reality cannot be fully understood in isolation from one another. The goal then is to apply the concepts of quantum theory to the brain in ways that will yield an understanding of consciousness and other mysteries of the mind and at the same time deepen understanding of quantum phenomena. A common criticism of these theories is that they seek to explain one mystery, consciousness, by appeal to another mystery, quantum phenomena. While this criticism has some validity – quantum phenomena are certainly puzzling and counter-intuitive – it does not seem to me entirely fair. Quantum theory is well established and tested and so the link with consciousness does point to a direction in which to look for serious explanations. Additionally, it is certainly possible that at the most fundamental level, consciousness and physical reality really cannot be understood separately. It would be folly to casually dismiss this possibility. But while the ideas are intriguing and deserve to be taken seriously, at this point they have little to offer to a cognitively oriented study of consciousness or, more specifically, to a study of consciousness in second language learning. So I will make no further mention of them.

Towards a Synthesis: Some Common Themes in the Theories

It is time now to step back from the individual theories and try to gain a broader perspective on the efforts that they represent to obtain a scientific understanding of consciousness. A number of important themes can be extracted from these efforts, which I see as pointing the way to a genuine understanding. These include the modularity of the cognitive system (or the brain) and, within this sort of system, the roles of activation (particularly synchronized activation), STM storage, executive control, attention, value and information. Here, I will discuss these various themes and how they might tie together, the goal being to lay the groundwork for my own proposal in Chapter 5.

Modularity

The first of the themes is modularity. Setting aside the quantum theories and those theories that I have labelled 'holistic', the theme is virtually universal in the literature. In general, the authors are not concerned about the details of modularity or of how their ideas relate to the work of Fodor and others who have explicitly discussed the nature of modularity, Jackendoff being the dramatic exception. The concept of modularity that they share is based on functional specialization. They hypothesize that the mind consists of various specialist units and that consciousness should be understood within a system of this sort, though considerable differences exist on the specific functions in terms of which the mind is differentiated and exactly how consciousness fits in.

Holistic theories of consciousness are commonly seen as the antithesis of modular approaches, but this contrast may do more to obscure the issues than to clarify them. A strong holistic element appears repeatedly in the modular theories. In these accounts, the modules are typically responsible for the specific contents of each conscious experience while the holistic element provides the essential means by which that content becomes more than just a matter of local, unconscious processing. Thus, holistic and modular approaches need not be in conflict. It seems to me very difficult, in fact, to imagine an adequate account of consciousness that does not include both elements. (Compare the discussion of 'global theories' by McGovern & Baars, 2007.)

Consider Greenfield's (2002) idea that the size of neuronal assemblies in the cortex varies as a function of neuromodulatory activity in the lower parts of the brain, which she offered as the basis for differing states of consciousness, including its absence. This holistic notion seems perfectly compatible with the various GW conceptions of consciousness, which explicitly acknowledge the necessity of such neuromodulatory activity for consciousness. Dehaene explicitly treats the workspace as dynamic, constantly shifting its boundaries. Even for modular theorists who do not make any such claim, there is no apparent reason why they could not; the idea that neuromodulatory activity underlies conscious states appears to be fully compatible with what they do claim. The modular aspects of these theories are intended to account for the specific contents of consciousness, while the phenomena that Greenfield is describing are about the general state of consciousness, an entirely different matter. Both are essential to a theory of consciousness.

This complementarity is shown nicely by what I would call the non-argument between Koch and Greenfield (2007). The article is presented, by the editors and the two authors, as a debate over the brain activity that corresponds to consciousness, but the only major difference revealed there is that Koch wants to focus on one aspect of the problem, the contents of consciousness, and Greenfield wants to focus on the other, the presence or absence of consciousness and its degree. Koch describes the way that an experience of seeing a patch of red, for example, is related to cortical activity. He acknowledges that all conscious experience depends on continuous activity, by arousal circuits, that originates from below the cortex and has very broad influences on cortical activity. But he has little to say about this aspect of the phenomena, focusing instead on the contents of consciousness. Greenfield dismisses most of Koch's comments by saying that the kinds of studies he does are about the *contents* of consciousness and are therefore not about consciousness but rather attention, a topic that she is not interested in discussing. Her interest is in how the varying sizes of neuron assemblies correspond to different states of awareness and non-awareness. The article does contain occasional hints of genuine disagreement, as when Greenfield accuses Koch of 'a 21st-century form of phrenology, in which different functions are related directly to different brain regions' (Koch & Greenfield, 2007: 81). But instead of offering a serious critique or an alternative account of how a particular percept can be conscious, she dismisses the whole subject as irrelevant. This debate is comparable to the one carried on by the blind men who felt different parts of an elephant's body and drew conflicting conclusions about what an elephant is really like.

Activation

Another theme that appears repeatedly in the literature, even in widely differing theories, is the importance of *activation*. This is in fact a traditional metaphor for consciousness (see Baars, 1988), according to which we are conscious of things that cause high levels of mental activity. A sudden loud noise is guaranteed to become conscious while a soft noise might well remain outside awareness. More generally, the louder a noise is, the more likely we are to become aware of it. A visual object that dominates our view, by virtue of its size, movement, colour, interest or whatever, is likely to become conscious, while a minor element of the scene is not. A strong emotional reaction to something makes it more likely to become and remain conscious. Such observations all point to the conclusion that it is the strength of a potentially experienced item – the activation that it produces in the mind/brain – that determines whether it reaches consciousness or not. This relation between activity and awareness can also be seen in research on subliminal perception and subliminal learning: in these cases in which we are not aware of a stimulus, there appears to be very limited activity involving that stimulus (Greenwald *et al.*, 1995; Kihlstrom, 1996; Merikle *et al.*, 2001).

It is not surprising, then, to find that the activation theme is present very generally in the theories summarized above. It appears in both cognitive and neural theories, and while the concept was created for distinct purposes in the two types of theory, they appear to be quite compatible, providing a fundamental link between the different levels of explanation. A representation in a cognitive theory corresponds to a network or *assembly* of neurons in a neural theory. An active representation corresponds to a network in which substantial physical (electrochemical) activity is currently taking place. General activation in a cognitive system corresponds to widespread activity in the brain, especially the cortex. In both cognitive and neural accounts, the activation can be divided into these two types, the general and the local. We can speak of activation of the local elements that constitute the current contents of consciousness and also of a more general, widespread activation that is associated with the local activity but goes well beyond it, establishing connections to additional modules/networks.

This point brings out a closely related theme in the various theories: the idea that consciousness requires widespread *synchronized* (or *integrated*) activity in the system. In GW accounts, this idea is at the heart of the notion of broadcasting. It is of course crucial for Tononi and Edelman as well. Their neural account focuses on the thalamocortical system. They also offer the need for integration as an explanation for the capacity limits of consciousness: too many subprocesses operating at once can disrupt the coherence of the dynamic core (Edelman & Tononi, 2000: 150). An approach with striking similarities to that of Edelman is offered by Llinás and colleagues (Llinás & Paré, 1991; Llinás & Ribary, 1993; Llinás *et al.*, 1998; see also Joliot *et al.*, 1994; Ribary *et al.*, 1991). Their emphasis is on the rich reciprocal connections between the thalamus and the cortex. Synchronized neural activity through this thalamocortical system binds the elements of a potential conscious experience together, producing an actual conscious experience. Greenfield's (2002; Greenfield & Collins, 2005) account of consciousness and the brain is quite similar as well.

The idea of synchronized activity underlying consciousness also appears in the accounts of Damasio (1999, 2003, 2010), Crick and Koch (2003, 2007), Koch (2004), Cooney and Gazzaniga (2003), Maia and Cleeremans (2005) and Kinsbourne (1988). Kinsbourne stressed that activity that does not become integrated with other activity does not contribute to awareness. A similar idea appears in the connectionist writings of McClelland (1997: 505), who suggested that partially activated elements participate in conscious experience if and only if they can be brought together with active elements in a coherent way: 'Consciousness reflects the contents of these coherent states'. The *supramodular interaction theory* of Morsella (2005) might also be seen in these terms. Morsella proposed that some response systems that involve control of the skeletal muscles must be integrated for the sake of adaptive behaviour, and phenomenal states (consciousness) make this integration possible. He described his theory, with some qualification, as one of many (including several discussed here) representing the *integration consensus* on consciousness.

Thus, coherent, integrated activity is widely seen as a necessary part of any account of consciousness. I will suggest in Chapters 4 and 5 that this coherence and integration is actually a special case of a far more general phenomenon, characterizing cognition in general rather than just conscious cognition.

Importantly, the synchronization referred to in these accounts is not synchronization of the entire system. Edelman and Tononi emphasize that truly system-wide synchronized activity is a mark of the *lack* of consciousness found in dreamless sleep and epileptic seizures. The synchronization associated with awareness is dynamic, constantly shifting in its details. The way I would characterize this is that system-wide processing must be focused on one particular representation or set of representations at a time, which then becomes conscious. In the absence of such a focus, there is no consciousness.

Llinás and colleagues distinguish two different thalamocortical systems (see especially Llinás & Ribary, 1993), a specific system providing the sensory content of awareness and a non-specific system producing more general synchronization. These ideas reflect themes that have since appeared repeatedly in the literature and can be connected to the idea of information sharing, as in Baars' GW: activation in the specific system, associated with a particular sensory modality, is broadcast by means of the synchronization in the thalamocortical system.

Thus, conscious experience is the combination of very widespread integrated/synchronized activity with a focus on some local representation, activation of the latter providing the contents of the experience. A theory of consciousness should incorporate both of these elements, along with the relation between them. The local activity has typically been associated with sensory processing (including internally generated sensory experience, i.e. memories, dreams, imagination, hallucinations, the voice in the head), but it should also include affective and related experiences, as well as the experience of self.

The contents of a short-term memory store

Another important view is that we are conscious specifically of the contents of an STM store. For Jackendoff, the contents of consciousness are intermediate-level representations that have been selected from among those currently found in STM. Kihlstrom (1987, 1997) hypothesized that working memory plays a central role in consciousness because it hosts the self; it is the place where other representations become associated with self and thereby become conscious. For Schneider and Pimm-Smith (1997), consciousness reflects the entry of modular information to their *inner loop*, which looks a great deal like an STM store. The association of such a store with consciousness is most explicit in the work of Broadbent (1958) and Atkinson and Shiffrin (1968). Their theories were not theories of consciousness as such, no doubt reflecting the low status of consciousness in the thinking of the time. But these authors did find a place for consciousness in the cognitive architectures they developed, namely the STM store. Baddeley's early ideas on working memory (e.g. Baddeley, 1986) showed similar thinking, associating consciousness with working memory, though not necessarily its contents as such. In his more recent work (e.g. Baddeley, 2007), as described above, consciousness is tentatively associated with a particular module of working memory, the episodic buffer.

This association of consciousness with (some of) the contents of an STM store has a great deal of intuitive appeal. When we think of holding some information in working memory, a telephone number for instance, what this seems to mean is keeping it either in consciousness or in such a condition that it can be very quickly brought back to consciousness. Thus, it seems quite reasonable, even compelling, to relate the elements that make up the current contents of STM with consciousness, treating them as a superset of the elements of which we are currently conscious.

Thus, the question of how this idea is to be reconciled with the other themes arises. A likely answer lies in a currently popular, though not universally accepted, view of working memory, described in Chapter 2 (see Cowan, 1993, 2001, 2005; Fuster, 2008; Miyake & Shah, 1999; Ruchkin et al., 2003). According to this view, working memory is precisely the elements of long-term memory that are currently active, with those elements possibly arranged in novel ways. There is no separate store, simply differing levels of activation. Given this view, the STM theme can be unified with the activation theme: saying that we are aware of the contents of working (short-term) memory is simply saying that we are aware of active representations. Recall that Jackendoff (1987) initially proposed that a representation must be active as a necessary condition for reaching consciousness but then replaced this requirement with a statement that it must be in STM. Given the activation view of working memory, the two become equivalent.

Executive control

As noted above, some early cognitive theories appealed to executive control, or a central processor, an operating system etc. While these terms are no longer common in the literature on consciousness, the concepts they represent can be found in other terms, as the original inspiration for their use remains valid. In neural accounts, the prefrontal cortex routinely exercises a limited sort of control function and is commonly given an important role in consciousness (but see Gazzaniga's work for a strong rejection of the idea that there is such a thing as executive control).

Executive control can also be seen in terms of self, further strengthening the theoretical links with consciousness. Self is a relatively stable, enduring framework of values, beliefs, goals and ways of interpreting experience, including internal experience. Additionally, it is clearly important for awareness. Even when something is just happening, i.e. is not being controlled in any familiar sense, the involvement of self is important. This idea emerges especially in the ideas of Kihlstrom, working from a cognitive perspective, and Damasio, working from a neural perspective. Baars treats self as the most important of the unconscious contexts that determine which representation becomes conscious at any given time: 'conscious experience in general can be viewed as information presented to prefrontal executive regions for interpretation, decision-making and voluntary control' (Baars et al., 2003: 673).

Executive control, in the form of self, is thus a feature that should be incorporated in an adequate theory of consciousness. A natural way to do this would be, once more, in terms of activation. The involvement of self, with its goals and values, is a major source of the activation and synchronization that characterize conscious states. In neural terms, the prefrontal cortex plays a crucial role in establishing the synchronized activity needed for awareness and in selecting the information that becomes the object of consciousness.

Attention

The concept of attention appears repeatedly in the cognitive and neural literature on consciousness. Its typical role is to pick out, in some sense, the representation that is to become conscious. A particular representation must somehow get tied into the broad process that yields awareness, and a standard account of how this happens is that attention selects that representation. For Dehaene and colleagues, attention is the way to amplify the activity of the neural representation that is to become conscious, a prerequisite for its achieving that status. As a result of this amplification, the representation is in effect plugged into the more general, synchronized activity that is the essence of consciousness. For Jackendoff (1987), attention selects a particular portion of a representation for more intensive processing, making it more vivid in consciousness. Schneider and Pimm-Smith (1997) placed consciousness within the attentional system. The importance of attention in selecting the contents of consciousness seems in fact to be nearly universal in current theories. Recall, for example, Greenfield's position that Koch actually studies attention rather than consciousness because he is concerned with the contents of awareness rather than its presence or absence.

Baars sees attention 'not as a separate system but rather as the name for the process of gaining access to global workspace by reference to long-term or current goals' (McGovern & Baars, 2007: 200). Given this view, which I more or less share, the role of attention in consciousness can reasonably be subsumed under the activation theme. Attention is the name for the complex, contextually dependent process by which a particular representation or series of representations comes to be the object of intensive and extensive processing. This is inseparable from the idea of the representation becoming part of the synchronized activity that characterizes consciousness.

Value (and its role in emotion)

In Chapter 2, I described value as the basis for the sense that something matters to the person. It includes the feature of positive vs. negative and a variable intensity. The roots of value are in biology, as the evaluation that leads an organism to seek or avoid aspects of its environment. All of our more sophisticated judgements of what we care about, good and bad, and how much we care about it, have their roots in these more basic, primitive evaluations.

The idea of value, in more or less this sense, has an important place in several of the theories considered above – including those of Mandler, Jackendoff, Dehaene, Damasio and Edelman – and is certainly worthy of such a place, both because of its inherent interest and because it is at the heart of emotion. The more biologically minded theorists – Edelman, Dehaene and Damasio – use the term exactly in the basic sense I have described: positive vs. negative (valence), along with a measure of intensity. Mandler and Jackendoff include this basic concept of value but treat it as one of a large number of value features (see Crick & Koch, 2000, for discussion and endorsement of Jackendoff's account of value). Chafe's (1996: 183) idea of 'evaluation' is close to Jackendoff's values, including 'emotions, attitudes, opinions, desires, aesthetic experiences, humor, and in general the assignment of values to whatever else is found in consciousness'. These treatments of value also have considerable overlap with the idea of the conscious *fringe* (see Mangan, 1993, 2007, who based his work on that of William James). Especially relevant are the fringe experiences of rightness and wrongness, which Mangan discussed in some detail. Interestingly, I have never seen these experiences connected to the concept of value.

Value has played several roles in the consciousness literature. Jackendoff emphasizes the point that value features give conscious perceptual experiences their 'feel'. For others, value plays a crucial role in determining what becomes conscious; in other words, what we are conscious of is closely related to what we care about, in general and at the moment. The other crucial aspect of value is that it underlies emotions and related experiences and mechanisms, as described in Chapter 2. An important limitation of the existing literature is that its focus is overwhelmingly on perceptual awareness. Consciousness of affect deserves far more attention than it has received. The concept of value, when recognized as the core of emotion, offers a good entry point for exploration of the subject.

On the subject of consciousness and emotion, the work of Jaak Panksepp deserves attention. I will not try to do justice to his very extensive work on the subject (e.g. Panksepp, 1998, 2003a, 2005, 2007), just mention some relevant points. Panksepp has for many years been a strong advocate of the position that emotion is fundamental to consciousness and its development, and that it must have a central place in research and theory on consciousness. In this respect, his thinking has clear affinities with that of Damasio. He sounds especially like Damasio when he says 'I assume that the evolution of consciousness was based on the ability of neural tissues to encode biological values' (Panksepp, 2005: 35). He does, however, have some important differences (see Panksepp, 2003b, especially), perhaps the most important being that he would put more emphasis on the *action* character of emotions, which makes them difficult to separate from motor systems. As a possibly oversimplified example, fear cannot be understood without reference to the acts it is associated with: fleeing, freezing, appeasing. Panksepp has thus hypothesized and developed a set of emotional action systems in some detail in his various publications.

Information

One of the most consistent themes in the literature is that information should be at the heart of a theory of consciousness. Baars (1988) argued, with considerable force, that informativeness plays an essential role in whether a representation becomes conscious and that the central function of consciousness can reasonably be seen as information sharing; this idea has been pursued by a variety of authors. Edelman and Tononi, for example, see information as the very essence of consciousness. The idea of information also appears in a variety of other theories, beginning with the early information-processing theories and continuing with more recent accounts, often in the form of 'novelty': an input representation that can be handled automatically, i.e. one that does not bring any new information, does not become conscious while one that does contain novel information does reach consciousness. In this sense, informativeness is at the heart of Pribram's holistic theory as well.

It is worth noting two additional theories that differ from the others in important respects but still include the focus on information flow within a modular system. Johnson and Reeder (1997) sought to explain consciousness within a relatively explicit cognitive architecture, the Multiple-Entry, Modular Memory System (MEM) framework of Johnson and colleagues, designed to explain cognition in general, with an emphasis on memory (see

Johnson, 1992). They used the term 'consciousness' in a broader sense than I use it; in their terms it is 'awareness' that I am interested in. They suggested that awareness comes from 'meta-processing that consists largely of monitoring the outcome of component processes' (Johnson, 1992: 282). This monitoring did not involve a fixed monitor but rather a more flexible relation between higher- and lower-level elements. Once again, we see the idea that consciousness is about dealing with information within a componential system. Similarly, Schneider and Pimm-Smith (1997) hypothesized that consciousness is a *message aware control mechanism* handling the transmission of information within the cognitive system. The system includes many specialized modules, the output of which is brought together in an *inner loop*. Because the amount of information that the modules can present to the loop is far too great for it to handle, an attentional system controls the flow from one system to others. Consciousness occurs within this attentional system.

Seen in its intuitive form, information is an outsider's perspective on the activity of the cognitive/neural system. But more useful definitions have been offered. Baars defines an informative representation as one which leads to adaptations by processors other than the one that produced it. Tononi provides a very explicit, formal definition based on Shannon's concept of information, and adds to it a quantitative measure. So information can be defined in sufficiently rigorous ways to make it a useful concept in a theory of consciousness.

However, an important limitation in the idea of information, has been brought out by Freeman (2003): what is important for an organism is not information but rather meaning, which he characterizes in terms of how information relates to successful action – the carrying out of intentions. Perception, for Freeman, is taking information from the senses and deriving meaning from it. The way I would frame this point is that information only matters if it has some value for the organism, if it somehow fits into the organism's system of values and goals. This point raises the question of whether information as such is the right concept to be used in studies of the mind/brain and, specifically, in the study of consciousness. Perhaps a better approach would be to follow Freeman and substitute meaning for information. The alternative that I will favour is to maintain the concept of information but place it in the context of value, an idea that will be developed in later chapters.

Information and informativeness, with the incorporation of value, have to be accommodated in a theory of consciousness. How they are to be incorporated is much less clear. Baars takes informativeness as a fundamental principle of his theory. An alternative approach would be to derive it from more general characteristics of the cognitive system. This approach, if it can be carried out in a way that does not add substantial complications to the theory, is inherently preferable, as it offers a more parsimonious account. I will pursue this possibility in depth in Chapter 5.

Conclusion

This chapter has considered a variety of approaches to the problem of explaining consciousness from a cognitive/neural perspective. I extracted several recurring themes in the literature, beginning with modularity, in its various forms, as a central feature of the cognitive/neural system within which consciousness is to be explained. The others are the association of consciousness with (a) activation, especially synchronized activity; (b) the contents of an STM store; (c) the workings of an executive function; (d) attention; (e) value; and (f) information. Temporarily setting aside information, I have argued that activation is the key to understanding all these themes, i.e. the others are important for consciousness exactly because they play a role in activation. The situation with informativeness is more complex and so I have not directly addressed its relation to activation here. In Chapter 5, I will return to this question in detail, concluding that within a suitable cognitive framework the role of information in consciousness can indeed be treated as a derivative of activation. There, I will also consider how an activation account, appropriately conceptualized and incorporated in a reasonable cognitive framework, can provide explanations for the major characteristics of consciousness.

Note

(1) I am simplifying the account here. A full description of the process would require a more detailed look at Jackendoff's cognitive theory, which I will not get into here.

4 MOGUL: A Framework for Understanding Consciousness and Learning

The best way to understand consciousness and its place in second language learning – perhaps the only way – is to put consciousness and second language learning in a cognitive framework that will provide a reasonably clear and explicit account of the mind and its workings. In Chapter 2, I described in general terms what such a framework should look like, focusing on the major elements that it should include. Now it is time to go beyond these general characteristics and present a specific framework, one that incorporates the important elements and also deals with second language learning. This is the Modular Online Growth and Use of Language (MOGUL) framework. In this chapter, I will give an overview of MOGUL, beginning with a brief general description and orientation, followed by a look at its architecture, its account of processing and the novel approach to learning that it incorporates. The place of consciousness in the framework will be the subject of the following chapter.

MOGUL: Its Nature, Goals and Applications

The goal of the MOGUL framework is to place research and theory on language acquisition, both first and second, in the context of cognition in general. It is not itself a theory but rather a framework within which specific theories can be developed. Thus, it does not directly address specific questions about language learning or make specific predictions regarding those questions; instead, it provides a framework within which the issues can be addressed. This is of course a limitation. But it is also a strength, as it ensures that any theories constructed within it will be connected to research and theory in related fields, in potentially productive ways, and that those theories will automatically capture some fundamental characteristics of (second) language learning, characteristics that I will describe in this chapter. Any such framework is necessarily provisional, and alternatives can and should be considered. But research that proceeds in the absence of such a framework is likely to leave an assortment of important aspects vague or to assume particular views on them without making these views explicit or trying to justify them. A much better approach, I suggest, is to adopt a framework that offers reasonably clear and explicit positions on the theoretical context.

The MOGUL framework has been developed in some detail (Sharwood Smith & Truscott, 2014; see Truscott, 2013b, for a brief summary), and has been applied, to varying extents, to a variety of topics in second language learning and beyond. These topics include the nature of the learning process and its relation to language processing (Sharwood Smith *et al.*, 2013; Truscott & Sharwood Smith, 2004), the distinction between knowledge of language and metalinguistic knowledge as well as the ways they are related (Sharwood Smith, 2004; Truscott & Sharwood Smith, 2004), consciousness and language (Sharwood Smith & Truscott, 2010; Truscott & Sharwood Smith, 2011), the nature of input and its relation to consciousness and learning (Truscott & Sharwood Smith, 2011), input enhancement (Sharwood Smith & Truscott, in press), language attrition (Sharwood Smith, 2007), optionality (Sharwood Smith & Truscott, 2006; Truscott, 2006), the paradox that learning is both continuous and stage-like (Sharwood Smith & Truscott, 2005), the development of inflectional morphology in second language learners (Sharwood Smith & Truscott, 2008), cross-linguistic influence (Sharwood Smith & Truscott, 2006, 2008), the initial state of second language learning (Sharwood Smith & Truscott, 2006; Truscott & Sharwood Smith, 2004), the issue of 'access' to 'universal grammar (UG)' (Sharwood Smith & Truscott, 2006; Truscott & Sharwood Smith, 2004), ultimate attainment in second language learning (Truscott & Sharwood Smith, 2004), second language instruction (Whong, 2007, 2011) and the nature of consciousness (this book). All of these topics are discussed in Sharwood Smith and Truscott (2014).

MOGUL is an information-processing approach in the literal sense of the term: it is about processors manipulating symbols in information stores – within a specific cognitive architecture. I will describe this architecture in the following section, then turn to the nature of processing within the framework and finally present the novel approach that it takes to learning.

MOGUL Architecture

The basics

MOGUL architecture is based on that of Jackendoff (1987, 1997, 2002, 2007), though it deviates from Jackendoff's proposals in important respects. As an information-processing framework, it consists of stores of information, in the form of representations, and processors that work on those representations. The system is modular, i.e. the assumption is that the mind is made up of a number of relatively independent units, each specialized for a particular function, prototypical examples being vision and syntax. In

MOGUL, a module is a processor–store pair, each such pair serving its own specialized function. Each uses its own distinctive code to represent information and each is connected to one or more others by interfaces, which serve to coordinate activity in adjacent modules.

Following Baars (1988: 384), a processor is 'a relatively unitary, organized collection of processes that work together in the service of a particular function'. The processes combine existing representations to form new ones. In other words, a processor is dedicated to a specialized function, which it serves by manipulating representations. A MOGUL processor embodies innate principles developed through natural selection, which do not change during a person's lifetime. This, then, is an invariant part of the architecture.

An information store begins with innate primitives appropriate to the particular domain, but the combination of these primitives is a learning process (possibly with some exceptions). A store thus contains all the acquired knowledge and beliefs, which are combinations of the primitives, created by the processor on the basis of experience, following its inbuilt principles. Distinguishing universal, inherent principles from those that have been constructed from the current social context (and could in fact be universal as well, if the contexts are) is of course quite difficult, and any specific proposal is guaranteed to generate controversy. More generally, as a framework rather than a specific theory, MOGUL does not include positions on the detailed nature of the various processors and stores. These are to be adopted, as appropriate, from specialist theories in the relevant domains.

A simplified sketch of MOGUL architecture is presented in Figure 4.1. At its heart is *perceptual output structures* (POpS), here shown in a greatly reduced form, which I will discuss in greater detail below. The system consists of paired processors (shown as rectangles) and information stores (octagons), each pair comprising a module. The processor half of the module is best seen as a composite entity made up of all the simpler (sub)processors that contribute to the overall function of the module. If one adopts a traditional principles and parameters view of syntax (Chomsky, 1986), for example, the syntax processor might be made up of all the 'modules' hypothesized by the theory, one handling x-bar structure, another handling movement, a third handling Case theory and so on. But MOGUL, as a framework rather than a theory, is not committed to any particular syntactic theory; others could be substituted.

The processors are the fixed 'hardware' responsible for manipulating the representations that make up the information stores. The information stores are specialized portions of long-term memory, and a representation is simply whatever is in a store, including primitives and combinations of them that have been produced in processing. I use the term 'representation' guardedly here, not intending any claims about how these mental objects relate to the world (see Jackendoff, 2002, 2003): a representation is simply a mental structure. The information stores are specialized in terms of the function their module serves, including phonological, syntactic, affective, conceptual, visual and auditory and the various other sensory modalities. The distinct modules are linked by interfaces (shown in Figure 4.1 as arrows), which have the function of connecting representations in adjacent stores and coactivating them during processing. The connections take the form of indexes: representations that are in different stores but share an index are thereby connected to one another. These indexes are themselves representations, differing from others only in that they are assigned and manipulated by interfaces rather than processors.

The specifically linguistic portions of the system, the 'core' faculty, are those on the left of the figure: the phonological and (morpho)syntactic components. These together make up what can be called 'the language module', though we might more properly speak of two distinct but tightly connected modules. In either case, the components of this portion of the figure are not to be equated with 'language' or its use, as all the other components also play a role in what we commonly think of as language. Note also that the inclusion of only a single syntax module and a single phonology module does not imply that only one language is present. Additional languages are represented in the same information stores and manipulated by the same processors. I will develop each of these points below.

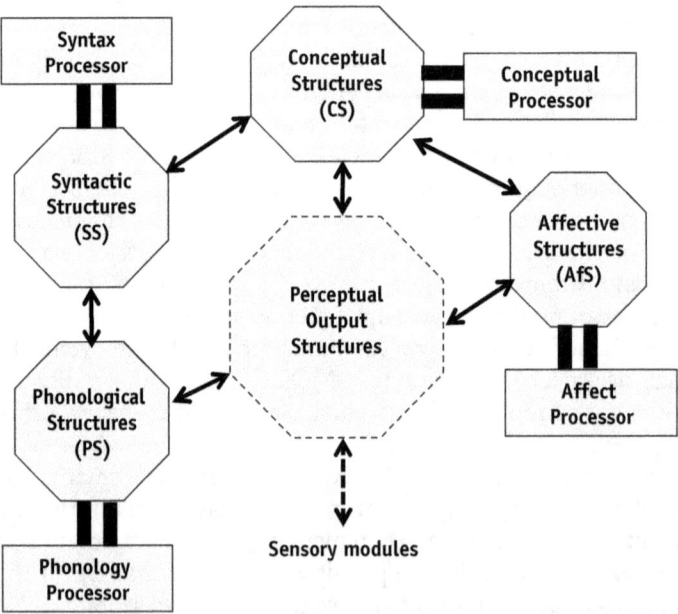

Figure 4.1 The basic architecture of MOGUL

Visual structures

In terms of Figure 4.1, the module called visual structures (VS) is included in POpS. Like all other modules, it consists of an information store and a processor that works with the representations that make up that store. The information store can also be thought of as visual memory. Its information is encoded in specifically visual terms, based on visual primitives. VS represents the output of the visual system. Most of the workings of the system are carried on in relative isolation, but its output is necessarily available to other systems, and interpreted partly in terms of what is going on in those other systems, particularly the conceptual system, which deals with abstract meanings, independent of any particular sensory modality. Knowledge of horses, for instance, includes both images of horses (VS representations) and the abstract idea of horse (one or more representations in conceptual structures [CS]). VS is thus connected to CS by an interface, the operation of which will be described below. This interface also allows the knowledge, beliefs, goals and expectations of CS to influence the output of visual processing. VS representations can also be active in the absence of input from the visual system, since we can have visual experiences based entirely on memory or imagination, as well as dreams and hallucinations. These experiences are the activation of VS representations by internal activity, separate from the sensory modules.

Auditory structures

The module called auditory structures (AS) represents the output of the auditory system, paralleling VS. It thus makes information from hearing available for further processing, including more abstract conceptual processing. When the sound of thunder is processed by the auditory module, for example, the resulting AS representation of the sound can trigger activity in CS constituting a recognition of the sound as thunder, with all of its associations. Like VS, and all other modules, AS consists of a processor and an information store (memory), the latter consisting of representations in the specific code of the module. As with VS, AS can be active independent of activity in the auditory module, as in inner speech, memories of songs, dreams and auditory hallucinations. Since the sounds of language are sounds, they are represented in AS as well. But these representations are not specifically linguistic. They are the sounds which the language system (specifically phonological structures [PS]) can subsequently interpret in terms of linguistic (phonological) knowledge. As far as AS is concerned, they are no different from the sound of thunder or of a fan blowing, the difference lying simply in the phonology module's ability to give them a linguistic interpretation.

Perceptual output structures

I have picked out the modules subserving hearing and vision because of their importance for any discussion of consciousness and learning. There are of course a number of other sensory modalities, the exact number depending on who is doing the counting and what criteria are adopted. Whatever the number and the details, each modality will be represented in the MOGUL framework by low-level modules, the details of which are not important for the framework or for the discussion of consciousness and learning. My concern, for the sensory modules in general, is with their outputs and specifically how these outputs are brought together.

To produce a focused and unified portrayal of significant current environmental events, these output representations are tightly integrated, meaning that their representations are connected to one another via interfaces and the connections (indexes) have very high activation levels. The effect of these strong connections is that processing in the various stores is constantly pushed towards synchronization. A representation that currently dominates one perceptual output store cannot be incompatible with one that currently dominates another. Other modules, especially CS and affective structures (AfS), also play an important role in this synchronization, which I will discuss further below and in Chapter 5. This integrated set of stores is POpS (see Figure 4.1).

The proposal of a common perceptual output store is not entirely novel. It bears a resemblance, for example, to Aristotle's hypothesis of a *common sense* where all the different senses come together (see Caston, 2002; Gregoric, 2007; Hardie, 1976). The most interesting parallel is with Baars' global workspace (see Chapter 3), a subject to which I will return in Chapter 5. Comparison can also be made with Atkinson and Shiffrin's (1968) *short-term store* (STS). The latter differs from POpS mainly in its separation of the STS from a long-term counterpart (see the discussion of working memory above) and its hypothesis of an additional sensory (iconic) memory store, which in MOGUL is treated as simply the immediate output of the sensory modules, the state of POpS before higher-level processing has had an opportunity to affect the products of sensory processing.

The POpS proposal also has interesting similarities and contrasts with Baddeley's working memory model (Baddeley, 1986, 2000, 2007, 2012; Baddeley & Hitch, 1974), described in Chapters 2 and 3. One apparent contrast between them is that research on working memory has focused on two modalities, visual and auditory, while POpS includes all modalities. But this focus can reasonably be seen as a reflection of the importance of these two modalities for humans. It is quite natural to treat all the senses as components of working memory, with dramatic differences in the relative importance of each. Baddeley has recently made tentative efforts to incorporate the remaining modalities (Baddeley *et al.*, 2011). In a sense, this incorporation was already implicitly carried out, as the episodic buffer deals with sensory information of all types. In Baddeley's (2007: 148) words, its function is 'to combine information from the loop, the sketchpad, long-term memory, or indeed from perceptual input, into a coherent episode'. The parallel with POpS should be clear. Another apparent, but not actual contrast lies in the term 'phonological loop'. The name suggests that it is specifically linguistic, in contrast to its MOGUL counterpart, AS, which is more general, representing all auditory processing. But Baddeley (2012) said that he was and is undecided on this point; he chose the term 'phonological' in the mistaken belief that it was neutral.

This formulation of working memory also leads into interesting issues about modularity, which I will do no more than mention here. An essential feature of Baddeley's model is the functional division of short-term memory into two components, verbal/acoustic and visuospatial, in effect treating these as distinct modules. Two open questions are how many divisions might be needed and what sorts of interaction might there be between the components. The MOGUL framework assumes a number of distinct working memory components, one for each processor–store pair, with specific, constrained interaction between them, namely coactivation of coindexed representations across stores. This hypothesis touches on some interesting empirical work but does not neatly correspond to any of the possibilities considered in it (cf. Caplan & Waters, 1999; Fedorenko *et al.*, 2006; Peretz & Hyde, 2003; Shah & Miyake, 1996).

The POpS proposal has interesting connections with ideas in neuroscience as well. Brain areas responsible for modality-specific processing are not difficult to find: books on neuroscience routinely identify visual, auditory, somatosensory, olfactory and gustatory regions. Specialization is also found within each modality. Visual processing, the most studied example, involves distinct regions for processing colour, motion and form, among others. All of this specialization, across and within modalities, raises the question of how the products of these diverse areas come to be unified. There does not seem to be any place in the brain where the various elements are combined. So how is it that we experience the world of our senses as a coherent whole rather than a collection of distinct experiences, each representing one modality or submodality? This is a central issue for neural research, where it is commonly referred to as the *binding problem*: how information from the various sensory cortices is integrated to produce a unified perceptual experience. A number of specific proposals have been put forward as possible solutions for the binding problem, typically involving *synchronization* of activity in the various areas. In Chapter 3, I described a number of such proposals, each of which can be tied to the MOGUL notion of POpS synchronization. Here, I will consider just one example, Damasio (1999, 2010).

Damasio (1999: 318) makes extensive use of the concept of *images*, which he characterizes as 'mental patterns with a structure built with the tokens of each of the sensory modalities — visual, auditory, olfactory, gustatory, and somatosensory'. These are POpS representations. It is noteworthy that Damasio (1999: 320) also uses the term 'representation' as a synonym for image (but see Chapter 3). He connects these images closely to the brain, hypothesizing that *image space*, containing all the images, is tied to *early sensory cortices*, by which he means all the cortical areas specifically associated with a particular sense, not just those that have been called the *primary* visual cortex, the *primary* auditory cortex etc. For vision, the early sensory cortex thus includes all those areas (V1, V2 etc.) that serve a distinctly visual function. In MOGUL terms, the early sensory cortices are thus the areas associated with POpS, either the output structures themselves or lower sensory areas that provide the input to POpS.

This proposal of an integrated perceptual store, POpS, is a central part of the MOGUL framework. It is crucial to the account of consciousness that I will develop in the following chapter and will then apply throughout the book.

The language module: Phonological structures, syntactic structures and interfaces

Language is an extremely broad and loose notion, covering a great variety of different types of knowledge and skill. As such, 'language' cannot be captured in a single module or even a small set of modules. Instead, we can speak of the 'core language faculty', which can be attributed to UG, and 'other' aspects of language. Core faculties include phonology, syntax and morphology, and these together constitute the language module. Syntax and morphology are difficult to separate; Jackendoff treats them as a single module, and MOGUL tentatively follows him on this point. The language module thus consists of two component modules – PS and syntactic structures (SS) – and the interfaces that connect them to each other and to other modules. This use of the term 'module' to refer to the combination of phonology and morphosyntax is rather loose, as this putative module does not have the single processor–store structure that makes up a MOGUL module nor does it have a single unique code. The term 'language module' is thus used as a matter of tradition and convenience.

CS, the general home of concepts, contains the meanings of words and other linguistic items but is not, in itself, part of the language module, though its connections to SS are. In addition to the meanings of linguistic items, CS is home to metalinguistic knowledge of all sorts, as well as the rich pragmatic and contextual associations that go with linguistic items. Other language-related knowledge is found in motor structures (MS), since language ability includes the ability to use muscles to produce linguistic utterances. The various POpS components, particularly AS and VS, also include language-related knowledge, as language sounds and written forms are inherently perceptual. All of these knowledge types are outside the language module, so the module itself is relatively narrow, given the extent of linguistic knowledge. Additionally, it may be more restricted than even this description suggests, as considerable knowledge that is traditionally referred to as phonological or syntactic may not be a part of the core language faculty. These are issues for linguistic theory, and I will not pursue them further here.

Turning now to the component modules, PS consists of a phonological store (memory) containing all the specifically linguistic representations of sound, and a phonology processor responsible for constructing from them representations of the input currently being received. The representations are all based on phonological primitives supplied by UG. The processor is innately established, by UG in this case, and does not change over the course of experience. MOGUL is not committed to any particular theory of the details of phonology, i.e. the nature of the primitives and of the processor. These are to be determined by specific theories of phonology. Phonological learning is the development of representations in PS and their connections to appropriate syntactic representations in SS and auditory representations in AS.

The nature of SS closely parallels that of PS. Like all modules, it consists of an information store, or memory, and a processor that manipulates representations in that store, combining them to form composite representations suitable for current input. The representations are all in a distinct syntactic code, based on syntactic primitives supplied by UG. The processor is also the product of UG constraints and does not change in any way during a person's lifetime. Syntactic learning is a matter of establishing appropriate representations and connecting them appropriately to phonological representations in PS and conceptual representations in CS.

In the brain, it is possible to roughly identify language-related areas, primarily in the left hemisphere for the great majority of people. They cover much of the temporal lobe, extending somewhat into the parietal lobe and the frontal lobe, specifically the back parts of the latter which are concerned with movement. This is not surprising, since speech is a kind of movement – as is sign language and the gestures that commonly accompany and may have preceded spoken language. These then are the language-related areas. But, again, 'language-related' is quite different from 'language module', which contains only the core areas, PS and SS along with their interfaces. The exact location of PS and SS (of UG-based grammar in general) is elusive. There could be very specific areas that have not yet been identified, or each linguistic module could be made up of a number of distinct brain regions (probably all within the general language area). The key to neural modularity is not localization but rather connectedness. If a large number of physically separated centres can work together effectively, then they can compose a single functional unit, i.e. a module, despite their physical separation.

Conceptual structures

CS is the home of concepts, including meanings of words and of other linguistic items. What distinguishes it from POpS is that it is amodal, i.e. its representations are not in the format of any specific sensory modality but rather in a form that is more abstract and more general, allowing knowledge and inference that are not closely tied to sensory/perceptual representations (but see Barsalou [1999, 2008] for arguments against the existence of amodal representations). Like other modules, it consists of a processor and an information (memory) store containing representations in the code of the module. The processor always seeks to establish a coherent representation in its store based on existing representations that are currently active there, that activity being the product of current activity in neighbouring modules and the lingering activation from previous processing. One interesting issue that remains open in the MOGUL framework is whether CS should be split into a number (possibly a very large number) of distinct modules, perhaps corresponding to the modules hypothesized by evolutionary psychologists (e.g. Cosmides & Tooby, 1992; Pinker, 1997; Tooby & Cosmides, 1992).

Neural research offers intriguing hints of how CS might be realized in the brain, but no clear answer. It might be associated with Damasio's dispositional space, which covers the majority of the cortex, possibly suggesting again that CS should be split into a number of smaller modules. However, there is substantial evidence for a more restricted area, namely the anterior temporal lobes (Lambon Ralph *et al.*, 2010; McClelland & Rogers, 2003; Pobric *et al.*, 2010). Neural work often refers to a 'semantic hub' located in this region. This hub is the site of amodal representations that link up features in the various sensory areas, plus motor and linguistic areas (the spokes), to make coherent concepts. This looks a great deal like CS.

While CS is not part of the core language areas (the language module), it does contain very extensive language-related knowledge. For one thing, its representations are the concepts that become attached to the strictly linguistic representations in the core areas, including words and functional categories, and so become the meanings of those linguistic entities. CS representations also constitute the contexts in which the linguistic representations are used. These points will be developed extensively in Part 2 of this book. One feature of CS that will assume great importance in Part 2 is its role as host of metalinguistic knowledge, i.e. the knowledge *about* language that was referred to in Chapter 2. This knowledge, which can be quite extensive, is an example of an S2 system, also described in Chapter 2. The language module, with its external connections, constitutes the specialist S1 system for language; the linguistic knowledge developed in CS provides a non-specialist way of dealing with language. I will refer to this non-specialist knowledge as *conceptual linguistic knowledge* or *extramodular linguistic knowledge* to distinguish it from knowledge in the language module.

The self

In the previous chapters, I discussed the concept of self and its importance for an understanding of the human mind, and especially of consciousness. Not surprisingly, then, it plays a significant role in the MOGUL framework. It is absent from Figure 4.1 simply because it is not a module but rather a representation in CS. It is a very important representation, with strong implications for consciousness and second language learning, and so I discuss it here in a section of its own.

The self is a product of natural selection, serving a crucial function in self-regulation (see discussion in Chapter 2). But it clearly develops through experience, especially childhood experience. The implication is that there is an innate component and there is also great potential for variability based on experience. In MOGUL terms, self is a CS representation, SELF, the development of which is guided by an innately specified processor. This might be seen simply as one aspect of the functioning of the conceptual processor. Alternatively, we might hypothesize a conceptual subprocessor embodying principles of self that have been established through natural selection. The subprocessor is innately specified, its function being to construct, maintain and update a representation of self that can serve the regulatory role for which the subprocessor evolved. The processor itself does not change during the person's lifetime; change is located in the information store.

In either case, the self is a conceptual representation (cf. Kihlstrom's analysis of self, described in Chapter 3). It therefore consists of other CS representations, selected and combined in accordance with the inbuilt principles of the conceptual (sub)processor. It begins life with innate primitives appropriate to its domain; the process of combining these primitives during processing, in accordance with the processor's inbuilt principles, is learning. The product of this learning is essentially the person – his/her characteristics and concepts of what he/she is. This crucially includes goals and motives, which are themselves CS representations, along with any conceptual representation that is about the characteristics of the system.

So far, I have referred to *the* SELF representation. But there is no apparent reason to think that only one such representation can exist. Given the regulatory function of the self, the conceptual (sub)processor might well construct more than one SELF representation in response to the demands of different contexts, such as work, school and family life. The natural result is the creation of multiple, overlapping selves (SELF representations). The overlap normally accounts for the overwhelming bulk of each self. When different SELF representations are genuinely separate in a person, we have a case of multiple personalities.

SELF is strongly connected to representations in other modules. In POpS, these include representations (primarily visual and somatosensory) of the body and especially the face, as well as the sound of one's own voice. Probably even more important than these, though, are the connections to AfS, where value is found. Self is, to a very large extent, about the value we assign to the things we are, the things we believe ourselves to be, the things we want to be and also to the things we do and experience. All of these are of the essence for self-regulation.

These associated representations are fundamental for the concept of self, so what we normally mean by self is perhaps best captured not by a single representation but rather by a collection of interconnected representations in different stores, all joined by indexes and therefore activated together. But we can reasonably think of the conceptual self as the core element and label it 'self', treating the other elements as associated features. For practical purposes, I will continue to speak of the CS SELF representation, with the understanding that it does not precisely coincide with our intuitive notion of self.

We also have the concept of things being 'not self'. The treatment of certain things – people, ideas, clothing styles, varieties of music, accents, etc. – as alien to us appears to be a fundamental part of human cognition. Thus the concept ALIEN or OTHER must be a general element of CS, no doubt appearing in a variety of combinations with other representations to indicate distance of those things from SELF. This concept is important for second language learning and so will be further considered in Part 2.

Affective structures

The content of AfS is the set of emotions, each constituting a representation. Each representation is, as is typical, composed of more basic representations, ultimately of affective primitives. The nature of these primitives in general is not well understood, but it is clear that all emotions contain the features of positive or negative, as described in Chapter 2, i.e. value. Positive and negative are thus basic (probably primitive) representations in AfS. The function of the affect processor, like all processors, is to establish a coherent representation in its store based on any currently active representations there. This processor may well have limited significance after early childhood, though, as adults have a relatively fixed emotional repertoire and so activity in the store will normally be a matter of one existing representation establishing a temporary dominance, based on current input.

The value representations are crucial components of AfS. I will refer to the positive one as !val!, for value. It is contained in all positive emotions. Its negative counterpart, contained in every negative emotion, will be referred to as !harm!. The logic of these names is that representations associated with !val! are representations of those things that have value for the organism (person), ranging from basics such as food, water and sex to more sophisticated items such as an art object, a favourite song, a happy memory, the face of a friend, an abstract ideal etc. Its activation underlies the various forms of pleasure, including happiness, physical pleasure, amusement, pride, relief, triumph, gratitude, sympathy (see Sauter, 2010). In contrast, the function of the !harm! representation is to label potentially harmful stimuli and actions and to encourage avoidance of them. The most basic cases are, again, biological in nature – threats to survival or physical well-being. Representations of such threats are thus associated with !harm!. As with !val!, this negative representation can also become associated, derivatively, with other sorts of negative objects and situations; it is connected to any representation of anything that we consider negative. These representations are typically those in POpS and CS.

AfS representations have very high activation levels and are extensively connected, explaining the fact (see Chapter 2) that they have great influence on activity throughout the system, affecting virtually all cognitive activity and body states. These connections also provide AfS with input from the perceptual modules and from CS, comprising emotional appraisal, and from the body, largely responsible for the high activation levels of its representations.

As described in Chapter 2, emotion is realized in the brain in what is called the limbic system. It is these regions that correspond to AfS. Value is associated with the projections, extending very generally throughout the cortex, from the limbic system and lower areas, as described in regard to a number of consciousness theories in Chapter 3. These projections correspond to the extensive connections of !val! and !harm!, which give them very broad influence throughout the cognitive system and make them especially important for learning, a point to which I will return below.

MOGUL Processing

The function of a processor is to make coherent representations from whatever is currently active in its store. Processing thus means activating existing representations and combining them into new ones. The coherence of a resulting representation is a function of the principles embodied by the processor; a representation is coherent if it is fully consistent with those principles. What is or is not a coherent representation will thus depend on the nature of the particular processor that is constructing it. We might also think of the processors as embodying principles of well-formedness and the resulting representations as being (or failing to be) 'well-formed' structures.

Language use is an example of this processing. Comprehension and production both involve activation and combination of representations, differing only in the primary direction in which information flows.

Activation

In MOGUL, every representation has an activation level. MOGUL follows the standard usage of the term, found throughout the cognitive literature, in treating the current activation level of a representation as determining its availability for processing (e.g. Anderson, 1993; Bock, 1986; Dijkstra & van Heuven, 1998; McClelland & Rumelhart, 1981; Saunders & MacLeod, 2006; Schwartz *et al.*, 2006). We can also speak abstractly of a representation's *resting* activation level, the level it has when not participating in any processing. It is abstract in that the dynamic nature of the system implies constant rises and falls in the current level for any representation. When a representation receives stimulation, its level will abruptly rise. When it is not receiving any stimulation, its level will slowly fall. The gradual nature of the fall is shown by priming effects, which can persist for a very long time after stimulation periods, leading a number of authors to tie together priming and implicit learning (Bock & Griffin, 2000; Chang *et al.*, 2000, 2003; Cleland & Pickering, 2006; Roediger, 2003), pointing to the conclusion that a change in activation level can be an enduring feature.

A representation can be stimulated in either of two ways. One is spreading activation within a store. When one representation becomes more active, all those representations in the store that contain it or are contained in it will also be activated (for spreading activation, see Anderson, 1983b; Collins & Loftus, 1975; Dell, 1986; McClelland & Rumelhart, 1981). The other source of stimulation involves the interfaces, the function of which is to match activation levels between stores. The indexes forming connections across stores are representations; thus, they also have activation levels. Whenever a representation is active in one store, its index will necessarily be active, through spreading activation, so the interface will stimulate that index in adjacent stores. Activation then spreads from it to any representations that it is part of. The effect is that corresponding (coindexed) representations in different stores will be activated together. This is very similar to the spreading activation of Levelt (1999; Levelt *et al.*, 1999), as perhaps should be expected given the parallels between Levelt's proposals and a Jackendovian architecture like that of MOGUL (see Jackendoff, 1997, 2002).

Consider then the activation levels that should be found in the various portions of the cognitive system as it is laid out in MOGUL architecture, beginning with POpS. Representations of current sensory input should have especially high activation levels; if they did not, information about the environment could be too easily overwhelmed by other activity, a situation that would not contribute to an organism's survival prospects. And these high levels are exactly what is expected given MOGUL architecture and processing. The integration of the perceptual stores implies that perceptual processing repeatedly converges on a single set of coindexed representations, each store being dominated by one member of this set. Each of these perceptual representations thus receives support from all the others (as well as from non-perceptual processing, as noted above). The consequence is that representations which currently dominate POpS stores are certain to have exceptionally high activation levels. This is, at least roughly, Baars' notion of competition for access to the global workspace, cast in terms of activation, a subject I will return to below.

The situation is quite different for other portions of the system. The sensory modules themselves, for instance, have nothing like the integration found in their output structures. Setting aside interesting debates over the 'cognitive penetrability' of low-level visual processing (see Jackendoff, 1987; Müller, 2005; Nakayama, 2000; Pylyshyn, 1999, 2003; Raftopoulos, 2005), each sensory module works largely on its own. Whatever integration there may be, it is nothing like that found in POpS, so extreme activation levels should not be expected for these representations. The same is true for the linguistic modules: PS and SS. Nor should MS be expected to show extreme activation levels.

CS is similar; there is no reason to attribute to its functioning any sort of multiprocessor integration along the lines of POpS, and so its representations should not be able to achieve high levels of activation. But there is one exception: SELF. This representation has to have a very high level because it is strongly connected throughout the mind and the body, is always active, is involved in virtually all processing and is relatively stable all through the person's life.

The other candidate for activation levels comparable to those found in POpS is AfS. The strong influence that emotions exert on thought, behaviour and physiological state suggests that their representations do routinely achieve very high levels of activation (for discussion of the centrality of emotion, see for example Damasio, 1994, 2003; Denton *et al.*, 2009; LeDoux, 1996; Panksepp, 1998). And this should be expected, given their rich connections throughout the cognitive system and especially throughout the body, reflecting their great value in survival. A reasonable conclusion, then, is that an active AfS representation is very active indeed, because of its inherently high resting activation level and because of synchronized activity temporarily integrating the AfS representation with body states and, secondarily, with the CS representations that are the appraisal underlying the emotion.

Intuitively, we might say that attention is a key to activation: a representation is activated when we pay attention to it. Based on the discussion in Chapter 2, attention is the name we give to the complex, diverse actions and interactions of processors that result in certain representations being activated and processed more extensively than others. Thus, attention should not be treated as a distinct source of activation, because such a treatment would be largely circular, giving the appearance of an explanation where none exists.

Competition, dominance and decision-making

Competition among representations provides a useful metaphor for processing. The competition is for temporary dominance of a store. This dominance is inseparable from the goal of every processor: to construct coherent representations in its store, using the currently active elements there. This is what processors exist for. It is all they ever do. The result is a constant tendency towards coherence in the activity in a given store. It is always in the context of a dynamic system, producing constant change, but the drive for coherence is a constant, universal characteristic of processing. When one representation is dominant, it precludes the possibility of any others being dominant at that point. The picture this suggests of activity in a given store is that of a series of coherent representations, one replacing the previous in rapid succession. Because of priming effects, the succession should typically not be to a radically different representation but rather to one that shares features with its predecessor. Exceptions occur when input from a neighbouring processing unit is both very different and very strong, strong enough to overwhelm anything else that is currently going on.

This looks a great deal like a picture of how a representation becomes conscious, including the ultimate coherence of the representation, the serial nature of the process, its continuous, flowing character and the exceptions to the flow, all as described in Chapter 3. This resemblance is by no means accidental, as will become clear in the following chapter. The coherent activity that played such a large and recurring role in the accounts of consciousness is simply one example of a far more general phenomenon. It is, I suggest, the normal, universal way that processing works.

This view of processing as an effort to establish a single coherent representation from currently active representations has interesting implications for decision-making. The options under consideration in the decision-making process are representations competing for dominance of CS. When one of these options comes to dominate the store, a decision has been made. Thus, decision-making may be best seen simply as normal processing.

One kind of decision-making, in its traditional understanding, is the decision to take a particular action. In MOGUL terms, actions are the domain of MS. When the representation of a particular motor plan dominates MS, the action is carried out. The question then is how this representation comes to dominate MS at a given point. The answer lies, at least to a large extent, in CS, with its goals and intentions. When a representation of an intention to act dominates CS, the CS/MS interface will trigger activity in MS that corresponds to that intention, either activating an existing representation that corresponds to it (is coindexed with it) or activating multiple MS representations that correspond to components of the CS intention, which the MS processor then assembles to produce a coherent overall motor plan.

This is simply normal processing, no different from that hypothesized in other processing units. All processing is about representations coming to (briefly) dominate a store. Those that do will have strong influences on the activity in all adjacent stores. In the case of MS, dominance will mean direct effects on muscles. Dominance on other stores will produce less overt effects; in other words, decisions, in the ordinary sense, commonly do not result in immediate action. But in such cases the decision is still a matter of a particular option, in the form of a representation, coming to dominate CS.

I want to suggest, then, that a theory of decision-making should not be a theory specifically of the things that have traditionally been called decision-making. It should be a reasonably direct application of general principles of processing, focused on how a given representation comes to temporarily dominate its store. From an alternative perspective, mental activity in general can be seen as decision-making, raising the possibility of generalizing decision theories beyond their original domain to include the process by which given representations come to dominate their stores in such areas as perception, memory retrieval, emotion and consciousness.

Most interestingly, for present purposes, language comprehension can be seen as decision-making, as can language production. More accurately, each is an integrated set of decisions. When a syntactic representation is constructed for current input, for example, each word can in principle be assigned any number of syntactic categories and the categorized words can be grouped into phrases in a variety of ways, the two types of processes inevitably interacting. Each possible outcome represents an option, and successful processing means deciding on one of these options. The decision has been made when one of them comes to dominate SS, if only briefly. In traditional language processing terms, this is the *selection* of a representation from among a set of active candidates. The decision in SS must of course be integrated with – and is therefore influenced by – decisions made in PS and CS. The same logic applies to language production. A CS representation of the intended message is a decision on the content of what is to be said. A great many syntactic representations can in principle be selected as expressions of this message. When a particular one comes to dominate SS, a decision has been made.

Value plays an important role in this broadened view of decision-making. As described in Chapter 2, a common view is that decisions are based, largely or entirely, on affective value. In MOGUL terms, the CS representations that instantiate the options under consideration are coindexed with !val!. As a result, their activation levels are influenced by those connections, and because AfS representations can reach extreme levels, this influence can also be extreme. !val! thus serves as a powerful amplifier, substantially raising the current levels of any coindexed representation, in proportion to the resting level of the index that connects it to that representation. Thus, when a choice is to be made between two or more competing options, the one that is more strongly connected to !val! is likely to triumph.

The !harm! representation also has an important role in processing (decision-making). Like !val!, its activity increases the activation level of conceptual, perceptual and motor representations with which it is coindexed. When a negative representation dominates CS or POpS, this dominance corresponds to dominance of !harm! or a representation that contains it in AfS. For action, the most important influence of !harm! is of course on MS. The exact nature of the influence depends on the active AfS representation of which it is a component. When it is active as a component of !fear!, for example, the effect is to raise the current level of avoidance representations in CS and MS, just as active !val! encourages seeking and approaching by activating the appropriate conceptual and motor representations.

This view of decision-making has close connections to the neuroscience work considered in Chapter 2, Damasio's (1994, 2003; Damasio et al., 1998) theory in particular. Damasio's somatic markers translate to indexes on CS representations that connect them to AfS representations. Because of these ubiquitous indexes, !val! is activated whenever a CS representation is active. Competition among active CS representations – decision-making – therefore reflects the affective value associated with each of the competing options.

The role of SELF in processing

SELF is a central part of decision-making in the sense just described; i.e. it has a profound and pervasive influence on processing and specifically on which representation comes to dominate a store at a given moment. Another way of putting this is that self is inseparable from executive control, as described in Chapter 3. Its immediate influence is of course on its own store, CS. But its effects inevitably extend to other stores as well.

The objective of a processor, always, is to make a coherent representation from active representations in its store, where coherence is defined in the processor's own inbuilt terms. The conceptual processor, in carrying out this function, is constantly faced with one particularly active representation, SELF. The implication is that it is extremely difficult for this processor to construct a representation that is incompatible with SELF. When such a representation *is* constructed, it is unlikely to dominate CS, at least not for any length of time. It is likely to be quickly replaced by another representation that is compatible with SELF or else to be adjusted, probably very quickly, to a form that is more compatible. The alternative is that SELF will be adjusted to accommodate the conflicting representation, a result that is only likely to occur if the latter is exceptionally strong (active) and/or exceptionally persistent, as when an idea has great emotional impact or is repeatedly activated in the person's experiences. In short, conceptual processing is to a large extent built around the demands of SELF. I believe this description captures, in broad outline, the known facts about the relation between self and cognition.

Goals and values are a crucial part of processing involving the self. A goal is a component of SELF that represents a desired state. Action plans compatible with the achievement of this state are activated when the goal is activated. Goals, in turn, are inseparable from value, i.e. from connections to !val! for positive goals and to !harm! for avoidance goals. In decision-making, when theorists speak of the most valued option winning, to a large extent the high value of the winner is based on its connection with SELF and the active goals that it includes. An option that is quickly eliminated from the competition because of its low value is likely to have that low value because of incompatibility with SELF and its goals. Such an option will have little chance of dominating CS.

The SELF representation also has important influences on perceptual processing, as a highly active conceptual representation will inevitably affect the activity of representations in POpS, via interfaces. Most interestingly, the highly active SELF representation plays a large role in the synchronization of POpS, described above, by simultaneously stimulating coindexed representations in the various perceptual stores. This point will be important for the discussion of consciousness in MOGUL in the following chapter.

Another aspect of self and processing that will become important later on involves what has been called *communicative competence* (see Savignon, 1991). The ability to speak a language includes the ability to use it appropriately in context, to achieve communicative goals. In MOGUL terms, this means that the language forms – the chains of representations in PS and SS – must be connected to CS representations not only of their meaning but also of the contexts in which their use is appropriate and of the communicative goals for which they are used. Goals are inseparable from self, so an essential element of this communicative competence is connections between language forms and the SELF representation in CS.

Acquisition by Processing Theory (APT)

The approach

If the mental system consists of processors and representations manipulated by them, then learning has to be changes in the processors and/or the set of representations. For the purposes of theory building, the complexities of acquired knowledge and ability could logically be placed in either, or could be distributed between them, in any number of ways. MOGUL adopts what I believe to be the simplest and theoretically neatest approach by assuming that the changes occur entirely in the set of representations, including the connections among them. Thus, learning is lasting changes that occur in the set of representations during processing. From another angle, learning is the establishment of appropriate representations in a way that includes an element of novelty – if the novel representations endure.

With this as background, the central principle of learning in MOGUL can be stated as follows:

Acquisition by processing:
Learning is the lingering effect of processing.

During processing, a novel representation is sometimes created in an information store in response to input received. It then lingers after the processing is complete, available for future use. This process is learning: the development of new items in a store through the combination of existing items in processing. It occurs purely as a part of the processors' work of making adequate representations for their current input – MOGUL does not hypothesize any mechanisms specifically for learning (Truscott & Sharwood Smith, 2004). The activation level of the new representation will initially be low but will gradually rise if it receives continued use in processing.

The other aspect of development in the system is the establishment and subsequent strengthening of connections between representations in different stores. Visual processing of a novel object, for example, can result in the creation of new representations both in VS, as the visual appearance of the object, and in CS, as the concept of that object, and these representations are necessarily connected. In MOGUL, the connections are, again, captured in the standard linguistic notation of coindexing (see especially Jackendoff, 1997, 2002). This establishment of connections across stores is essentially the establishment of new composite representations and so it is not fundamentally different from the development occurring specifically within a store. Recall that an index is a representation. When it is attached to some representation in a store, the result is a new, composite representation. What makes this type of case special is that the combining is carried out by the interface rather than by the processor within the module.

It should be emphasized that the creation of new representations is not an intelligent effort to improve the system. The process is intelligent only in the sense that processing is intelligent – it typically ends up with a coherent interpretation of the current input. It is not a matter of evaluating the current state of the grammar as a whole (or even a portion of it), judging what gaps need to be filled in or adjustments made and then hypothesizing a new version of the grammar. It is simply a matter of coming up with a way to construct an acceptable representation for current input. If that can only be done by inserting an element that has never been used before, then the processor is likely to do so. In terms of the development of the system, this is very much a hit-and-miss process; the result in any given case is not likely to produce the solution that will be most useful for processing in general in the long term. Gradual development is possible not because the system makes intelligent hypotheses and then intelligently evaluates them on the basis of evidence, but because it has an enormous number of opportunities to deal with novel input. Some of these will result in the creation of representations that prove useful in the long run and so gradually become strengthened through extensive use.

This approach has a selectionist flavour to it, seeing learning primarily as a matter of selecting suitable representations, suitable in terms of their usefulness, from a vast array of possibilities, rather than as a deductive or inductive problem-solving process. So we might call it *representational Darwinism* or a *theory of representational selection*, paralleling Edelman's (1987) neural Darwinism and theory of neuronal group selection. Enormous numbers of representations are created in response to processing needs in individual cases. Most of these will prove to have little value beyond the individual case for which they were created; they fade away or simply become irrelevant. Some prove to be highly valuable and so acquire a firm position in the system. There is no figuring out the language, no hypotheses being tried out, no inferences across the different cases, no 'aha' as the correct option is identified. There is just processing and success or failure therein.

This conception of learning is not generally accepted in psychology or in language learning, but it is actually much less alien than it might seem at first glance. The common term *memory trace*, for example, expresses the idea that processing leaves behind a trace of its activity, which is a memory. Also common in the cognitive literature is *automatic encoding*, the idea that attended items are automatically stored. Similarly, Eichenbaum and Cohen (2001: 507) see storage of memories as 'an integral part of ongoing information processing'. APT also has significant similarities to learning as hypothesized in dynamic systems approaches (e.g. de Bot, 2008; Edelman, 1992; Smith & Thelen, 2003), where the term 'growth' is sometimes used in place of 'learning' (e.g. van Geert, 2008). More limited similarities can be found with emergentist and connectionist approaches (see Sharwood Smith & Truscott, 2014, for discussion).

The APT concept also fits well with work on distributed representations referred to in Chapter 2. Memories are stored in the same places in the brain where the initial processing took place. In the words of Martin (2007: 25): 'information about salient properties of an object — such as what it looks like, how it moves, and how it is used — is stored in sensory and motor systems active when that information was acquired'. If storage is the lingering effect of processing, this is expected. If processing and storage are distinct processes, it is not.

Some implications of the approach

The MOGUL approach to development directly predicts some fundamental characteristics of acquisition (see Sharwood Smith & Truscott, 2005; Truscott, 2006; Truscott & Sharwood Smith, 2004). First, acquisition involves gradual, quantitative movement towards the target grammar, not sudden discovery of correct features. In almost any aspect of language learning, we find that when learners start to use a form properly, they do so only a fraction of the time. They progress by gradually increasing the percentage of correct uses until the right form comes to be used consistently. Accompanying this feature is another that is equally ubiquitous and equally important: optionality. During the period in which the correct form is gradually becoming more common, an incorrect form is also commonly used, its frequency gradually declining as that of the correct form increases. A learner might, for example, treat the target language sometimes as a pro-drop language and sometimes as a non-pro-drop language. Standard generative approaches assume that a grammar has one parameter setting (feature value) or another, with no intermediate possibilities, and so do not allow for such phenomena (for an alternative approach, see Amaral & Roeper, 2014; Roeper, 1999; also Truscott, 2014).

MOGUL directly predicts the phenomena. All options (pro-drop and non-pro-drop, for example) exist in the grammar, as representations in SS. Each has its own activation level, which determines its availability for use in comprehension and production. In the early stages of learning, when little relevant input has yet been processed, their levels are comparable, and we should expect to see both options used. As more input is processed over time, the activation level of the correct value will gradually rise and the incorrect value will become increasingly irrelevant. Throughout this process, both values will appear in the learner's performance.

The MOGUL approach also handles a closely related problem that is standard in generatively oriented accounts of learning, first and second: how success is possible in the face of noise in the data that learners must rely on. The background assumption in most generative work is that learners have available to them consistent, unambiguous evidence pointing to the correct option. This assumption abstracts away from a number of potential problems. First, exceptions to parameter settings and feature values are the rule, and they do not come marked as exceptions. Learners are also likely to be subject to input from other dialects or registers, which could point them in the wrong direction. They sometimes hear sloppy speech. They sometimes encounter noise in the literal sense, which could lead to misunderstanding of what was said. Distraction could have a similar effect. The current, imperfect state of their grammar could lead to misanalysis of input that would suggest a false conclusion about the grammar. Altogether, such factors are certain to mislead learners at times, resulting in the adoption of inappropriate parameter settings or feature values (depending on the particular linguistic theory adopted). The problem is how such errors are to be undone. In traditional generative approaches the answer is far from clear.

In the MOGUL approach, it is reasonably clear. As mentioned in the discussion of the gradual nature of learning, both options are available from the beginning. If bad input or misinterpretation of input favours the wrong value, and therefore raises its activation level, this could lead to a temporary and probably weak dominance by that value, but the effect will be only temporary. Continuing experience with the language will result in more and more cases of the correct value being used in processing, with the result that its activation level will gradually rise to the point at which the incorrect value cannot appear in use, or can only appear rarely, under special conditions. If the input leading away from the correct value is not simply a mistake, but is rather a genuine exception or belongs to a special register, the situation is different. The inappropriate representations will remain in the grammar, as MOGUL has no mechanism to remove representations.

Value and learning

As described above, linguistic competence includes appropriate associations between value representations (!val! and !harm! and other AfS representations that contain them) and the chains of representations that are language forms. The issue for learning is how the value representations become connected to other representations, such as those comprising linguistic knowledge, and how these connections influence the growth and use or non-use of knowledge/skills. The basic answer is that the connections are formed through associative learning: when two representations are simultaneously active they become connected. This type of learning is usually contrasted with modular, UG-based conceptions of learning, but there is no problem of principle in unifying the two. The associative learning occurs within the constraints imposed by the innately specified modular architecture, associating representations that are either innately present or are created as combinations of innately given representations, combined in accordance with UG principles.

When !val! is active at the same time as some other representation, its index is assigned to that representation, the activation level of the index depending on the activation levels of the representation and !val! at the moment. The activity of !val! during learning also raises the initial resting activation level of the new representation, making it more likely to be used in subsequent processing. This likelihood is further increased by its continuing connection to !val!. The associative learning begins, very early in life, with innate associations between !val! and other representations, such as those involved in eating and drinking, i.e. those that by nature have value. New associations (valuations) are formed on the basis of these. In other words, new experiences acquire value through association with others that already have value. From a neural perspective, it is inevitable that

!val! will become connected very widely, because the limbic system is active virtually all the time and so representations in AfS are routinely coactivated with those in other stores.

This concept has clear parallels with the classic behaviourist idea of reinforcement. MOGUL, of course, does not accept the concept as used in behaviourist psychology, in which talk of mental representation was not even allowed. But the MOGUL concept is very compatible with current neural 'reinforcement theory' (see Montague, 2006). A central phenomenon is the 'dopamine surge' or 'dopamine burst' (Cohen, 2005; Cohen et al., 2002; Schultz, 1998), a neural mechanism for labelling a stimulus or action as rewarding and, accordingly, for reinforcing it. In MOGUL terms, when a representation that has value (is coindexed with !val!) is activated, !val! is thereby activated as well. Another representation that is active at that point will therefore get !val!'s index, or if it already has it then the activation level of that index will rise. This is the dopamine burst.

There is also a negative version of value learning – new representations can be connected to !harm! instead of or in addition to !val!. This learning occurs in the same way as described above for its positive counterpart, by innately constrained associative learning. The association with !harm! gives the new representation a higher resting level and makes it more likely to be used in subsequent processing, both because of this higher resting level and because of the support it will receive from !harm! during processing. But this use will take a form opposite to that of !val!, i.e. it will encourage avoidance of the object.

Context, self and learning

In language learning, success is not simply a matter of achieving a good knowledge of abstract grammar and word definitions. Language is used in contexts, for purposes, and this purposeful, contextualized use must be developed as an integral part of learning. From a MOGUL perspective, linguistic representations must be connected to additional CS representations, beyond simple definitions. These representations are of the contexts in which given elements of linguistic form are used and the goals for which they are used. Goals, again, are inseparable from self, so successful learning necessarily includes connecting language forms with the SELF representation in CS.

These aspects of language are acquired in the same way that form is acquired – as the lingering effect of processing. Psychological research established long ago that context is a fundamental part of learning: when we learn one thing, elements of the context are stored with it. And language learning is no exception. It always takes place in some sort of context, even if it is a very artificial one. This context is processed, to varying degrees and in varying ways, which means that representations of it are active in CS and in other stores during learning. Active representations in one store become coindexed with active representations in adjacent stores, as a normal part of processing. The activation level of the new indexes will typically be quite low initially and will remain so unless the indexes are reactivated repeatedly. Repeated activation will occur if and only if the particular combination of form and context recurs, which hopefully means that the form has been found useful in that sort of context. If the use of particular forms successfully achieves the speaker's communicative goals, then those forms and those goals (i.e. the CS representations of them) will become associated. With each subsequent use, the forms will become more readily available for use when those goal representations are active.

Conclusion

The description of MOGUL presented in this chapter is necessarily brief and incomplete in many respects (for a fuller presentation, see especially Sharwood Smith & Truscott, 2014). Some additional aspects will be developed in the remainder of this book, starting with the place of consciousness in the framework, in the following chapter.

I want to emphasize at this point that MOGUL is not a theory, of second language learning or of anything else, but rather a broad framework within which specific theories can be formulated and developed with an eye to research and theory in related areas. Theories formulated within this framework will automatically incorporate some fundamental features of second language learning, including the fact that it is a gradual, quantitative process and that during this process learner grammars routinely display conflicting features (optionality). They will have an account of the nature of input and how it can influence or fail to influence acquisition. They will automatically be connected to research and theory on processing. They will have available research-based accounts of various aspects of the cognitive system, including working memory, the nature and place of affect in the system and consciousness and its place in (second language) learning.

None of these features is set in concrete, so an aspect that proves unfruitful in its current form can be adjusted or even replaced, within limits, the goal always being a framework that will provide maximum understanding and maximum potential for fruitful research. A constructive critique of the framework should look at how it meets or fails to meet these goals. Criticism of MOGUL as 'unfalsifiable' would be a category error. No single experiment or set of experiments can tell us if a broad framework is valid or not.

These are overall goals for MOGUL. In the context of this book, the goal is to use the framework to explore consciousness in second language learning. To that end, I will develop the place of consciousness in the framework in the following chapter and then, in the second half of the book, apply that cognitively contextualized understanding of consciousness to fundamental concerns in second language learning.

5 Consciousness in the MOGUL Framework

In this chapter, I will propose a parsimonious account of consciousness based on the Modular Online Growth and Use of Language (MOGUL) framework, as presented in the preceding chapter. The primary focus of MOGUL is on second language acquisition, the goal being to provide a framework within which research and theory from a variety of related areas can be brought together and thereby brought to bear on ongoing second language research. It was not originally intended to be an account of consciousness. But I will suggest in this chapter that it offers a straightforward way to understand central aspects of consciousness; specifically, that it supports a parsimonious account of what we are and are not conscious of at any given moment. After presenting the approach, I will discuss the relations between this account and several prominent views of consciousness, as described in Chapter 3. I will then describe the way that this approach can explain various important characteristics of consciousness.

Ultimately, the ideas developed here will serve as the basis for an exploration of consciousness in second language learning, presented in Part 2 of this book. However, much of the discussion in this chapter is only indirectly related to that exploration, aiming instead at providing a reasonably thorough explanation and defence of the approach that I take to consciousness. So readers who are not interested in such matters can safely skip large portions of this chapter. The only section that is strictly necessary for an understanding of Part 2 is the first section – 'The MOGUL/Activation Account'. The two sections after it – 'Informativeness and the Activation Hypothesis' and 'Relations to Some Prominent Theories of Consciousness' – are intended for those who do wish to see a more detailed presentation of the account and its justification. The final section – 'Accounting for Some Major Characteristics of Consciousness' – is not strictly necessary for a reading of Part 2, but is likely to be of value.

The MOGUL/Activation Account

In Chapter 3, I extracted several prominent themes from the theories of consciousness reviewed there. First, consciousness should be explained within a modular system that provides a reasonably explicit and inclusive account of the mind and its workings. This theme is straightforwardly accommodated in the modular architecture and processing of the MOGUL framework. The other themes all involve the contents of consciousness. Specifically, these contents are associated with the following:

(a) activation, particularly synchronized activation;
(b) the contents of a short-term memory store;
(c) executive control;
(d) attention;
(e) value;
(f) information.

These themes represent higher-level characteristics of consciousness, to be incorporated in the MOGUL/Activation account in the following discussion. The last theme, information, is a particularly large subject and so it will make up a section of its own.

What becomes conscious and under what conditions?

One crucial question that can be answered within a cognitive framework, but probably cannot be answered in a meaningful way without one, is what sorts of entities become conscious. The objects of consciousness have been characterized, often quite vaguely, as information, mental elements, structures, contents, input, stimuli etc. If we want a clearer characterization, an important guide is the observation commonly attributed to Karl Lashley (1923) and since repeated by many others, that we are never conscious of processes, just the results of them. In MOGUL, processing consists of processors constructing representations in their associated information stores. The representations are thus the products of processing. The initial conclusion, then, is the following:

The objects of consciousness
The potential contents of awareness are representations, and only representations.

This conclusion fits well with a number of previous proposals. Jackendoff once used the term *representation* in almost exactly the way that I use it here but has more recently replaced it with *structures,* based on a concern that *representation* carries unwanted implications regarding relations with the external world. The *schemas* of Mandler are the same type of entity. In neurally based theory, Damasio's *images* and Edelman's *scenes* are also quite similar (though Edelman would no doubt object to the kind of representational account of consciousness that I am proposing; but see also Edelman et al., 2011). Below, I will offer a somewhat revised view of images and scenes.

The next question of course is *which* representations become conscious and under what circumstances. The MOGUL framework suggests a ready answer, in terms of the most important of the main themes in theories of consciousness: activation. I argued in Chapter 3 that the other themes considered there can reasonably be understood in terms of this central and essential notion. We should therefore explore the possibility that consciousness can be explained by a maximally simple, one-factor account.

The Activation Hypothesis
A representation is conscious if and only if its current activation level is above a given threshold.

In the remainder of this chapter, I will explore the implications of this hypothesis, beginning with its application to perceptual output structures (POpS) and the way that this application incorporates the central themes identified in the theories of consciousness considered in Chapter 3.

Perceptual awareness

I suggested in Chapter 4 that representations in POpS routinely reach exceptional activation levels, partly as a result of POpS integration. Given the Activation Hypothesis, it follows that those representations should routinely dominate conscious experience – as they in fact do. Researchers have long been aware of the 'perceptual bias of consciousness' (Baars, 1988), though this awareness has played a surprisingly limited role in the theories. In global workspace (GW) theory, in particular, it is an incidental feature of consciousness, with no principled explanation. Note that it makes no difference whether the perceptual representation is a product of sensory experience or memory, imagination, dreaming or hallucination. All such cases involve POpS representations, with the same processes applying.

In discussing the various theories of consciousness in Chapter 3, I suggested that the major recurring themes found in them hinted at an underlying unity, which could be brought out if those themes were appropriately reconceptualized within a suitable framework. I believe that MOGUL provides a suitable framework. The appropriate reconceptualization involves seeing how the other themes are all related to one logically central theme: *activation*. It is difficult to find a theorist who does not treat activation, explicitly or implicitly, as a crucial element of consciousness. But none of these theorists, even Kinsbourne, sees it as sufficient for consciousness. So the reconceptualization I am suggesting is a substantial one.

In the MOGUL/Activation approach, a representation that becomes exceptionally *active* thereby becomes the object of awareness. This representation is in a *short-term memory store* simply because a short-term memory store is best conceptualized as the set of currently active items in long-term memory. When it attains the exceptional activation level needed for awareness, this state is brought about by widespread *synchronized activation* that is focused on that particular representation and/or a set of representations that includes it. The focus on one particular representation rather than another is the product of various influences, one of which is the SELF representation, with its goals, drives, motives and such. As the self is a form of executive – the ultimate executive – it is no surprise that *executive control* has been associated with consciousness.

Value is associated with consciousness primarily for the same reason. Values guide processing because the things that matter to us are naturally the target of more frequent, more intense and more sustained processing. Values are in fact difficult to separate from the goals, drives and motives that are central to SELF. *Attention* is a cover term for these complex and varied processes. With this recognition, one can easily understand why it has frequently been seen as central for consciousness. Finally, the relevance of *informativeness* to consciousness is due to the fact that informative input is, almost by definition, input that receives more processing and more sustained processing. This greater processing opens the door to very high levels of activation, which are the key to consciousness. As this treatment of informativeness has proven contentious, I will return to it in some detail below.

And so, I suggest, the various pieces really can be fit together to make a coherent picture. A crucial aspect of this fitting together is that it is done within a broad cognitive framework, MOGUL in this case. The approach is, in fact, very nearly a direct consequence of MOGUL architecture and processing, making it a parsimonious account. And if the unification of the various themes under activation is accepted, this account has another important advantage in terms of parsimony.

An additional issue of parsimony concerns the common practice of postulating two or more distinct types of consciousness, one built on top of the other, as in the theories of Damasio and Edelman, for example. I see little to be gained by dichotomizing consciousness in this way. When very limited cognitive functions exist, consciousness is necessarily limited to those functions. When higher types of cognition develop, this development is accompanied by the possibility of our being aware of them, directly or indirectly. Some authors see the development of awareness of our own consciousness as a fundamental break in evolution. But this is nothing more (or less) than awareness of the self and its activities. Once the self is established as a solid part of the cognitive system there is nothing special or surprising about its becoming another object of awareness. While the phenomena that are discussed in terms of higher forms of awareness are real and important, explaining them does not require a new theoretical entity such as 'higher-order consciousness'. So, while the application of this account will cover a variety of forms of cognition and mental contents, I will not speak of two different types of consciousness, only the application of a unified account to differing areas.

Awareness of affect and value

Another portion of the cognitive system identified above as a site of exceptional activation levels is affective structures (AfS). Its representations are highly active because of inherently high resting activation levels and because of synchronized activity temporarily integrating the AfS representation with body states and with the conceptual structures (CS) representations that constitute the appraisal underlying the emotion. And these are representations that routinely appear in awareness, as predicted by the Activation Hypothesis.

At the heart of all affective experience is value, i.e. the !val! and !harm! representations in AfS. Activation of these representations is typically accompanied by activation of larger affect representations that contain them, and so they commonly appear in awareness as part of a larger composite experience. In other words, what we experience in such cases is a particular emotion, which includes awareness of !val! if the emotion is positive (e.g. joy) or of !harm! if it is negative (e.g. fear). But the value representations, in themselves, have some of the highest activation levels found anywhere in the system, so they should be expected to pop up in their relatively pure forms, i.e. unaccompanied by any specific emotion. When they do, the result is the experience of rightness (pure !val!) and wrongness (pure !harm!).

Activation of !val! follows from the activation of any representation it is coindexed with; it is experienced simply as rightness when the experience is not strongly coloured by other representations. An example is the case of coming up with the right word after seeking it for some time. Its appearance yields a clear and relatively strong experience of rightness. But this event differs from normal lexical access only in that difficulty occurred, creating a delay and extra associated processing. All instances of retrieving a word should involve activation of !val! in a similar manner, but usually at a low level. And word retrieval is also just one example of an extremely pervasive process. Rightness accompanies normal reading and listening, for example, in essentially the same way that it accompanies lexical retrieval. When the process is going on smoothly, with understanding, a subtle, low-level rightness is present. When difficulty occurs, it is replaced by a feeling of wrongness. When understanding suddenly comes, with it comes a clearer and stronger experience of rightness, just as in the case of finding the right word. The same phenomenon can be seen in the linguist's grammaticality judgements. Anyone who speaks a language can look at or listen to a sentence in that language and judge, by feel, whether it is acceptable or not. This again is a feeling of rightness or wrongness.

The phenomenon is by no means restricted to language. When you figure out who the murderer is in a movie, the realization is accompanied by a feeling of rightness. If you then think of some evidence that contradicts your conclusion, the rightness is likely to be replaced by wrongness. When you are in the process of walking or driving towards a particular destination, low-level feelings of rightness are subtly present, becoming more salient when you choose a proper turn or recognize a landmark which confirms that you are going in the right direction. Perhaps the most basic, and the most general case of rightness involves making decisions. When we choose a dish from a menu, for instance, settling on that particular dish means connecting that option with a sense of rightness.

Such experiences are the norm in everything we do. They typically involve relatively low-level activation of !val! and !harm!, with only a subtle conscious experience of rightness and wrongness, or even none at all. When a sudden change occurs, the activation is more clearly experienced, as when the right word finally emerges or you run into a problem understanding a part of what you are reading, or when the sight of a landmark confirms that you are going in the right direction. These enhanced experiences naturally reflect an increased focus of processing on the goal and its match or mismatch with the new input, meaning greater activation of !val! or !harm!. It should also be clear that rightness and wrongness are not mutually exclusive. A particular choice from the menu can involve a feeling of rightness because it is what you really want but also a feeling of wrongness because it is so expensive or because choosing that item means foregoing another item that also seems desirable.

Consciousness and other modules

The primary conclusion to this point is that representations in POpS and AfS can and do achieve the activation levels necessary for awareness. Representations in other portions of the cognitive system do not reach such high levels and therefore are not conscious. There is no awareness, for example, of linguistic representations, syntactic or phonological. If there were, linguistics would become largely an introspective endeavour: most of the work of linguists would centre around direct examination of the representations that are active during language processing. The aspects of language that do appear in consciousness are sounds and written forms (see especially Jackendoff, 1987). In MOGUL terms, representations in auditory structures (AS) and visual structures (VS) become conscious but those in phonological structures (PS) and syntactic structures (SS) do not. Similarly, motor structures (MS) are not objects of consciousness; we are aware of sensory feedback from muscles but not of the representations that are directly responsible for planning and executing movements.

The case of CS is more complex. Concepts, quite generally, do not have phenomenal properties, as described in Chapter 3 (see also discussion in Baars, 1988, 1997; Jackendoff, 1987, 1996). A reasonable conclusion is that they are never the objects of consciousness. The common feeling that we are aware of ideas, goals and such may be due to their close association with perceptual representations and with the conscious feeling of understanding or not understanding, i.e. rightness and wrongness, that accompanies their use. This lack of awareness is natural because there is no reason to expect the kinds of activation levels found in POpS and AfS to be found in CS.

But this reasonable conclusion must be treated with some caution. We cannot dismiss the possibility that awareness, of a more modest and nebulous sort, actually is associated with CS. When we quickly review the day's events, for example, there is a feeling that we are aware of the specific events, even when there is little or no accompanying experience involving language or images. In terms of their exact phenomenal character, such experiences are quite slippery, and they might or might not be explicable in terms of fleeting POpS representations, feelings of rightness and perhaps knowledge that we can make the events conscious through language if we choose to.

This discussion connects to the classic controversy over the possibility of thought occurring without any perceptual experience, which has recently taken the form of the 'unsymbolized thinking' debate (e.g. Carruthers, 1996; Hurlburt & Akhter, 2008; Persaud, 2008). A traditional and still common view is that such thought is impossible, that in apparent cases of unsymbolized thinking the perceptual experience is actually present but is too fleeting to be available for report. This issue is extremely difficult, if not impossible to resolve, so we cannot rule out the possibility of CS awareness: that the levels of activation reached by a CS representation when it is the focus of processing, while not comparable to the levels found in POpS and AfS, are sufficient for a weak, ill-defined sort of awareness.

A possible alternative analysis is that this apparent conceptual awareness is actually awareness of the indexes on perceptual representations that link them to conceptual representations. This approach might explain the presence of awareness (the indexes are representations in POpS), the sense that it is awareness of concepts (the indexes are in effect tokens of the concepts) and the typically nebulous character of the experience when it does not involve specific perceptual representations (we should not expect an index to have clear phenomenal properties). But I will not pursue this idea any further here. The essential point is that this possible awareness, whichever interpretation is given to it, is what we would expect given the Activation Hypothesis: it is categorically below the rich phenomenal experiences associated with the extremely active representations found in POpS and AfS.

There is an additional, more important complication regarding awareness and CS. One conceptual representation appears to be exceptional, as described in Chapter 3: SELF. It is involved in virtually all processing, meaning that it is richly connected to POpS and AfS and other portions of the system, strongly influencing almost everything that goes on. It thus has a continuously high current activation level and therefore is continuously part of conscious experience. In Chapter 3, I suggested that the theme of executive control can be understood partly in terms of self, which is the closest thing to a general controller and is intimately associated with the prefrontal cortex, which is generally assigned an executive function in neural research (e.g. Goldberg, 2009).

Conclusion

The facts of what we are and are not aware of fit well with the Activation Hypothesis. A representation in POpS or AfS readily becomes the object of consciousness when it is the focus of processing, and these are the two locations where exceptional activation levels should be expected. CS representations in general should not be able to achieve such levels, fitting with the observation that they have no phenomenal qualities. The SELF representation in CS is the exception that proves the rule, as it is exceptional both in activation level and in appearing in consciousness. Representations in other modules should not be expected to ever reach sufficient activation levels, corresponding to the observation that their representations are never the objects of awareness.

An additional appeal of an activation approach is that it may be the most parsimonious means of explaining what does and does not become conscious. The concept of activation is used here in the familiar processing sense, particularly as is customary in the psycholinguistics literature. It is thus independently motivated, serving a function that is essential for any adequate cognitive theory, independent of its use in explaining consciousness. The concept of activation is of course crucial for understanding brain function as well, and the two uses are closely associated. Thus, a simple, one-factor account of consciousness based on activation is probably the most parsimonious account imaginable. The MOGUL/Activation account also successfully incorporates the major themes considered in Chapter 3 – though the theme of informativeness remains to be considered. This is the business of the following section.

Informativeness and the Activation Hypothesis

In the preceding section, I argued that the Activation Hypothesis, in the context of the MOGUL framework, can incorporate the major themes of consciousness theories identified in Chapter 3. But one of those themes has not yet been considered: the informativeness of conscious representations. There is much to be said on this matter, and it has generated some strong reactions, so I will need to deal with it in some depth. Again, readers who are not interested in this issue are welcome to skip over this section.

Baars (1988) showed that informativeness plays an essential role in whether a representation becomes conscious and that the central function of consciousness can reasonably be seen as information sharing. More generally, it is probably fair to say that all mind/brain processes – conscious and unconscious – are sensitive to informativeness. Thus, there is no disputing the importance of informativeness for cognition in general, nor is there any doubt that high levels of informativeness are characteristic of conscious representations. The issue is how these facts are to be explained. Do theories of consciousness, and cognitive theories in general, need to include an explicit informativeness principle or can the effects be derived from more fundamental characteristics of representation and processing?

At the heart of this question are the *redundancy effects*, habituation and automatization, which served as the basis for Baars' (1988) argument that an explicit informativeness condition is needed. In these phenomena, a representation fades from awareness when it should be gaining activation, an apparent contradiction with the Activation Hypothesis. What this seems to imply is that informativeness is also a necessary condition for a representation becoming conscious, since a loss of informativeness is the essence of the redundancy effects. Thus, these phenomena seem to show that activation is not a sufficient condition for consciousness; an informativeness condition must be added. So if the proposal presented in the previous sections is to be viable, these effects must be explained within that proposal; i.e. redundancy effects must be derived from the character of representation and processing in MOGUL.

In this section, I will first show how this can be done, exploring the issue of redundancy effects. I will then turn to the question of why, within MOGUL, consciousness is biased towards informative events and, more generally, what informativeness is within this framework. The section will conclude with a brief look at some additional applications of the ideas presented.

Habituation

Habituation is an adaptation to a continuing or repeated stimulus. The phenomenon has been much studied, though most of the work has been with animal behaviour and so has not dealt with consciousness (see Thompson, 2009). Focusing on the awareness aspect (see Baars, 1988), initially the stimulus is, or at least could be, informative and so its occurrence consciously registers and may lead to a response. But after the adaptation has occurred it loses its value as information and so comes to be ignored, to the point at which the person is no longer aware of its continuing presence or its reoccurrence. An ordinary example might be a bathroom fan that is connected to a light switch and so is automatically turned on along with the light. A person turning on the switch for the first time will almost certainly be aware of the sound and consciously realize that it is the sound of a fan and that the fan is connected to the light switch. But after the person has this experience many times, the awareness is likely to fade. Eventually, the person might not even be able to say, without careful consideration, whether there is a fan in the bathroom or, if so, whether it goes on automatically with the light.

The apparent problem for an activation account of consciousness is that the representation of the sound of the fan in that context should be getting *more* active with each stimulation and so awareness of it should at least continue and probably even grow stronger, contrary to the facts. But the MOGUL/Activation account does not in fact make this prediction. Representations related to the sound do gradually rise in activation with each reoccurrence, but these are the conceptual representations that interpret the sound and others that ready the body for responses to it. While the activation levels of these representations rise, that of the auditory (POpS) representation of the sound will steadily decline, resulting in a gradual loss of awareness.

The logic is that a representation's rise to consciousness involves a gradual increase in the activation level over a substantial period of time, substantial in neural terms, that is (see below). If this process is terminated before the consciousness threshold has been reached, the representation will not become conscious. In the case of the bathroom fan, the potentially conscious representation is in AS. In the first experience, its activation level rises enough to cross the consciousness threshold partly because it receives support from activity in other modules, which are attempting to interpret it and prepare for possible responses. This support allows it to win the competition against other potentially dominant POpS representations, to become the focus of perceptual processing. But once these non-perceptual processors have dealt with it adequately, their representations will no longer provide such support. With repeated occurrences of the stimulation, the non-perceptual representations acquire higher resting activation levels and so can deal more quickly with the AS representation of the fan sound. When they become able to do so before the AS representation's activation has risen to the consciousness threshold, the loss of their support will mean that this representation's rise in activation level will be terminated short of the threshold – it will not become conscious.

In this description of habituation, I said that a POpS representation receives 'support' from activity in other modules. This should not be read as a decision by a processor that the representation is interesting and therefore deserves its support. What I am suggesting is an unintelligent process. A POpS representation, by virtue of its (somewhat) elevated activation level, triggers activity in CS (for example), because anything in CS that is coindexed with it will be automatically activated by the interface and thereby become immediately available for processing in CS. If the conceptual processor does then use these newly activated representations, their activation level will rise further as a result. The interface connecting them to POpS will then further stimulate the POpS representation that started the process, further raising its activation level. It is in this sense that CS activity can support perceptual representations and help them to become conscious.

Habituation depends on non-perceptual modules developing the ability to deal quickly and efficiently with the recurring stimulus, because their relevant representations acquire high activation levels. One implication of this account is that this ability is specialized; it developed specifically to deal with that particular stimulus. When a change occurs in the stimulus, a change in the volume or pitch of the fan sound for example, these representations are no longer adequate to deal with it and so the system loses its ability to respond quickly. The result is that the AS representation of the altered stimulus can receive support from non-perceptual processors long enough for its activation level to rise to the consciousness threshold, and so it can return to awareness. Thus, the phenomenon of *dishabituation* (see Baars, 1988) also receives a ready explanation.

Automatization

Automatization is about the changes that occur in the way a skill is performed as a person acquires extensive practice with it (see Moors & De Houwer, 2006; Schneider & Shiffrin, 1977; Shiffrin, 1988; Shiffrin & Schneider, 1977). The traditional explanation is that the effects reflect a gradually diminishing need for attention. The subject has generated considerable confusion regarding exactly what the criteria are for labelling a process automatic, a great many characteristics being suggested with only limited agreement among researchers (see Bargh, 1992; Kahneman & Treisman, 1984; Logan, 1988; Rawson, 2004; Shiffrin, 1988). For present purposes, the important aspect is the loss of awareness that accompanies extensive practice. A relatively simple example is learning to tie shoelaces. In the early stages, the person must attend to all the details of the hand movements and the current state of the laces. Accompanying this attention is a clear awareness of these details, which gradually fades with practice.

The MOGUL/Activation account offers essentially the same explanation as that provided for the loss of awareness in habituation. Non-perceptual processors become better able to deal with a task quickly and efficiently and therefore complete their work before the relevant representations in POpS have had a chance to reach the activation levels needed for consciousness. They then cease to support that representation, with the result that its activation level never reaches the consciousness threshold.

In the shoelace example, the task necessarily makes use of a number of distinct representations in CS (the intention to carry out the action), MS (the plans for executing the action), VS (the sight of the laces and the hands) and somatosensory structures (sensations from the hands). To avoid unnecessary complications, I will focus on MS, which is responsible for actually carrying out the task, and VS, which provides visual input to the motor system in this case. For the motor processor to carry out its task, MS must contain a series of representations of the movements required at each point, coindexed with VS representations of the state of the laces and the hands at each point. Successful execution of the shoelace tying procedure requires that these motor representations successively dominate MS: at each step the VS representation of the current state of the laces and the hands activates the MS representation of the action that is to follow. The procedure is automatic when this sequence occurs quickly and efficiently.

The process is initially slow because of the low resting activation levels of the motor representations and the indexes that link them to the corresponding VS representations, limiting their availability for processing. In this state, they require considerable stimulation from their VS counterparts if they are to dominate MS and trigger the appropriate actions. Under these conditions, the VS representations must reach very high activation levels if they are to adequately activate the MS representations; they are therefore conscious whenever the tying process is carried out successfully. Automatization involves the gradual rise in the resting levels of the MS representations and the indexes, increasing both the chances of these representations coming to dominate MS and the speed with which they can do so. This rise is brought about, as always, by their repeated use in processing. As their resting levels become higher, they require steadily less stimulation from VS to achieve the current levels at which they can dominate MS. The ultimate result is that even when the current activation levels of the VS representations are still relatively low, they are sufficient to activate the corresponding MS representations to the point that they can dominate MS and trigger the motor activity, i.e. the series of actions involved in tying the laces. Under these conditions, dominance of VS shifts quickly from one representation to the next, each being replaced before it has the opportunity to reach activation levels sufficient for consciousness.

This account of automatization is simplified in a number of ways. But the simplifications do not affect the point, that the gradual loss of awareness that accompanies automatization can be explained purely in terms of activation levels, without any explicit reference to informativeness.

Why are conscious percepts biased towards informative events?

A central point of Baars' (1988) work on consciousness was that conscious events have a strong tendency to be informative. It is as if conscious processing seeks out informative events and dismisses anything that does not contain worthwhile information. This description is no doubt valid as a high-level, external perspective on how the system works, and is a plausible account of why it developed into its current form. But the observation does not imply that the system contains an explicit informativeness condition. I suggest that from a system-internal perspective there is no focus on informative events and no seeking for information. Processors blindly carry out their function of making legitimate representations from whatever input they are presented with.

The MOGUL processor is a much less intelligent entity than the information-seeking view would require. Its only concern, always, is to construct a legitimate representation from the input that is presented to it. Informative input is, more or less by definition, input that it cannot handle in an automatic fashion, i.e. for which processing is necessarily less efficient and – more to the point – slower. So it necessarily takes more time to construct representations for informative input than for uninformative input. Thus, a general characteristic of the cognitive system is that a loss of informativeness results in reduced activity by processors, because of a reduced need for activity. Thus, habituation is not limited to representations that are initially conscious; the phenomenon should be (and is) found throughout the system.

The central concern here, however, is with cases involving potentially conscious POpS representations. Here, a lack of informativeness means limited processing activity, which means only a limited rise in the current activation level of the POpS representation, which means a reduced opportunity for that representation to become conscious. Informative input is input that requires more processing and therefore has a better opportunity to reach the activation levels needed for awareness. From a MOGUL perspective, this is why consciousness is biased towards informative percepts. Interestingly, this association of novelty with additional processing and additional time has parallels in holistic theories of consciousness. For Pribram and Meade (1999: 213), 'When the formation of axonal patterns takes time (a temporal hold) because of the novelty of the input, they become experienced consciously'. Also worth noting is Kinsbourne's (1988, 1997, 2006) use of 'duration' as a factor contributing to consciousness.

One implication of this discussion is that it may be possible to remove the informativeness condition not only from accounts of consciousness but also from cognitive theory in general. Given a suitable framework, the effects of such a principle can be derived from the basic characteristics of the system.

Additional applications: Some phenomena closely related to redundancy

The redundancy effects are about POpS representations not reaching activation levels that are sufficient for awareness, and in this respect they are closely related to some additional phenomena. The difference is that in these other phenomena the representations that fail to become conscious fail not because they are not informative – they typically are – but because circumstances do not allow them a chance to attain high activation levels. Thus, the MOGUL/Activation approach offers a unified account of why stimuli do not become conscious, both in cases in which they are not informative and in those in which they are.

One of the relevant phenomena is subliminal perception (Greenwald et al., 1995; Kihlstrom, 1996; Merikle et al., 2001). Its essence is that sensory input appears in POpS but too weakly to become conscious, just as in habituation or automatization. The crucial difference is that in the case of the redundancy effects, non-perceptual processors have already acquired the ability to deal effectively with this limited input, while no such development has occurred in the case of subliminal perception and so only limited processing of the input is possible. Priming effects show that the unattended items, not reaching consciousness, are represented in POpS. The problem is that their activation level never becomes very high and so they do not reach consciousness and, for the same reason, cannot have more substantial effects on non-perceptual processing.

The situation may be the same for blindsight (Stoerig & Cowey, 1997; Weiskrantz, 1986, 2007). When blindness results from damage to visual areas of the brain, the patient can sometimes accurately judge the location of objects in the visual field without any awareness of their presence. A likely explanation is that VS representations can still be constructed but are too weak to cross the consciousness threshold (and are possibly incomplete as well). Analogous phenomena have been found involving other modalities: hearing (Engelien et al., 2000; Garde & Cowey, 2000), smell (Henkin & Levy, 2002) and touch and proprioception (Rossetti et al., 1995). In the MOGUL/Activation account, these effects are expected, since there is no reason why the other POpS stores would differ from VS in this respect.

Inattentional blindness (Mack & Rock, 1998; see also Mack, 2003) might also be seen in these terms. When instructed to focus on a particular portion of the visual field, a person tends to be unaware of a stimulus that is briefly presented elsewhere in the field, even when it is fixated on. Perceptual representations are constructed of the apparently unseen stimuli, as shown by priming effects. The problem is that POpS is dominated by a different representation, that of the portion of the visual field on which processing focused, so representations of other portions can only be briefly present. As a result, they cannot attain the activation levels necessary for awareness and can have only limited effects on processing outside POpS.

Inattentional blindness comes in a variety of forms, some of them far more dramatic than that revealed in the Mack and Rock experiments. Simons (2000; Chabris & Simons, 2009), basing his experiment on earlier work by Neisser, had participants watch a film of two intermingled teams, one wearing white shirts and the other black, passing a basketball among themselves. Participants were instructed to count the number of passes made by one of the teams, disregarding the other team's actions. In the midst of the action, a person in a gorilla suit slowly walked into the middle of the scene, paused and then walked off. The striking finding is that approximately half the people who watch this film are completely unaware of the gorilla, and this blindness occurs even when their gaze is clearly fixated on it at some point.

Chabris and Simons (2009) discuss many other cases of this sort (see also Chun & Marois, 2002; Most et al., 2005; Rensink, 2002; Simons & Rensink, 2005). Within the MOGUL framework, these findings all receive the same explanation. A representation of the missed item is formed, but the circumstances prevent it from being processed extensively enough to achieve a high activation level, and therefore to become conscious.

It is worth noting that there is no principled distinction between what we call inattentional blindness and ordinary, unproblematic perception. The perceptual system cannot possibly process all aspects of a visual scene beyond the most superficial level, so perception necessarily involves picking out certain aspects of the scene for in-depth processing and abandoning all the other aspects. When the category of abandoned aspects includes items which we feel it should not include, we call this inattentional blindness. When the choice of items to be abandoned is unobjectionable, the process is seen as normal perception.

Finally, note that exceptions are commonly found to these findings that unattended stimuli do not reach consciousness. They typically involve representations that have special significance to the person, such as his/her own name (e.g. Mack & Rock, 1998; Moray, 1969; Shapiro et al., 1997). In the MOGUL/Activation account this is expected because these are exactly the representations that should have unusually high resting activation levels, meaning that they require considerably less stimulation to reach the consciousness threshold.

Conclusion

I have argued in this section that the redundancy effects do not pose any obstacle to the development of an activation theory of consciousness, if that theory is developed within a suitable general framework. The essential point is that while redundancy produces high activation levels in some parts of the cognitive system, it can – and should – lead to reduced levels in POpS and therefore to the disappearance of the relevant representation from consciousness. This account illustrates the value of addressing issues of consciousness within a relatively explicit framework. Discussions of habituation have typically been framed in terms of changes in the activation of an externally defined 'stimulus' or 'object'. But the phenomenon cannot be understood unless we look inside the black box and consider the multiple levels of processing and representation that are triggered by that stimulus.

I also argued that the general tendency for conscious percepts to be informative can be accounted for without any appeal to an explicit informativeness condition: informative percepts are those that require more extended processing and therefore have a better opportunity to reach the activation levels needed for awareness. This is not to dismiss informativeness as a genuine – and central – characteristic of conscious representations.

Sharing of information is an essential function and the need for this sharing was presumably a major factor in the development of the system. However, there is no need for an explicit informativeness condition in a theory of consciousness. The effects can be derived in a natural way, the essential feature of the derivation being the natural split between the *de facto* seat of consciousness, POpS, and the locations at which follow-up processing goes on.

Relations to Some Prominent Theories of Consciousness

This proposal is naturally related to and contrasts with many existing theories of consciousness, including those described in Chapter 3. Those theories have a great deal in common, often more than is readily apparent. I suggest that casting their central ideas in MOGUL terms brings out crucial similarities among the various theories, similarities that are hidden behind the differing terminology, emphases and orientations. Again, readers who are not interested in the issues of consciousness, in themselves, are welcome to skip over this section.

Baars' global workspace theory

The approach I am suggesting here was originally inspired by Baars' GW theory and has much in common with it. Most importantly, POpS resembles the hypothesized GW in many respects. It is necessarily connected widely to other portions of the cognitive system, its representations being read by a great variety of processors and at the same time being influenced by them. The GW is about using these connections to share important information throughout the system. The information that is most important to share is that of the senses, particularly so when the various modalities converge on a single set of representations, across modalities, that can together form a coherent whole. It is quite natural then to identify the common sensory output store with the seat of consciousness (the GW) and to identify the representations on which it converges as the bearers of the information to be shared. POpS thus carries out the function of the GW. In addition to information coming directly from the senses, POpS (like the GW) supports representations of perceptual memories and imagination, which involve largely the same brain systems involved in awareness of immediate perceptual representations (Behrmann, 2000; Jackendoff, 2002; Kosslyn *et al.*, 2001; Pinker, 1997). When a representation of this sort comes to dominate POpS, it becomes conscious (is broadcast), in place of any representation of current sensory information.

But while the MOGUL/Activation approach was inspired by GW theory, it differs from it in crucial respects. Perhaps the most important contrast is the lack of an explicit informativeness condition, which is at the heart of Baars' theory. I discussed this point above in some detail and here will focus instead on two additional differences. One contrast is that in the MOGUL account consciousness is not inherently associated with any particular part of the cognitive system. Any representation anywhere in the system can in principle become conscious, if its current activation level is sufficiently high. Thus, POpS is not a system designed to produce or house conscious representations. The fact that its representations dominate conscious experience is the product of the high activation levels that they routinely reach. A virtue of this approach is that it correctly predicts that an additional type of representation, affective, also routinely becomes conscious, as does the one special CS representation: SELF. Another contrast with GW theory is that POpS is in one respect much more limited than the GW, as it contains exclusively perceptual representations. But this apparent distinction in fact strengthens the resemblance. The GW hosts conscious representations, and conscious representations are predominantly perceptual, as Baars (1988) noted.

The MOGUL account has another important advantage over GW theory. Baars (1988) was concerned about a paradox that emerged in his theory. If a representation is to be broadcast (become conscious), the information it contains must lead other processors to adapt to it. But the response from those processors cannot be determined until after the broadcast has occurred. The apparent solution to this *threshold paradox* is to hypothesize preliminary, subliminal broadcasts that serve to give the processors a taste of what is available. They respond to these preliminary broadcasts by supporting those representations that appear to be informative to them, the ultimate result being that the most informative will win the competition for dominance of the GW.

These subliminal broadcasts are not a natural part of GW theory; instead, they constitute an *ad hoc* complication. They are a natural consequence, however, of the MOGUL/Activation account. Each sensory processing system is constantly trying to establish a representation in its POpS store: the sight of the words on the page, assorted sounds in the room, the smell of food from the next room, the feel of the chair and so on. The result is that a number of representations are briefly and weakly active in the various POpS stores. Active representations in one store always trigger activity in others, via the interfaces, so each of these weakly active POpS representations will influence activity by a variety of processors. On any given store, CS for instance, this influence could turn out to be decisive (for the moment), the activated representations becoming the centre of activity in that store. Or it could be only fleeting, use of the newly activated representations being quickly overwhelmed by other activity. In the former case only, the CS representations activated in response to the initial POpS activity further rise in activation level, thereby triggering a corresponding rise in the level of the associated POpS representation. If several processors respond to a particular perceptual representation in this way, each raising its activation level, it can come to dominate POpS and become conscious. In the MOGUL/Activation account, this is the process by which a candidate representation reaches consciousness. In this process, the subliminal broadcasts turn out to be nothing more than ordinary processing activity.

Dehaene's global neuronal workspace

Dehaene's theory is close to GW theory in most respects, so only limited comments are needed here. His is very much a modular approach, rejecting the idea of an executive controller. Worth stressing is the idea of an active local representation and its connection to the synchronized activity of the broader network that makes it the content of consciousness. Largely implicit, but nonetheless central in this account, is activation: the local representation is necessarily active and the synchronization is synchronization of activity. Dehaene also incorporates value, in the form of reward signals. In all these respects, his theory parallels the MOGUL/Activation account.

Cooney and Gazzaniga's account of consciousness in certain neurological disorders

The approach to consciousness sketched by Cooney and Gazzaniga is very similar to that of Baars and Dehaene, so most of the comments made above are also relevant here. Especially worth noting is their concern with both the local module that provides the contents of a conscious experience and the global neuronal network which makes those contents conscious as well as the relation between them. They do not explicitly consider activation, but it is implicitly central in their proposal. Consciousness requires a 'coherent network state', and the coherence is a matter of coherent *activity*. Gazzaniga's view of the self as pure illusion, with no causal effect on what goes on in the mind, is a stronger position than most would be willing to take on the subject, and the MOGUL account does not follow him on this point. But this strong claim does have the virtue of bringing out the more widely accepted point that the mind is highly modular and that control comes from many different sources.

Damasio's body- and self-oriented account

I argued in Chapter 4 that Damasio's picture of the brain fits reasonably well with the picture offered by the MOGUL framework, at least in the aspects that are especially important for an understanding of consciousness. His early sensory cortices (representing image space) can be associated with POpS, and his association cortex (dispositional space) with the interfaces connecting the various POpS stores to one another and to non-perceptual modules. I suggested above that his sensory *images* might be more or less equated with POpS representations, but it is more accurate to see them as the *sets* of coindexed POpS representations, one in each perceptual store, that together form a unified portrayal of significant environmental events.

A significant point of difference is that for Damasio, image space does not literally contain the images but only the material that is used for (re)constructing them, using the instructions in dispositional space. The validity of this separation is very much unresolved. In any case, this contrast can reasonably be taken as a difference between neural and cognitive orientations. Note that in the MOGUL framework, a stored representation is not activated in isolation from other representations. As described in Chapter 4, a store is a web of interconnected representations, with additional, more limited connections to other stores, via interfaces. An inevitable consequence is that activation cannot be isolated to one representation but instead involves a great deal of coactivation throughout the store and beyond. This activity can greatly influence the conscious experience and can alter the activated representations, topics to which I will return in later chapters. Thus, the (re)constructive nature of memory is recognized by both approaches.

For Damasio, the current content of consciousness consists of an active image. It becomes conscious through the synchronization of activity across wide areas of the brain, with self playing a crucial role in the synchronization. At a more fundamental level, value appears to be the key (or at least one very important key) to consciousness, serving a function very similar to that of attention in various other approaches. With some important qualifications, this picture also corresponds reasonably well with that hypothesized in MOGUL. Representations in POpS become conscious when their current activation level is raised to an exceptional level through the synchronization of activity in POpS and beyond. Self and value are important influences on this synchronization. Damasio does not explicitly give activation the central place that it occupies in the MOGUL/Activation account, but it is clearly present and crucial for his account. He places body and self at the centre of his proposal to a much greater degree than I do, but those elements are nonetheless important for the MOGUL/Activation account.

Edelman's dynamic core

Edelman presents his theory in terms that are quite different from those of the MOGUL/Activation account. But this apparent contrast hides a strong underlying resemblance. A concept that is logically central in his account, but receives only limited development, is *scene*, which, like Damasio's *image*, looks a great deal like the set of coindexed POpS representations hypothesized as targets of consciousness in the MOGUL framework. For Edelman, a unified scene is produced by the synchronization of processing in the various senses plus value-category memories, all through re-entrant signalling. From a MOGUL/Activation perspective, this is a neural account of how representations can achieve exceptional activation levels. It is quite compatible with the idea of the synchronization of representations across POpS, with the crucial involvement of conceptual and affective modules, the latter associating value with the content representations.

The appearance of incompatibility between Edelman's account and that offered here stems in part, of course, from the fact that Edelman's account is neural. But no less important is his rejection of representation. One consequence of this rejection is that he does little to develop the core concept of scene, which is an inherently representational idea. If he did so, I believe a strong resemblance to MOGUL representations would become clear. Closely related is his de-emphasis of the local element in consciousness, which contrasts with my emphasis on the representations that are the objects of awareness. These particular representations are the focus of processing and therefore have the extreme activation levels that make consciousness possible. Naturally, this local element also plays a crucial role in GW theory and related theories. Edelman shows little interest in it, but it is very much present in his account, and is indeed essential, as in the 'blue' example considered in Chapter 3.

Tononi's information integration theory

Tononi (2007, 2012) proposed that consciousness results from the integration of large amounts of information. Any system in which this occurs is conscious. On Tononi's rather complex analysis, an extremely modular system is not conducive to consciousness because the information in the various modules is integrated only locally. But nor is a modular system in which all elements are connected to all others. Maximal information integration occurs in a system that is composed of distinct modules that have strong interactions with one another. This is a reasonably good description of the MOGUL framework and especially of POpS. Information integration might in fact be seen as the essential function of POpS: it ties together the information coming from the various sensory modules and connects it to conceptual and affective processing. The association between POpS and consciousness is thus reasonably compatible with Tononi's information integration theory. The claim that information integration is behind consciousness can be readily translated into activation terms. A natural consequence of large-scale integrative processing is that the representations that embody the integration are the focus of intensive processing and therefore have exceptionally high activation levels. It is not clear, however, how such an analysis can be extended to affective processing or the sense of self.

Kinsbourne's dominant focus model

One of the contrasts with GW theory is that the MOGUL/Activation approach does not hypothesize that consciousness is inherently tied to any particular system; any representations can in principle reach consciousness if they are sufficiently active. In this respect, it resembles a rival to GW theory: the *dominant focus* model of Kinsbourne (1988, 1997, 2006; see also Cohen, 1997), which I considered in Chapter 3 under the heading 'Some Holistic Treatments of Consciousness'. In this model, consciousness is about general activity in the system, not about special structures designed to support it. The MOGUL/Activation approach adopts this position as well but with the twist that certain structures, namely perceptual and affective, are incidentally suitable for consciousness because they can attain very high activation levels, while others have no opportunity to reach such levels and therefore cannot become conscious.

Kinsbourne hypothesized two or three factors determining whether a representation becomes conscious, the first of course being activation. Duration is also important. In many cases a representation is replaced so quickly that it has no chance to become conscious. I suggest that this factor can reasonably be reduced to activation. It takes a substantial amount of time (in neural terms) for a representation to become conscious (see below), during which its activation level gradually rises towards the consciousness threshold. If the process is terminated too quickly, it will have no chance to reach the threshold. Thus, duration can reasonably be seen as simply one factor behind its activation level rather than a direct cause of a representation becoming conscious. I will not consider the third factor, *congruence*, because Kinsbourne (1997) discussed it only in his relatively early work and not since.

Jackendoff's intermediate-levels theory

Jackendoff (1987, 1996, 1997, 2007) associated consciousness with the intermediate levels in the cognitive system, between early sensory processing and later conceptual processing, neither of which, Jackendoff argued, involves conscious representations. An intermediate-level representation that is currently in working memory is chosen for awareness by a selection function. Attention then focuses on portions of this representation for more intense processing, making those parts more vivid in consciousness. The 'feel' of an experience comes from value features that are associated with the representation that becomes conscious. We become aware of particular value features because they are attached to the content representation and so essentially get a free ride to consciousness.

Translated into MOGUL terms, the intermediate levels correspond to the output of perceptual processing, POpS. Jackendoff (1987) characterized linguistic awareness as 'phonological' but hedged considerably on this description, noting that we are not conscious of the details of a phonological representation. In MOGUL, awareness of (spoken) language is simply awareness of AS representations, which represent all the sounds processed by the auditory system, linguistic or otherwise, in a purely auditory format. One criticism of Jackendoff's approach is that it is not clear why PS should be considered an intermediate level. It is an abstract, linguistic level representing further analysis of the products of perceptual processing, much like CS. If its intermediate status is based on its falling between the perceptual and the conceptual, then it is not clear why syntax should not also qualify. But syntactic representations are never the objects of awareness. No such issues arise in the MOGUL/Activation account.

Jackendoff (2007) tentatively suggested that what makes the intermediate level special is that it is where top-down processes become a substantial part of processing and where attention first plays a role. He added the important qualification that it is not clear why these characteristics should be associated with consciousness. Within an activation account, it is clear. What Jackendoff is describing is the intersection of sensory, bottom-up processes with conceptual, top-down processes and with attention (however it is interpreted). This is precisely where we should expect to find the highest activation levels. Representations that are influenced by a variety of processors should be representations that have the potential to reach exceptional levels of activation.

Jackendoff's account of how an intermediate-level representation becomes conscious includes the requirement that it be currently in working memory. In MOGUL terms, this means it must be currently active. Jackendoff does not seem to distinguish levels of activation, characterizing a representation as either active or not active. Among items in working memory (i.e. active items), one is chosen by the selection function, which in MOGUL terms is an abstraction from ordinary processing, as described in Chapter 4. Jackendoff also has a role for attention. A mechanism directs attention to the appropriate portions of the conscious representation, which then receive extra processing, making them more vivid in consciousness. MOGUL does not have a mechanism specifically serving this function. As described in previous chapters, the focus is, again, the result of all the factors that influence processing.

Baddeley's working memory model

I discussed the similarities and differences between POpS and Baddeley's working memory model in Chapter 4, especially the episodic buffer, and will simply add one note here. Baddeley (2007: 316) said that he was 'inclined to identify the episodic buffer with the representation of events that are currently in conscious awareness'. The parallels between the two proposals thus extend to the hosting of conscious experience. (For interesting discussion of awareness in the working memory model, see McGovern & Baars, 2007.)

Accounting for Some Major Characteristics of Consciousness

The final business of this chapter is to consider what the MOGUL/Activation account has to say about a variety of phenomena that need to be explained in any adequate theory of consciousness. This amounts to asking what we know about consciousness. It seems bold to speak of what we know on a subject that has generated so much confusion and controversy, but consciousness has been the subject of a great deal of scientific research, which has much to teach us. Perhaps of even greater importance is the ordinary experience that we all have with consciousness. In a sense, we are all experts on the subject and the problem is to figure out exactly what it is that we already know. So here is my effort to identify some things we know about consciousness, based on both research and ordinary experience, and to show how the account that I have offered in this chapter can explain them. This effort is necessarily somewhat subjective, as everyone has his/her own way of thinking about the problem and his/her own emphases (for examples of other people's lists, see Baars, 1998; Shallice & Cooper, 2011: 446–447).

Most of what goes on in the mind/brain is unconscious

In Chapter 1, I presented evidence that we are primarily unconscious creatures. Given the MOGUL/Activation account, this fact is expected, as exceptional activation levels can only be achieved in particular contexts. Specifically, they can be achieved in POpS and AfS, and by one special conceptual representation, SELF, that is involved in virtually all processing. And by no means does all activity in POpS and AfS result in awareness; only representations that come to dominate one of the stores can achieve sufficient levels, so a great deal of more brief and/or lower-level activity remains unconscious. Lower-level perceptual processing offers no opportunities for very high activation levels and therefore no opportunity for consciousness. The same is true for MS and nearly all activity in CS. No activity in these parts of the system can result in activation levels comparable to those reached in POpS and AfS. Most of what goes on in the mind is necessarily unconscious.

Conscious experience is continuous, flowing from one experience to another

One of the most familiar features of experience is the continuity found in the stream of consciousness. Experience does not normally jump from one topic to another without some identifiable relation between the two. Instead, the current contents of consciousness are typically replaced by something closely related to them. Thoughts of a particular friend will be followed by thoughts of experiences with that friend, or of characteristics of that friend or of other people associated with him/her and so forth. In a good theory of consciousness, this stream of associated experiences should make sense, as should the exceptions to it: cases in which an external stimulus overwhelms the current mental activity, as when a sudden loud noise occurs.

The continuity of conscious experience is most naturally explained in terms of activation as a continuously varying feature of representations. When the activation level of a given representation is high enough to cross the threshold, it will remain elevated for some time afterwards, only gradually falling back to its resting level, as will all the unconscious contextual representations whose activation contributed to its rise to consciousness. Thus, all these representations will strongly influence the activity that immediately follows, producing the continuity that is observed in conscious experience. This is essentially Baars' (1988) account, explicitly phrased in terms of activation levels. The exception to the continuity is when an external stimulus is so strong that it can overwhelm the currently active representations, as in the case of a sudden loud noise. In MOGUL terms, the auditory module processes the sound to produce a very active representation in AS, which is strongly reinforced by a fear representation in AfS that is connected to auditory representations, probably innately.

Conscious experience is dominated by perceptual elements

Ordinary observation tells us that conscious experience typically comes from our sensations of the world around us and of our own bodies: the sight of the words on the page, the sound of someone's laughter, the feel of a book in one's hand, the dryness in one's mouth, the ache of an overworked muscle, the butterflies in one's stomach. And when we are not actually experiencing the world or our bodies, these perceptual elements are replaced largely by internally generated perceptual experience. We see images in our heads, images that can be memories of past experience or can be our own inventions. We hear the words that represent our thoughts, the 'voice in the head'. Even in dreaming, conscious experiences are primarily perceptual. The fact that conscious experience is dominated by perceptual representations has long been recognized. Baars (1988) wrote of the 'perceptual bias of consciousness', tracing it far back into history. But this central fact has generally not received its due in theories of consciousness. A satisfactory theory of consciousness should explain why perceptual elements have this privileged status.

In GW theory it is an incidental feature, which Baars (1997a) discussed only briefly, tentatively attributing it to the phylogenetic age of the perceptual system relative to that of the conceptual system; in other words, in the evolution of the brain the perceptual system appeared before the conceptual system and so maybe it is not surprising that consciousness is especially tied to perception. This idea has appeal, but it is the appeal of interesting but undeveloped speculation. In the MOGUL/Activation account, it is a natural consequence of the architecture of the system, requiring only the addition of the Activation Hypothesis. Because of their integration (and therefore synchronization) and their rich connections throughout the system, perceptual output representations can achieve exceptional activation levels, while their conceptual counterparts, for example, cannot. Therefore, we have conscious perceptual experience but only indirect experience of concepts.

Emotion is also a prominent part of conscious experience

The prominent place of emotion in consciousness is clear from ordinary experience. The explanation for this prominence is equally straightforward. As described in the previous chapter, affective representations routinely reach extreme activation levels, like POpS representations. So they necessarily play a prominent role in conscious experience.

The experience of self plays a role in all conscious experience

A crucial characteristic of conscious experiences is that they are not simply experiences but rather *my* experiences, an experience as I am experiencing it. In other words, self seems to be a universal element of conscious life. In the previous chapter, I described self as a representation that is involved in virtually all processing. This role ensures that it has an exceptionally high resting activation level. The notion of a resting level, in the sense of the level it falls back to when not receiving stimulation, may not even be a meaningful concept for the self representation, because it participates in virtually all processing and therefore has little or no opportunity to fall back very far. Given the Activation Hypothesis, it follows that this representation will continuously be a part of conscious experience. It is not clear if self even can be removed from experience. Possible cases of this sort include meditation and the *flow* experience (Csikszentmihaly, 1990).

Conscious perceptual experience is coherent and serial

Conscious experience is of one thing followed by another. The 'thing' can include a variety of features, such as colour, shape and size for a visual object, or volume, tone and stress in speech perception. But these features necessarily fit together to form a single coherent whole. If this coherence is lacking, the different features can only be experienced separately, one after the other. The coherence can cross modalities, a single thing including both visual and auditory elements, for example. But elements in the different modalities cannot conflict with one another, or else one will drive the other from awareness.

Within the MOGUL/Activation approach, these characteristics follow naturally from the nature of POpS as described above, particularly the way that its integration leads to the synchronization of the processing activity. The extreme activation levels needed for awareness are a product of this synchronization. When POpS activity does not converge on a single set of representations, no perceptual representation will have a high enough activation level to cross the consciousness threshold. When it does, all those that participate in this synchronization can contribute to the contents of consciousness; one can be simultaneously aware of the sight, sound and smell of an object, for example.

The limits of coherence/seriality: Emotional and perceptual experience co-occur

While the coherence/seriality requirement has been widely recognized, surprisingly little attention has been given to a striking exception to it: the experience of emotion. To be simultaneously present in awareness, two perceptual elements must be combined into a coherent whole, but this is not true of a perceptual element and an emotion. Feelings of anxiety, for example, can indefinitely coexist with essentially any perceptual experience, whether or not the latter has any relation to the anxiety. A person who is feeling strong anger can go on feeling that anger while consciously dealing with, and experiencing, any type of ordinary matter. A person who is happy can maintain the feeling of happiness while doing those exact same things. One might dismiss such observations by defining conscious experience as coherent: if two elements are experienced simultaneously then they are by definition part of a single coherent experience. But beyond this arbitrary preference there is no apparent reason to treat the emotion and the perceptual experience together as a single thing. A single conscious experience can include both a perceptual element and an emotional element.

The MOGUL/Activation account predicts this exceptional status of the perceptual–affective combination. If awareness is not tied to any particular part of the cognitive system, there is no reason why exceptions to seriality/coherence should not occur. The only requirement is that the two potentially conscious representations should attain exceptionally high activation levels at the same time. This rules out representations in most parts of the system, since they are not able to reach such levels, regardless of what is happening elsewhere. Additionally, it cannot occur with two perceptual representations, as described above, because a perceptual representation can only reach those high levels if it receives general support across POpS, something that cannot happen simultaneously with two incompatible representations. The only remaining possibility for simultaneous awareness is that one of the representations is perceptual and the other is affective, because each can achieve the necessary levels and because processing in AfS is largely separate from that in POpS, meaning that strong activation of one will not prevent strong activation of the other.

POpS and AfS activity do influence each other, due to the general connectedness of the cognitive system as a whole. But this influence produces only a *tendency* to feel happy during a 'happy' perceptual experience. We might well observe something that in itself would make us happy and yet feel sad or angry as the result of previous experience which has become part of the background, no longer present in awareness. This situation is in striking contrast with the absolute demand for perceptual coherence.

Within the MOGUL framework, coherence and seriality are not characteristics specifically of consciousness. They are, rather, general characteristics of processing within a given module. Representations constantly compete for dominance in a store. When one is dominant, it precludes the possibility of any others being dominant at that point. The coherence/seriality requirement is a principle of how dominance in a store occurs. It translates into a principle of consciousness in exactly those cases in which the currently dominant representation achieves a current activation level sufficient for awareness.

The place of self should also be considered in regard to coherence and seriality. Virtually all conscious experience includes self as the experiencer. Self thus freely coexists with perceptual and affective representations in consciousness. This coexistence inevitably yields coherence, though. It is difficult to imagine any experience with which self as the experiencer would not be coherent. So the presence of self in consciousness is not an exception to the coherence/seriality requirement, though it is a case of fundamentally different types of elements appearing together in consciousness.

Consciousness is slow, by the standards of cognitive/neural processes in general

It takes a surprisingly long time for something to become conscious. A typical neuron can fire in only a few milliseconds and a great deal can be done in the mind/brain over spans of tens of milliseconds. But for something to become conscious, approximately 500 milliseconds are required (Libet, 1966, 1982; Libet *et al.*, 1991). By the standards of cognitive and neural activity, this is a very long time. A theory of consciousness should explain why the process takes so long: what is happening during this relatively extended period, and why must these things happen before consciousness is possible? The common answer in neurally oriented accounts is that consciousness is a product (or entailment) of the synchronization of activity across separate regions of the brain. This synchronization requires a considerable amount of back and forth communication between the regions (re-entrant signalling), which is naturally a time-consuming process. In the MOGUL/ Activation account, this translates in part to the synchronization of activity in the various processing units that make up POpS, focused on a particular perceptual representation. As this representation is selected by activity in other processing units, notably CS and AfS, the synchronization naturally includes these as well. The result is a gradual increase in the representation's activation level, eventually taking it over the consciousness threshold.

Conscious experience shows limited capacity

A striking observation about consciousness is how limited conscious processes are relative to the immense capacity of the human brain (Baars, 1988, 2007). The MOGUL/Activation account suggests a way of thinking about this fact that parallels Baars' GW explanation but sees things from a different angle. First, to clarify the question: in this account there is, strictly speaking, no such thing as a conscious process, only representations that can become conscious, given the right circumstances. The circumstances are large-scale synchronized processing that focuses on a particular representation or coherent set of representations and thereby raises the activation to exceptional levels. Given that awareness arises specifically from this intense focus of resources, it is no surprise that conscious activity is severely limited, that one cannot simultaneously do a variety of things consciously. This is essentially the same phenomenon as coherence/seriality, though the slow speed with which an item becomes conscious also imposes limits on the capacity of conscious activity. So the limited capacity feature of consciousness is not a separate characteristic but rather an aspect of other characteristics.

Concepts play a background role in conscious experience

I suggested above that conceptual representations are never present in conscious experience, remaining instead in the background, where they exert important influences on the experience without being an actual part of it. This observation makes sense in terms of the MOGUL/Activation approach. CS representations cannot achieve the activation levels necessary for consciousness, but they are coindexed with POpS representations which can. Because of these connections, strong activation of AS or VS representations – strong enough to make them conscious – implies that their CS counterparts are also active, dominating CS. Thus, conscious experience of the voice inside the head, for example, coincides with conceptual processing. When we say to ourselves 'Mary needs a vacation', the accompanying concepts – MARY, NEED and VACATION (among others) – are active in CS and combined in a way that corresponds to the silent utterance. The perceptual representations thus serve in a sense as proxies for their conceptual counterparts.

This might be seen in terms of Baars' (1997a: 86) suggestion that concepts 'may ride on fragments of conscious images, basic brain elements that allow us to use the ancestral sensorimotor system to think'. In any case, thought is a complex interplay between conceptual representations in CS and perceptual representations, especially auditory (usually linguistic) and visual, in POpS. The concepts are crucially present and involved in thought, but only the perceptual elements appear in awareness.

The other, more subtle conscious elements in these experiences are the feelings of rightness and wrongness (see Mangan, 1993, 2007) that routinely accompany other conscious experiences. In MOGUL, these are affective representations – relatively pure expressions of !val! and !harm! – and so their appearance in conscious experience is natural. When the content of the experience is not understood or seems wrong in some sense, the feeling of wrongness is a normal part of conscious experience. When things fall into place, it is replaced by a feeling of rightness. These feelings also play a crucial role in reading or listening to speech. Understanding a spoken utterance, for example, does not involve any conscious experience of the concepts that are being understood. What it does involve is the unconscious establishment of a conceptual representation of the utterance, accompanied by a feeling of rightness, or understanding.

Conscious states can have very wide influence throughout the cognitive system

One of the central characteristics that Baars (1988) attributed to consciousness is *vast access*: consciousness makes the contents of an experience available for use by a vast array of mental systems, giving the person access to enormous amounts of relevant information. When we hear someone say 'It's raining', an array of language processors immediately go into action, analyzing the sound, form and meaning of the utterance. After this processing, we can then think of any number of things related to the utterance. We can access the written forms of the words. We have thoughts of objects associated with rain, such as umbrellas and raincoats. We bring up memories of experiences with rain. We think of our plans for the day and how the rain will affect them. Our feelings associated with rain are awakened. We can think of metaphorical uses of 'rain'. At the same time we can identify characteristics of the speaker's voice, the feeling behind the utterance, the location of the speaker, along with countless additional associations. And these lists barely scratch the surface of the information that can be evoked by one simple, consciously perceived sentence. This very broad influence of conscious states should make sense within a theory of consciousness.

It is a natural consequence of the MOGUL/Activation approach. POpS has a central position in the cognitive system. A dominant POpS representation embodies the information that has been in some sense selected as most important out of all the currently available information. If the system is to make any sense, particularly in terms of survival value, this information *must* be widely available. What this means is, first, that POpS is very widely connected and, second, that extremely active representations necessarily produce strong influences, both within the store in which they are found and beyond it. The function of interfaces is to propagate elevated activation levels to coindexed representations in adjacent stores. Extremely elevated levels mean especially strong propagation, i.e. especially strong influences on activity in other modules.

It is important to note that Baars, like most others, focuses on *perceptual* consciousness. When he identified 'vast access' as a characteristic of conscious states, he was speaking of the access enjoyed by conscious perceptual representations. The same logic applies to affective representations and the SELF representation, though. Their broad connectivity, with their accompanying high activation levels, was discussed above and in previous chapters. Note particularly the place of !val! and !harm!, the core of every AfS representation, with their very extensive connections in the mind/brain.

Conclusion

I have offered here a proposal in which activation level is the necessary and sufficient condition for determining which representations are conscious at any given time. The key to the proposal is to place the issues within a general cognitive framework, in this case provided by MOGUL. At the heart of this framework is POpS, the common output of sensory processing and the primary seat of consciousness. POpS has a clear resemblance to Baars' GW but differs in important respects, especially in being limited to perceptual representations, a characteristic that captures the perceptual bias of consciousness, and in the lack of any claim that it was designed for consciousness or has more than an incidental relation with it.

I argued that this approach has a number of virtues, especially that it can account for the central characteristics of consciousness in a parsimonious manner. The account is very nearly a direct consequence of the architecture and processing of the MOGUL framework. The only addition required to produce an account of consciousness is the Activation Hypothesis itself, which is perhaps the simplest conceivable answer to the question of what distinguishes conscious from unconscious representations. One example of this parsimony is the elimination of an explicit informativeness condition, which is essential for many other theories but would be redundant in this account. Again, this is not to deny the importance of informativeness in cognition, simply to say that there is no need for an explicit informativeness condition in an account of consciousness. Another example involves the *threshold paradox* that Baars found in his theory, as described above. To deal with the problem, Baars needed to complicate his theory with an *ad hoc* hypothesis of subliminal broadcasts preceding conscious broadcasting. In the MOGUL account there is no paradox and no need for extra complications.

With this discussion of the MOGUL account of consciousness, the framework is now in place for an exploration of consciousness in second language learning. I will begin this exploration, in the following chapter, by offering a rather critical review of previous work in the area. This will be followed by two chapters directly applying the MOGUL account of consciousness to second language learning and a final chapter putting things together and providing a general perspective.

Part 2

Consciousness in Second Language Learning: Applying the Framework

6 Consciousness in Second Language Learning: A Selective Review

In Chapter 1, I described two general views on consciousness and human nature. One sees people as essentially conscious creatures and so naturally emphasizes conscious processes. The other is more sceptical about consciousness and holds a much higher opinion of unconscious processes. Both perspectives can be found in the literature on second language (L2) learning. It would in fact be only a small exaggeration to say that the conflict between these two perspectives characterizes much of the history of the field. I will begin this chapter with a relatively quick overview of the ways that these views have appeared, often implicitly, through the history of the field. I will then consider in a bit more detail the place of consciousness in Krashen's Monitor Model, the kindred view of consciousness found in universal grammar (UG) approaches, and some major critical reactions to Krashen's ideas. Finally, I will take a very critical look at the two ideas that dominate current thinking in second language acquisition (SLA) about consciousness: 'noticing' and the distinction between implicit and explicit knowledge and learning.

Consciousness and the Language Teaching Tradition(s)

How to teach or learn an L2 has been an issue for millennia, while discussions of the role of consciousness are only a recent phenomenon. But despite this apparent contrast, beliefs about the role of consciousness in learning have played a central role in ideas about teaching throughout the history of language teaching. A classic disagreement is about whether it is best to explicitly teach (study) the form of the language or to acquire it through natural experience. This is a question of whether awareness of form is necessary and/or important for language learning. The immediate (though often unstated) goal of most grammar instruction is to give learners conscious knowledge or understanding of grammar. Naturalistic approaches reject or downplay this goal and instead seek to impart linguistic ability implicitly, through unanalyzed experience with the language, especially experience in processing linguistic input.

These contrasting approaches can be seen clearly in the modern history of language teaching (the following discussion is based partly on Howatt, 1984). A prominent example of an experience-oriented theorist was Joseph Webbe, who in the 1620s rejected grammar instruction and instead emphasized unconscious assimilation of grammar through reading, writing and speaking. After Webbe, this view was largely dormant until Lambert Sauveur resurrected it in the 19th century and the direct method teachers then systematized it. In more recent times, its main proponent has been Stephen Krashen, with his natural approach (Krashen & Terrell, 1988), though Prabhu's (1987) Bangalore Project is also noteworthy. But while experience-oriented approaches, with their reliance on unconscious processes, have repeatedly appeared, approaches that take explicit grammar more seriously have probably been more the norm over the centuries, a situation that continues today.

In this contrast, it is not hard to see the two conflicting views on consciousness and human nature described in Chapter 1. An approach that downplays the role of explicit knowledge and explicit learning in favour of a reliance on naturalistic experience is a consequence of the second view, while a focus on explicit knowledge and learning fits well with the first, seeing people as essentially conscious creatures. This should not be taken as a categorical distinction, though. Both conscious and unconscious components are commonly recognized, authors varying greatly in the emphasis they place on each. Modern communicative approaches, which are quite variable themselves, often see a need for conscious knowledge of grammar while emphasizing the need to practice its use in communication. Howatt (1984) distinguished this view from a 'strong' communicative approach, in which communication *is* the acquisition of linguistic knowledge rather than just a way to practice using it.

Also common has been the idea that there are two different types of learning and/or two different types of knowledge, one primarily conscious and the other primarily unconscious. This dichotomy is an instance of the distinction drawn in Chapter 2 between the workings of specialist and non-specialist processes. A good example is Palmer's distinction between *spontaneous capacities* underlying natural, unconscious language acquisition and *studial capacities* involved in classroom learning (see Howatt, 1984). It is echoed in Krashen's acquisition–learning distinction and is also a largely implicit feature of UG-oriented views of learning, both of which I will consider below.

Krashen's Monitor Model

The most developed and most influential version of the naturalistic approach, emphasizing the second view of consciousness and human nature, is Krashen's Monitor Model (Krashen, 1981, 1982, 1985), rooted in the creative construction approach of Dulay and Burt (summarized in Dulay et al., 1982). Krashen hypothesized two types of knowledge, acquired in two different ways: *learning* is a conscious process producing knowledge that is conscious and can only be used consciously, while *acquisition* is unconscious and yields knowledge that is unconscious. The latter is what underlies fluent use of the language; learning, on the other hand, has value specifically as a conscious monitor, observing and modifying the products of the unconscious system.

Given what we know about the mind in general, this sort of distinction is quite natural and can reasonably serve as a default assumption. Recall again the distinction, described in Chapter 2, between the functioning of expert systems and that of processes that can be applied to the same domains as the expert systems but are not specialized for any of them and are generally inferior in their performance. Krashen's distinction is a logical application of this general phenomenon to L2 learning. It is particularly natural because of the consistent association of consciousness with non-specialist processes ('learning' in this case) and its absence in the workings of the specialist system ('acquisition').

It is important to clarify exactly what Krashen's claims about consciousness did and did not include, as considerable confusion has occurred on this point. In particular, it is important to distinguish between awareness of input and awareness of the linguistic form embodied in the input. The claim of a theory of unconscious acquisition, such as Krashen's, is that awareness of form plays little or no role in acquisition (distinct from learning). It is not that consciousness in general is unimportant. A theory which took the latter position would amount to a claim that we can acquire a language while asleep or while absorbed in a task that has no relation to the language. No claim of this sort was made by Krashen or by any other serious proponent of unconscious acquisition. Thus, Krashen's view did not include a claim that consciousness plays no role, only that awareness of language form is peripheral. This point deserves emphasis because much of the subsequent discussion of conscious and unconscious acquisition in SLA has confused these two very different claims.

Universal Grammar Approaches

Krashen's model was based to a large extent on the ideas of Noam Chomsky on the nature and acquisition of first languages (e.g. Chomsky, 1965). The details of these proposals have changed enormously since the time that Krashen developed his model, but the leading idea remains: the human mind includes an innate module that guides language learning, based on principles that are specific to language rather than belonging to cognition in general. Actually, in a Chomskyan perspective, we should not even talk about 'learning' but rather 'growth' of language. Among UG-oriented linguists, there is little discussion of whether this growth is conscious or unconscious – its unconscious nature is taken for granted. This position is inevitable, given the nature of linguistic knowledge commonly hypothesized in Chomskyan theorizing: the principles are so abstract and unintuitive that we can safely assume that learners are never conscious of them (see Roberts, 1994).

Not surprisingly then, when UG approaches are developed within SLA the unconscious nature of learning is taken for granted. It is in fact quite rare to see in this literature any mention of consciousness, presumably because it is so clear that the kinds of knowledge that are being discussed are not a part of the conscious knowledge of anyone other than the linguists who hypothesize them. In other words, unless these approaches are entirely misguided, the competence they explore and the process by which it develops are quite obviously unconscious.

This does not mean, though, that UG theorists treat *all* L2 knowledge and learning (or even all morphosyntactic knowledge and learning) as unconscious. It is generally accepted that people can also acquire metalinguistic knowledge – conscious knowledge *about* the language – independent of the competence that develops in the language module. Especially noteworthy here is the early work of Bonnie Schwartz (1986, 1993), who sought to develop Krashen's learning–acquisition distinction in a way that would fit well with UG theory, based on Fodor's (1983) account of modularity. She hypothesized two kinds of linguistic knowledge. *Competence* is the knowledge found in the language module, which is based on UG and so is the object of study for UG theorists. *Learned linguistic knowledge* (LLK) corresponds to Krashen's consciously learned knowledge.

Another prominent SLA theorist who works from a UG perspective is Bill VanPatten (1996, 2002, 2011). Especially noteworthy here is his notion of 'stubborn syntax' (VanPatten, 2011), the idea being that efforts to explicitly teach/learn the syntax that rests on UG tend to show limited results. Another of VanPatten's contributions to the topic of consciousness in L2 learning is a critique of the concept of noticing (VanPatten, 1994), which I will describe below.

Krashen's Critics

Krashen's work has been very widely cited and has drawn strong reactions. While some have been positive, even a casual reading of the SLA literature over the past three or four decades will make it clear that the critics have dominated the discussion. So it is worthwhile here to take a critical look at some of the criticisms. I will be selective, looking only at some of those that are concerned with the place of consciousness in SLA, an issue that, in Krashen's work, naturally centres on the acquisition–learning distinction.

The acquisition–learning distinction

This distinction drew strong criticism, but the central point, that two types of linguistic knowledge exist and that one is much more meaningful than the other, has actually received very wide acceptance. Fundamental differences exist on the nature of the two types and especially the relation between them, but the existence of such a distinction is very broadly accepted (e.g. Ellis, 1988; Felix, 1987; Lightbown, 1985; Long, 1977; Schwartz, 1986; Zobl, 1995). Empirical support can be found in research which shows a dissociation between conscious knowledge of the language and ability to use it (e.g. Frantzen, 1995; Kadia, 1988; Schumann, 1978a, 1978b; Terrell et al., 1987) and in studies that found the loss of initial learning from formal instruction when it was tested after a delay period, apparently indicating that the instruction had given learners conscious knowledge of grammar but had not altered their primary, unconscious grammar (Harley, 1989; Lightbown, 1983, 1985, 1987; Lightbown et al., 1980; Pienemann, 1989; Weinert, 1987; White, 1991).

The relevance of such a distinction to consciousness is seen in what has in recent years become the most popular way to characterize it in SLA: *implicit* knowledge/learning vs. *explicit* knowledge/learning. These notions, originating in the psychology literature, will be discussed in some detail below. For present purposes, the important point is that a number of authors within SLA have adopted them.

This general recognition of two distinct kinds of processes is appropriate, based both on SLA findings and on the general nature of the human mind. Recall, again, the very general distinction between the functioning of expert systems and that of other mechanisms that can carry out similar functions but typically much less accurately and efficiently. These other mechanisms are strongly associated with consciousness, in contrast to the expert systems, which function largely if not entirely without awareness. So it is reasonable to expect something of the sort in L2 learning. Krashen's hypothesis of two distinct types of development – acquisition and learning – is thus a fairly straightforward application of what is known about the human mind to this research area, and it fits well with what is known specifically about L2 learning. As such it is the appropriate default assumption for L2 research. It has, however, been the subject of strong criticism.

Perhaps the strongest critic of the learning–acquisition distinction was McLaughlin (1978, 1987), who dismissed it along with essentially everything else that Krashen did (for Krashen's response, see Krashen, 1979). His central point was that the concepts are not clear enough to be testable and therefore are not to be taken seriously. There is an important issue here: how can we empirically distinguish the use of consciously learned knowledge from that of unconsciously acquired knowledge? But this problem is not specifically a product of Krashen's theory. It occurs in any theory that hypothesizes both an unconscious grammar underlying fluent performance and some form of explicit learning – that is to say, it arises for any viable theory.

When knowledge is explicitly acquired, there can never be a guarantee that it will be successfully incorporated in the unconscious grammar, regardless of one's views on the nature of learning or of the grammar (the point applies to McLaughlin, 1990, for example). This integration is by no means unproblematic, based on both theory and empirical findings. And any knowledge that is not incorporated (or has not yet been incorporated) has a status comparable to that of Krashen's consciously learned knowledge: it is distinct from the unconscious grammar and will presumably have its own distinct influences on performance. The familiar question then arises: how can we empirically distinguish the effects of this secondary knowledge from those of the implicit grammar? This is the same issue as how to distinguish Krashen's learned knowledge from his acquired knowledge.

The best – if still imperfect – way to answer the question is to look at the use of the knowledge under two types of conditions, one allowing or encouraging deliberate, conscious use of that knowledge and one requiring spontaneous, communicative use, without a focus on the knowledge itself. If what we have is simply explicit knowledge, it is likely to have considerable value in the first condition but little in the second. The explicit variety can involve, and has involved, a variety of test types, such as manipulating sentences as a grammar exercise, selecting the appropriate verb form to use, making explicit judgements of whether a sentence obeys the rules or constructing a sentence under constrained conditions. More spontaneous, communicative use is found in conversations or writing assignments done for the purpose of communicating ideas and information. A key element of such testing is avoidance of a focus on the points being tested.

Using and analyzing communicative tests is more challenging than using and analyzing formal grammar tests, and various complications inevitably arise, some of which I will consider below. But testing of this sort is already reasonably common and such complications are the norm in serious research. No matter how well the research is done, this approach has its limits, as does all research: we can never fully rule out a role for explicit knowledge in spontaneous production. But a look at research on grammar instruction in these terms provides considerable data, pointing to a reasonably clear conclusion.

From decades of empirical research on instruction and correction of grammar, probably the clearest, most consistent finding is that the success of the treatment is a function of the way that learning is measured. When the tests are amenable to the use of consciously held knowledge, particularly when they encourage learners to focus on the correct use of the instructed knowledge, the typical finding is that the instruction was very beneficial.

When learners are required to demonstrate their learning in spontaneous, communicatively oriented tasks, where the focus is on meaning rather on the instructed form, the observed effects are quite limited (see Truscott, 1996, 1998, 2004, 2005, 2007a, 2007b). This is a point that Krashen has made all along (see especially Krashen, 1992, 1993), and time and further research have only served to strengthen it.

The contrast can be seen clearly in studies, mentioned above, that examined both types of abilities (Frantzen, 1995; Kadia, 1988; Schumann, 1978a, 1978b; Terrell et al., 1987). In Terrell et al.'s study, for example, after instruction in the Spanish subjunctive, learners received scores of over 90% on formal tests but were less than 10% successful in their subjunctive use in conversation.

The other way to examine the possible contrast is by comparing studies that used communicative testing with those in which the testing allowed or encouraged the use of explicit knowledge. Especially interesting here is Norris and Ortega's (2000) meta-analysis of experiments on instruction of L2 forms, essentially grammar instruction. The authors synthesized a large number of studies of various types and included secondary analyses that divided the studies in various ways, including by the type of testing used. Norris and Ortega identified four distinct types of tests, only one of which could be considered a measure of learners' ability to use the instructed forms in realistic, communicative ways. This group included eight studies. In Norris and Ortega's (2000: 486) words, the remainder of the studies they surveyed tested learners' ability to apply 'explicit declarative knowledge under controlled conditions'.

This research review thus provides a good opportunity to check for differential effects of instruction on ability to use knowledge in spontaneous, communicatively oriented tasks versus in tasks that invite the use of consciously held knowledge. For the three groups of studies of the latter type, the average effect sizes obtained were 0.82, 1.46 and 1.20, all falling in the category of 'large effect'. The more communicative testing yielded an average effect size of 0.55, putting it at the lower end of the 'medium' category. This number was not significantly different from zero; in other words, if these eight studies are treated as a single experiment, their combined results are not significant and we cannot reject the null hypothesis that instruction actually had no effect at all. And these modest results were obtained largely from immediate posttests, where we should expect the effects to be at their strongest (an expectation that was confirmed in the overall sample).

This meta-analysis thus found a dramatic difference based on testing type (see Truscott [2004] for more detailed discussion of all these points and reasons to believe that the effects of the instruction on communicative ability were actually even smaller than this discussion suggests). These findings fit well with Krashen's acquisition–learning distinction, with its two types of knowledge/learning. Form-based instruction gave learners conscious knowledge that was very useful for tasks that could be done primarily with conscious knowledge but had only limited (and possibly no) value for tasks that required spontaneous communicative use of the forms.

What this all suggests is that Krashen was right to hypothesize two distinct types of linguistic knowledge, one unconsciously acquired and underlying spontaneous use of the language, the other consciously learned. The acquisition–learning distinction is now commonly treated as an early mistake that the field has since moved beyond, but there is no justification for such treatment. Some aspects of the proposal are open to criticism and modification, notably as a result of Krashen's lack of interest in automatization (see below), but the reflex rejection that characterizes much current thinking is misguided. A better approach is to seek appropriate refinements and adjustments.

Can consciously 'learned' knowledge become unconscious 'acquired' knowledge?

A crucial aspect of Krashen's model is the claim that knowledge which comes from conscious learning will remain forever separate from the unconsciously acquired knowledge that underlies spontaneous use of language: learning cannot become acquisition. This point is especially interesting because it is strongly (if somewhat unclearly) associated with ideas of modularity. It has also been strongly criticized. Here, I will focus on the critique offered by Gregg (1984), for whom the interest of the acquisition–learning distinction was specifically in the claim that learning cannot become acquisition.

Gregg challenged this claim on the grounds that experience clearly shows that we can come to use a rule quickly and accurately through study, without input (i.e. through learning rather than acquisition). As this type of use is, for Krashen, possible only with acquired knowledge, it certainly appears, intuitively, that learning can become acquisition. And so, Gregg suggested, there is a considerable burden on Krashen to demonstrate that it cannot, something he had not done. One example Gregg used was his own learning of Japanese past tense verb forms. He mastered these forms through memorization, with virtually no input, in the space of 'a couple of days', after which he exhibited 'error-free, rapid production'.

The point that consciously learned rules can come to be used quickly and accurately certainly has some validity – for linguistic rules just as for a wide variety of other areas. We learn to do arithmetic that way, and while 'error-free' seems a bit optimistic, we can and often do develop considerable accuracy and efficiency. If we can do this with numbers, it would be quite surprising if we could not also do it with words and other linguistic tokens. In terms of consciousness, a common outcome of conscious learning and practice is automatization, which typically involves a reduction or loss of awareness. There is no apparent reason why the phenomenon should not apply to manipulation of linguistic tokens.

But there is much more to be said about the kind of experience Gregg described and the implications it does and does not have for the acquisition–learning distinction. Most importantly, nothing was said in that description about the contexts in which he could use the forms rapidly and without error. If he was talking about normal, communicative use of the forms, this would make him a truly remarkable learner. I, for one, would feel that a heavy burden of proof falls on him to show that he really had achieved such success, since the problems of going from memorization to fluent and accurate communicative use are clear from the experience of both learners and teachers and have been repeatedly confirmed by research. So when Gregg referred to his rapid, error-free use of the memorized forms, was he talking about performance in drills, where correct use of the specified form was the focus? This would seem the most likely interpretation.

This kind of successful use – comparable to arithmetic – is exactly what should be expected to result from deliberate memorization and practice. More to the point, it has no implications for the question of whether the consciously learned knowledge and skills have become part of the unconscious grammar – whether learning has become acquisition. The best way to address this question is, again, to see how well the knowledge can be used in spontaneous, communicatively oriented speech. And, again, the evidence strongly suggests that very little success occurs.

This evidence cannot be considered conclusive. But if there is no conclusive demonstration that learned knowledge cannot turn into acquired knowledge (and it is difficult to see how such a demonstration could ever be made, even in principle), there is also no demonstration that consciously learned knowledge *can* turn into the kind of unconscious knowledge that underlies fluent, spontaneous use of language. DeKeyser (2003), perhaps the strongest advocate of such a claim, offered a lengthy discussion of this issue. As I read that discussion, he more or less acknowledged (section 3.3) that he could not provide any demonstration that explicitly acquired knowledge ever becomes acquired knowledge, in Krashen's sense. The best he could offer was a study of his own (DeKeyser, 1997) that used a simple artificial language, with four grammar rules, and tested learners on computer-based tasks involving the use of these rules after eight weeks of practice with them. The study showed that the rules could become automatized and that the characteristics of the learning fit well with those observed in other types of learning. But the same points discussed above apply here. This is too far removed from genuine language and, especially, genuine use of language, to be taken as anything more than a demonstration of what we already know: that with enough practice, people can explicitly learn to manipulate symbols of almost any kind. It cannot tell us what sort of role such skills play in actual language learning and use.

It is important to recognize that the burden of proof here does not fall specifically on the claim that consciously and unconsciously acquired knowledge remain separate. It is perhaps better placed on those who hold that some sort of merger occurs, or that the implicit grammar is the product of consciously acquired knowledge. A crucial issue for any theory which hypothesizes that the products of explicit learning become incorporated in the implicit grammar is exactly how this incorporation occurs. There is a need, in such a theory, for an additional mechanism, one that either converts explicit knowledge into implicit or somehow merges these two fundamentally different types of representations. Given this complication, the natural default position would seem to be the no-interface claim, that there is no such mechanism. The burden of proof then falls on those who hold that such a mechanism does exist – i.e. on those who maintain an interface position – to show how the merger between knowledge types occurs, and *that* it occurs. In the absence of such a demonstration, the preferred assumption has to be that the two types of knowledge, initially encoded in fundamentally different ways, remain forever distinct, each type influencing performance in its own way.

And while there is no conclusive demonstration on this issue, the available evidence clearly supports the no-interface position. As I argued above, empirical research has found that knowledge acquired through conscious attention to form has quite limited value for the communicative use of the language, suggesting that it remains separate from the unconsciously acquired grammar.

In this context, it is interesting to examine the views of Rod Ellis, who has been a prominent advocate of conscious attention to form. Interestingly, Ellis does not argue that the kind of knowledge acquired through formal instruction can become the kind that underlies fluent, spontaneous use. His claim, rather, is that it can help the development of the more important sort of knowledge. He called this a weak interface position, though from a theoretical perspective it is better seen as a no-interface position (Paradis, 2009) with an important footnote attached.

The argument he offered for this position, though (R. Ellis, 2002), could just as well be taken as an argument that one type of knowledge does turn into the other (i.e. that Krashen's separation was wrong), and it has no doubt been taken as such by many who are not overly concerned with the niceties of theoretical disputes. So it is worthwhile to critically examine this argument. Ellis reviewed a set of 11 studies that used communicatively oriented tests. He argued that their findings, taken together, showed that instruction on language form is successful in this crucial sense. I will suggest here that the work he reviewed actually points to the opposite conclusion. The following critique largely follows Truscott (2007b), where a more detailed version can be found.

First, Salaberry (1997) and Williams and Evans (1998) obtained negative results, as Ellis acknowledged. Long *et al.* (1998) looked at form-focused interaction under idealized conditions and yet obtained only very weak results and did not try to determine if these unimpressive effects endured. Mackey (1999) found interaction helpful but her study provided no means of judging what aspect(s) of the interaction led to the positive results, making the findings consistent with virtually any theoretical position, including Krashen's. Lyster (1994) found instruction successful on what Ellis characterized as 'formulaic' language, entirely distinct from the grammatical learning which is the issue in disagreements regarding the interface question. Harley (1989) found only very small benefits of instruction in immediate testing and no difference between instructed and uninstructed students on follow-up tests. VanPatten and Sanz (1995) did not carry out any follow-up testing and found immediate benefits only on a written test, not on the oral version, which provided a better measure of spontaneous communicative use. Muranoi (2000) found benefits on immediate posttests using communicative and non-communicative measures. He also used delayed posttests of both types but declined to present the results obtained on the communicative measures, offering instead a composite of the results from the two test types. Day and Shapson (1991) obtained positive results using an analysis that disregarded inappropriate uses of the instructed forms, introducing a strong bias towards positive results.

Doughty and Varela (1998) obtained good results on an oral test, which consisted of students presenting answers to the same questions they had previously responded to in writing. Students knew, based on what had been done all through the term, that things would be done in this way and that the teacher was especially interested in the grammar points that were being examined on the test. So this test is best seen as a measure of prepared speech, prepared and delivered with those particular grammar points in mind. The testing and scoring methods also largely removed from consideration the errors that these students were most likely to make, namely errors of overuse. The observed success can readily be attributed to the combination of this bias and the use of explicit knowledge. Mackey and Philp (1998) used two grammatical treatment groups and two different analyses for each. On one analysis neither group benefitted from the treatment; on the other the authors claimed benefits for only one of the groups. In this seemingly more successful case, the gains actually did not significantly differ from those of the genuine control group that they used,[1] despite some important biases in the testing and analysis (again, see Truscott [2007b] for more detailed discussion of this and the other studies; Truscott, 2005, for Doughty & Varela, 1998).

There is little in these findings to suggest that conscious attention to form has any meaningful effects on communicative, meaning-oriented tasks. There is considerable reason to think it does not (see Truscott [2004] for reasons to think this discussion actually understates the failure of instruction in these studies). What this suggests is that the two types of knowledge remain quite separate, as Krashen suggested. In Modular Online Growth and Use of Language (MOGUL) terms, there is grammatical knowledge centred on the language module and grammatical knowledge centred on conceptual structures. The latter does not become the former, and its ability to facilitate the development of modular knowledge appears to be quite limited.

The meaning of 'conscious' and 'unconscious'

McLaughlin (1978) and Gregg (1984) pointed out a significant ambiguity in the use of the words 'conscious' and 'unconscious'. A statement that some knowledge is unconscious could mean either that the knowledge *is not* conscious or that it *cannot be* conscious. In discussions of L2 learning, and elsewhere, it is important to be clear about which meaning is intended. Similar clarifications are needed for 'conscious knowledge'.

Richard Schmidt (1990), whose work I will discuss in some detail below, pointed out several different meanings of 'conscious' and 'unconscious', meanings that can be and have been confused. One problem is that incidental learning has often been referred to as unconscious when in fact it could just as well be conscious. Suppose a learner is reading something simply for understanding, with no intent to learn any aspect of language from it, but during the process consciously notices something about language form and thereby learns it. This learning is both incidental and conscious. In more legitimate uses of 'unconscious', Schmidt tried to distinguish subliminal learning from implicit learning, the former referring to learning that occurs on the basis of features that never become conscious in the input and the latter to learning that occurs unconsciously on the basis of features that had consciously registered in the input previously. I will consider this distinction further below.

Schmidt did not address what I consider the most important problems of clarity in uses of the word 'conscious'. One of these problems is confusion between awareness of form and awareness of a task that involves use of the form (the latter paralleling the psychologist's notion of *attention to the task* – Carr & Curran, 1994; Curran & Keele, 1993; Dienes *et al.*, 1991; Nissen & Bullemer, 1987; Winter & Reber, 1994). When someone is reading a sentence that includes a past tense form, awareness of the text, its meaning and the act of reading it is not at all the same thing as awareness of the past tense form that it contains, nor does it imply any such awareness. A very similar confusion is that between awareness of input and awareness of particular forms in that input. A statement that learners need to be aware of input would provoke no controversy; it is simply a statement that learning cannot occur on the basis of 'input' that occurs when the learner is asleep or is focused on something else. I am not aware of anyone in the field who would dispute this. A claim that learners need to be aware of forms in the input is more interesting. It is the essence of fundamental disagreements that have been with us throughout the history of language teaching, and remain divisive today. I will return to these points below.

The relative value of implicit and explicit learning

Peter Robinson, a student of Schmidt, took up the critical approach to Krashen's theory in a series of experiments (Robinson, 1996a, 1996b, 1997; Robinson & Ha, 1993), the results of which were offered as evidence that implicit (unconscious) learning is not superior to explicit (conscious) learning and can in fact be inferior, contra Krashen. But in fact these findings were fully compatible with Krashen's claims. The research relied on explicit, decontextualized testing, with a focus on language form, making it a paradigm case of his conscious learning. The finding that such knowledge is best acquired explicitly is not surprising and is not a problem for Krashen. For the findings to comprise a challenge to his claims, it would have to be shown that the explicit treatment had benefits for learners' spontaneous production. But this point was not investigated. More generally, in work of this sort there is a serious issue of ecological validity. When the learning and (especially) the testing are done in such an artificial context and manner as they were in this research, it is not clear that anything can be concluded about how learning occurs in real life (for further critical analysis of this work, see Schachter, 1999).

Sharwood Smith's concerns

Another prominent, early critic of Krashen's work was Sharwood Smith (1981). His primary criticism was that the claims were overly strong given the available research at the time, and that their application to teaching was premature. This was not a rejection of Krashen's theory but rather a call for further research and for caution while that research was ongoing. Sharwood Smith's own views on acquisition are in fact rather similar to Krashen's. He has always accepted the distinction between two types of knowledge and two types of learning, in roughly the forms that Krashen presented them, along with the centrality of input for acquisition. He has a somewhat higher regard for the conscious variety of learning than Krashen does, but nonetheless sees unconscious processes as central in L2 learning and has maintained a healthy scepticism regarding the value of explicit learning. His term 'consciousness raising' appears to put consciousness in a prominent position, but the practice that it refers to, at least as Sharwood Smith described it, does not make any claims or assumptions of that sort. This point was clarified in his subsequent replacement of 'consciousness raising' with 'input enhancement' (Sharwood Smith, 1991, 1993).

Conclusion

Krashen's account of consciousness in L2 learning, like any other, has weaknesses. Some of its concepts are not as clear as they could be. The treatment of consciousness as definitional for the two types of knowledge and learning needs to be weakened, to allow for automatization of consciously learned knowledge.[2] And I would like to see more in the way of theoretical development, going inside the black box. But these points should not obscure the basic soundness of the approach. To me, the primary conclusion is that Krashen's account of consciousness in L2 learning, as far as it went, was essentially right.

Noticing

One notion of conscious learning has been institutionalized in SLA, both as a theoretical idea and as a part of pedagogy. This is Schmidt's *noticing* (Schmidt, 1990, 1993, 1994, 1995, 2001, 2010; Schmidt & Frota, 1986). Because of its importance, I will devote a considerable amount of space to describing it and, especially, to critically analyzing it (for more extensive critiques, see Paradis, 2004, 2009; Truscott, 1998; Truscott & Sharwood Smith, 2011; VanPatten, 1994).

Noticing and the Noticing Hypothesis

Schmidt proposed his concept in response to Krashen's claims about acquisition occurring unconsciously; specifically, he took a position against those claims. He argued that if a linguistic feature is to be acquired through input, the learner must be aware of its presence in the input – its presence must consciously register. This awareness is called noticing, and Schmidt's claim that it is necessary for learning is the Noticing Hypothesis (NH). Another way to state that hypothesis is to say that noticing is necessary for the conversion of input to intake. To support such a role for awareness, he sought to marshal evidence from cognitive psychology and SLA. Much of the cognitive evidence came from drawing a close association between awareness and attention and then using research on attention to make the argument that consciousness is necessary for learning.

But while arguing for the importance of conscious processes, Schmidt recognized that a complete denial of unconscious learning is not realistic. It is not plausible to claim that successful learners, especially successful informal learners, are aware of all the complex grammar underlying their L2. So he sought a concept that would stake out a place for awareness of form while at the same time allowing a significant role for unconscious processes. This is a very ambitious goal, and I will suggest below that it has not worked out well.

Perhaps the most important thing to understand about noticing is that it is not just awareness of input. It is about learners being aware of formal features of language in the input. If it is simply about input as such, then the NH says nothing that would challenge the views of Krashen or anyone else now active in the field. A theory of unconscious acquisition does not say that you can learn from input that you are completely ignoring or that is going on while you are asleep – and this is what it would mean to say that awareness of input is not necessary. If the NH does not rule out anything more than this, it is entirely uncontroversial and contributes nothing to the debate over consciousness and learning. Thus, noticing must be awareness of the presence of linguistic features in the input, and this is the way that Schmidt has typically presented it.

Confusion in the concept of noticing

Schmidt sought to support the NH by arguing that evidence from cognitive psychology shows that awareness is necessary for learning in general and that SLA research has found attention to form important specifically for L2 learning. I pointed out the problems with this interpretation of the cognitive evidence long ago (Truscott, 1998) and responded to claims of this sort about the SLA evidence above and in much greater detail in a number of previous papers (see citations above). I will not repeat those points here, but focus instead on the confusion found in the concept of noticing, as used by Schmidt and others.

Notice what?

One point on which Schmidt and others have been vague is the question of what, according to the NH, needs to be noticed and what does not. More than two decades after the hypothesis was first presented, and after considerable work has been done in relation to noticing, we are still virtually clueless on this point. This limitation is especially important because Schmidt's approach implies a two-step learning process in which the targets of noticing play a central role. First, the learner must notice a set of basic elements in the input. Once this has been accomplished, these elements can be used unconsciously in the construction of an implicit grammar. I have never seen Schmidt explicitly state such a theory (though Schmidt, 2010, comes close), but the things he does say seem to require it, and Ellis (2005) has been explicit about it. But Ellis is no clearer than Schmidt on the identity of the elements that have to be noticed. I argued some time ago (Truscott, 1998) that establishing them is a serious problem, and the absence of any progress since then would seem to show that the concern was justified.

One aspect of the problem is that work on noticing has relied on the familiar assumption that language is nothing special. Schmidt based his claims on work in other areas and took it for granted that this work is directly applicable to language and its acquisition, an assumption which can certainly be disputed (VanPatten, 1994) and which may help to explain the vagueness regarding the objects of noticing: if the important thing is the general nature of learning, not its target, maybe we do not have to be very concerned about the nature of language. I will return to this 'nothing special' assumption below, and in the following chapter I will re-examine noticing in terms of the MOGUL/Activation account of consciousness, which rests on a different assumption about language and its place in the human mind.

Awareness and input

It is worth repeating that noticing cannot be just awareness of input, or else the NH becomes simply the uncontroversial statement that we cannot learn while asleep or while focusing on something unrelated to the target language. It has to be awareness of particular linguistic features in the input. And Schmidt almost always presents it this way. Surprisingly, though, he occasionally does sound as though he is treating noticing as simply awareness of input. Schmidt (1990: 134) said that learning without noticing means not noticing 'stretches of speech'. In discussing the example of learning the English verbal affix –s, Schmidt (1995) said the requirement is that learners must notice a sentence that contains it. Schmidt (2001: 31) presented the NH as being about awareness of sounds and words and their meanings, apparently leaving grammar out. Such claims are fully consistent with ideas of unconscious learning, which he presents the NH as a rejection of.

Not surprisingly, applications of noticing have reflected this confusion. We repeatedly find authors treating input itself as the target (e.g. Egi, 2004; Mackey, 2006) or describing learners 'noticing' feedback (e.g. Nicholas *et al.*, 2001) independent of any particular form. These authors cite Schmidt as the source of the concept they are using, but that concept in fact has nothing to do with his theorizing (unless of course we treat the exceptional statements cited in the previous paragraph as what Schmidt really intended).

Awareness and understanding

Noticing must be awareness of linguistic features in the input. But in order to leave room for implicit learning, it should not be awareness of anything more than that, or at least not much more. In other words, there must be an upper boundary on the domain of noticing and the NH. Schmidt sought to establish this boundary by distinguishing noticing from awareness at the level of understanding. The latter refers to awareness of rules, generalizations and abstractions of all sorts, and this sort of awareness is explicitly excluded from the NH. In other words, the hypothesis says nothing about whether learners are, or should be, aware of these things; it only deals with the intermediate level of awareness that Schmidt called noticing.

The distinction between noticing and awareness at the level of understanding is no less problematic than that between noticing and simple awareness of input. The question of exactly what the objects of noticing are reappears here, in a more confusing form. Schmidt's descriptions make it clear that all the standard rules and principles that linguists and teachers talk about are outside this category, because they represent generalizations and so awareness of them cannot be simple registration of their presence in the input. The question is what sorts of objects do *not* represent abstractions or generalizations. Even a simple linguistic feature such as 'noun' is necessarily an abstraction. The presence of a noun in the input registers only by virtue of a recognition that some perceived object has the various features that define a noun. It is far from clear how to draw a principled distinction between 'the input includes a noun' and 'the input includes an instance of wh-fronting'. There is always, inevitably, some degree of understanding involved in the perception of a linguistic object, so defining noticing in terms of the absence of understanding is problematic, to say the least.

The problem is compounded by Schmidt's current position on awareness of meaning in the NH. This position has shifted over the years. Schmidt (1994) explicitly excluded form/meaning relationships from the NH. Schmidt (1995) said that awareness of a word's meaning is a matter of understanding, not noticing. But Schmidt (2001, 2010) wrote of the need for attention to (awareness of) both forms and their meaning. This second view is confusing: it is hard to see why awareness that *-ed* means 'past' should not qualify as conscious understanding.

Applications of noticing have, again, extended the confusion found in the original work regarding the distinction between noticing and awareness at the level of understanding. Authors who try to use Schmidt's concept have routinely disregarded his statements that awareness of rules is not noticing (e.g. Egi, 2004; Kowal & Swain, 1997; Mennim, 2007). Perhaps more disturbing are efforts to use noticing as a theoretical foundation for grammar instruction in general, without concern for whether any given grammar point is or is not a legitimate object of noticing for Schmidt (e.g. R. Ellis, 1993, 1994, 1995; Long & Robinson, 1998; Nassaji & Fotos, 2004). A genuine application of Schmidt's concept of noticing would have to take this issue seriously and, as a result, would have to be quite humble in its selection of grammar points to include, leaving out especially all those things that can be considered rules or general principles. Given the mismatch between the typically broad aims of grammar instruction and the relatively narrow scope of Schmidt's noticing, it is perhaps not surprising that pedagogical approaches tend to be applications of noticing in name only.

Attention and learning

Schmidt has always treated consciousness as more or less equivalent to attention, an equation that is by no means generally accepted by those who study these topics (see, for example, Anderson, 1995; Baars, 1997b; Koch & Tsuchiya, 2007, 2012), and so attention has been a significant part of his presentations of noticing. Schmidt (2001: 3) in fact shifted his focus from awareness to attention, arguing that 'for all practical purposes, attention is necessary for all aspects of L2 learning'. Here, we return to the problem, discussed in Chapter 2, of what exactly is meant by 'attention'. Schmidt (2001) clearly recognized that the word covers an assortment of very different things, conceptualized in a variety of ways by different theorists. But in making his strong statement about the importance of attention and going through the various areas to which he wanted to apply it, he did not say what sense of the term he was using, either in general or in the individual cases. The list of things that attention can be, in Schmidt's summary, includes alertness, which is little more than being awake, so his claim that attention is necessary for learning might be taken to mean simply that you cannot learn in your sleep. He obviously had something much stronger in mind, but he did not make clear exactly what that something was. The discussion thus shows a vagueness paralleling that found in presentations of noticing.

Noticing the gap

Finally, a word is needed regarding Schmidt and Frota's (1986) idea of noticing the gap. The idea was based on Krashen's (1983) mini-model of acquisition, which hypothesized an unconscious process of comparing current input to the learner's existing L2 grammar. Schmidt and Frota adopted this model and added the claim that the comparison must be carried out consciously. This revised version is noticing the gap. As with noticing, applications have been quite loose. The unifying theme is recognition by the learner that something is wrong, based on a comparison of two things. But the nature of the two things that get compared depends on who is using the term. One additional confusion that must be avoided is between noticing the gap and what might be called registering the gap. In some sense, learning must involve a comparison between input and the current state of the interlanguage, with observed inconsistencies leading to adjustment of the interlanguage. But this in itself is not noticing the gap and has no special association with Schmidt's work. It becomes noticing the gap only with the added claim that the registration is necessarily conscious. I suspect that this confusion has made a significant contribution to the popularity of Schmidt's view. The idea that a comparison process must occur seems intuitively compelling, while the idea that it cannot occur unconsciously – the actual claim – does not; it represents a very debatable hypothesis about learning.

Conclusion

Noticing and noticing the gap have acquired a central place in SLA. The good side of this development is that it has brought attention to important issues and introduced significant cognitive research to the field. The downside is that these notions are badly confused and have nonetheless come to be uncritically accepted and treated as foundational for most of what goes on in the field in relation to consciousness. Not surprisingly, their applications in SLA tend to be far removed from Schmidt's own version.

Schmidt (2010) seemed to show a recognition of this large gap between his concept and the applications it has received, saying that varying definitions of noticing are used in the literature and that he does not own the concept. But I believe there is more cause for concern than these liberal comments suggest. An enormous amount of work clearly went into Schmidt's efforts to develop his concept and build a case for it. When others use the term 'noticing' and cite Schmidt as its source, they are claiming – whether the claim is explicit or not – that their use rests on this work, when in fact it typically does not. The result is a widespread belief that research and pedagogy in the area of L2 learning are now being guided by a firmly established concept, rooted in extensive review and analysis of research and theory in psychology. But this appearance is an illusion. The reality, whatever one thinks of Schmidt's noticing, is that most of the relevant work is guided by nothing more than a loose, intuitive notion that consciousness is somehow important.

Implicit and Explicit Learning

I suggested earlier that SLA has not given sufficient attention to theoretical or empirical research on consciousness from other, more basic fields. The main exception is work on implicit learning. The application of this literature is now the primary focus of SLA work on consciousness. In this section, I will briefly describe the source literature and then the way it has been applied in SLA, adopting a critical perspective.

Implicit and explicit learning in psychology

A common, though by no means universally accepted view in cognitive psychology is that two distinct types of learning occur, corresponding to two distinct types of knowledge. Implicit learning occurs unconsciously and yields knowledge that is unconscious. Explicit learning relies on conscious processes and results in conscious knowledge, though it might be possible for use of that knowledge to subsequently become automatic and unconscious.

This distinction is related to but should not be confused with that between the domain-specific learning that constitutes development of the language module, corresponding to Krashen's unconscious acquisition, and the more general, non-specialist form of learning that produces linguistic knowledge outside the module. The standard view among cognitive psychologists (reflected in the views of the SLA theorists who use this distinction) is that both implicit and explicit learning reflect domain-general learning mechanisms – that language is nothing special. The hypothesis that language *is* something special leads to a more complex view, according to which the implicit–explicit contrast is a product of interactions between the particular part of the cognitive system that is involved and the particular conditions under which the learning is occurring – a view that will be developed in Chapter 7 (see also Chapter 9).

The implicit–explicit distinction is based in part on findings that damage to particular parts of the brain, centred on the hippocampus, results in the loss of ability to acquire declarative knowledge but leaves intact other types of learning, notably including the acquisition of skills. These findings naturally led to the idea that there are two distinct types of learning/knowledge in the brain (see Schacter & Tulving, 1994; Squire, 1992; Squire & Kandel, 2000). The distinction has taken varying forms, perhaps the most common being that between declarative and procedural knowledge, or declarative and non-declarative, the latter including procedural as well as a number of other types. The explicit–implicit distinction, defined by the presence or absence of consciousness rather than by the uses to which the knowledge is put, imperfectly corresponds to declarative–procedural (the limits of the correspondence are discussed by Ullman [2005] and Paradis [2009]).

The neural research is supplemented by extensive laboratory research in the cognitive domain. Experimenters design tasks that will limit the possibilities for explicit learning and then see if learners' ability to carry out those tasks improves in the absence of conscious (explicit) knowledge. If their performance significantly improves but they show no evidence of awareness of what has been learned in the process, the conclusion is that implicit learning has occurred.

The classic example of such experimenting involves artificial grammar learning (see Reber, 1989, 1993). Participants are shown large numbers of strings of letters or numbers, all generated by a simple grammar, exemplified by the following (in which S stands for 'start' and the other letters are arbitrary symbols):

(1) S → ABa
(2) A → Bba
(3) A → aa
(4) B → Abb
(5) B → ab

Strings are produced by first applying (1) to produce ABa, then applying other rules to the A and the B, and proceeding in this way until only lowercase letters remain. Examples of 'grammatical' strings, i.e. strings that can be generated by this grammar, are *aaaba*, using rules (1), (3) and (5), and *abbaaba*, using (1), (2), (5) and (5) again. In contrast, the grammar cannot generate the string *aaabaa* (there is no way to get two *a*'s at the end) or any string that begins or ends in *b*. So all these strings are ungrammatical. After extensive exposure to grammatical strings ('input'), participants are asked to judge a number of additional strings, saying whether they are grammatical or not. Their conscious knowledge of the grammar is also probed, in a variety of ways. These experiments have commonly found that participants' ability to make accurate judgements improves in the absence of any conscious understanding of how they do it.

Based on work using this and related paradigms (see, for example, Berry, 1994; Carr & Curran, 1994; Cleeremans, 1993; Dulany *et al.*, 1984; Ericsson & Simon, 1993; Hayes & Broadbent, 1988; Kihlstrom *et al.*, 2007; Knopman & Nissen, 1987; Lewicki, 1986; Mathews *et al.*, 1989; Nissen & Bullemer, 1987; Nissen *et al.*, 1987; Perruchet & Pacteau, 1990, 1991; Pothos, 2007; Reber, 1989, 1990; Shanks & St. John, 1994), it is now generally accepted that implicit learning does occur. This work has nonetheless generated considerable controversy, especially regarding how abstract the implicitly acquired knowledge is: do participants actually acquire the abstract grammar or just instances of its application, which can be used, with varying success, to judge new instances? But here I am more interested in another important question about implicit and explicit learning/knowledge: do they represent two distinct memory systems?

The affirmative answer to this question is popular now, but alternative accounts of the findings can be and have been proposed (e.g. Bowers & Marsolek, 2003; Carr & Curren, 1994; Kinder & Shanks, 2001; Moscovitch *et al.*, 1993; Nosofsky & Zaki, 1998; Roediger & McDermott, 1993; Shanks, 2003; Shanks & Berry, 2012; Shanks *et al.*, 2002; Wallach & Lebiere, 2003). One such proposal is particularly interesting here, namely that of Cleeremans and colleagues (Cleeremans, 2006; Cleeremans & Jiménez, 2002; Destrebecqz & Cleeremans, 2001, 2003; Jiménez *et al.*, 2006). On their account, representations are 'graded' in terms of their 'quality', based on several criteria, and the quality of a representation affects both its influence on processing and its availability to consciousness. I will return to these ideas in the following chapter, proposing an incorporation of them in the MOGUL framework.

Research and theory on implicit and explicit learning have received considerable application in the field of SLA. But before moving on to discussion of this application, one additional point should be made – that the debate over implicit learning is fundamentally different from the debate over noticing. The implicit learning literature contains no concept comparable to noticing. Critics of implicit learning do not claim simply that aspects of the target must register in sensory experience – be noticed. Their argument has always been the much stronger one that abstract principles cannot be learned without the learner being aware of those principles. Translated into Schmidt's terms, this is a claim that awareness at the level of understanding is necessary for learning, which of course is entirely different from the position that Schmidt adopted. Schmidt's (1990) original goal, in fact, was essentially to identify a place for awareness in learning while at the same time leaving room for implicit learning. This novel and very challenging endeavour naturally resulted in some confusion, as described above.

General limitations of the application of implicit learning to SLA

Ideas about implicit learning in SLA have largely been imported from psychology, and they inherit the strengths and the limitations of the work in the source field. I am particularly interested in two related limitations: the problem of ecological validity and the assumption that implicit learning is just implicit learning – that it does not make much difference what the target of the learning is.

One important limitation of research on implicit learning is that it is, overwhelmingly, controlled laboratory work. Participants in the experiments are taught – and more importantly, tested – on laboratory tasks, under laboratory conditions, with little relation to actual L2 learning. This type of research has a good side and a bad side, an ambiguity that is probably best seen in terms of the 'experimenter's dilemma' (Jung, 1971). Careful controls are needed if we want to make reliable inferences from research, and these are the strength of laboratory research. But the more tightly an experiment is controlled, the more removed it is from real life, i.e. from the things we want to make inferences about, raising doubts about whether the experiment is actually studying what it set out to study rather than some artificial phenomenon created by the experimental design. On the other hand, research that studies a phenomenon as it naturally occurs, without imposing any controls on it, is strong in terms of ecological validity but will have great difficulty drawing convincing conclusions about what caused what to happen.

Implicit learning research is very much on the control side of the experimenter's dilemma: it is generally high-quality laboratory research that shows little concern with ecological validity. In other words, we can be confident that conclusions drawn from the research are valid within the laboratory context but cannot be confident that these conclusions tell us anything about more natural, realistic learning – in particular, about how people acquire language. This limitation dictates some caution in the way the research is applied to SLA.

To me, the most important feature of the implicit learning literature is one that is closely related to the first but goes well beyond it. For implicit learning research to have reliable implications for L2 learning, that research should be about implicit learning in L2 learning, at least approximately as the latter occurs in real life. When SLA researchers make use of work that is not specifically about L2 learning, as it occurs in real life, they are relying on a very questionable assumption: that implicit learning is simply implicit learning; that it does not make much difference if the object of the learning is natural language grammar or patterns found in sequences of lights or any of countless other targets. Perhaps not surprisingly, this assumption has been imported into SLA along with the idea of implicit learning. Thus, while it is now widely accepted that implicit processes are important in acquisition, the notion of implicit learning assumed and developed in SLA work is a generic one.

This assumption of generic implicit learning is in conflict with the very plausible idea that language is a distinctive part of evolved human nature. If this idea is accurate (as I argued in Chapters 1 and 2), there should be something special about the way we learn it, something that distinguishes it from the way that we learn chess, for example. Thus, it is quite conservative to say that the view of implicit learning as a single generic process is not compelling. SLA research and theory that assume a generic form of implicit learning must be treated with some caution. They cannot be lightly dismissed, but nor can the more modular view according to which language development is based to a large extent on specifically linguistic mechanisms. This is the view developed in this book and elsewhere.

Implicit learning in the SLA literature

Implicit learning has been the subject of considerable research and discussion in SLA. Notable among this work is the large collection of papers in N. Ellis (1994a), the smaller but more up-to-date collection in Sanz and Leow (2011) and the efforts of Ellis et al. (2009) to establish the differing characteristics of implicit and explicit knowledge (see also, among many others, Bialystok, 1979; DeKeyser, 1994; Green & Hecht, 1992; Hulstijn, 2005; Hulstijn & Hulstijn, 1984; Leung & Williams, 2011; Robinson, 1995, 1996a; Rosa & Leow, 2004; Sanz & Morgan-Short, 2004; Williams, 2005). I will forego discussion of most of this work, focusing instead on one particular theory, that of N. Ellis (2002a, 2002b, 2005, 2006a, 2006b, 2011;

Ellis & Larsen-Freeman, 2006), which is perhaps the most developed and influential treatment of implicit learning in SLA (for previous critiques of Ellis's approach, see Gregg, 2003; Paradis, 2009).

Ellis sees language as a dynamic system (see de Bot, 2008; Smith & Thelen, 2003; van Gelder, 1998), or a complex adaptive system (Five Graces Group, 2009). Its development is 'usage-based' and emergentist, i.e. the regularities of language emerge from the learner's experience with the language. To some extent this is true of any theory of language and its acquisition; the variable is the directness of the relation between the experience and the development of the internal language system. Whereas a Chomskyan approach would have the relation very strongly mediated by innate linguistic principles, a usage-based approach rejects such principles and seeks to make the relation as direct as possible, minimizing mediation of all sorts.

Acquisition for Ellis starts with explicit establishment of some basic linguistic representations (the nature and identity of which have never been made clear), through noticing. This is followed by implicit restructuring and consolidation: the basic representations are connected to one another on the basis of their repeated co-occurrence in the input and the connections are strengthened (consolidated) as a function of the frequency of co-occurrence. For Ellis, most learning is thus unconscious (implicit), but awareness of form still has the important role of providing the basic items with which implicit learning works. This approach seems to include the view that implicitly established representations cannot serve as the basis for the consolidation and restructuring, or maybe cannot fill this role nearly as well as explicitly established representations. Altogether, this is a relatively neat account of implicit and explicit knowledge and learning and the relations between them: explicitly acquired instances are connected in appropriate ways by implicitly acquired associations, forming a tightly integrated system consisting of both implicit and explicit knowledge.

Ellis, like Krashen, stresses that implicit and explicit knowledge are inherently distinct and that neither can ever turn into the other. But, unlike Krashen, he holds that a great deal of interaction occurs between them, with explicit knowledge significantly influencing implicit learning. If explicit knowledge is held in working memory while an utterance is being processed, it will influence implicit processing, possibly resulting in beneficial changes in the implicit system. If I understand correctly (I find the presentation a bit confusing on this point), automatization and proceduralization are relevant specifically to implicit knowledge. Thus, when a person is apparently learning to use some consciously acquired knowledge automatically, what is actually happening is that the explicit knowledge is exerting an influence on implicit learning which eventually results in the development of an entirely implicit procedure. The explicit knowledge does not undergo any changes during this process. Its use can be speeded up, however, possibly giving the appearance of automatization, but this speed up is actually an entirely different process. The relation between the explicit knowledge and the ultimate implicit procedure is quite indirect and the development of the latter is necessarily slow, so one could question whether this approach offers a convincing explanation of the apparent automatization of explicit knowledge (consider the discussion of Gregg [1984] above).

An important principle of the theory is that the two knowledge types are represented separately in the brain. This raises questions, which I will not pursue, regarding the difference between the declarative–procedural distinction, on which this separation is typically based, and the explicit–implicit distinction that Ellis uses (see above). More significantly, perhaps, observed separations in the brain appear to be problematic for his theory. If implicit knowledge and learning consist of associations among explicitly acquired items, then all acquisition and use of implicit knowledge will necessarily include activation of explicit knowledge as well. It should be literally impossible to separate implicit processing from explicit processing.

The reliance on the confused notion of noticing is also a problem. The theory crucially assumes that certain things must be noticed in order for implicit learning to occur, but we have essentially no idea what those things might be, and no one has yet given a coherent account of what it would even mean to notice them. This problem stems, to a large extent, from the widespread lack of concern in the field, and beyond, with the general nature of the objects of consciousness. SLA researchers refer to awareness of 'input', 'language', 'language form', 'items of the language', 'instances of language', 'information', 'stimulus events', with no clear notion of what these things are, within a cognitive theory, or what it means to be aware of them. Such questions can only be adequately addressed within an account of representation and processing, an account which specifies, if only provisionally, the general nature of the processing system and how the information it works with is represented within that system – a cognitive architecture. Emergentism, with its allergy to innate structure and its focus on the dynamic, does not seem inclined to produce answers to these questions. The result is vagueness in central aspects of the explanation.

Ellis' empirical claims can also be challenged, particularly regarding the very extensive influences that explicit knowledge is claimed to have on implicit learning. For this position, he relies, all through his writing, on the popular claim that research has found explicit instruction of form beneficial for language learning. He repeatedly appeals, in particular, to Norris and Ortega (2000), usually citing only the overall findings without mentioning contrasts among test types (see above). Ellis (2011) included a reference of this sort and then later in the paper noted the issue of test types but treated it as very secondary, and did not mention that the results of all the relatively communicative tests, taken together, did not even reach statistical significance, or that these modest results were based almost entirely on immediate posttests. Such findings do not support his position that interactions between implicit and explicit knowledge have substantial benefits for implicit learning. What they suggest is that explicit knowledge has only limited influence on the development and functioning of implicit knowledge.

Interestingly, though, it is not clear that this is a problem for Ellis' theory. He does take a strong position in favour of beneficial effects occurring, but whether this position is a consequence of his theory is very much in doubt. The explicit influence he hypothesizes on implicit learning is a very indirect sort of influence. The real learning is always the slow 'statistical tallying' that constitutes implicit learning for him; influences of explicit knowledge must work through this very slow process. Should we expect to see the effects of such influences in the relatively short-term studies that characterize the research? Given Ellis' view of implicit learning, it seems more likely that any benefits found in such research represent a direct application of explicit knowledge rather than a (surprisingly quick) improvement in implicit knowledge. And that, again, is exactly what *is* indicated by the dramatic split between the results of communicative and non-communicative tests. If any genuine effects on implicit knowledge occur, the theory would seem to predict that they will show only much later, probably after learners have repeatedly activated their explicit knowledge during language use over a lengthy period of time.

This is still maintaining a relatively optimistic view. In Ellis' theory, the actual influence of explicit knowledge on implicit learning is very uncertain. The state of the learner's implicit knowledge, the way it is used and the way it develops are, by definition, unknown to the learner, and to the teacher. Thus, when the learner holds some particular explicit information in working memory, we simply do not know what effect, if any, it will have on implicit processing, and therefore on implicit learning. It is not even clear that when effects do occur they will be desirable ones. In Ellis' writing it seems to be taken for granted that holding the explicit knowledge in working memory will seldom or never be harmful to the implicit learning process. But it is difficult to see any basis for this implicit optimism. There is no apparent reason why the presence of the explicit knowledge in working memory could not get in the way of implicit processing, pushing it in directions that would retard the emergence of the desired grammar.

Of course, we cannot know that this will happen. And this ignorance is precisely the point. When we hypothesize that learning is primarily unconscious, we are acknowledging that we do not know what is going on at any given point. In the absence of such knowledge, efforts to alter what is going on are little better than groping in the dark.

This point, regarding the possible benefit (or harm) resulting from explicit–implicit interactions, is not a criticism of Ellis' theory as such. He could just as well present the interactions the way he does but then conclude (as he does not) that their practical implications for learning and teaching are unclear, or that there is likely to be only limited practical value. As far as I can see, such a conclusion would not dictate any changes in the theory itself.

The other points that I raised, previously, *are* criticisms of the theory. I do not mean to suggest by them, however, that this theory, or others that rely on a generic implicit–explicit distinction, should be dismissed. The approach adopted in these theories needs to be taken seriously. We should also recognize that there are important points of contact between Ellis' theory and the MOGUL framework. One important agreement is that unconscious learning is central. Another is our shared emphasis on the point that perception is at the heart of learning and that much can be learned about the acquisition process through a consideration of how input is processed (perceived). Indeed, most of the concepts that Ellis works with have (or can have) a home in the MOGUL framework. The crucial difference, again, is that MOGUL rejects the 'nothing special' view of language, according to which there is no innate language module and therefore no distinction between modular and extramodular linguistic knowledge and acquisition.

Conclusion

There is now a widespread recognition in the SLA literature of the importance of the topic of consciousness, which bodes well for the future. In reviewing this literature, I have expressed the concerns I have about the way the topic is commonly approached, including the limited attention to work on consciousness in psychology and neuroscience, the uncritical reliance on the very confused notion of noticing and the questionable assumption that there is nothing special about language and its acquisition. I believe that these points call for the development of a somewhat different approach. In the first half of this book, I laid the groundwork for such an approach, in the form of the MOGUL framework and its treatment of consciousness. In the remaining chapters, I will use this framework to explore the place of consciousness in L2 learning.

Notes
(1) Mackey and Philp did not explicitly make this comparison in their paper; see Krashen (2002).
(2) And I will suggest below that the typically conscious variety of learning is only *typically* conscious.

7 Perception: Processing Input

Dividing the topic of second language (L2) learning into distinct parts, for separate discussion, is always challenging and always somewhat arbitrary. In this and the following chapter, the somewhat arbitrary division I will adopt is based on cognitive categories. The first deals with the way that L2 representations come to exist in the mind – perception. The second is about how those representations subsequently acquire a firm place in the mind and how they are adjusted – the topics of memory consolidation and restructuring. In this chapter, I will consider the perception aspect, looking first at the nature of perception in L2 learning and its relation to consciousness and then, more briefly, at how consciousness is involved in efforts to manipulate the perceptual process in order to facilitate L2 learning. Memory consolidation and restructuring will be the subjects of the following chapter.

Perception: Input and Intake

In Chapter 2, I described perception as the multistage construction of representations for input from the senses. In Modular Online Growth and Use of Language (MOGUL) terms, this translates to the establishment of a perceptual output structure (POpS) representation in response to environmental stimulation. It is necessarily a multistage process, involving not only the construction of the POpS representation but also all the sensory processing that goes on prior to this ultimate stage. This is perception in the most basic, traditional sense.

But it is too simple a notion, in two respects. First, we do not normally process a stimulus in isolation from the context in which it appears. Aspects of the context inevitably play a role in perception. Second, the affective system is routinely active during processing of all sorts, evaluating everything we perceive in terms of its significance for us. The way we value the things around us determines to a large extent whether we pay attention to a stimulus at all, as well as what aspects of it we are likely to focus on and how we interpret it, to say nothing of whether we remember it – and if so, how we remember it. The 'how' in this case primarily means valuation, determining if it is good or bad and to what extent. In this section, I will first consider the notion of input and the relatively straightforward interpretation it receives in the MOGUL framework and then turn to the more abstract (and perhaps dispensable) idea of intake.

Input

In the context of L2 acquisition, perception is processing of linguistic input. Second language acquisition (SLA) research has typically worked with a simplistic idea of input, treating the utterance or written text itself as the input, as if perception were a matter of importing something from the environment into the mind, rather than the complex, multistage construction process that it actually is. Input must be understood in the context of this construction process, as was convincingly shown by Carroll (1999, 2001). She defined input in terms of individual modules. Stimulation from the senses triggers the construction of a representation in one module, which then serves as input to the next module and so on. There is thus a chain of separate inputs, corresponding to the chain of modules. Input to conceptual structures (CS) comes from syntax; input for syntax comes from phonology; input for phonology comes from auditory processing, which is itself the product of lower-level processing.

For MOGUL, based on the same Jackendovian architecture that Carroll assumed, input to the language module is primarily representations in POpS, which are themselves products of extensive processing by lower-level sensory modules. Strictly speaking, a POpS representation is input specifically to phonological structures (PS) and only indirectly to syntactic structures (SS), the latter receiving its direct input from the phonology module and then providing the input to CS. POpS representations also serve as input directly to CS, though, providing the basis for conceptual learning, including metalinguistic learning and the assignment of meanings to forms in the language module. It must also be recognized that information does not flow in just one direction: conceptual representations, for example, can also serve as input to the syntax. My focus here will be on information that comes from sensory processing.

Because context and affect are crucial parts of perception, we need a broadened notion of L2 input to accommodate them. Input is not simply the linguistic information contained in an utterance. The context in which the information appears must also be recognized, along with the value that is attached to it. This recognition is crucial for an understanding of L2 learning, and the place of consciousness in it.

Starting with context, many factors can be part of the context of linguistic input. For oral input, enormous variation can occur in the setting: an exchange with a waiter in a restaurant, a casual conversation between friends, an academic lecture, a TV drama. Within the setting, important variables include the identity of the speaker (in terms of the listener's concept of that person) and the communicative goals of the speaker, or, more accurately, the learner's perception of those goals. These in turn are tied up with facial expressions, body language, perceived reactions of other people who are present and a variety of other factors. As long as these elements are perceived, consciously or unconsciously, they are part of the input that the learner receives. Setting of this sort may be less variable and less important for written input, but it is nonetheless present.

This is not to say that all these things will be remembered in any given case; we cannot expect complete memory of context any more than we can expect all the strictly linguistic information contained in input to be remembered. The point is that they are all pieces of the picture, no less than the linguistic information itself. If we look only at the linguistic information, we are looking at a very incomplete picture of the input.

From a cognitive perspective, contextual factors are relevant only if they are mentally represented. Thus, we have to talk about the 'internal context' of the input, i.e. the mental representations of the contextual factors and the current state of activation of those representations. In a specifically MOGUL perspective, this primarily means conceptual (CS) representations. Internal context is not limited to representations that correspond, in any sense, to aspects of the current environment. It consists of any conceptual representations that are active and therefore influencing current processing. In this sense, SELF is very much a part of internal context, as it is by nature active during perception, and so can reasonably be considered part of the input in the broad sense assumed here.

Affect might also be treated as a part of internal context. But it will be more useful to restrict the term 'internal context' to representations in CS and to treat affect as a distinct domain, and a distinct element of input. At the heart of this domain is value – what the input means to the person. The value of the input inevitably influences the way it is processed, as well as the way it is stored and subsequently used, so value should be a prominent concern in discussions of input.

Intake

In SLA, input has traditionally been distinguished from intake, beginning with Corder (1967). The idea behind the distinction is that not all input is used by learners; that which can be used is called intake. The presence in the input of –s on the verb *walks*, for instance, might not register at all or might register in only the most superficial manner, having no impact on acquisition. This is a case, then, in which input does not become intake. The input–intake distinction has been used extensively in SLA work on consciousness, notably in Schmidt's hypothesis, described in Chapter 6, that noticing is essential for the conversion of input to intake.

Intake is a very abstract notion, and we should probably not expect to find anything in the cognitive system that corresponds to it. This situation contrasts with that of 'input', for which we can readily point to given representations and identify them with the term. Intake refers to whatever information is useful in these representations, which is highly variable and dependent on the situation. To understand intake in processing terms (or specifically MOGUL terms), we have to ask what particular processors can do with a given input representation under given conditions.

To be useful for the development of interlanguage, a POpS representation has to contain linguistic information, and it must be the right kind of linguistic information for the given module (phonological, syntactic, conceptual). This information is necessarily implicit in the perceptual representation, simply because it is a perceptual representation, and so the processor must be able to make it explicit, to extract appropriate information. Its ability to do so depends on an interaction between the nature and current state of its module, on the one hand, and the character and availability of the input on the other. Because the information is implicit, extracting it could require the extended availability of the representation and a number of intermediate steps, depending on how novel the input is and how far removed it is from a form that the processor can use. On the other hand, if the processor is able to automatically extract the information it needs – i.e. already-existing routines allow it to do so quickly and efficiently – then these requirements will be greatly reduced. I will return to these points below.

Intake also has an affective component. This can be illustrated by the concept of 'speaker models' (Dulay et al., 1982) or 'input preferences' (Beebe, 1985). The idea is that learners select the input that they receive by attending to the speech of some people but not to that of others and therefore come to speak like the models they prefer, even if they have received extensive exposure to the dispreferred models. In other words, the speech of some people becomes intake while that of others does not. The standard preferences that have been identified in the research, and in casual observation, are peer over teacher, peer over parent and own social group over other social group. Beebe pointed out that these preferences can occasionally be reversed ('marked choices'). This is to say that people can vary in their values; a certain student in a certain situation could well place higher value on the teacher's dialect than on that of peers. Such variation is in principle explicable in terms of social and psychological factors, including the variable and sometimes conflicting influences of status and group solidarity. If intake is to be a useful concept, it will have to incorporate such factors.

One conclusion that can be drawn from this discussion, though, is that intake might not be a very useful concept. Perhaps instead we should directly talk of how a given processor can and cannot use particular information contained in particular representations under particular conditions.

Consciousness and Perception

With this understanding of input, questions can now be addressed regarding input and consciousness. What input can be conscious? What makes it conscious? The basic answers follow directly from the account of consciousness presented in Chapter 5 and the discussion of input above. The primary input to the language module is POpS representations. Awareness is of representations. So awareness of linguistic input means awareness of a POpS representation of a sample of language. It becomes conscious in the same way that any representation does. When its current activation level becomes sufficiently high, we become aware of it. But given the broader notion of input presented above, we also have to consider awareness of the context and of the value associated with the input.

Awareness of POpS representations

Several possibilities can be identified for the relation between perceptual input representations and awareness. These include (a) no awareness at all, (b) simple awareness of input, (c) awareness of a follow-up representation consisting of one selected portion of the original input representation and (d) awareness of representations that are more removed from the original input and come from analysis of that input.

No awareness of the input representation

At one extreme, the POpS representation that constitutes the perceptual input might never come to dominate POpS and so never achieve the activation levels necessary for awareness. This would mean it never received intensive processing, either because of the way it was presented or the state of the person when it was presented. In laboratory research, this limited processing is often induced by the experimenter's manipulations: the stimulus is presented too briefly for conscious perception, or its presence is masked by another stimulus presented before or after it, or participants are encouraged to pay attention to a different location from where it is presented or to focus on an unrelated activity. In language learning situations, a failure of the input representation to dominate POpS and become conscious could result from competition from other perceptual representations; in more common terms, the person's attention could be elsewhere. Lack of awareness could also be caused by drowsiness or an anxious state that constantly shifts processing from one possible input to another, not giving any of them the chance to dominate POpS.

In such cases – when the input representation never becomes conscious – if any information in that representation influences subsequent processing, this is subliminal perception. Any new representation that is established as the result of this processing is a product of subliminal learning. In practice, it is difficult to draw the distinction between no awareness of the input representation and very brief, fleeting awareness of it. This is the zero-point problem discussed by Schmidt and others. For my purposes it is not particularly important whether a given case involves no awareness of a representation or extremely little awareness, and so I will not pursue this issue.

Simple awareness of the input

Of course, we do routinely become aware of input representations, consciously hearing a person's utterance, consciously seeing the words on the page or the movements of sign language, consciously feeling the words presented in Braille. In these cases, the input representation has come to dominate POpS and so reach awareness. This could result in various options for subsequent processing, with varying consequences for awareness of subsequently constructed representations. The minimal outcome could be called *simple awareness of input*. The term refers to cases in which any processing that results from the input representation does not produce another conscious representation related to the linguistic information in the input. This does not imply that no further linguistic processing occurred, just that any such processing did not lead to a POpS representation with a sufficiently high current activation level to reach consciousness.

Awareness of a follow-up representation

Often, though, the processing that follows construction of an input representation will involve awareness of some additional representations, i.e. the processing will go beyond simple awareness of input. One possibility is that the perceptual representation contains linguistic information that is especially interesting in some respect and/or is difficult to understand. In such cases, a follow-up representation might be constructed of the interesting or difficult portion, in effect zooming in on one part of the input representation. In the context of language learning, this follow-up representation could be based on the presence in the original representation of a novel word, an inflection, a sequence of words showing a particular order (an adjective following a noun, for instance), an interesting construction, a pronunciation, a spelling or any of countless other linguistic characteristics.

This phenomenon might be seen in terms of *apperception* (see Gass, 1988, 1997), the process that identifies a certain portion of a perceptual representation as significant in some sense and thereby triggers further processing of it. In the case of L2 learning, the significance could be that this portion of the input does not fit with existing knowledge and therefore deserves closer consideration in some sense. Note the overlap with the concept of attention. But, like attention, a process of this sort is very much an abstraction from ordinary processing, i.e. there is no intelligent decision that a part of the input deserves further attention. Instead, there is an interaction between conceptual and perceptual processing in an effort to construct acceptable representations from currently active items in the respective stores. If a limitation in existing linguistic representations (the learner's current grammar) makes it difficult to deal with the input in POpS, a likely result will be that this portion receives extended conceptual processing in an effort to incorporate it in the overall conceptual representation under construction. This extended processing naturally triggers construction of a perceptual counterpart, i.e. the selected portion of the original input representation. If the conceptual processing involves sufficient activity for a sufficient time, this new representation can reach an activation level sufficient for awareness.

Awareness of additional follow-up representations

This conscious follow-up representation could well lead to further conceptual processing, constituting analysis of that representation, especially if it was constructed specifically as a result of its novelty. Conscious representations make especially good material for additional processing, because they become conscious by virtue of dominating a store; this dominance implies that they are strongly present for an extended period and therefore very available for use by other modules. One possibility would be that a representation of a noun-adjective sequence would trigger conceptual processing involving linguistic notions of syntactic category and word order. For a discussion of awareness, the question then becomes whether the subsequent processing results in additional perceptual representations crossing the consciousness threshold. The answer depends to a large extent on which modules are involved, a point to which I will return below.

An example

To understand these rather complex and abstract ideas on the relation between input and consciousness, we need a more concrete consideration of what goes on during the processing of input. Suppose, then, that a learner encounters, in spoken form, the following sentence.

Bill saw Mary yesterday.

I will assume that a representation of the sentence is constructed in auditory structures (AS), based on lower-level auditory processing. Several possibilities exist for subsequent processing of this auditory representation and for the resultant presence or absence of consciousness.

In some circumstances, the representation will never come to dominate POpS, will never achieve a high activation level and so will never become conscious. The person would probably not be able to repeat the sentence if asked. In this case, any influence that the sentence has on subsequent processing would indicate that subliminal perception had occurred. The failure to reach consciousness could result from a loss in competition with other perceptual input. Maybe the person was listening to a radio broadcast when a friend uttered the sentence, or was trying to monitor multiple conversations at a party and lost this particular thread. Or it could result from simple inattention or perhaps drowsiness.

Under more normal circumstances, though, this AS representation will come to dominate POpS, achieving a high activation level and so becoming conscious: the person is aware of hearing the sentence and might be able to repeat it if asked. This is simple awareness of input. As far as consciousness is concerned, this could be the end of this line of processing: the input would likely stimulate construction of other representations in various stores but none of these representations achieve the activation levels necessary for awareness.

Alternatively, a portion of the sentence might stimulate additional processing that results in additional conscious representations. Suppose, for example, that the listener is a low-level English learner who has learned some words but so far has little or no grasp of English grammar. In this case, the sequence *saw Mary* might stimulate further processing because it instantiates interesting information about grammar, namely that the object follows the verb. The result is construction of a new AS representation specifically of this sequence. If this new representation comes to dominate POpS, we then have something beyond simple awareness of input, namely awareness of the presence of a particular linguistic feature, order of verb and object in this case.

This awareness indicates that the follow-up representation has come to dominate POpS and so is especially available for use by adjacent modules. Thus, further processing, based on it, is a strong possibility, including processing that constitutes analysis of the input representation. Such processing might go beyond simple registration of an instance of VO order, to the construction of a more abstract conceptual representation, one expressing the information that verbs precede objects in English. This is particularly likely if previous instances of this order have been stored and are activated by the current processing (this would be a natural case of spreading activation based on shared features).

This new representation, being conceptual, could not itself be conscious. But its existence and activation could lead to the construction of a new POpS representation corresponding to it, such as an AS representation of the words 'objects come after verbs' (probably said in the person's native language) or an image of a V appearing before an O or possibly another, more idiosyncratic perceptual expression of the idea. This is an additional variety of awareness resulting from an input representation. It is distinct from the previous types in that it is further removed from the original input and constitutes analysis of that input.

The processing steps that can occur in this example, and the awareness that accompanies each, can be summarized as follows.

- The sound of the utterance, *Bill saw Mary yesterday*, registers in the auditory system.
    - no awareness at this point
- An AS representation of the utterance comes to dominate POpS.
    - awareness of the sounds of the utterance
- A CS representation of the meaning is constructed while the AS representation remains active.

- o   indirect awareness of the meaning
- A CS representation expressing the VO order is constructed.
- An AS representation of *saw Mary* is constructed and comes to dominate POpS.
  - o   awareness of this AS representation
  - o   indirect awareness of VO order in the phrase
- A CS representation is constructed of the concept that objects follow verbs in English.
- An AS representation expressing this concept is constructed and comes to dominate POpS.
  - o   awareness of the AS representation
  - o   indirect awareness of the concept that objects follow verbs in English

The line of processing could terminate at any point, and of course these steps are not the only possibilities, simply those that are important for the current discussion.

I have focused here on the interaction between perceptual and conceptual processing and not addressed that which might occur between perception and processing in the language module. Where morphology and syntax are concerned, this focus is natural. Direct interaction between morphosyntax and perception is not a possibility, because the phonology module separates SS from POpS. If development of the phonology module is under consideration, interesting possibilities arise from the adjacency of this module to POpS, but I will not consider these issues here, because of my focus on syntax and morphology.

Noticing revisited

I discussed the idea of noticing in Chapter 6 and argued that it is a very confused idea. We might ask now if the discussion of consciousness and perception in this chapter can provide some clarification.

Noticing might have a place in the classification, given above, of types of relations between input and awareness. It looks a great deal like the construction of a conscious follow-up representation consisting of one selected portion of the initial perceptual representation. In the example above, construction of a perceptual representation of *saw Mary* in response to construction of the original *Bill saw Mary yesterday* might be interpreted as noticing of the VO order, assuming that the new representation becomes conscious. We might define noticing then as the construction of a follow-up perceptual representation consisting of a selected part of the original input representation.

But any such definition must also refer to the CS activity that gave rise to this follow-up representation. A single perceptual representation of linguistic input could instantiate any number of linguistic features. When an

AS representation of *saw Mary* is constructed as a follow-up to *Bill saw Mary yesterday*, this could constitute noticing of VO order. But this more focused representation is not inherently about word order. It also instantiates a particular meaning, a particular collocation, a verb phrase, the appearance of a noun with no accompanying determiner, the absence of overt agreement between verb and object, a series of phonemes, the influence of a word-initial nasal consonant on a preceding vowel, a stress pattern and an intonation pattern; and this list could no doubt be expanded considerably. For this follow-up representation to be an instance of noticing verb-object (VO) order, there must be a recognition that *saw* is a verb and *Mary* an object and that they are in a particular order. In other words, the perceptual representation must be associated with, i.e. coindexed with, a CS representation of this information. A possible interpretation of noticing, then, is the following:

> Noticing linguistic feature x (e.g. VO order) in the input means (a) a follow-up POpS representation (of *saw Mary*) is constructed which instantiates x by virtue of being coindexed with a conceptual representation of x, and then (b) this POpS representation reaches an activation level sufficient for awareness.

Note that this idea of noticing is quite close to conscious apperception.

This discussion offers a way to understand the confusion, discussed in Chapter 6, regarding the involvement of meaning in Schmidt's noticing. Meaning takes the form of conceptual (CS) representations, which cannot themselves be conscious due to the limited activation levels they can achieve. So meaning cannot literally be noticed. But its background role in the construction and activation of POpS representations makes meaning an intimate, if indirect, part of our awareness of those representations. If a representation of *saw Mary* is constructed and becomes conscious partly because of its coactivation with a conceptual representation of word order, then we are indirectly aware of word order. Awareness of the plural affix on *days* is awareness of the sound or written form, but can also be considered indirect awareness of the concept of plural, i.e. the CS representation PLURAL, if it is coindexed with the latter.

This approach seems to give noticing a clearer interpretation. But a problem remains. Noticing, as characterized by Schmidt, must be distinguished from awareness at the level of understanding, and there is still no apparent way to do this. The background representation of the linguistic feature is inherently an understanding of it. The understanding can be very thorough or very limited or anything in between, but to say that a particular feature has been identified in the input representation with literally no understanding of it would be nonsense. The apparent conclusion is that the distinction between noticing and awareness at the level of understanding cannot be maintained, unless perhaps noticing is treated as the hypothetical end point of a continuum or as the lower region of the continuum. Defining degrees of understanding is very difficult but not necessarily impossible.

Noticing the gap revisited

Finally, consider the idea of noticing the gap in light of this discussion. I interpreted noticing in terms of a follow-up representation consisting of one portion of the original input representation, constructed because unconscious processes (apperception) in effect selected that portion. The reason for the focus on that particular portion of the input representation can be that it reveals a problem with current knowledge. In other words, a gap has registered. It is important to distinguish this 'registering the gap' from noticing the gap. The latter, by definition, is a conscious phenomenon, while the former might or might not be. Registering the gap becomes noticing the gap if and only if the registration is accompanied by a conscious experience.

The exact nature of this conscious experience is an interesting issue. A natural part of it is the feeling of wrongness. Awareness of a follow-up representation that instantiates the relevant linguistic feature probably accompanies it. What other representations might be constructed and become conscious would make an interesting research question, which I will not pursue here, simply noting that in this way the concept of noticing the gap might become an interesting topic for theoretical development. This approach also establishes the missing connection between noticing the gap and noticing.

Awareness of value and affect

Another important aspect of input awareness is value, and the affect of which it is part. This again is awareness of representations. For value, it is awareness of the !val! and !harm! representations in affective structures (AfS), possibly along with emotions that include them. Awareness of !val!, in its purest form, is the feeling of rightness, while awareness of pure !harm! is the feeling of wrongness. These can of course take on more complex forms, as the result of activation of affective representations that contain them. Rightness could become happiness, pride, satisfaction or any other positive emotion. Wrongness could become fear, anger, shame or any other negative emotion.

Affective representations are always active, as evaluations of current experience and what should be done about it. So affect is consistently a part of perception and therefore of linguistic input. Awareness of value/affect representations can thus accompany any linguistic input. When the situation is perceived as positive, !val! is activated, possibly as part of a positive emotion. When the situation is intimidating, the affect could be fear, i.e. activation of the !fear! representation in AfS, which includes !harm! as a component. Anxiety is probably best seen as a steady and relatively low-level activation of !fear!. Whatever the specific affect, its simultaneous activation with an input representation can establish a lasting relation with that input, with consequences for subsequent use and development.

A different form of affective awareness is awareness of the value associated with the language in general. All learners of English as an L2, for example, presumably have a concept of English, i.e. a CS representation of the idea. And this representation can be connected to !val! and !harm! just like any other, as a product of individual experiences with the language. This valuation could well colour a learner's subjective experience of input, a positive view of the language making the input more positively valued than it would otherwise be, a negative view having the opposite effect.

Awareness of context

Awareness of context is a more complex matter. Context, at least as it is relevant to linguistic input, consists primarily of conceptual information, i.e. CS representations, which never achieve the activation levels needed for consciousness. So awareness of context cannot be direct awareness of conceptual information. Instead, it reflects the usual indirect association between CS and awareness. Conceptual representations are coindexed with POpS representations. When the former are active, the latter become active as a result. If this activity is sufficient, the POpS representations reach consciousness, in effect serving as proxies for their CS counterparts in awareness. Note that this is indistinguishable from awareness of meaning, including the meaning of linguistic items. The meaning is a CS representation; its activation is associated with activation of a perceptual representation, which can become conscious, creating an indirect awareness of meaning.

The one CS representation that is a direct part of conscious experience is, again, SELF. It is by nature active during perception, forming a part of the context in which linguistic input is processed, which is to say part of the input in the broad sense assumed here. Because its activation level is consistently very high, it is inevitably a *conscious* part of the input. My awareness of an input representation is never simply awareness of that representation; it is also awareness of *me* perceiving it.

Conclusion

In this section, I have considered some ways in which consciousness can be associated with input, emphasizing awareness of POpS representations and their implicit linguistic content. First, when there is no association at all between an input representation and consciousness, we have (a) subliminal perception; the representation of linguistic input in POpS does not come to be dominant and does not achieve an activation level sufficient for awareness. If it does achieve such a level, we have (b) simple awareness of input. This awareness could be followed by awareness of representations beyond the immediate input. One possibility is (c) a conscious follow-up representation consisting of a portion of the original that instantiates some linguistic feature. Finally, there could be (d) awareness of a representation that is more removed from the original input representation, constituting the conscious outcome of analysis of that initial representation.

We might take (c) as an interpretation of noticing and (d) as an interpretation of awareness at the level of understanding. But the interpretation of noticing as (c) requires the involvement of an additional background representation that provides the nature and identity of the linguistic feature being noticed. As this necessarily involves some degree of understanding of the input, the idea of registering the occurrence of a feature in the input without understanding it, crucial for Schmidt's concept of noticing, is probably not meaningful. It is very difficult, and probably impossible, to draw a line between noticing and conscious understanding. The difference is at best a matter of degree.

The Establishment of New Representations in Perception

According to acquisition by processing theory (APT), new representations are created during processing, as part of processors' attempts to construct adequate representations for their current input. The question then is how awareness of input representations is associated with the creation of these new representations.

In the MOGUL framework, the most important point is that awareness of a representation implies that the representation has reached very high activation levels. This means it will have a strong influence on activity in other modules and, because the rise to such high activation levels takes considerable time, other modules will have an especially good opportunity to use whatever information it contains. Note that when we talk about the place of consciousness in processing, this is not necessarily about consciousness *doing* something; when it is involved in processing (including learning), we cannot assume that its involvement takes the form of an actor; it could instead be an incidental product of processing. Any conclusions on that sort of question would go well beyond this discussion, and well beyond any evidence that we might come up with. The issue here is association rather than causation.

Investigations of the place of awareness in establishing new knowledge commonly focus entirely on the linguistic aspects of this knowledge. But the discussion should not be restricted to awareness of linguistic representations or awareness of linguistic information, because the establishment of new representations is not simply about the language forms. We also have to consider context, for one thing. What association, if any, is there between awareness of context and the establishment of new linguistic representations? Also crucial is the significance of the input for the person, i.e. its value. Thus, the strictly linguistic representations that are established through perception necessarily include associations with context and affect, especially value. Does it matter if we are aware of the affect and its connection to the strictly linguistic representation? Does it matter if we are aware of the context?

This broader view of consciousness of input might be compared to Schmidt's hypothesis that every aspect of L2 knowledge must be noticed, including pragmatics, though his focus has always been on grammar. He presumably was not saying that we have to be aware of pragmatic principles, as this would clearly constitute awareness at the level of understanding for him, so this looks like a claim that learners must be aware of context and its relation to the form that is being learned. To my knowledge, Schmidt has never applied his hypothesis to affect or value, though.

In this section, I wish to consider these issues regarding the relation between awareness of input and the establishment of new linguistic representations. In the MOGUL framework, it matters a great deal which type of linguistic knowledge is being considered, modular or extramodular, and so I will divide the discussion accordingly.

Establishing linguistic representations in CS

Extramodular linguistic knowledge consists of representations in CS, typically with connections to perceptual representations of sound (AS) and spelling (visual structures [VS]) of linguistic items. An extramodular word is thus a sound in AS and a spelling in VS, coindexed with a meaning in CS, the latter combined with the representation WORD. An extramodular noun is a CS representation NOUN, composed of whatever elements make up the concept for that particular person. Once established, it can be combined with CS representations of individual words, in effect identifying those words as nouns. The establishment of representations of categories allows the creation of representations of rules such as ADJECTIVE PRECEDE NOUN, with which ENGLISH can be combined to form a representation of a language-specific rule.

These representations are established during perception, as part of processing. A new representation is necessarily a combination of smaller representations, brought together by the processor in its usual effort to make a single unified representation from whatever is currently active in its store. This processing typically involves activity in POpS and AfS, and therefore, potentially, consciousness. The different types of awareness of input described above have important implications for the establishment of new representations in CS. Roughly speaking, the more awareness, the greater the possibilities for the successful establishment of new representations.

No awareness of the input representation

When there is no awareness of an input representation, this means that the representation never comes to dominate POpS and never achieves a very high activation level. A representation of this sort is unlikely to have large effects on processing in other modules, because it will stimulate only weak activation of representations in those modules and because those modules will have only a brief opportunity to use the information it contains. This prediction matches the observed limits of subliminal learning (Greenwald *et al.*, 1995; Kihlstrom, 1996; Merikle *et al.*, 2001; Schmidt, 1990).

Simple awareness of the input

If the perceptual representation does become conscious, it follows that this representation dominated POpS and achieved very high activation levels. The implication is that it can have much stronger influences on processing in adjacent modules, greatly enhancing the possibility of new representations being formed in those modules in response to the information it contains. These possibilities are still greatly limited, though, by the fact that the input representation is perceptual not conceptual and so any information it contains that is relevant to conceptual processing is only implicitly present. In the aural or written form of *Bill saw Mary yesterday*, for example, the VO order is not explicitly present; the conceptual processor must in effect extract such information from it. This process will be made easier and more likely to occur if the representation containing that information is actively present in POpS for a more extended period and in a form that is more amenable to the extraction of the information.

Awareness of a follow-up representation

A minimal step in making the representation more amenable is to construct a follow-up representation that consists specifically of the relevant portion of the original and is therefore closer to a direct representation of the relevant information. This would mean, for example, following up a perceptual representation of *Bill saw Mary yesterday* with one of *saw Mary*, the latter containing exactly the portions of the original that instantiate the VO order. The construction of such a representation makes that linguistic information more available for additional use. If this follow-up representation becomes conscious, this means that it is especially active, dominating POpS for a period, and is therefore especially available for use. This is an interplay between perceptual and conceptual processing, each leading the other to construct particular kinds of representations, which could lead to the creation of CS representations that constitute new linguistic knowledge.

Awareness of additional follow-up representations

But to this point the interplay is very limited, involving only two conscious perceptual representations and the conceptual processing that follows from each. If the interplay is extended, the chances of meaningful development in CS are increased. Continuing with the example of VO order, the high activation level of the follow-up representation *saw Mary* can set up additional conceptual–perceptual processing. During the relatively extended period in which this representation is active in POpS, with a high activation level, CS processing could respond to its presence by constructing a related conceptual representation such as OBJECT FOLLOW VERB (assuming that VERB, OBJECT and FOLLOW are already present in CS). Given APT, this representation would then linger in CS, constituting knowledge (or at least belief) about word order in English. The active presence of this new representation in CS could then lead to the construction of a related POpS representation, such as an image of V followed by O, or the voice in the head saying 'English is VO' or 'objects follow verbs'. If this representation comes to dominate POpS, we have indirect awareness of the new knowledge of word order.

Establishing representations in the language module

Modular linguistic knowledge consists of chains of coindexed representations in PS and SS and extending beyond the language module's boundaries, again through coindexation, to CS and beyond. Linguistic knowledge is thus a system of multistore units, prominently including words and functional categories. I will first describe the units that are to be established, then the way they are established in perception, and finally the place of awareness in this process.

Words

Words are primarily chains of coindexed phonological (PS), syntactic (SS) and conceptual (CS) representations. These three representations can be considered the core of the word, but a complete description of any word must also include contextual representations in CS, giving for example whether it is formal or not and what kinds of situations it is used in, plus AfS representations of emotion associated with it, most notably its value. The concept expressed by the word will often involve perceptual qualities as well. The word *tree*, for example, is associated with visual images of trees, the sound of leaves rustling in the wind, the feel of the leaves or the bark and so on. Perceptual representations of these qualities, in POpS, will then be part of the extended chain, as will other perceptual representations of the spelling of the word and its pronunciation.

Functional categories

A different kind of example of modular linguistic knowledge is the set of functional categories in SS. These representations make up the heart of the linguistic system, so it is important to consider their establishment and their connections to representations in other stores. Functional categories have received a great variety of treatments in linguistic theory, and generative thinking on them is in a constant state of development. The MOGUL framework does not include a commitment to any particular version; the discussion here should be taken as illustrative rather than definitive.

In the approach I will assume here, a functional category is a representation in SS that establishes the frame for any representation of a sentence or phrase. An example is Number (Num), a category involved in establishing the frame for a noun phrase. It can be combined in SS with either of two feature values, [strong] and [weak], each of which is itself a simple SS representation. The [strong] value has the effect of moving the noun to the left of any adjective that appears with it, producing the word order typical of Spanish, as shown in the following example:

la casa roja
the house red

The [weak] value leaves the noun in place, resulting in the standard English order. Thus, SS can contain Num+[strong] or Num+[weak] or both. Indexes connecting the functional category to PS and CS representations are also a part of the composite representation. In English, this functional category is coindexed with the CS representations PLURAL and SINGULAR. In PS, the phonological representations /s/, /z/ and /əz/ bear the index of PLURAL, while SINGULAR shares an index with a null PS. The functional category in SS bears all these indexes.

Lardiere (2008, 2009) addressed some more complex cases of cross-linguistic variation in the ways that features are combined, in terms of her Feature Assembly Hypothesis. For Lardiere, acquisition involves assembling features from a universal inventory, provided by universal grammar (UG), into combinations that are appropriate for the language, a view that fits comfortably within the MOGUL framework. One example is the +past feature that appears widely in the world's languages, including English, Somali and Irish, all discussed by Lardiere. In English, the feature appears on verbs and auxiliaries. In Somali, it combines with determiners and adjectives, in addition to verbs, while in Irish it can also be found on complementizers. When a native speaker of one of these languages is learning another of them as an L2, this feature must be combined, during processing, with those SS representations that are appropriate for that particular L2, differing from the first language (L1).

The other aspect of establishing a functional category involves the indexes that connect it to PS and CS representations, i.e. to the sounds and meanings associated with them. I will focus on the meaning side. In the case of +past, important cross-linguistic contrasts occur in the meanings that the form can express in its various combinations. The idea of past can reasonably be taken as the central concept, but the form can also express such concepts as perfective, habitual, alienable possession and various others, depending on the language in which it appears. This is a matter of coindexing between the SS form, in its various combinations, and the CS representations that constitute its various meanings.

How the multistore units are established in perception

Each of these representational chains – words, extended functional categories and various others – is established in essentially the same way. During the processing of linguistic input, i.e. during perception, auditory representations are activated/constructed to represent the input from lower-level auditory processing. These representations then serve as input to PS, where phonological representations are activated/constructed to establish an acceptable overall representation that is consistent with this input. This PS activity is then the input to SS, where the syntax processor seeks to establish from active representations an acceptable overall syntactic representation. This process continues at CS and beyond.

In each module, the process might require the processor to create one or more new representations, by combining existing representations that were activated during the processing. Any such new representation will linger in the store after the processing is complete. A fundamental part of processing is coactivation by interfaces based on shared indexes. A new representation becomes connected to another on the other side of the interface and so receives the index of that representation. This assignment is in fact part of the creation of the new representation, as the index is itself a component part of that representation.

Given the frequent complexity of the representations, the noise that commonly occurs in the input and the ambiguity that can often be found even in high-quality input, acquiring these aspects of the L2 is by no means a simple matter of perception. In each instance of perception, a chain of representations will be constructed and/or activated to handle that particular input. In many cases – perhaps the great majority of them – the result will be far from optimal for the language as a whole. When a more generally appropriate representation *is* established in this way, it will have to be gradually strengthened in further processing, at the expense of the less suitable ones that were also created during perception, and it will probably have to change as well, in ways that will make it more suitable for the bulk of future processing. I will return to this topic in the following chapter, in the context of memory consolidation and restructuring.

The place of awareness in the process

Consider, then, how awareness might be involved in the establishment of new representations during perception. The most fundamental difference between development within the language module and development of conceptual linguistic knowledge is that the language module is, from the beginning, a language processing system and so it automatically extracts linguistic information from any input presented to it.

In the case of establishing the English representation Num+[weak], for example, an AS representation of a sentence such as 'The grandmother lived in a red house in the woods', in which *red* precedes *house*, should be sufficient, assuming that the words have been adequately acquired already. From this AS, the phonological processor should be able to construct a PS representation, from which the syntax processor can then establish the Num+[weak] representation, based on the order of *red* and *house*, or activate it if it was already established in previous processing.

Thus, it should not matter how implicit the information is in the input representation. In other words, there is no need for the construction of follow-up representations that focus on specific implicit information, nor is there any need for a back and forth interplay between linguistic processing and perceptual processing, corresponding to the perceptual–conceptual interplay described above (and of course in the development of SS there cannot be any direct interplay between the module and POpS, because the two are separated by PS). And so we should not expect to find additional perceptual representations reaching consciousness as they did in the case of conceptual development. Because of the automatic, specialized character of processing in the language module, the only requirement for its use of information in a perceptual representation is that the information should be implicitly present in the input representation and that this perceptual representation should be sufficiently active for a sufficient period for the extraction to occur.

The issue then is how much activation and how much time are sufficient. No matter how automatic a process is, it cannot occur instantaneously, and so there must be a threshold of some sort for duration, probably a variable one. There must also be a threshold for the activation level. If the perceptual representation is only minimally active, the interface will only minimally activate appropriate linguistic representations. This limited stimulation will be in the context of residual activation from previous input and of stimulation coming from other sources, specifically CS. This other stimulation might well overwhelm that which is coming from the perceptual input representation.

It is reasonable, then, to suppose that if the linguistic information contained in a perceptual input representation is to be incorporated in the language module, that representation should at least briefly dominate POpS. This in turn suggests at least some degree of awareness of the representation. The possibility of a subliminally perceived perceptual representation contributing to the growth of the language module cannot be ruled out, but we should not expect much, if any, development to occur this way. The key level of awareness here is simple awareness of input, which provides optimal conditions for modular growth. Input that falls below that level is not likely to be helpful. Input that goes beyond it, to conscious follow-up representations in POpS, has little or no relevance for the establishment of new representations in the module.

Reinterpreting the Noticing Hypothesis

Earlier in this chapter, I offered a reinterpretation of noticing based on an analysis of the various ways in which consciousness can be related to perceptual input representations. I suggested that one of these ways corresponds reasonably well, if imperfectly, to noticing as Schmidt has characterized it. This was the case in which a follow-up perceptual representation is constructed specifically of a portion of a prior perceptual representation, constructed because it instantiates a particular linguistic form. I suggested that this type of case might be interpreted as noticing of that linguistic form, if the follow-up representation reaches an activation level sufficient for awareness. If this interpretation is accepted, provisionally, the Noticing Hypothesis (NH) should then be seen as a claim that this sort of awareness is necessary for learning:

> *The Noticing Hypothesis reformulated*
> Establishment of a new representation of a linguistic form requires that the learner be aware of a POpS representation that was constructed specifically as an instance of that form.

As explained above, the POpS representation becomes an instance of the form by virtue of coindexation with a conceptual representation of the form. This formulation is, in important respects, clearer than the standard version.

Advantages of the reformulation

The original version tried to limit the application of the hypothesis by appeal to the presence or absence of understanding, an extremely problematic distinction. The revised version recognizes that noticing necessarily involves some degree of understanding and establishes the limits of the NH instead by restricting noticing to awareness of an immediate follow-up representation consisting of the relevant portion of the original, excluding awareness of the outcome of subsequent processing that results from that representation.

The revised NH also makes a clear distinction between noticing and simple awareness of input, a distinction that is crucial for making sense of the hypothesis. This point deserves emphasis, because it has been an important source of confusion in the literature. The NH, as Schmidt and others have presented it, cannot simply be a claim that awareness of input is necessary for learning. Schmidt has always presented his hypothesis as a rejection of claims, especially Krashen's, that acquisition is unconscious, and this is the way that it has been consistently used by others as well. But a claim about the need for awareness of input is fully consistent with Krashen's position, and with the position of virtually everyone else who takes unconscious acquisition seriously. Rejecting the need for simple awareness of input would amount to claiming that we can learn language from input that occurs while we are asleep or while our attention is fully taken up by some unrelated task. I do not know of anyone who would now make such claims, certainly not Krashen.

So if the NH is read as a statement that awareness of input is needed, it is simply saying something that everyone assumes as background – it then has no significance for any disagreements about the place of consciousness in L2 learning. For the NH to be interesting it must be taken as a claim about a level above simple awareness of input, i.e. the awareness it refers to must represent at least a conscious registration of the presence of a particular linguistic feature in the input. And this is the way it has almost always been used, by Schmidt and everyone else who takes it seriously. In MOGUL terms, this means awareness of a follow-up representation that was based on the relevant linguistic feature.

The Noticing Hypothesis without the 'nothing special' assumption

Schmidt, like nearly everyone else who has addressed consciousness in SLA, worked under the assumption that there is nothing special about language, and so his hypothesis is a single general claim about the place of consciousness in the development of linguistic knowledge, without any distinctions between types of linguistic knowledge. For MOGUL, and other approaches which assume that there *is* something special about language, there are two distinct types of linguistic knowledge, that which is centred in the language module and that which is centred in CS. So to evaluate the revised NH within the MOGUL framework, we have to ask how well it works for the development of each kind of knowledge.

For the acquisition of linguistic knowledge in CS, the revised NH looks plausible. Only under rare conditions will CS processing be able to automatically extract relevant linguistic information from a perceptual representation. This extraction should require more extended conceptual processing, which will naturally be reflected in POpS activity. Awareness of the POpS representations is significant because it reflects intense, sustained activity and because it gives conceptual processing ideal opportunities to make use of any information implicitly present in the perceptual representations.

In contrast, the language module is by nature specialized to extract linguistic information from perceptual representations and so should be able to do so automatically, given only that the representation dominates POpS at least briefly. So, for the development of the language module, simple awareness of input provides optimal conditions for development. The NH, which states a requirement for higher levels, is plausible when it is taken as a claim about CS development, but not when applied to the language module (cf. Truscott, 1998).

Value

Value is an integral part of L2 learning and use. Linguistic items are connected, directly or indirectly, to AfS representations, and these connections are a constant part of language use. They are established and strengthened as a function of the value that is assigned to input during perception, so we have to ask how *awareness* of value in the input relates to learning. Is this awareness necessary? Do higher levels of awareness result in more successful learning? To my knowledge, there is little or no empirical basis for any answers to these questions. The goal here is not to offer answers but to raise the questions and hopefully frame them in ways that can encourage serious investigation.

Learning and awareness of value

Value, expressed as feelings of rightness or wrongness, is a strong candidate for awareness in any sort of processing, because the !val! and !harm! representations are always active and can easily reach very high levels of activation. When they do reach such levels – and are therefore conscious – they will have increased influence on processing throughout the system, including the coindexing of representations across modules. We should thus expect awareness of value to be related to the establishment of connections (possibly indirect) between value and linguistic representations.

It seems unlikely that such awareness, beyond perhaps a very subtle, fleeting variety, is a requirement for learning, though this should be considered an open research question. But a *relation* between awareness and learning seems quite plausible. Investigation of this possibility should consider the distinction between modular and extramodular (CS) linguistic knowledge.

The good side of !harm!

Negative valuation has a good side that should be recognized: it serves the valuable function of identifying input that does *not* belong to the linguistic system that is being developed. Many varieties of a language exist, and a learner may well be exposed to input from a number of 'other' varieties. Coindexation with !harm! labels them as outside the variety being learned. This does not mean that no learning of those varieties occurs but rather that they become labelled as alien, undesirable to varying extents or desirable only within narrow contexts. Here, the question for consciousness is how awareness of !harm! – i.e. a feeling of wrongness or of a negative emotion containing it – is related to the labelling process.

Value and input preferences

This approach has interesting applications to the idea of speaker models, or input preferences, considered above. Dulay *et al.* (1982) used speaker models, specifically the preference for peer over teacher, to account for the limits observed for acquisition in immersion contexts (e.g. Snow *et al.*, 1989; Swain, 1985). Students prefer the non-native input they receive from peers over the native input from the teacher. They therefore attend, consciously or unconsciously, to the former rather than the latter.

This account seems compelling, as does the general idea of input preferences, but I would revise it in one crucial respect. I suggest that input preferences are best seen not as a matter of attending or not attending to particular models but rather of *valuing* some models over others. Immersion students who come to speak like each other, rather than like the native speaker teacher, have typically been fully successful in learning to comprehend the teacher's speech. In other words, they *have* taken in this input and *have* acquired the dispreferred dialect that it represents; they just do not value it and therefore do not use it in their production. I am not talking here about a conscious choice to avoid that dialect (though this can also play a role); it is not an intellectual decision so much as the way things *feel* – speaking a certain way feels right and speaking a certain other way does not.

From a MOGUL perspective, this is a matter of input valuation: connecting !val! and !harm! to input, based on existing valuations of the speaker. Part of the perception process is valuing the input in terms of positive or negative, along with degree, the latter being the activation level of the indexes connecting the affective (value) representations to the perceptual representations and therefore indirectly to the linguistic representations. The establishment and subsequent strengthening of these connections is a straightforward consequence of APT. When !val! is active at the same time as a perceptual representation, the two become coindexed; if the index already exists, its activation level rises. The activation of the value representation comes from activation of any representation that it is already coindexed with. If the speaker is valued, then !val! will be active when he or she is speaking. The input thus inherits value from its context.

During production – i.e. activation and construction of the linguistic representations that will underlie the act of speaking – connections to !val! will encourage use of the items representing the preferred dialect; their chances of being included in production will be enhanced in proportion to the strength of the connections. Connections to !harm! will discourage use of the dispreferred items. So valued representations will usually win the competition for inclusion in the representations being constructed and so will usually surface in production. When they do (i.e. in the person's normal speech), the established preferences are expressed by a feeling of rightness, reflecting an active !val!, though this experience could be quite subtle, depending on the degree to which !val! is activated. If the person does use forms from the dispreferred dialect, possibly requiring a substantial effort, this use is likely to be accompanied by a conscious experience of wrongness, reflecting a very active !harm! representation.

To illustrate these points, consider the case of immersion students avoiding the use of past tense forms in contexts that require them. These students have encountered such forms repeatedly, but specifically in input from the teacher, while input from their peers has included uninflected forms instead – in past time contexts. The past tense forms will be present in their grammars as a result of the input from the teacher. But if these forms are coindexed with !val! at all, the connection will be much weaker than that between !val! and the uninflected forms, because the teacher is not valued as highly as peers, or is not valued at all as a linguistic model. The past tense forms are likely to be associated with !harm! as well, probably in association with the ALIEN representation in CS. The overall result is that the uninflected forms will enjoy a huge advantage in the competition for use in production.

This situation could change if the students subsequently receive appropriate input from a valued person, perhaps a peer who is a native speaker of the target language and is liked. This experience could result in the past tense forms becoming strongly coindexed with !val! and therefore being used in production, though this would require successful competition with the uninflected forms.

Context

The remaining issue regarding input, consciousness and the establishment of new linguistic representations is the involvement of context, as a part of the input. Internal context consists of CS representations that become associated with representations of linguistic knowledge. It can include, for instance, conceptual representations of the speaker, the speaker's goals, any background knowledge that is currently active as the result of recent use or spreading activation, and the setting, as well as the listener's own attitudes and reactions. Cognitively, these things are mainly CS representations. To say that they are the context of linguistic processing is to say that they are active during that processing.

Contextual learning is potentially problematic in L2 learning due in part to the artificial situations in which learning often occurs. If the setting is a classroom and the goal is to complete a particular classroom task or to understand the teacher's instructions, the linguistic representations could become connected specifically to these contextual factors and therefore remain far removed from the contexts that will enter into their use in real life. The more similar these contextual connections are to those that would be active during actual use of the language outside the classroom, the better prepared the learner will be for such use. The issue of input preferences also comes up here. If the unmarked preferences are operating, as they typically are, input from peers will have a greater impact than that from teachers or parents, with lasting effects on fluent, accurate use of the linguistic representations in production.

Modular vs. extramodular knowledge

The relation that linguistic representations have with contextual representations is essentially the same relation they have with meaning. Partly for this reason, it is quite different for modular versus extramodular linguistic knowledge. For SS representations, the relation with context is a matter of coindexing the representation with one or more CS representations, which constitute the context for their use, just as assigning meaning to an SS representation consists of coindexing it with one or more CS representations. In the case of extramodular linguistic knowledge, establishing associations between linguistic forms and contexts is not a matter of coindexing items in different stores, since both are in CS. It is, rather, about forming larger composite representations in CS that include the context.

Consider, for example, the case of a Spanish learner acquiring second person pronouns – formal (*usted*) and informal (*tu*). Acquiring modular linguistic knowledge of this context means coindexing the PS and SS representations of the pronouns with the FORMAL and INFORMAL representations in CS. Acquiring conceptual linguistic knowledge, on the other hand, is a matter of incorporating one of these in the CS representation that is the conceptual knowledge of the pronoun.

In one sense, development of the conceptual linguistic knowledge might be a more straightforward process than that involving the language module, because it does not require the operations of an additional interface, that between SS and CS. On the other hand, the SS–CS interface is a part of the language module and evolved for the purpose of making appropriate connections. Exactly how these points play out in L2 learning is a large issue that I will not try to address here.

Awareness of context

Being aware of context as a part of input means exactly what being aware of CS representations usually means: strong activation of the conceptual representation is accompanied by strong activation of a coindexed perceptual representation, which in effect serves as its proxy in consciousness. This awareness can be accompanied by a feeling of rightness, or understanding. An interesting research question then is to what extent and in what ways these types of awareness during perception are important for learning. The contrast between modular and extramodular knowledge should be important here. CS representations normally have perceptual counterparts in POpS, allowing an indirect awareness of extramodular linguistic knowledge, while SS is an additional step removed from POpS, and therefore from consciousness. Awareness (indirectly) of CS representations is thus a better reflection of extramodular than modular knowledge.

One aspect of context that deserves additional attention is the ALIEN representation described in Chapter 4, which will be coindexed with any input perceived as alien to the self. Input is perceived as alien if representations that contain ALIEN as one of their components are active in CS during the perceiving. A typical example would be the speech of a person who is perceived as 'other'. This perception is based on – or simply is – the active presence of ALIEN in the conceptual representation of the speaker. If this representation is active in CS, it becomes coindexed with representations of the current linguistic input, which are henceforth alien to the self (recall the input preferences discussed earlier in this chapter).[1]

Perception and Learning: Implicit, Explicit and Subliminal

Putting together various points from the discussion in this chapter, we can establish general characterizations of three types of perception and the learning that is based on each of them. In this section, I will describe the three types – subliminal, implicit and explicit – and their basis in the nature of processing. I will then consider the implications for the development of the language module and of extramodular linguistic knowledge.

Types of perception and learning

Two characteristics of a perceptual representation determine whether information it contains can be used for the development of particular linguistic knowledge. One is its activation: a perceptual representation that is highly active for a relatively long period of time will exert a strong influence on processing and will give processors good opportunities to deal with the information it contains; one that is only briefly active and only at a low level will have little influence on processing and will offer little opportunity for processors to use its information. The second characteristic of the perceptual representation is the explicitness of the potentially useful information it contains. Perceptual representations directly contain only perceptual information; if non-perceptual information implicitly contained in them is to be used by other processors, it requires an extraction process, one that could be simple and direct or could be very complex and extensive, involving multiple intermediate steps.

These two variable characteristics – the availability of the input representation itself and the availability of the relevant information that it implicitly contains – underlie the differences among three general types of perception and learning: subliminal, implicit and explicit. The types reflect the possibilities of information that is implicitly contained in an input representation (i.e. a POpS representation) registering in the system, i.e. somehow influencing subsequent processing. The three types are as follows:

- *Subliminal perception*: Perception occurs with no awareness of the input representation containing the information.
- *Implicit perception*: Perception occurs with awareness of the input representation but no awareness of the information it contains.
- *Explicit perception*: Perception occurs with awareness of the information contained in the input representation.

Explicit perception has varying degrees, or levels, of awareness, involving anything from a single follow-up representation focused on the relevant information (compare noticing) to a long series of representations each constituting a conceptual analysis of that information. In terms of the four types of awareness discussed above, the *explicit* category thus includes both (c) and (d).

This classification can be directly extended to learning: *subliminal learning* is learning that occurs on the basis of information that is subliminally perceived; *implicit learning* is learning that occurs on the basis of information that is implicitly perceived; and *explicit learning* is learning that occurs on the basis of information that is explicitly perceived. Explicit learning of course has the same variable levels as explicit perception.

Explaining the types

The characteristics of these three types of perception and learning can be derived from the following principles:

A. Processors work with active representations.
B. The more active a representation is and the longer it remains active, the more a processor can do with it.

C. Conscious representations are those that have achieved sustained high levels of activation.

Principle A is standard in processing and is virtually a definition of activation. Principle B is a reasonably straightforward consequence. C is the Activation Hypothesis adopted by MOGUL, possibly the most parsimonious account of consciousness possible. Together, I suggest, they provide a simple, intuitive approach to the different varieties of perception and learning and particularly their relation to consciousness.

The issue is the state of the POpS representation containing the information that might be useful for learning. In the *subliminal* case, this representation never comes to dominate POpS and therefore does not become conscious. In this case, the information has very low availability because the representation implicitly containing it is only minimally active and/or is active for only a brief time. Use of that information remains a logical possibility, but little more than that. This is subliminal perception; any learning that results from it is subliminal learning. A second possibility, the *implicit* case, is that the POpS representation is the subject of awareness, but the relevant information it contains is not. In this case, the information will be more available, because the awareness implies that the input representation is highly active, in a relatively sustained manner. But the potential for use is limited by the implicit nature of the information it contains. This is implicit perception; learning that occurs on this basis is implicit learning. The third possibility is that the input representation becomes conscious and additional processing then results in (indirect) awareness of the information it contains. This is explicit perception of the information, the basis for explicit learning.

Explicit perception and learning

Consider in more detail now the nature of these three types, beginning with the explicit variety. Its essence is that (a) information implicitly present in a perceptual representation becomes explicitly represented in another module, such as CS; and (b) a perceptual counterpart of this new representation becomes conscious. This follow-up awareness could take a variety of forms, including the voice in the head (an AS representation), saying for example 'the adjective is before the noun', or maybe a visual representation of an A followed by an N. In its weakest form, the experience is only a fleeting awareness of the new representation, accompanied by a conscious experience of rightness, showing understanding.

Explicit perception of information in a POpS representation can comprise not just one new representation but rather a series of them, each constituting knowledge gained on the basis of the original input representation. In the adjective-noun example, there could be for instance a representation of the A-N order in the input sentence, followed by a representation of the idea that this is a principle of English, followed by one that contrasts English and Spanish order, followed by another of the information that the order might depend on the individual adjective. For each of these representations there is the possibility of a coindexed POpS representation developing and becoming active enough to reach consciousness.

In each case, if such a representation is formed and does become conscious, this is, first of all, an indication that the new representation dominated its own store for a time and will therefore acquire a reasonably high resting activation level. Beyond reflecting the condition of the new representation, the presence of the dominant POpS representation with which it is coindexed will also help sustain it, making it more available for further processing and ultimately contributing to its resting activation level. The maintenance of the new representation's activation will also facilitate further processing based on that representation, constituting additional analysis of the information in the original input representation. Each step in this processing could result in a new representation, developed as a product of explicit perception and learning.

It is important to note that this is, so far, a very incomplete picture, as it does not take into account the nature of the processor that is involved, a factor that I will take up shortly. The conclusion at this point, though, is that explicit perception and the learning that is based on it allow and encourage rich development of knowledge.

Subliminal and implicit perception and learning

The situation is very different for subliminal and implicit perception and learning. A representation that is established on the basis of an input representation that is never strong enough to reach consciousness should be of very low quality and should have an extremely low activation level. One that is established on the basis of information that remains implicit in a conscious input representation is likely to have similar, though less severe, limitations. (I will add a very important qualification to this point shortly, namely that it depends on the particular processor that is involved.) Since processors use active representations, such representations will have only a limited role in processing.

But any representation that is present in a store can affect the activation of other representations there, i.e. it can prime those other representations. These limited-use representations can be compared to the *low-quality traces/ representations* of Cleeremans and colleagues (Cleeremans, 2006; Cleeremans & Jiménez, 2002; Destrebecqz & Cleeremans, 2001, 2003; Jiménez et al., 2006). These authors argued that implicit learning produces low-quality representations, which can only influence subsequent processing through priming. This account also provides a natural approach to the problems of amnesics. They have trouble with declarative knowledge because they have lost the ability to establish the high-quality memory traces that can be used for explicit tasks.

In the MOGUL interpretation, traces can be low quality in two senses. First, they have a very low resting level, as just described. Second, because they were constructed on the basis of perceptual representations that the processors had only limited opportunity to use, the new representations (traces) may well be low quality in the more direct sense. Thus, 'low quality' is not in itself a kind of representation. It describes representations that are likely to result when processors have only limited opportunities to work with the information on which they are to be based.

Cleeremans' notion of low-quality traces does not distinguish the products of implicit perception from those of subliminal perception, placing both under the heading of 'implicit', while in the analysis I am suggesting they are likely to involve two different degrees of low quality, reflecting differences in the circumstances in which they are created. Subliminal perception, in which the initial perceptual representation itself never becomes conscious, is likely to yield lower-quality representations than implicit perception, in which we have the lesser problem that the relevant information within the perceptual representation is never consciously represented. I will return to the subject of low-quality representations briefly below and in more detail in the following chapter.

Processors and automaticity

So far, I have abstracted away from differences in the nature of the processors, specifically differences in their inherent ability to use information of a given kind. For most input, most processors can do little or nothing with it, regardless of how good an opportunity they are given. A visual processor cannot handle sounds. A phonology processor cannot make sense of visual input or of non-linguistic auditory input, such as the sound of thunder. So principles (A–C) above are only relevant to a fraction of processor–input combinations, namely those for which successful processing is possible in principle. More interestingly, perhaps, two processors that are both able to handle a given type of input can differ greatly in how quickly and efficiently they are able to do it (and of course in what they do with the information).

Processors and specialization of function

The conceptual processor has no inherent ability to extract linguistic information from perceptual representations, simply because it is a conceptual, not linguistic, processor. Thus, the discussion to this point can be taken as a description of how linguistic representations in CS develop. An essential feature of the account is that the conceptual processor can only construct good representations from POpS input if the POpS representation is available to it at some length, and a considerable amount of back and forth processing between CS and POpS is likely to be needed. In other words, explicit learning should generally be superior, the more explicit and extensive, the better. Implicit learning should be possible but limited, and subliminal learning is quite unlikely. Recall, though, that I am speaking here only of the kinds of representations that can be established in perception. Regarding the limits of implicit learning, especially, the question arises as to what might become of implicitly established representations in the long run, but this is an aspect of memory consolidation and restructuring, which I will consider in the following chapter.

Extraction of linguistic information by the language module differs fundamentally from extraction of such information by conceptual processing. It is in the nature of the module to extract specific types of (linguistic) information from input representations and to use that information for highly constrained construction of specific types of linguistic representations. A system of this sort, when confronted by a perceptual representation that implicitly contains useful linguistic information, should often be able to extract that information quickly and efficiently, despite the implicit status of the information in the perceptual representation. This is to say that implicit learning is the norm in the language module.

Automaticity

This difference between linguistic processing in CS and in the language module can be understood in terms of automaticity: the ability of a processor to deal with particular kinds of information in a fast, efficient manner. Automaticity has traditionally been discussed entirely in terms of learning – a process becomes automatic through practice. But there is nothing in the nature of automaticity that implies such a limitation. The automaticity of a process could just as well be inherent in that process. Good candidates for such built-in automaticity are the low-level sensory processes that handle sensory input, each in its own modality.

Another good candidate for built-in automaticity is the language module. As described above, the nature of the module is to extract specific types of information from perceptual representations for the purpose of constructing specific, narrowly constrained types of linguistic representations. This is exactly the kind of process that should be inherently automatic, not requiring more than the presence of a strong input representation, the specifically linguistic content of which remains implicit. The automaticity is a combination of the phonology module's ability to use input from POpS to construct its representations and the syntax module's ability to use the input it receives from the phonology. I will skip over the details of the phonology and consider development of SS.

One part of the syntax module's inherent automaticity is the process of assigning lexical categories, such as noun and verb, to units (words) established by the phonology. The features underlying the categories are innately present in SS, and the syntax processor has the inherent ability to combine them in ways that reflect both its inbuilt principles and the nature of the input. Establishment of lexical categories makes possible the subsequent establishment of the functional categories in SS, specifically their combination with appropriate feature representations. For the case of the functional category Num and its strength feature, considered above, the syntax processor will automatically combine [weak] with Num when the active representation in SS includes an appropriate adjective-noun sequence and will automatically combine [strong] with Num when it includes a noun-adjective sequence.

The essence of all these processes is that they are pre-established and operate automatically whenever conditions allow them to, namely when appropriate input is encountered. Two clarifications should be added. First, 'input' here refers not to the utterance but rather to the intermediate representations constructed from it; it is these representations that must provide the material with which the automatic processes work. Second, the automaticity of a process does not ensure that its output will be correct in any given case. The processes apply blindly to whatever input they encounter. Since any particular input is limited, and possibly wrong, the output in a given case will very often not be the final, desired result. Successful learning involves an enormous number of applications of automatic (and non-automatic) processes over a long period of time. I will consider the way this occurs in the following chapter.

If the implicitly developed representations in the language module are established automatically, by processes designed specifically to construct them, then in general these representations, unlike those that are implicitly developed in CS, will not be low quality in the sense of being poorly constructed or unsuited for their function. However, they *will* begin life with very low activation levels, like those of low-quality CS representations. It follows that the linguistic processors are using representations that are quite low in activation in comparison with other parts of the cognitive system. The representations they work with in any given instance of processing are those that are active *relative to other representations in their stores*. These points reinforce the previous conclusion that representations in SS and PS can never be conscious.

Conclusion

This discussion has assumed a distinction between two different kinds of 'unconscious' learning. Implicit learning occurs when the perceptual representation is conscious but there is no awareness of any follow-up representations that contribute to the extraction of linguistic information from that representation. This sort of learning is normal in the development of the language module but unlikely in the development of extramodular linguistic knowledge.

Subliminal learning refers to learning in the absence of awareness even of the perceptual representation. Its prospects are very limited, regardless of what type of knowledge is involved. Note that this idea does not correspond to the concept of subliminal learning presented by Schmidt (1990), which referred to learning in the absence of noticing rather than in the absence of awareness of the perceptual representation implicitly containing the relevant linguistic information. On the other hand, on occasion he did seem to be treating subliminal learning as complete unawareness of input (see Truscott, 1998; Truscott & Sharwood Smith, 2011). This is one point of confusion in work on noticing, confusion that hopefully can be avoided.

An important feature of this approach is that it avoids the assumption that implicit learning is a single, unified phenomenon, that its operations are the same regardless of the domain in which it is operating. This is because the degree/duration of activation that is needed for a given case of processing varies with the nature of the input and the nature of the processor and, especially, the interaction between the two. Processors operate in real time. If they are to do their work successfully, the requirement is that the input must be available to them in a manner that is sufficient given their ability. A given processor might be able to make full use of a given type of representation, automatically, even if the information contained in it is available only implicitly and only for a relatively brief time. Note that automaticity is not a yes or no matter, but rather one of degree. *How* quickly and efficiently can a given processor handle given input?

Enhancing Input

To this point, the focus has been on how linguistic ability develops as a by-product of conscious and unconscious processing activity, with only passing concern given to how that activity is or can be influenced by outside intervention. In this section, I turn to the more applied side of the issues, exploring the effects of various forms of intervention, all of which can be called input enhancement, though I use the term somewhat differently than it has been used in the past. The concept originated as *consciousness raising* (Sharwood Smith 1981), but its originator later decided that the use of 'consciousness' in the name was inappropriate and so replaced it with *input enhancement* (Sharwood Smith 1991, 1993, 2013; Sharwood Smith & Truscott, in press). Neither term was intended to refer specifically to making input or aspects of it conscious, or more conscious, but this is generally what it has amounted to in its applications, and this is essentially the issue I am interested in: how the various ways of altering input (and therefore processing) influence awareness and how these changes might affect learning.

The other terminological issue is the scope of 'input enhancement'. The term has typically been used specifically for a particular type of enhancement, what is sometimes called textual enhancement, the goal of which is to make selected aspects of form more salient in written input (for example Alanen, 1995; Berent *et al.*, 2009; Overstreet, 1998; Park & Han, 2008; Simard, 2009; J. White, 1998; see Gascoigne, 2006 and Han *et al.*, 2008, for useful overviews of this type of research). A limitation of this work is that it focuses on language forms and their meanings. I suggested above that input also includes the context in which the form is encountered and the affect associated with it, value especially. If input is more than the strictly linguistic aspects that have been the focus of previous work, then input enhancement logically encompasses more than enhancement of these strictly linguistic aspects. The standard notion must be expanded to include contextual enhancement and enhancement of value.

The issue then is how efforts to alter the processing of input, in terms of linguistic form, meaning, context and value, influence awareness and how any such influences on awareness might be related to learning. In exploring these questions, I will consider, specifically, textual enhancement (including input flood), oral enhancement, efforts to improve comprehension, contextual enhancement and affective enhancement, leaving out of the discussion some more explicit types of intervention that Sharwood Smith treated as types of input enhancement. Throughout the discussion, I will refer to the four levels of awareness in perception identified in this chapter.

Textual enhancement

Textual enhancement has, again, been the standard form of input enhancement, or at least the form of intervention to which the term is most commonly applied. The usage is not surprising, since this is the form of intervention that most neatly captures the idea of *enhancing* the input. It consists of efforts to make a selected linguistic feature more salient, and therefore more likely to be subject to in-depth processing, by increasing the salience of that portion of the visual input that embodies the feature. This can be done with highlighting, font size, bold or italics, for example. Increased salience of this sort is difficult to separate from increased likelihood of awareness, so textual enhancement is very much about consciousness.

Textual enhancement in MOGUL terms

The immediate influence of such an intervention is on a visual (VS) representation: the portion of that representation that embodies the linguistic target will be different from the rest of the representation in some way. But altering the perceptual representation is only important as a means to the end of influencing subsequent linguistic processing. The normal goal is to encourage *explicit* processing of the target form. Based on the discussion above, this change could have a significant impact on the development of extramodular linguistic knowledge, though this is only a theoretical possibility. That analysis also suggests that it will have no direct impact on the development of the language module. Simple awareness of the perceptual representation (input) is optimal for such development; enhancement that aims at producing further awareness should not be relevant. Empirical research has not found more than limited effects for textual enhancement, on any kind of measure (Han *et al.*, 2008; Han & Peverly, 2007; Lee & Huang, 2008), suggesting that this sort of enhancement does not greatly contribute to the development of linguistic knowledge, modular or extramodular, though this evidence should not be considered conclusive.

Input flood

A variant of textual enhancement is the 'input flood', in which learners are presented with a very large number of instances of input embodying the target feature, normally in unaltered form. The goal here is not to make the target feature more salient, at least not within any given instance of input, but rather to create a great many opportunities for that feature to be processed. If consciousness is the concern, this is about creating many instances of simple awareness of input, with the possibility of more explicit processing in any given instance.

We can imagine this technique benefitting development in the language module, at least in principle, as simple awareness of input is well suited for this development. Probably the biggest question mark is uncertainty regarding the exact nature of the module and its processing. The selection of a target form is based on an outsider's perspective of what counts as a real unit of language. It is far from clear that this choice will correspond to anything real in the language module. And if it does, a serious possibility exists that development of this unit would require input containing particular other sorts of information, which the flood did not provide. Another issue is how much input (of the right sort) would be needed. Successful development of L2 knowledge in the module often involves competition with well-established L1 items, a topic that I will consider further in the following chapter. So even if the flood is done properly, it might have to be truly extreme if it is to have any discernible effects. Another important issue is the context and value that are associated with the flood.

For the development of extramodular knowledge, it is not clear whether success should be expected from this approach. The higher levels of awareness are associated with success here, and an input flood is oriented towards the lower level. A number of very small, cumulative gains are possible, but if success is to occur, the flood, again, would presumably have to be very extensive indeed. On the empirical side, research has not found impressive effects of any sort for the input flood (see Leow *et al.*,

2003; Trahey & White, 1993; for review, see Han et al., 2008), suggesting that it does not make meaningful contributions to the development of extramodular knowledge.

Oral enhancement

Oral enhancement is the natural counterpart of textual enhancement, seeking to make a selected portion of oral input more salient, that particular portion being selected because it embodies a linguistic feature that is being targeted. The enhancement can consist of adjustments in volume, length or intonation, or through pauses. It might also come in the form of visual input, such as gestures and facial expressions. In any case, the ultimate goal is to encourage more in-depth processing of a linguistic feature that is implicitly present in the perceptual representation and thereby allow its establishment in the mental grammar. The perceptual representation in this case is in AS and is not to be confused with phonological (PS) representations.

Enhancement of degraded input representations

From a theoretical perspective, oral enhancement is most clearly significant when it is the only way that a target feature can get represented, implicitly, at the POpS level. In casual English speech, for instance, final *–s/z* is often dropped. If this occurs when the ending is supposed to be marking plural, as in *books*, then the perceptual input representation will contain nothing that could contribute to the development of a plural representation. More careful speech, clearly including the final *–s*, could then be a useful enhancement.

Another possible cause for the absence of an important item in the input representation would be that the sound was lost during auditory processing as the result of competition from well-established L1 representations that have no place for it. This might happen, for instance, in a Chinese speaker's processing of English final consonants. When a word such as *books* is processed, the final *–s* might not appear in the AS representation because competing representations based on the L1 dominate processing, and these representations do not allow final consonants. As a possible treatment for this problem, this portion of the perceptual representation might be enhanced, lengthening the *–s* or saying it more loudly or making it a full syllable. The hope is that this treatment would make that phone more likely to appear in the auditory representation, despite the influence of the L1 competitors. If successful, the treatment might be beneficial for both modular and extramodular knowledge, as no growth is possible on the basis of an element that is not even implicitly present in the perceptual representation. Such success would probably be associated with awareness of at least an auditory representation including the *–s*.

Enhancement for salience

Perhaps more common are situations in which the target form *is* already implicitly present in the perceptual representation and the goal of the enhancement is to encourage more explicit processing. In the example of plural, added stress on –*s* might lead to construction of a follow-up representation specifically of this portion of the auditory representation, quite possibly followed by further analysis based in CS. If the enhancement is successful in this respect, it might be expected to benefit the development of extramodular linguistic knowledge, as the additional processing reflected by the higher level of awareness is precisely the way to develop conceptual representations. It should be irrelevant for modular development, though, because simple awareness of input is sufficient for such development, and processing in the module is not sensitive to the higher levels of awareness.

Efforts to make input more comprehensible

The end of perception is meaning – understanding of the information coming from the senses. In MOGUL terms, this means construction of an appropriate CS representation. For language, it is specifically construction of a CS representation of the meaning of the utterance or text. Failure in this construction of meaning is thus a failure of perception. It can also mean failure for the development of linguistic knowledge. This suggests another form of intervention (enhancement) that could in principle help both perception and linguistic learning: assisting learners in understanding the input they receive. This is not, of course, an entirely original suggestion, but rather an incorporation of familiar ideas, especially from traditional comprehension-based approaches (cf. Courchène *et al.*, 1992; Krashen & Terrell, 1988; Winitz, 1981).

One form the assistance in comprehension can take is selection of input – finding reading and listening materials that are suitable for learners. For some target languages, especially English, there is a vast wealth of reading and listening material available; finding material of a suitable level should not be difficult, though for other languages the situation varies tremendously. The more important form of assistance, in the present context, is providing support for learners' efforts to understand their input. This type of assistance could take a very general form, not targeting any particular features of the language but rather trying to help with the meaning of the material.

Enhancement for comprehension can also be done with a particular learning target in mind – such as the development of English passive forms. If the learner is processing the input sentence *Bill was kissed by Mary*, clarification of the meaning might help not only comprehension but also development, including development of the language module. This is because interfaces – in this case the SS/CS interface – push adjacent modules towards agreement in their currently active representations. If CS contains an active representation of the concept of Mary kissing Bill, and SS produces a regular active representation for *Bill was kissed by Mary*, a conflict will occur, creating pressure for one or the other to change. One possible result is that the CS representation will be altered in a way that makes it consistent with the SS representation, in which case no development will occur. The other possibility, though, is that the adjustments will instead be in the SS representation, making it compatible with its CS counterpart. This would mean assigning the sentence a passive structure. Passive could become established in SS in this way and could subsequently be consolidated in the same way, through further input.

The enhancement in this case could be provided in a variety of forms, including an explicit statement of the meaning of the sentence, a picture showing a woman kissing a man (or a demonstration) or a story that gives disambiguating information. In any case, the added input could help with the perceptual process and thereby with learning, in either the language module or CS.

In enhancement for comprehension, the issue for consciousness is awareness of meaning, in the standard indirect sense in which we can be aware of conceptual representations. The most consistent involvement of awareness here is likely to be the feeling of rightness that accompanies successful comprehension, or the feeling of wrongness when comprehension fails. Such awareness should be associated with successful acquisition. Higher levels of awareness, of the meaning of passive forms for example, are likely to be related to the development of conceptual linguistic knowledge but not of the language module.

Contextual enhancement

Contextual enhancement might be seen as an idea that has been around for some time but has not been thought of in these terms, and has not been pursued as seriously as perhaps it should be. In traditional audiolingual and grammar translation approaches, and to some extent in the more cognitive approaches that followed, language was seen as a system of linguistic items and rules and the assumption was that inculcating that linguistic information in learners equalled L2 learning. The movement towards communicative teaching was to a large extent a recognition that purely linguistic knowledge is not sufficient, that language is by nature used in contexts and with particular goals in mind, with the implication that any learning which abstracts away from these features is likely to be of only limited practical value. So contextual factors, in the form of internal context, must be appropriately connected to representations of linguistic knowledge. The goal of contextual enhancement is to assist this process.

Contextual enhancement in MOGUL terms

In MOGUL, items in the language module are connected to a variety of CS representations – providing the internal context of their use – and are used by virtue of these connections. Extramodular linguistic knowledge, if it is to be used for communication, must also be tied to context, but in this case it is not a matter of connections but rather the creation of complex CS representations that include both the linguistic information and the internal context. For both kinds of cases, enhancing input in terms of context means establishing the link in the input between linguistic information and contextual representations. The key in both cases is for the context representations to be active at the same time as the representations of the linguistic information.

Enhancement thus means making appropriate contextual representations more active while the linguistic representations, or perhaps the perceptual representations that gave rise to them, are active. This might be accomplished by drawing learners' attention to the context, either explicitly or by trying to make certain features of the context especially salient. The hope is that this intervention will increase the chances of the contextual representations becoming coindexed with the linguistic representations, preferably with the indexes having a relatively high activation level.

Awareness and contextual enhancement

The question then is the place of awareness in this process. Being aware of context does not mean being directly aware of the contextual representations, which is not possible. It means awareness of perceptual representations coindexed with them. When the issue is the development of extramodular linguistic knowledge, in CS, we can ask about the prospects for encouraging simultaneous or near-simultaneous awareness of the linguistic and the contextual representations, the awareness being indirect in both cases. Awareness of modular representations, on the other hand, is not possible, even in the indirect sense, so we must consider awareness of contextual representations occurring at the same time that modular representations are likely to be (unconsciously) active.

In each case, modular and extramodular, we can ask how the awareness is related to the successful establishment of the contextual representations and, especially, their connections to linguistic items. Will enhancements that yield higher levels of awareness result in more successful learning? In principle, we should expect the answer to be yes, because awareness implies higher activation levels. But this type of enhancement faces the same practical issues associated with enhancement in general. To my knowledge, there is little or no empirical basis on which to judge the actual effects. The point here is to raise the questions, hopefully in ways that can be seriously investigated.

Affective enhancement

Affect has not played a major role in SLA theory, at least not within cognitive perspectives (but see, for example, Dewaele, 2005; Sharwood Smith, 2014). But there does nonetheless seem to be a general awareness of its importance in L2 learning. At the heart of this importance, and the heart of affect itself, is value. Input that acquires a high positive value will have a very different impact on the linguistic system than input that is negatively valued or is neutral. The question is how the value of input might be influenced for the better; in other words, how can input be enhanced in terms of its value? And, of course, what difference does it make if the learner is conscious of the input's value?

In MOGUL, affect is representations in AfS and their connections (i.e. indexes) with other representations throughout the system. Connections to linguistic representations are established during perception, when the affect representations are active at the same time as the purely linguistic representations and so can be connected to them, directly or indirectly. We therefore have to ask how intervention might encourage this process, particularly in regard to the !val! and !harm! representations, and how consciousness of value fits in. The other side of the question is how we might avoid or minimize harmful connections, perhaps the best example being the effects of anxiety on learning. In an anxious context, !harm! is continuously active. A new representation established under these conditions will therefore acquire its index, encouraging subsequent avoidance of that representation, or at best a hesitant use.

Ways to enhance input value

Affective enhancement of input thus means encouraging the creation of positive links and strengthening those that already exist while avoiding or diminishing harmful affective links. In this section, I will consider several possible ways to go about this.

The most obvious way is to encourage a positive atmosphere for learning and one that minimizes anxiety. This is a familiar theme in language teaching and so I will simply note its relevance. The same can be said for encouragement of positive attitudes towards the target language and the culture it is associated with, helping learners see the value of the language. The idea of acculturation is relevant here (Schumann, 1978a, 1978b). A learner who identifies with the culture associated with the target language is likely to be more successful than one who does not. To some extent this familiar point can be attributed to the influence of value. Acculturation implies strong positive value associated with native speaker input, for example.

An important element of value is the perceived usefulness of the forms that are being learned. This point is probably clearest for vocabulary. If learners perceive a particular word as especially useful for them, that word will naturally become associated with !val! and benefit from that association. On the other hand, a word that they are learning simply because they have been told to learn it will not have the benefit of a value boost. A possible moral is that it is a good idea to focus instruction on words that learners are likely to consider useful and/or to convince them of the usefulness of the words that are being taught. Such efforts would constitute affective enhancement of the input.

A closely related source of value is success (or failure) in communication. For someone struggling to master a foreign language, there can be little that is more rewarding than understanding something spoken or written in that language or having his/her own production understood. On the other hand, failure to understand or, especially, to be understood can be a source of considerable negative value. For the comprehension side, this is a familiar matter of positive or negative value (!val! or !harm!) being coactive with linguistic input and therefore becoming associated with the linguistic forms. For the production side, we are talking about a form of *auto-input* (*virtual input, backdoor learning*; see Schmidt & Frota, 1986; Sharwood Smith, 1981; Terrell, 1991): learners perceive their own output and it thereby becomes input for them. In this case, the important point is that the value associated with communicative success is active along with the perceptual and linguistic representations that were used and the input therefore includes this affect.

In this respect, enhancing value means helping learners succeed in their efforts at using the language. This can involve support from the teacher, texts and videos, as well as from other learners. It can mean careful selection of learning tasks to avoid making things too difficult for learners. Of course simplicity is not everything. Understanding or producing overly simple language is not a particularly rewarding experience. So a degree of challenge is also important. The value of communicative success is an aspect that is also important in contemporary grammar-oriented activities but does not receive much recognition there. These activities are often designed to establish a need for learners to use selected target forms to complete the task (e.g. Batstone, 1994). This design has an affective component, which is usually not recognized. Completion of a task of this sort can result in the target forms being associated with value, simply because they were a salient part of the success.

Enhancing the value of input can also mean reducing or eliminating negative value. Anxiety, in particular, is clearly a problem for L2 learning. It could be brought about by any number of factors, involving the general nature of a class, conflict with the teaching style or the teacher's personality, or particular activities, such as forced production or correction. And these factors can interact with the traits of the individual learner.

In MOGUL, anxiety is steady, relatively low-level activation of !fear!, which of course includes !harm! as its central component. If input is received in this state, !fear! will become coindexed with the POpS representation of that input and so with any resulting linguistic representations. Subsequent activation of these representations, for possible use in production or comprehension, will activate !fear!, encouraging avoidance of the negatively valued representations or leading to slow, hesitant use. So enhancement that eliminates or reduces the activation of !fear! during perception could have a beneficial effect on learners' practical abilities. This is not a novel observation or novel advice, of course. Teachers have long recognized the importance of creating a positive, low-anxiety environment for learning, and it is not difficult to find specific suggestions in the literature, so I will not go into details. The novel aspect of this discussion is the interpretation of the phenomena within a general framework for understanding L2 learning.

A word is in order here about possible positive effects of negative affect. Negative emotion can clearly make an experience more memorable, as when a learner feels embarrassed after being corrected for a particular error and so maintains a clear and strong memory of the error and the correct form. A memory of this sort is about !harm! becoming connected to the experience because of its high activation level during that experience. This connection can subsequently amplify the activation of the memory. The problem is that the negative associations are likely to remain and to exert a harmful influence on production that should use the form, possibly resulting in avoidance of it or hesitant, uncomfortable use. There is also a danger of such experiences harming the learner's overall attitude towards the language, with more general negative effects on learning and use.

Awareness and affective enhancement

Awareness of affect is a normal aspect of conscious experience, and feelings of rightness and wrongness are a normal part of affective awareness. So we might expect enhancement of affect/value to be especially related to consciousness. In the previous section, I described a direct kind of enhancement, involving !val!, and an indirect variety involving reduction or avoidance of !harm!.

One of the direct varieties was the development of a positive attitude towards the language and the culture with which it is associated. Any positive experience should strengthen the association between !val! and the CS representation of the language. Because of the typically high activation level of !val!, we might expect this experience to be typically conscious, though the influence of unconscious positive experience cannot be easily dismissed.

The second type of direct enhancement depended on perceived usefulness of a linguistic form. We might expect that when learners come to see a particular word, for example, as useful for expressing their ideas, they will consciously experience positive affect as a result. Actual use of it could then include feelings of rightness and perhaps additional affect, satisfaction for example. Whether the success of the enhancement depends on this conscious experience is less clear, though.

Closely related to perceived usefulness is the enhancement of a sense of success in communication. It seems intuitively clear that success in communication is often accompanied by conscious positive affect, reflecting the activation of !val!. This could well mean that a linguistic representation is becoming strongly associated with !val!. In this respect, affective enhancement could in principle be valuable for modular development, as well as extramodular development. On the other hand, when there is awareness of value associated with a particular form and its use – awareness that a particular form has value – the form in question should be a CS representation, because representations in the language module would not be associated with a conscious experience. What this suggests is that awareness of this sort is relevant specifically to the development of extramodular linguistic knowledge. Its relation to modular development is at best uncertain. But a sense of success that is not consciously tied to a particular form could well be relevant to modular development, because *some* representations are likely to be active in the module at the time and so become associated with the positive affect.

We can also ask whether the harmful effects of anxiety depend on the anxiety being a conscious state or if a more subtle, background sort of anxiety can have the same effect. The natural expectation is that awareness is not necessary for the effect but is directly related to its strength. Research might explore this question, since low levels of anxiety have physiological correlates that can be measured. The question of awareness in enhancement of the input takes on an odd form in cases like this, because the enhancement, if successful, consists of a reduction or elimination of activity in a particular representation and so there may be no active AfS representation to be aware of. If, on the other hand, the anxiety is replaced by more positive affect as a result of the enhancing activity, the situation becomes essentially the same as that considered above for more direct instances of input enhancement.

Input preferences and affective enhancement

Above, I described input preferences, discussing the case of immersion students whose production settles into a grammatically non-standard form even after very extensive input has given them native-like comprehension skills. I tentatively attributed the phenomenon, following Dulay *et al.* (1982), to learners' input preferences; specifically, they value peer input over teacher input and so come to sound like their classmates rather than their teacher. This naturally raises the question of how input that reflects the favoured language form might be enhanced in a way that would make it more likely to become the learners' standard form of production.

A preliminary observation is that if the problem for these students really is input preferences, then we should not expect much benefit to result from instruction in proper language form, 'proper' meaning the form used by the teacher rather than the peers. This approach could well give them more conscious knowledge of the target speech, but the negative value associated with it would remain. Such instruction, in itself, would more likely reinforce students' perception of this dialect as belonging to the teacher rather than to the preferred models.

A more promising approach would be to provide models that use standard speech and are likely to be highly valued by the learners as speakers. The models could be peers who are native speakers of the language, ideally as regular members of the class. Appealing videos could be an alternative or supplement, presenting students with standard speech produced by people they might identify with or admire. The possibility of encouraging 'marked' input preferences (Beebe, 1985) should also be investigated. In some circumstances, the status of the teacher and/or the standard dialect can make that dialect the preferred option for learners, though this is very much the exception and the feasibility of efforts to deliberately bring it about is uncertain. Such efforts would probably have to involve somehow getting the learners to recognize, in a gut sense, the practical value of speaking the way the teacher does. For consciousness, the question would then be whether this shift requires awareness on the part of the learners who make it, or perhaps whether greater awareness goes with greater success.

Conclusion

The focus of this chapter was on perception as it applies to L2 learning, specifically on the implications of the framework developed in the first half of the book for the processing of linguistic input and for the place of consciousness in that processing. One important theme is awareness at different levels, i.e. differences in what exactly it is that learners are aware of. Awareness defines three types of perception and learning: subliminal, in which there is no awareness of the input representation; implicit, in which there is awareness of the input representation but not of the target information that is implicitly contained in it; and explicit, involving awareness of the information. Interacting with this theme is that of two distinct types of linguistic knowledge, modular and extramodular. Discussion of the place of consciousness in learning must consider each; the questions cannot be adequately explored in terms of an undifferentiated notion of language learning. A final theme is that we must include in the discussion contextual factors and affect, especially the *value* attached to representations. All these issues are best addressed in the context of a cognitive architecture and the position it takes on the nature of processing. In the final section of the chapter, I considered the possible implications of this understanding of perception for efforts to improve learning by adjusting the input that learners receive, concluding that such efforts are much more promising for the development of extramodular linguistic knowledge than for the development of the language module.

Note

(1) This account of the role of ALIEN should be supplemented by an account of the role of SELF, but this will probably require a more sophisticated notion of SELF than has so far been developed in MOGUL, perhaps distinguishing between a perceiving self and an acting self. I leave this for future development.

8 Memory Consolidation and Restructuring

In the previous chapter, the focus was on perception: specifically, the way that new linguistic representations and connections are established as part of perception and the place of consciousness in this process. The next question is what happens to those representations after they have been established and, again, how consciousness is involved. We can ask whether the new representations become significant parts of the language system or fade away; whether they remain in essentially their original form or undergo substantial changes, and how all of this is related to awareness. This is about memory – its consolidation and its restructuring.

Memory, as described in Chapter 2, is the information side of information processing. Importantly, it is not any one thing and it is not found in any one place in the mind/brain. Instead, it is functionally distributed, most clearly in terms of the various sensory modalities but also more generally. I suggested in Chapter 2 that each mental component (module) has its own memory store and that this is true for both long-term and working memory. The relation between the two is activation: working memory is the set of long-term memory representations that are currently active. The other aspects of memory discussed in Chapter 2 are consolidation and restructuring. Memory consolidation does not involve changes in the nature of a representation or its connections to other representations but is instead a matter of strengthening the representation and the connections, in their current form. This strengthening makes a representation more durable and more available for use. It also makes any future use more likely to include the other representations to which it is connected. Memory restructuring, on the other hand, is changes in the nature of the set of representations.

Learning, as it is normally understood, is changes in memory. According to acquisition by processing theory (APT; see Chapter 4), learning is not a mechanism or even a set of mechanisms but rather the lingering effect of processing. In other words, changes in memory occur in processing and as a part of it. These changes are of two general types, reflecting two general areas of processing. One is perception, the processing of sensory experience. Its essence is the construction of representations that make sense of the experience. The other type of processing, and therefore of learning, is memory consolidation and restructuring. A new representation constructed during perception is by nature a weak and relatively isolated entity. If it is to be a meaningful sort of knowledge, it must be strengthened – i.e. its resting activation level must be raised – through additional processing experience. It must also be integrated with existing representations and with those constructed in subsequent perceptual processing. These changes in memory are all lingering effects of processing.

In this chapter, I will first consider memory consolidation and then memory restructuring as they apply in second language (L2) learning, and the place of consciousness in each process, continuing to assume the terms of the Modular Online Growth and Use of Language (MOGUL) framework.[1] But first, a familiar clarification is needed. A recurring theme of this book is that the underlying reality of the mind is the architecture and the general processing principles; the various topics discussed in psychology do not pick out genuine, distinct components of the mind but are useful abstractions from the architecture and the processing. This point extends to the topics of consolidation and restructuring: considerable overlap exists between them.

Specifically, representations can become stronger and more available for processing in two ways. One is the phenomenon that I am calling 'consolidation', while the other is a consequence of restructuring. The first is about the resting activation level of the representation. The higher that level, the more available it is for processing (more 'retrievable', in traditional terms) and the less vulnerable it is to forgetting. The level is raised through use in processing and so consolidation in this sense is simply a matter of use. This is about a representation becoming stronger (more solid) in itself. On the other hand, a representation can also become stronger by virtue of the place it acquires in the system as a whole, i.e. the relations it develops with other representations, both within its own store and across stores. These associations make it more available for use in processing and less subject to forgetting. This is about restructuring. In the following discussion, I will use the term 'consolidation' specifically in the first sense, that of a representation becoming stronger in itself. The kind of strengthening associated with restructuring will be considered within the context of restructuring.

Consolidation and Consciousness

The topic of this section is how new representations created as part of perception become (or fail to become) solidly established in the learner's linguistic system and how consciousness is involved in this consolidation process. After discussing the general nature of consolidation, particularly within the MOGUL framework, I will consider its application to modular linguistic knowledge, including the role of competition, automatization, connections to contextual and affective representations and the possible role of production in consolidation. The final section will look at the consolidation of extramodular linguistic knowledge.

The nature of consolidation[2]

Recall the notion of representational Darwinism discussed in Chapter 4. A very large number of representations are naturally formed during processing, most of which turn out to be of little lasting value. The overwhelming majority of sentences that a person hears, for instance, can safely be forgotten, and are forgotten. In the typical case, if anything is remembered of a sentence, it will be the meaning (Clark & Clark, 1977; Sacks, 1967), and in most cases this too is of only limited long-term value. Conceptual information that turns out to be useful is likely to remain in the system and receive further use, as is information that the language module can use in its own development. There is, then, a selection process at work. This selection process is consolidation. Its outcome is that the particular representations that turn out to be useful are especially available to the processors and so dominate processing, while those that receive little or no consolidation never come to play a significant role in processing and in effect fade away.

In MOGUL, consolidation is about activation level. When a representation is first established during processing, it is likely to have a fairly high *current* activation level, simply by virtue of it being used in current processing. But if it receives no further stimulation, its activation will soon fall to a very low level because it had no previous use that could have established a higher resting level. The same is true for indexes linking it to representations in other stores (recall that indexes are themselves representations, subject to the same principles as others). So consolidation is an essential part of L2 learning. If the changes that constitute learning are to be meaningful, the new representations must be repeatedly reactivated in processing.

Successful consolidation is clearly related to the frequency with which an item is encountered in the learner's input. It is important to recognize, though, that when we are talking about the traditional sense of 'input', this is an indirect relation. The more often something is encountered, the more opportunities the system has to use the representation(s) associated with it and therefore the more opportunities for consolidation of those representations. But the presence of an item in the input does not guarantee that it will be a part of processing. When *sings* appears in the input, for example, the final *–s* might not register, especially if the learner's native language is one that makes little or no use of final consonants and consonant clusters. In such cases, the appearance of the affix in the input has no bearing on consolidation.

Less commonly, the system might mistakenly include the affix in mental representations of the input even when it was not actually present in that input. This could occur, for example, if the word following *sing* begins with /z/. For the purposes of consolidation of the affix's mental representation, such cases are indistinguishable from those in which the affix actually does appear and is properly analyzed. We thus have to distinguish the *external frequency* of an item – how often it appears in the input – from its *internal frequency*, i.e. how often it is processed. The latter is what is important for consolidation. External frequency is important exactly to the extent that it is reflected in internal frequency.

Within a store, consolidation means strengthening the new representation. A new representation is necessarily a combination of simpler existing ones, so consolidation is in a sense a matter of strengthening connections among component parts. But, as described in the previous chapter, I will restrict the term *connections* to the coindexing of representations in different stores, as in the case of a visual percept (in visual structures [VS]) connected to its meaning (in conceptual structures [CS]) and the emotion associated with it (in affective structures [AfS]). Each of these is a composite representation in its own store, and in each case consolidation means reactivating that representation, including the indexes that connect it to other representations.

As noted in previous chapters, there is a strong parallel between the cognitive notion of activation found in MOGUL and the concept of activation commonly used in neural work on consolidation, where the term 'reactivate' is common. The 'fire together, wire together' idea that is standard in neural work and neurally inspired work also has a MOGUL analogue in coindexation and the coactivation associated with it. An interface between adjacent stores will seek to coindex representations that are simultaneously active in the stores. Once they are coindexed, the resting activation level of the shared index will rise with further shared firing, consolidating the connections.

The consolidation process in the language module

If linguistic knowledge centred on the language module consists of multistore units, we must consider both the representations in the module themselves and their connections, in the form of indexes, to representations in other stores. In the previous chapter, I considered two kinds of examples of multistore linguistic units, words and functional categories.

Words consist of chains of coindexed phonological (phonological structures [PS]), syntactic (syntactic structures [SS]) and conceptual (CS) representations, with extensions to contextual representations (also in CS), as well as AfS representations that are the value and the emotional associations of the words, perceptual representations of appearance, sound and other sensory qualities and additional perceptual representations of spelling and pronunciation. The second example of multistore units that are centred on the language module is the set of functional categories in SS, each with its connections to PS and CS representations. In each case, we can talk about direct consolidation of a representation within a store as well as consolidation of its connections to representations in other stores.

The distinction is actually just a matter of convenience, as the connections (indexes) are themselves component representations and so consolidation of connections is an element of consolidation of the representations, each within its own store.

Words

Beginning with the example of words, consider the way that the representations which make up these multistore units are consolidated in comprehension (I will explore the role of production below). In comprehension of the spoken form of a word, processing in the auditory system culminates in an AS representation, which serves as the input to linguistic processing in the language module. If this representation is already present in the store, its resting activation level will undergo a very small increase, larger if it comes to temporarily dominate the store. In other words, it is consolidated, though only in a small way, since only one instance of reactivation is involved.

This process then extends into PS, where phonological representations coindexed with the active auditory representations are activated and combined and then serve as input to syntactic structures, where the activated representations are combined by the syntax processor to make an acceptable overall representation. Syntactic activity leads to conceptual activity in CS in the same way. At each level, active representations, particularly those that come to dominate their store during processing, end up with a slightly increased resting level; in other words, they undergo consolidation. These active representations include the indexes that connect the different levels, so consolidation operates both within a store and across stores, encompassing multistore units.

Functional categories

Consolidation of functional categories in comprehension is quite similar to consolidation of words. There is in fact some overlap between functional categories and words, as some of the former take the form of words, an example being the determiner category in English, which is realized as articles (*a*, *the*) and demonstratives (*this*, *that*, *these*, *those*). A more interesting case, though, is provided once more by the example of Number (Num) in English learning, already considered in Chapter 7 in regard to perception. The main issue is consolidation of the SS representation Num+[weak], which must become a solid part of L2 use if that use is to be accurate. But the connections of Num+[weak] to PS and CS are also essential.

The consolidation process works largely the same way it does with words, the primary difference being that Num need not have an overt sound. In the phrase 'the old book', for example, Num is implicitly present and must be a part of the SS representation, but there is nothing in the auditory or phonological form of the input that corresponds to it. In such cases, the functional category representation receives its activation entirely from within SS, through spreading activation and the demands of the syntax processor, though this activity is based on PS representations and so is at least an indirect product of the input. But the source of the activation does not affect consolidation; the relevant point is that Num+[weak] *is* strongly activated, becoming a part of the overall representation constructed for the input. If this condition is met then the functional category with its English feature value has progressed towards consolidation.

An important note is that processing is not one-directional as this simplified presentation suggests. The activity of an interface constantly works in both directions, so if the conceptual processor, for example, has trouble constructing an acceptable CS representation from the items that have been directly activated from SS input, the result may be a reverse activation, influencing SS to use a somewhat different set of representations or to combine them in a somewhat different way. The same phenomena can occur in interactions between SS and PS. In the functional category example, activation of Num and its inclusion in the overall SS representation might result in the activation of a null representation in PS, which can then become a part of the overall PS representation.

Consciousness and the consolidation process

Is consciousness involved in this consolidation process? Representations in the language module are never conscious, nor are they directly connected to perceptual output structures (POpS) representations as CS is, so there is no possibility of the kind of proxy awareness that CS representations enjoy. So the linguistic representations themselves cannot be objects of awareness during the consolidation process. The question then is whether the more peripheral aspects of the process can be conscious and, if they are, how this awareness might be related to consolidation of knowledge in the module. These peripheral aspects should be primarily perceptual representations, the standard objects of awareness. And perception is an integral part of the consolidation process. When a representation is consolidated through comprehension, construction of an appropriate POpS representation is a prerequisite, since POpS is the gateway to the language module.

This leads us back to the discussion of awareness in perception and its relation to the establishment of new representations. If there is no awareness of a perceptual representation, then the information that representation contains is not likely to have more than very limited effects on processing anywhere in the system; in other words, subliminal perception is limited, and subliminal learning even more so. This point applies as much to consolidation as it does to the initial establishment of representations. The very minimal activation involved in subliminal perception should make little if any contribution to consolidation. Simple awareness of input (i.e. the POpS representation), on the other hand, is sufficient to yield full-fledged processing in the language module of information implicitly contained in that input, with the implication that normal consolidation is going on.

The point, familiar from the previous chapter, is that development of the language module is associated with simple awareness of input. Note that this is not awareness, in any sense, of *what* in the module is being consolidated. It is awareness that conditions are right for consolidation of whatever representations might be involved in processing the current input. Thus, awareness of the POpS representation is an indication that something related to consolidation of modular linguistic knowledge is going on, but it is nothing more than this. Modular consolidation, like the establishment of new representations, is essentially an unconscious process.

There is another sort of indirect relation between awareness and consolidation of modular knowledge. Whenever CS activity occurs, the possibility exists of indirect awareness of that activity, in the form of coindexed POpS representations. And CS activity is very much a part of consolidation of meaning, both word meaning and meanings of functional categories such as Num. Indirect awareness of the meanings reflects, if imperfectly, dominance of CS by the relevant representations, which in turn implies that those representations are undergoing consolidation. Indirect awareness of conceptual consolidation is feasible, and this awareness is another indication that some sort of consolidation is going on in the language module.

Consolidation and competition

Consolidation is especially important in L2 learning because L2 representations must compete with already-established, highly active L1 representations for use in processing. If there is a general failure to successfully compete, there is a general failure of acquisition. The consolidation (reactivation) process is the key to success in this regard, as it can eventually result in high resting activation levels for the L2 representations, allowing them to successfully compete.

Consolidation through success in competition

Paradoxically, a representation becomes able to compete in general by successfully competing in many individual cases. In L2 use, representations belonging to each language are activated (e.g. Martin *et al.*, 2009; Spivey & Marian, 1999; Thierry & Wu, 2007; Wu & Thierry, 2012). Use of the L2 thus involves a constant competition between L1 and L2 items (in addition to competition within each language). Sometimes one will be used and at other times its competitor will appear. This is the phenomenon of *optionality*: 'the simultaneous presence in a learner's grammar of two features that should be mutually exclusive' (Truscott, 2006: 311). L2 acquisition, when it is successful, is characterized by a gradual, quantitative increase in the use of correct L2 forms and an accompanying decline in the use of the inappropriate forms that compete with them (see Sharwood Smith & Truscott, 2005). These phenomena – optionality and gradual, quantitative movement towards the use of appropriate forms – can be found in virtually all aspects of L2 learning.

This understanding incorporates the *full transfer, full access* idea of Schwartz and Sprouse (1996; see Sharwood Smith & Truscott, 2006). L1 representations are present and involved in L2 learning (full transfer), because there is only one PS, one SS and one CS containing all the representations for all languages the person knows. This characteristic of the system underlies competition and optionality. The principles of universal grammar (UG) are fully available (full access), as they are embodied in the processors, which do not change. One implication of this 'access' is that there is no principled limit on the success of an L2 learner. L1 competition and a variety of situational factors can make it very challenging and result in most learners falling short, but the native-like skills achieved by many learners show that these factors are not absolute barriers, suggesting in turn that the guidance provided by UG principles is present in the acquisition of an L2. This success, when it occurs, is to a considerable extent a product of consolidating L2 representations, often in the face of competition from entrenched L1 representations.

An example

Consider again the example of the functional category Num. A Spanish speaker acquiring English as an L2 will begin the process with the Num+[strong] representation in SS, based on phrases such as *casa roja (house red)*, and this representation will have, by SS standards, an extremely high resting activation level because it has undergone enormous amounts of use in comprehension and production of the native language. Num+[weak] will probably exist as well, because the adjective-noun order does sometimes occur in Spanish, but with a resting level far below that of its rival. The two will compete in Spanish production, with the strong value winning whenever no special internal context is present to greatly raise its rival's current level.

When English input is being processed, Num+[weak] *should* consistently appear in SS representations, as it is the value that accurately captures English word order (*the red house* rather than *the house red*). But Num+[strong] will often take its place, because processors favour highly active representations and the strong value is highly active as a result of L1 experience. If learning is to be successful, the resting level of Num+[weak] must rise considerably, i.e. the representation must be consolidated. This can happen despite the greatly higher resting level of Num+[strong] because English input sentences routinely show the adjective-noun order that requires the [weak] value and so the PS representations constructed for such input should almost always contain the words in that order. An SS representation that includes Num+[strong] will be extremely difficult to reconcile with this order in the phonology, which serves as input to SS. The incompatibility would virtually force the syntax either to use Num+[weak] or to produce some alternative analysis of the input, one in which an adjective did not precede a noun. In at least a significant percentage of the cases, the result should be that Num+[weak] appears in the representation that comes to temporarily dominate SS. This representation should therefore gradually become consolidated.

The place of awareness in all of this is essentially as described above. There cannot be any awareness of the representations in the module or of the gradual changes in their resting activation levels that constitute consolidation. The competition that occurs in processing within the module is unconscious as well. There can be awareness of the effects that the changes in activation levels have on performance: the learner can in principle observe that he/she is producing noun phrases with the proper order more consistently and fluently. But this is not awareness of the representations or of the processing in the module. It is the same awareness that an outside observer could have.

The example of Num has an interesting additional element in that the effects of this particular functional category might well be mimicked by extramodular knowledge. This is a subject I will consider below.

Automatization as consolidation

In Chapter 5, I described the automatization process, focusing on the place of consciousness within it. The essence of the process is a gradual rise in the resting activation levels of a set of representations and the indexes that connect them to one another across stores, this rise resulting from repeated use of the representations together. In the example of tying shoelaces, the relevant stores include VS and somatosensory structures, containing representations of the current state of the laces and the position of the fingers; motor structures, containing representations of the specific movements to be carried out; and CS, containing representations of the overall action and the intention to carry it out. The process of tying shoelaces has become automatized when each of the relevant representations, including the indexes connecting them, has achieved a sufficiently high resting activation level to make the process run quickly and efficiently.

For present purposes, the interesting point is that this is nothing more than consolidation. In this case, the consolidation necessarily goes beyond single representations, to include multiple stores and the connections among them, but in this respect it does not differ from many other examples of consolidation. This is again the 'fire together, wire together' principle.

Not surprisingly, then, automatization of language use is also a matter of consolidation. Fluent speech, for example, requires that the various linguistic representations be readily available for use by their respective processors, i.e. that their resting activation levels be relatively high. It also requires strong connections among them, i.e. high resting levels for the indexes that connect them. The representations in motor structures that are responsible for articulation must also achieve high resting levels, as must the indexes that connect them to the linguistic representations. And these factors, together, are the essence of fluent speech, which is impossible without them. In each case, these elevated resting levels are the product of consolidation.

One of the central features of automatization, as it is commonly discussed, is the gradual loss of awareness that accompanies it (see Chapter 5). A person developing a skill, such as tying shoelaces or playing piano, is initially aware of the individual low-level actions involved, but this awareness fades with practice and increased mastery. These standard examples differ from uses involving the language module in a crucial respect: for automatization within the language module, the individual representations there cannot cease to be conscious, since they were never conscious in the first place.

Limited automatization of processes involving the language module – or limited development there in general – can result in another type of awareness, namely awareness of problems in speaking. When a problem occurs it is likely to be accompanied by a feeling of wrongness, i.e. by activation of the AfS !harm! representation. This awareness of a problem could be followed either by an alternative formulation of the utterance, coming from the language module and necessarily produced unconsciously, or by the intervention of conceptual linguistic knowledge in CS. The latter could involve varying degrees of awareness.

Context and consolidation

If linguistic forms are to be used successfully, it is also important to consolidate their connections with contextual representations in CS. These connections are the indexes, and consolidating them means the same thing it means for the linguistic representations themselves: the indexes must be repeatedly activated. This is best accomplished through input that will activate both the linguistic forms and the contextual representations with which they are coindexed. In other words, processing of the forms in appropriate contexts is likely to produce the best results for consolidation.

Regarding the place of awareness in the consolidation of context, the same issues arise as those considered in the previous chapter regarding the initial establishment of the connections in perception. The CS representations that constitute context cannot themselves be the objects of consciousness, because they cannot reach the necessary activation levels. Awareness of them is instead a matter of direct awareness of perceptual representations that are coindexed with them and therefore coactivated with them. Awareness of context in consolidation is this indirect awareness of contextual CS representations that have already been coindexed with the given linguistic representations. As this awareness reflects strong activation of the representations and, most importantly, of the indexes connecting the linguistic and contextual representations, we should expect it to be related to the success of consolidation.

The one CS element that is directly part of conscious experience is the SELF representation, which is always highly active and therefore always present in awareness. It makes up a crucial part of internal context and so it is important for a discussion of consolidation of context. Consolidation of existing connections between SELF and linguistic representations means, as always, activation of the indexes that connect the representations, best accomplished through simultaneous activation of the linguistic representation and SELF. The extent of this activation, and therefore the extent of the consolidation that occurs, depends on the extent to which the self is involved in the language use. A stronger sense of involvement implies stronger consolidation. As awareness is a function of activation, we should expect awareness of self and its involvement to be related to successful consolidation.

Affect and value in consolidation

As affect and especially value are crucial elements in the successful use of linguistic forms, the consolidation of their connections to the linguistic representations is essential, particularly the indexes connecting linguistic representations to !val!. This consolidation occurs in the usual way, as a product of repeated activation of the indexes in processing. This means processing the linguistic forms in the context of suitable affect, particularly !val!; in other words, using the forms in processing that is in some sense positively valued. In Chapter 7, I discussed various ways that !val! can be activated in the context of language use, notable among them being success in communication. When that success activates !val!, linguistic representations that are still active will become coindexed with it or have existing connections with it strengthened, i.e. their resting activation levels will rise. Consolidation of linguistic knowledge, in contrast to the initial development of that knowledge, means activating connections (indexes) that already exist rather than establishing new ones.

Regarding the place of awareness in the consolidation process, the same considerations discussed in Chapter 7 apply here. The indexes were originally established through coactivation of representations in different stores, and they are consolidated by further coactivation. So awareness of consolidation is essentially the same phenomenon as awareness of initial learning.

Affect is not only an object of consolidation, though. It also plays an important role in consolidating other representations. In the extreme form, the presence of strong emotion during perception yields the 'flashbulb memories' (Brown & Kulik, 1977) commonly associated with dramatic events such as 9/11 or the assassination of President Kennedy. The emotion makes the memory especially strong and vivid. But such cases are not qualitatively distinct from ordinary memory; they represent the end of a continuum. Emotion strengthens a memory (see Chapter 2), and the stronger the emotion the stronger the facilitative effect. The presence of affect during perception is thus a kind of fast-track consolidation. Note that it makes perfect sense for the cognitive system to be built like this. Things that provoke a strong emotional response are things that are important to us and therefore things that we have reason to remember. Those which provoke little or no emotional response are things that do not matter and can therefore be ignored.

In MOGUL terms, affect influences consolidation because highly active AfS representations (which, by the nature of AfS, are *very* highly active) further activate the representations they are coindexed with, resulting in a greater increase in the resting levels of those representations. Awareness should be strongly but variably associated with this effect. Strength of emotion is based on the current activation level of an AfS representation, which, by the Activation Hypothesis, determines whether and to what extent we are aware of the emotion. The degree of consolidation that occurs is also a function of this activation level, so successful consolidation should be closely related to awareness of the affect that is experienced during language processing. In other words, if you feel good about the way you are using the language, you are probably making progress towards consolidation of your grammar.

The role of production in consolidation

Consolidation is a matter of activation, and existing representations are activated during production, so production is a means of consolidation. In other words, any representation that is used in production will, because of that use, have a slightly higher resting level afterwards, the extent of the increase reflecting the extent of the activation it undergoes during processing. A representation that comes to dominate a store should have a relatively substantial increase in its resting level as a result, while one that is only briefly and weakly activated will experience only very tiny changes. When two or more representations in different stores are used simultaneously, especially when one or both come to dominate their stores, the index(es) linking them will undergo the same increase in resting level.

These points suggest that output practice may be a good way to consolidate linguistic knowledge and is therefore a valuable part of language learning. A learner who uses the L2 in appropriate ways should have an advantage over one who does not. But 'appropriate ways' is important here. They should include contextualized use of language involving realistic communicative goals, with positive affect. Extensive output practice of this sort should be expected to have a positive influence on the general consolidation of linguistic knowledge. It is important to distinguish this general, communicative use of language from focused practice, which has the aim of trying to consolidate a selected aspect of the language. This is a different issue.

For development of the language module, the prospects for focused output practice appear to be poor. Given the unconscious nature of its representations, along with the complexity of the linguistic system and its connections to other modules and the limits of our current understanding of that system, the focused use of output practice as a way to consolidate representations in the language module can amount to groping in the dark. If you want to manipulate the contents of the black box for a particular purpose, you first have to understand those contents and the ways that they relate to the rest of the system. One lesson is that any use of production practice for the purpose of consolidation should be guided by what is known about language as it is represented in the human mind, not by pedagogical grammars or intuitive notions of how language works. Another is that, as far as development of the language module is concerned, we should not expect much from focused output practice at this time.

Consolidation of conceptual linguistic knowledge

To this point the discussion of consolidation has focused on the development of the language module and its connections to other stores. In this section, I turn to the other type of linguistic knowledge – extramodular.

The consolidation process

Extramodular linguistic knowledge is centred in CS, though an important aspect of this knowledge is connections to perceptual representations of the sound (AS) and spelling (VS) of linguistic items, primarily words. The CS representations are formed, as always, through a combination of existing representations, as described in the previous chapter. Consolidation of these representations occurs through repeated activation in processing. The more frequently and the more strongly they are activated, the more their resting levels will rise, which is to say the more successful their consolidation will be. In terms of representational Darwinism, these representations are selected over the huge number of less useful ones that are constantly being created in processing.

This selection process often has a significant role in the development of extramodular linguistic knowledge. A great many people have the CS representation ADJECTIVE, for example, typically established through explicit input. For those acquiring a language through formal instruction, such a representation could prove very useful in the instructional context, making its consolidation virtually certain. For those who encounter it only briefly, in regard to the grammar of their first language (L1; and probably find it quite boring), its usefulness will be relatively limited and its consolidation will therefore be limited as well.

More interesting, though, is the case of the L2 learner who repeatedly encounters concepts of this sort. Such learners are likely to also develop a number of more complex linguistic representations in CS, embodying rules or generalizations about the language, such as ADJECTIVE PRECEDE NOUN. Repeated use of such representations – in listening to lectures, doing exercises, deliberately producing sentences with this order or simply thinking about the language and the learning process – will gradually consolidate them. The extent to which students have learned the grammar, in the sense of acquiring knowledge *about* the language, is in part the extent to which they have consolidated such representations (the other part is restructuring). Consolidation of CS representations is in fact what grammar exercises are mainly about.

Consciousness and consolidation

Consciousness should be strongly associated with this process of consolidating extramodular linguistic knowledge. It is necessarily indirect awareness, because CS representations cannot themselves be the objects of consciousness. Awareness of them is thus awareness of perceptual (POpS) representations that are coindexed with them. Awareness of the conceptual representation ADJECTIVE is awareness of the auditory representation of the word *adjective*, or of a visual representation of its spelling, or perhaps a perceptual representation of some more idiosyncratic association that the individual speaker has with the concept. It can be strong and sustained or it can be simply a vague, fleeting awareness.

The presence and extent of the awareness should be directly related to the success of consolidation. Awareness of the AS representation of the word *adjective* implies that this perceptual representation is highly active, and this in turn is strongly associated with the activation level of the CS representation with which it is coindexed, ADJECTIVE. Consciousness of the sound is thus a good indication that the concept is being consolidated, and the extent of the consciousness is strongly related to the degree of consolidation. This relation should hold regardless of whether the concept is a relatively simple one (ADJECTIVE, for example) or a more complex generalization or rule.

Automatization as consolidation

I said above that automatization involving the language module is simply an example of consolidation. The same is true for conceptual linguistic knowledge, the only difference being that the latter more neatly fits the prototypical notion of automatization in that it typically involves a gradual loss of awareness. Automatization of conceptual knowledge, in general, is in fact exactly the type of case for which the notion was established.

Consolidation of implicitly acquired representations

In Chapter 7, I described the construction of new representations based on information that is perceived only implicitly. These representations, or 'low-quality traces', are constructed on the basis of very limited processing. They are therefore low quality in the sense that the processors may well have been unable to use the information as effectively as they would have if it had been more fully available. They are also low quality in the sense that this limited processing leaves them with very low resting activation levels, with the result that they can play only a small role in processing, affecting it mainly by priming other representations that are capable of a more substantial role. Memory consolidation offers the possibility of these representations coming to play a larger role in processing, through increases in their activation levels, and eventually achieving the indirect consciousness that characterizes more explicitly acquired conceptual representations.

As always, extramodular linguistic knowledge must be distinguished from modular linguistic knowledge. For the latter, there is little that is new to say here. Establishment and consolidation of representations in the language module are based entirely on implicitly perceived information. These representations are low quality only in the sense that their activation levels are relatively low. They are not low quality in the more literal sense, because the processors construct them by automatically processing very specific information in the input and using it in very constrained ways, for which they are innately specialized. The question of what happens to these implicitly acquired representations is simply the question of how the language module develops, as it has been explored throughout this chapter.

The more interesting question is the fate of implicitly created representations in CS. Many of these representations should receive at least some minimal stimulation during processing, possibly a great many times. The result should be a very slow rise in their resting activation level. If this process goes far enough, the possibility exists of these representations eventually becoming active enough to show in conscious experience. A CS representation cannot itself be conscious, but one that has been substantially consolidated in this way might well have conscious reflections in POpS. In other words, its activation will be associated with sufficiently strong activation of a coindexed perceptual representation for the latter to become conscious.

A possible example is conceptual knowledge of subject-verb inversion in English questions. A learner might process many interrogative sentences, in which the inverted order occurs, without any conscious awareness that this order represents a principle of English question formation. But this lack of awareness would not imply that the information is not represented in CS. It is quite possible that a representation of the generalization had been constructed but its activation level was initially quite low. Afterwards, it might be activated, and thereby consolidated, each time an instance of the inversion is processed. As its activation level gradually rises in this way, its influence on other processing increases, with an increasing likelihood that a POpS representation corresponding to it will be established and will at some point achieve an activation level sufficient for consciousness. The result could then be an 'aha' experience, in which the learner suddenly experiences a metalinguistic understanding of this aspect of the L2.

Context

Consolidation of contextual knowledge, as it relates to extramodular (CS) linguistic knowledge, is essentially the same process as consolidation of the linguistic knowledge itself. The knowledge that *moreover* is used in formal contexts, for example, is a composite CS representation consisting of a representation of the word (the concept of the word, more accurately) and FORMAL. Consolidation therefore consists of repeated use of this composite representation, resulting in gradual increases in its resting activation level. Unlike the case of modular linguistic knowledge, there is no issue of coindexation or coactivation of representations across stores. The fact that the consolidation occurs entirely in CS implies a more direct relation between awareness and the linguistic representations. Learners can be aware of the composite CS representation, in the usual sense of awareness via coindexed perceptual representations. And this awareness should be correlated with the success of the consolidation, as it implies that the CS representation achieved a high activation level.

Value and affect

Consolidation of associations with affect is a somewhat different matter, as these associations involve connections across stores, namely CS and AfS. Positive feelings about a particular word or construction are based on coindexation of a conceptual linguistic representation in CS with the !val! representation in AfS (or a larger affective representation that includes it), resulting in coactivation of the two. Consolidation is thus about processing in which both are activated simultaneously. In other words, it is about repeated use of the linguistic representation in ways that are positive to the person. We should expect consciousness to be strongly related to the success of this consolidation. If there is no awareness of the positive affect, this would imply that the activation of the AfS representation was relatively weak, while a clear awareness of the feeling would mean a high level of activation and therefore better prospects for consolidation of the index connecting it to the linguistic representation in CS. Awareness of the CS representation would mean that it was quite active, with the same favourable implications for consolidation.

The role of production

In the discussion of modular knowledge above, I suggested that production practice may be a useful means of consolidating linguistic knowledge but that this favourable conclusion probably does not apply to focused practice, i.e. the effort to practice particular, selected aspects of linguistic knowledge. If the goal is the development of extramodular knowledge and the ability to put it to use, though, the conclusion might be somewhat different. The central problem for intervention in consolidation in the language module is that the module has considerable inherent structure, what Corder (1967, based on Mager, 1961) called a 'built-in syllabus'. This structure is still poorly understood, creating obvious problems for efforts to intervene in its functioning.

Conceptual structure no doubt has its own inbuilt nature, but it is unlikely to be as constraining in regard to the development of language, since it did not come into existence for the purpose of constraining the possible forms that linguistic knowledge can take, as the language module did. CS is also much closer to awareness, and so we can make much better judgements about its contents – this particular black box is not nearly so black as the language module. So focused output practice as a means of consolidating linguistic knowledge appears to be at least somewhat more realistic when applied to extramodular knowledge than when applied to the module.

But in evaluating the potential benefits of production practice, we have to ask not only what should be practiced, but also what context the practice is and should be in – context in the broad sense that includes communicative goals. If these do not support the kind of practical use that we want to prepare students for, the value of the practice is doubtful, even if the right things are being practiced. This is to some extent manipulable, especially because a strong internal context can be reflected in conscious experience.

A final question is what affect is associated with the production practice, particularly regarding value. Activation of negative value during the practice will result in a lasting association between the linguistic forms and !harm!, which will discourage future use. This could well result, again, from practice that is not enjoyable and for which learners do not see practical value. But it should be possible to manipulate the affect that accompanies the practice, at least to some extent. Affect, particularly when it is relatively strong, is associated with awareness, enhancing the possibilities for such manipulation.

To summarize, while focused production practice is probably not a realistic possibility for intervening in memory consolidation in the language module, the prospects are better for the case of extramodular linguistic knowledge. Getting content, context and affect right is certainly a challenge, but as far as the development of extramodular linguistic knowledge is concerned, we should not dismiss the possibility that this can be achieved. At the same time, though, the limits of such knowledge, however consolidated it may be, should be recognized.

Conclusion

The primary conclusion from this exploration of consciousness and consolidation is the familiar one, that development of knowledge in the language module – consolidation in this case – involves awareness only peripherally. Development (consolidation) of extramodular linguistic knowledge is much more closely associated with consciousness, though here again the association is primarily an indirect one. An important note on this discussion is that a badly flawed grammar can be consolidated as well as an accurate grammar. Successful consolidation is a necessary part of successful language learning, but it is not sufficient. The other necessary element, restructuring, is the subject of the following section. These two aspects of learning, consolidation and restructuring, are intertwined. The conditions that lead to consolidation are to a large extent the same conditions that lead to restructuring, and the effects are not always clearly distinct.

Restructuring and Consciousness

In this section, I am concerned with the way that linguistic knowledge changes, both within the language module and outside it. I will begin with a general description of restructuring, as it is understood within the MOGUL framework. This will be followed by a more specific look at the way it occurs in the language module, considering not only linguistic representations but also the links between them and contextual and affective representations, as well as the possible role of production. I will then turn to restructuring as it applies to linguistic knowledge in CS.

At the beginning of this chapter, I noted that restructuring often has the effect of strengthening existing representations and making them more readily available for use in processing. It might therefore be seen, in a great many cases, as including consolidation, though I reserved this term for the more direct sort of strengthening, namely increases in a representation's resting level resulting from repeated use in processing. The restructuring form of strengthening, on the other hand, involves integration with other representations. This can mean inclusion in more complex representations that develop in the same store or it can mean connections, in the form of indexes, to representations in other stores. An example of the latter case is the chain of representations – PS, SS, CS and beyond – that comprise a word; activation of one results in activation of all the others. In either case, the representation is likely to be more available, more often, for use in processing, simply because its activation will follow from activation of the representations that are associated with it. This increased use will also result in consolidation proper, i.e. increases in its resting level.

The nature of restructuring

From the perspective I have adopted in this book, i.e. the MOGUL framework, restructuring is to be explained in terms of a single central principle, one that is familiar from research on memory, particularly on inaccuracies in memory. This is the principle that active representations influence each other, and can be synthesized. It is both a central feature of memory and a logical consequence of the MOGUL framework. The nature of a processor is to construct a legitimate representation – legitimate according to its own inbuilt principles. When two representations are active in a store and they can be legitimately combined in a reasonably straightforward way, the processor will do so (setting aside potential complications from the possible presence of additional active representations in that store).

This sort of combining is in fact a necessary element of cognition. There has to be a means of bringing together closely related information obtained at separate times. Different views of a person's face (or of any other object for that matter) must be stored as belonging to that one person. Information on the rules of chess must be combined with existing knowledge of chess, including the nature of the board and the pieces and any rules that have already been learned. This is, and has to be, the universal nature of memory. We could not function in the world if our memories consisted of vast numbers of isolated bits of information. New information that is brought in must be reconciled with existing information. This reconciliation is memory restructuring, and it is readily explained in terms of the most basic principle of processing – that processors seek to combine active representations in their stores.

The downside of this good process is that not all resulting combinations will be desirable. In Chapters 1 and 2, I briefly described the research on false memory. In the classic example (see Loftus, 1997, 2005; Frenda et al., 2011), Loftus showed participants pictures of an automobile accident and afterwards asked them leading questions about it, i.e. questions that would encourage them to add new, and false, information to what they had seen. She then found that this information was often incorporated in subsequent reports of the accident. The straightforward explanation for this phenomenon is that the original memory was active at the same time as the false information and could be readily combined with it, so the conceptual processor made a new composite representation that included both. In subsequent processing, this new representation competes with the old; its victory in the competition is the phenomenon of false memory. This is a variety of memory restructuring.

The traditional term 'restructuring' is in a sense misleading. Representations in general are combinations of simpler representations, and are constructed from those simpler representations during processing. Restructuring thus means constructing new combinations during processing, combinations which typically will closely resemble existing ones in terms of component representations. The original representation still remains afterwards and can compete with the new one in processing. It is therefore better to refer to restructuring of a memory store as a whole rather than restructuring of individual representations.

Restructuring of a store can be seen in terms of the representational Darwinism discussed in Chapter 4. As described there, learning is to a large extent a matter of selecting useful representations from a vast array of possibilities rather than a reshaping of representations to give them more appropriate forms. These possibilities consist of all the representations that were established during processing, each because it was useful for some particular input, not because it was a good fit for the target language more generally. The creation of this vast store of representations was thus, in a sense, a matter of accident. On the other hand, the creation of each new representation was strongly influenced by those that already existed, and most strongly by those that had proved most useful so far. Each was established as a combination of existing representations, and the components tend to be representations that have high resting levels, indicating that they have been found useful in past processing. Thus, the creation of a series of new representations might well be seen as a progressive refinement, reflecting (inconsistently) increased suitability for the task of dealing with the language. So restructuring is a reasonable way to think of the process, though it must be kept in mind that this is a somewhat abstract perspective.

Another necessary clarification involves the distinction between restructuring of existing representations and establishment of new representations in perception. This is only a loose, heuristic distinction, useful for breaking up a complex phenomenon but not to be taken too literally. Just as there is no clear line between perception and the higher-level processing that logically follows it, there is no clear line between establishing new representations and restructuring existing ones.

The restructuring process in the language module

In the discussion of consolidation in the language module, I used the examples of functional categories and words. I will return to these examples here to illustrate restructuring.

Functional categories and restructuring

The case of Num, as considered above for consolidation, provides a very simple example of restructuring. The existence of exceptional cases and noisy data in general can easily lead to a combination of Num with the feature value that is not appropriate for input in general. In Spanish, for example, adjectives typically follow nouns but a number of exceptions occur; early processing of one or more exceptional cases could result in the establishment of a Num+[weak] representation in SS. Restructuring then means combining Num with the more appropriate feature, [strong]. This more useful combination is then likely to be consolidated, at the expense of the alternative, in subsequent processing.

A more interesting example is the [+past] feature considered in the previous chapter. Establishing the combinations in which it occurs in the L2 can be a very complex process, as Lardiere's (2008) discussion makes clear. Combinations that are initially formed in perception, and have some value in future processing, are not likely to be fully adequate, or even very close to it. In other words, learning here is by no means a simple matter of forming representations that are appropriate for this aspect of the language and then consolidating them. The development of variations on already-established representations is an inevitable part of learning in such cases, at least if learning is to be successful. This restructuring process constantly interacts with consolidation. Some combinations created in restructuring will prove more useful than others and will therefore be gradually consolidated, at the expense of the less useful alternatives. This is, again, the representational Darwinism considered in previous chapters.

The same considerations apply to coindexation of the SS representations with PS and CS representations. These connections can vary across languages in quite complex ways and therefore are unlikely to be established in an adequate form in a single instance of input processing. Restructuring, again interacting with consolidation, must therefore extend to this coindexation, in addition to the purely SS-internal restructuring just described.

All of this restructuring must occur in the presence of well-established L1 representations that compete with the new L2 representations in processing. Whenever the L1 representations win the competition, their use blocks restructuring and consolidation of appropriate L2 representations. This situation poses probably the most serious challenge to learners' ultimate success. It does not rule out ultimate success, in the sense of native-like proficiency, but if such success is achieved it is likely to be only after very many years of intensive experience with the language, and there are no guarantees no matter how much time and effort goes into the learning process.

Word meanings and restructuring

The other example I will consider of SS-based restructuring is the assignment of meanings to L2 words, further pursuing the discussion of consolidation of word meanings above. Word meanings, again, are CS representations that are coindexed with PS representations giving the sound of the words and SS representations giving their morphosyntactic aspects, along with extensions of the chains into AfS, AS, VS and other perceptual modules. Acquisition of word meanings is a combination of restructuring the CS representations that constitute the meanings and restructuring the SS representations to assign appropriate indexes connecting them to the CS representations. As in the case of functional categories, L2 acquisition begins with well-established cross-store connections among the representations that constitute L1 words, including the CS representations that constitute their meanings. The indexes that constitute these connections typically have high resting levels, as do the CS representations that are the word meanings, though this level varies with the frequency of the word and how often the concept is used independently of the word. These strong representations, with their strong connections to SS, will compete with any new L2 representations for use in processing, as was the case for the Num example. Successful learning means both connecting the SS representations to CS representations that are more appropriate for the meanings of the L2 words and restructuring CS to *make* representations that are more appropriate for those meanings.

At one extreme are cases in which the necessary concept is entirely absent prior to learning the L2 word. An example of a concept that exists in speakers of one language but probably not in those of another is the idea expressed by the Chinese word *xuejie* (literally 'study older sister'), which can be translated as 'fellow student or ex-student in the same institution who is older and is female'. For Chinese speakers this is a routinely used word, and we can safely assume that they all possess the concept. While we cannot rule out the possibility that at least some monolingual English speakers also possess this concept, it seems unlikely that it could be a standard part of conceptual structure for English speakers. Those who learn Chinese must construct it from its component features (representations), which they certainly do possess already. This constitutes restructuring of CS; the involvement of the language module is the coindexing of this new representation with the PS/SS of the new word.

At the other extreme are cases in which the L2 word has a meaning that is for all practical purposes identical to that of an already known L1 word. Among the clearest examples are numbers and names for days of the week. In such cases, restructuring is a relatively simple matter of adding the index of this existing concept to the new L2 word, which is inseparable from comprehension of the word, because comprehension *is* activation of the appropriate CS representation(s). When this representation is active at the same time as the PS/SS of the new L2 word, its index will automatically be placed on that SS.

The more common situation is that in which the meaning of the new L2 word is very similar to that of an existing L1 word but significant differences exist. In these cases, restructuring involves both adding the index of the L1 CS to the new L2 word and restructuring CS to make that representation more suitable. As an example, consider the case of *wear* and its Chinese counterparts. Simplifying a bit, Chinese has two common words that translate as *wear – chuan*, used for basic articles of clothing, and *dai*, used for belts, hats, glasses and such.

When a Chinese speaker learns the English word through exposure to it in context, the PS/SS of *wear* will become coindexed with whichever of the Chinese meanings (for convenience, call them DAI and CHUAN) fits the observed use, because this CS representation will be active. So *wear* might initially be treated as equivalent to *chuan* if the learner's first encounter with *wear* involves a shirt, for example. Additional experience in which *wear* is applied to a hat, for instance, is likely to add the index of DAI to the new PS/SS. If DAI and CHUAN are simultaneously activated in future processing, further restructuring of CS is likely, yielding a composite representation that includes both meanings and so more closely approximates the actual meaning of *wear*. This combination would occur simply because the conceptual processor, like all processors, always seeks to make a unified representation from whatever is currently active in its store. Simultaneous activation of the two CS representations could occur in ordinary input processing or if the learner is told that *wear* has both of those meanings.

An English speaker learning one of the Chinese counterparts of *wear*, *dai* for example, is likely to initially coindex the newly established PS/SS of *dai* with the CS representation (call it WEAR) that is already established as the meaning of the English word, i.e. is coindexed with the PS/SS of *wear*. The natural result is overuse of *dai*: the learner uses it in contexts in which it is appropriate and also in contexts in which *chuan* should be used. Subsequent exposure to *chuan* in a context that makes it comprehensible could result in the establishment of a new PS/SS for it and coindexing of these representations with WEAR, the result being that the two L2 words are wrongly treated as synonyms. Separation of the two meanings might eventually occur through ordinary input processing. Individual words naturally become associated with features of the situations in which they are encountered, such as the fact that glasses were the topic of conversation, simply because they are active at the same time. The features that are associated with *dai* and *chuan* will overlap but will be distinct. With continued processing, these distinct features become more strongly associated with the respective words (the CS representations that include both the word and the contextual features acquire higher activation levels). In production, the word that more closely matches the context will thus have an advantage in the competition with the other, an advantage that will gradually increase with further processing of input. The result, hopefully, is that the learner will eventually come to use *dai* in contexts that include belts, hats, glasses, etc. and *chuan* in contexts that include basic articles of clothing.

This restructuring does not entail any awareness on the part of the learner. But a more explicit restructuring is also possible. This is in fact a case in which explicit processing could well be of value for the learner. Being explicitly told that *dai* is only used with particular items (or consciously drawing that conclusion without being explicitly told) can certainly result in potentially useful conceptual knowledge, in CS. Its effect on connections to the SS and PS representations of the words is more uncertain. If the CS representations BELT, HAT and GLASSES are active at the same time as the PS and SS representations of *dai*, they could become more strongly associated with that PS/SS combination. Awareness of these CS representations is an indication that they are especially active and that this favourable development is therefore more likely.

Consciousness and restructuring in the language module

Regarding consciousness in the restructuring of functional categories, the situation is essentially the same as that described in the discussions of perception and consolidation as these processes apply to the language module. There is no possibility of awareness of the functional category representations in SS or of the restructuring process. If the restructuring is based on a perceptual input representation, awareness of that representation is important, but any higher level of awareness, of the representation's linguistic significance in particular, would not be relevant. Restructuring involving indexes that connect the functional category to meanings – CS representations – can be a step closer to awareness, as these representations of meaning can be directly connected to POpS representations and so can become indirect objects of awareness. But in regard to SS, this awareness is simply an indication that some sort of restructuring occurred, nothing more specific than that.

Turning to word meaning, in all the cases considered here restructuring in the language module is a matter of coindexing PS/SS representations of linguistic forms with CS representations of the meanings of those forms. This coindexing necessarily involves significant activation of the CS representations. It is not clear whether this activation has to be substantial enough to entail indirect awareness of the representations via direct awareness of their perceptual counterparts. But it is reasonably clear that such awareness should be strongly related to successful coindexing. This conclusion fits well with N. Ellis's (1994b) argument that learning of word meaning is to a large extent an explicit process. Once again, the awareness could well include an input representation containing the information used for the restructuring. The PS/SS forms that participate in the coindexing are of course unconscious.

Restructuring of context

Contextual representations and their connections to linguistic representations are involved in essentially all language use. Each instance of language processing thus creates opportunities for changes in linguistic context, i.e. restructuring. This is fortunate, since the one initial context of acquisition is not likely to be sufficient. For representations in the language module, restructuring of context is actually indistinguishable from restructuring of meaning, because meaning and context are themselves inseparable, both being primarily the CS representations with which linguistic representations are coindexed. Thus, there is relatively little to say that is new here.

The exception is the case of SELF, the most important and most consistently relevant contextual representation. Virtually any representation, from the time it is first established, will have some connection to SELF, because SELF is active all the time and so is likely to get coindexed, directly or indirectly, with virtually all new representations. Changes that occur in the relation of linguistic representations to SELF are thus in the strength of the connections, which is a matter of consolidation rather than restructuring. But there is another, very different way in which relations between self and language can change: the SELF representation itself can change, or a new, L2 SELF can develop alongside the basic self (for relevant discussion, with references, see Mitchell & Myles, 2004, Chapter 8). Changes in SELF might allow a coindexing with L2 linguistic representations that would not otherwise occur. A Western woman learning Japanese, for example, might find some aspects of 'women's speech' inconsistent with her normal identity. If the motivation to speak Japanese in a native-like manner is sufficiently strong, the result could be adjustments in her SELF. Or she might develop a special Japanese identity for appropriate occasions while retaining her original SELF for the rest of her activities.

A variant of this case is one in which a normally confident, outgoing person adopts a quiet, humble identity in the L2 as a result of feeling inadequate in L2 ability and/or ability to deal with the environment in which the new language is spoken. This new L2 SELF could well be just transitional, losing its reason to exist once the person becomes more adept at dealing with the L2 and the environments in which it is used. The opposite development is also possible, namely a gradual consolidation of the L2 SELF and its increasing dominance, at the expense of the original SELF.

For my purposes, the central issue is the association between these various changes and awareness. It seems likely that the development of a new SELF or substantial adjustments in the basic SELF would involve some degree of awareness, though the possibility of largely unconscious changes should not be ruled out, especially if the changes are very gradual. This general issue would make an interesting research question, as would more specific questions regarding exactly what the learners might be aware of.

Affect and value in restructuring

Activity in AfS is a constant element of all perceptual processing, so any linguistic representations established on the basis of input will have affect, particularly value, associated with them, i.e. they will be coindexed, directly or indirectly, with representations in AfS, notably with !val! and/or !harm!. Additional experiences with the language and its forms always come with associated affect as well, and this affect may or may not be consistent with the original associations. If it is consistent, the effect of this additional experience is to further consolidate those associations, i.e. to raise the activation levels of the indexes connecting the linguistic forms to AfS representations. If it is not consistent, new indexes are added to the linguistic representations, connecting them to different affective representations. As the indexes themselves are representations, this addition is the creation of new composite representations, and so this is an example of restructuring.

What all this means for the practice of L2 learning and teaching is that affect probably never loses its importance in L2 experience. Negative attitudes towards the language and its acquisition cannot simply be erased, but they can be overwhelmed by subsequent positive experience. Likewise for particular elements of the language. Those that initially became coindexed with !harm! as a result of their use in unpleasant contexts can become more strongly coindexed with !val! if they are subsequently used in ways that are positive to the person. As these positive connections become stronger than their negative counterparts (indexes with !val! come to have higher resting levels than those with !harm!), affect can come to support language use rather than hinder it. This restructuring is associated with consciousness in that the more active the affective representations are, the more likely they are to be conscious and the stronger their connections to linguistic representations will be.

Positive affective connections can also be overwhelmed by subsequent negative experience, sometimes with good consequences. The bad cases are of course those in which initially positive experience with the language and its forms is replaced by negative experience, as when a beginning language class that is valued by a learner is followed by a class that he/she does not value, or when a learner who initially enjoys communicating in the L2 then experiences an embarrassing failure to communicate. Positive cases, on the other hand, involve linguistic elements that should not be part of the learner's standard repertoire – including aspects of non-target dialects, or simply errors – but have been inappropriately associated with !val!. Subsequent experience can result in their being associated with !harm!.

With consolidation of this connection and appropriate alternative forms, they might gradually become irrelevant for L2 processing. This restructuring, like that in which !val! comes to dominate !harm!, is strongly associated with consciousness, and for exactly the same reason.

Awareness is naturally present in affective restructuring, specifically awareness of the affect. Affect associated with an activity – enjoyment or boredom, for example – becomes connected to whatever linguistic representations are active during that activity, for better or for worse. The stronger the awareness of the affect the higher the activation level of the AfS representation and therefore the more strongly the connection is being made. Thus, meaningful restructuring of affective connections is likely to involve awareness of the affect, though the possibility certainly exists of restructuring occurring in the absence of such awareness. Awareness of the linguistic forms in the language module is, as always, not a possibility, so affective restructuring of modular knowledge can only involve awareness of affect.

The role of production in restructuring

Processors do not operate any differently when they are producing language than when they are comprehending it, so production can in principle be a source of restructuring. But it is not a good source. If learning is to be at all successful, comprehension must play the main role in restructuring because it provides information about the nature of the language, information which the processors must deal with. Input carries information, for example, on how the features that make up functional categories are bundled in the language, and this information can exert strong pressure on SS for use of appropriate bundles. In production, on the other hand, the actual nature of the language does not constrain activity in SS – all that is available is the current state of the mental grammar. As a result, changes in the content of SS during production are unlikely. If they do occur, they might not be beneficial.

One implication is that general communicative output practice does not have the value for restructuring that it has for consolidation. Focused output practice is no more promising as a means of intervention in the restructuring process, for the same reasons considered in regard to consolidation.

Restructuring of conceptual linguistic knowledge

There is rich potential for restructuring in CS, because CS does not have the linguistic, UG-based constraints that characterize the language module, and so the range of extramodular linguistic representations that can be constructed in CS is virtually unlimited. But it is these UG constraints that are responsible for high levels of success in language learning, so rich potential in this case is not an entirely good thing. It does mean that extramodular knowledge can in principle be improved indefinitely, but in the absence of UG guidance it is very much *in principle*.

As an example of restructuring in CS, consider the learning of English tense forms. A learner might initially develop a CS representation of the information that a particular form, *-ed*, means past. Additional input, possibly through formal instruction, could then result in the creation of a more complex representation, including the information that this form can also indicate politeness, for example. Further input could then produce further changes, yielding a more complex representation that gives the form additional meanings or restricts its uses – indicating that it does not apply to the cases covered by perfect forms, for instance.

As in this example, the restructuring is most naturally conscious in the sense that learners are likely to have indirect awareness of the conceptual linguistic representations. It might be too much to say that such awareness is strictly necessary for restructuring of conceptual linguistic knowledge, but then a claim of this sort might not be too far off the mark.

Restructuring context

In the case of linguistic representations in CS, context consists of additional CS representations that are combined with them. So restructuring here means combining two or more existing conceptual representations. This process, occurring entirely within CS, is closer to POpS and therefore to consciousness than is the process of coindexing modular representations with CS representations of context (or meaning). We should thus expect to find a much greater involvement of consciousness in the development of context for extramodular than modular knowledge. It is still, however, the indirect sort of awareness repeatedly discussed in regard to conceptual processing. This awareness, of form and context, should be strongly related to the success of the restructuring.

Affect and value in conceptual restructuring

I said above that in affective restructuring of modular linguistic knowledge, the only awareness is of the affective representations. Affective restructuring of conceptual linguistic knowledge, on the other hand, might well involve indirect awareness of the forms, in addition to awareness of the affect. Such restructuring is a matter of assigning alternative indexes connecting conceptual linguistic representations in CS to AfS representations. Awareness of the CS representations – indirect, as always – is quite feasible and should correlate with the extent to which the restructuring is effective.

The role of production

As described above, production practice is unlikely to have much value for restructuring in the language module, whether it is focused practice or general communicative use of the language. For communicative use, the same conclusion applies to conceptual linguistic knowledge, for largely the same reasons. For focused production activities, the situation is more complex. Such activities are designed by teachers or textbook writers to encourage accurate use of forms that the learner has not yet mastered. Given the relatively unrestricted nature of conceptual linguistic knowledge, production practice of this sort might result in adjustments in CS that match, to some extent, the intentions of their designers. Success should be related to learners' awareness of the forms, made possible by the fact that they are in CS rather than the language module. Possible limitations of this sort of activity come from the challenges of dealing appropriately with affect and context, as described above. Thus, restructuring extramodular knowledge through production practice might be feasible, though getting it right is challenging and results should therefore be inconsistent. I believe this prediction fits well with the findings of research on pushed output.

Conclusion

Linguistic representations, like other representations, are established in perception, as an integral part of the process of making sense of (representing) input. The topic of this chapter has been what happens after a representation or set of representations has been established, i.e. once it is a part of memory; in other words, what effect subsequent processing can have on the new representations. Two kinds of things can happen: (a) they can be strengthened by further use, becoming more solidly present in memory and more influential in processing, and (b) their position in the store, as well as the store itself, can be altered. Thus, I divided the discussion into the two topics of consolidation and restructuring, while recognizing that this division is somewhat arbitrary.

Paradoxically, restructuring is a natural consequence of the process by which a representation is consolidated, a point that has been noted in the neural literature (e.g. Hupbach et al., 2007). Consolidation relies on reactivation, but reactivation is inherently destabilizing, as active representations are exactly those that are vulnerable to alteration, simply because their elevated activation level makes them available for use by processors.

The place of consciousness in consolidation and restructuring depends crucially on the distinction between modular and extramodular linguistic knowledge. Representations in PS and SS constitute the heart of linguistic knowledge, underlying the great bulk of successful language use, and so their status is the central issue. These representations cannot be conscious and so consolidation and restructuring in these stores are by necessity largely unconscious processes. Their connections, direct and indirect, to representations outside the module are another matter, though. The connections I considered involve conceptual representations of meaning and context, including the SELF context, and affective representations in AfS.

Consolidation and restructuring of these connections involve consciousness to the extent that these associated representations can be conscious.

Linguistic representations in CS, in contrast to those in PS and SS, lend themselves to the indirect but important sort of awareness, via coindexed perceptual representations, that is commonly found with conceptual representations. Consolidation and restructuring here can and typically do involve this type of awareness, in regard to both the linguistic representations themselves and their connections. Conceptual linguistic knowledge plays a very secondary role in language learning and use, and so the emphasis should be placed on development within the language module and the connections between its representations and those found outside the module. But it is worthwhile to consider the possibilities and limitations of conscious – explicit – L2 learning as well.

Notes

(1) One intriguing aspect of the topic will only be mentioned here: the role of sleep. Research has established that consolidation and restructuring go on during sleep, and this would appear to be crucial (see Diekelmann & Born, 2010; Walker & Stickgold, 2006). But current understanding of the phenomena is still limited.

(2) The neural literature sometimes draws a distinction between consolidation and reconsolidation. My use of the term 'consolidation' corresponds to the latter.

9 Conclusion: Consciousness in Second Language Learning

In Chapter 1, I described two views of human nature, based on fundamentally differing views of the place of consciousness in it. One view sees people as essentially conscious creatures, downplaying any role of unconscious processes, while the other prefers to put consciousness in a more humble role, emphasizing the importance of the unconscious. The two views were presented in a somewhat exaggerated form, suggesting a sharper line than usually exists. Most of us are willing to grant meaningful roles to both conscious and unconscious processes. But the difference in emphasis, and of course detail, is real and important.

It is not difficult to see the influence of these two views in second language acquisition (SLA), and in language teaching in practice, one view pointing to a strong concern with conscious understanding of language, the other to a downplaying of such awareness in favour of a greater reliance on a natural, realistic experience with the language. And, again, this is typically not an all-or-nothing matter. Nearly everyone recognizes, in one form or another, that both conscious and unconscious processes are important. Schmidt, who is strongly associated with the view that consciousness is central in learning, has always been open to the possibility that implicit learning also plays an important role. For Krashen, who is strongly associated with unconscious acquisition, awareness of the input and its meaning is essential, conscious efforts to obtain appropriate input and to comprehend it have obvious value and knowledge that is consciously learned does have a role to play in language use, if only a limited one.

In disagreements about the place of consciousness, the central issue is awareness of the particular aspects of the language that are being acquired. For those who favour conscious processes, such awareness is at the very least highly valuable and is more likely essential. The logical implication is that instruction should at least draw learners' attention to formal features and possibly seek to give them a conscious understanding of those features. Proponents of unconscious acquisition are inclined to say that such awareness has little value.

The popularity of the two views has varied over the years. My own feeling is that too much emphasis is now being placed on explicit approaches to learning – and too much faith is being expressed in their effectiveness. Consciousness must be given its due, but unconscious processes deserve centre stage. In what follows, I will summarize the view that emerges from the discussion in this book, namely that (a) second language (L2) learning is primarily unconscious; (b) consciously learned knowledge can nonetheless contribute to language use; and (c) conscious processes can support unconscious learning. I will then conclude the chapter, and the book, with some general observations.

Second Language Learning is Primarily an Unconscious Process

Representations in the language module, because of the limited activation levels they achieve, can never be conscious. Since these representations and their connections constitute the heart of linguistic knowledge, for first language and L2, the natural conclusion is that language learning is primarily an unconscious process. When we are aware of linguistic knowledge as such, it is necessarily conceptual representations, in conceptual structures (CS), associated with consciousness by virtue of their connections to perceptual representations of sound and written form.

On this modular view of language, knowledge that is acquired consciously (i.e. with awareness of that knowledge) is fundamentally distinct from the core linguistic knowledge that comprises the language module, and remains forever separate from it. This is in an important sense a 'non-interface' position. Below, I will suggest that explicitly acquired knowledge interacts with modular knowledge in language use and I will consider the various ways in which it might also influence the development of the language module.

The conclusion that L2 learning is primarily unconscious is supported by the extensive empirical research examining the effects of grammar instruction, in all its varied forms, on the development of L2 knowledge and ability. As described in Chapter 6, such instruction is quite valuable for the development of knowledge that can be used in contexts which allow and, especially, encourage a conscious focus on it. But the findings indicate that it has little value for communicative language use, the type of activity that can offer insights into the state of the language module. The appropriate conclusion again is that the language module, the heart of linguistic knowledge, develops in an essentially unconscious manner.

Consciously Learned Knowledge can Contribute to Language Use

There is no disagreement over the point that consciously learned knowledge can play a role in language use – both comprehension and production – and it is difficult to see how there could be disagreement. The interesting questions are the extent of that role and the processes underlying it.

I will begin with the processes. How exactly does conceptual linguistic knowledge, in CS, influence language comprehension and production? Consider first the comprehension side. Suppose that CS contains representations of the features of the English passive, for example, naturally including the overt cues to it, namely the *be-en* forms and *by*. When a person hears a passive sentence, the resulting perceptual representation of the sentence, in auditory structures (AS), may contain those cues as component representations. If so, they will activate the CS representation PASSIVE, which will then influence the CS processing that seeks to establish a meaning for the input sentence, simply because the conceptual processor works with whatever representations are currently active. The result might then be the construction of a meaning that reflects the person's conceptual knowledge of the passive, treating the subject as the underlying object. This could occur even if the language module cannot, at this stage of development, process the sentence as passive, illustrating the possible benefits of consciously acquired knowledge.

The key here is the direct connections between perceptual output structures (POpS), where the sound or written form of the input sentence is represented, and CS, where the conceptual linguistic knowledge is found and where the meaning of a sentence is constructed. This is a direct path from sound to meaning and conceptual analysis, which can be used as a supplement to the basic route through the language module.

This supplemental path can also be used in the opposite direction, i.e. for production. The first step in any instance of production is the activation or construction of a conceptual representation of the meaning to be expressed. This active representation will trigger activity in the language module to construct corresponding syntactic and phonological representations, the latter serving as the basis for the articulation of output, and will also be reflected in auditory structures (AS) activity. But the activation of the CS representation can also spread within CS to conceptual linguistic representations, if they share any features with it, say, PLURAL. Their activation will influence activity in AS, which will then influence phonological structures (PS) activity (and, again, be influenced by it). The result is two streams of processing:

(a) modular: CS → SS → PS → articulation;
(b) extramodular: CS → AS → PS → articulation.

The two converge at PS and so the representation constructed there – the input to articulatory mechanisms – will be influenced by both. The extramodular route might, for example, be able to insert a final –s on a noun, marking plural, if the language module, in its current state, failed to do so.

The relative influence of the two streams should vary greatly, reflecting the state of both the language module and conceptual linguistic knowledge, as well as the particular circumstances of the speech act. Consider an extreme case. If I consciously learn a few words of some language along with some basic rules of word order, I can produce a sentence or two in that language (quite possibly an ungrammatical one, probably with horrendous pronunciation, all of which is besides the point), even though I have had no opportunity for any unconscious acquisition. In this case, the language module has essentially nothing to work with apart from the first language, so the final form of the utterance, particularly its morphosyntactic form, should be a reflection of consciously acquired conceptual linguistic knowledge. At the other extreme, very successful modular development and/or very weak conceptual linguistic knowledge should result in utterances that show little or no influence from the latter.

This analysis of the role of consciously learned knowledge in language use does not logically imply awareness of any of the representations that are involved. Awareness is, however, a function of the activation level, which is the main determinant of how much influence there will be, so the possibility of a conceptual influence on the output should be strongly correlated with awareness of the activity in that stream.

From a theoretical standpoint, it thus makes sense that consciously learned knowledge can influence language use. But there is nothing in the discussion to this point to indicate how great the influence will be, or how much it will be affected by the situation in which the language use occurs. There is in fact little theoretical basis for a judgment on these matters. We can imagine the effect being anywhere from negligible to quite strong (recall the discussion of N. Ellis' theory in Chapter 6). But the empirical basis for a judgement is reasonably solid. The evidence described in Chapter 6 indicates that consciously learned knowledge has very large effects on production in artificial tasks in which the application of that knowledge is the focus, but has little effect on communicative performance. While the theoretical significance of the interactions is considerable, for practical purposes they are probably of only limited interest.

However, it should be added that communicative ability is not always the goal of teaching or learning. If the learner's goal is to be able to use the language in very controlled ways, then consciously learned knowledge may have considerable value. Controlled uses could include, for example, very limited forms of communication, as might be important in travel or performance on formal tests.

Conscious Processes Support Unconscious Learning

Language learning is primarily unconscious, in the sense that awareness of the formal features of the language has only limited value. But, again, this does not mean that conscious processes are unimportant. In the previous section, I suggested that they can contribute to language use. In this section, I am concerned with their possible effects on the development of the language module, including the effects of both conscious processing and the conceptual products of that processing. Conscious processing includes the planning and management of learning.

Awareness of perceptual representations

Conscious perception is clearly important for modular development. When a person is speaking in the target language but the learner is unaware of the utterances, this 'input' will not be of any value. When the learner's gaze passes over the words on a page while he/she consciously thinks of other things, no development will result. Consciousness in this respect is necessary for modular development. However, an essential clarification, is that the necessary awareness is of the input representations in themselves, not of follow-up representations specifically of the information that is to be incorporated in the module.

If awareness of perceptual input representations is important, the possibility exists, at least in principle, of conscious processes making those representations better suited to contribute to modular development. This is input enhancement, discussed in Chapter 7. The cases in which it is most likely to be meaningful in regard to the language module are those in which input representations are routinely impoverished in such a way that they lack information which could be important for modular development. A good example is the case in which final consonants that are essential for the acquisition of English tense are absent from AS representations, possibly as a result of influence from the first language. The more common type of enhancement, aimed at making existing features of the input representation more salient, may be useful for conceptual linguistic learning but is not likely to be of value for the language module.

Awareness in the development and use of conceptual representations

Consciously acquired conceptual knowledge can also aid comprehension and might thereby contribute to modular development. During the processing that constitutes comprehension of input, the construction of appropriate representations in syntactic structures (SS) is inevitably influenced by the representations constructed in CS, which constitute the meaning of the input, because the SS/CS interface coordinates the activation levels of coindexed representations in the two stores. Thus, if the learner can use conceptual linguistic knowledge to determine the meaning of an utterance – i.e. to construct an appropriate CS representation for it – the construction of appropriate SS representations might be more likely. If consciously acquired conceptual knowledge can be used to improve comprehension, it can also be used to improve production, with the additional possibilities of benefits for modular development. In particular, such knowledge can be used to make the output more accurate. The grammatically improved utterances might then serve as useful input to the language module. Available evidence, however, suggests that the theoretical possibilities described here may be little more than that: there does not appear to be any substantial effect of conceptual linguistic knowledge on modular development (see Chapter 6).

Awareness in the establishment of the language module's external connections

Another way in which conscious processes might support unconscious learning is in the establishment of connections between representations in the language module and those in other modules, particularly CS, constituting the meanings of the linguistic items. This process necessarily involves activation of the representations that are to be connected (coindexed). Those in the language module will never reach levels sufficient for awareness, but indirect awareness of the conceptual representations via their perceptual counterparts is a possibility. This indirect awareness of the meanings should be related to success, and quite possibly necessary for it, as its absence would suggest that the CS representations were not especially active. The very important limitation here is that there is no way to know what representations are active in the language module and so no way to know which are being connected to the active conceptual representations. So the indirect conceptual awareness, while important and possibly necessary, cannot provide any assurances that anything positive is occurring in regard to the language module. Any awareness of what the conceptual representations are being connected to is awareness of representations in AS or visual structures (VS), and possibly others in CS.

Planning and managing second language learning

An area in which consciousness is clearly important is the planning and management of learning. There is presumably no implicit module that tells learners how to go about these things, so they are naturally and necessarily done in a largely explicit way. It is possible to suggest ways to carry them out on the basis of the view of language and learning taken throughout this book, along with more general considerations.

The most basic consideration is goals. If the learning is to be planned and managed effectively, this must be done in terms of what the learner wants to accomplish. The goals might be, for example, to communicate through the spoken language, to read a particular type of material in that language, to blend into the L2 culture, to pass a particular test or any combination of these and other goals, with different priorities for each. These goals might be set by the individual learner or by others, such as teachers, parents or educational systems at the national or local level. In any case, decisions of this sort fall very much in the domain of conscious processes.

Closely related is the topic of learning strategies, which received considerable research attention in the past but appears to have fallen on hard times. A learning strategy, as the idea is usually understood, is very much a way to use conscious thought to guide learning. The use of such strategies could in principle be of great value, though I personally have always found this literature befuddling. It contains a huge assortment of strategies, varying greatly with the particular author, and classified in a variety of overlapping and conflicting ways that do not always make sense to me. On the other hand, individual learners and teachers who are not overly concerned about such general issues might be able to select ideas from this literature that are of value to them.

Also crucial is the problem of maintaining motivation, or of finding ways to keep going in the face of sometimes flagging motivation. This can mean setting up a regular schedule and establishing constructive habits. It can mean rewards for sticking to the schedule. Maybe the most important element, though, is making learning as enjoyable as it reasonably can be, through the intelligent selection of materials and tasks, i.e. finding those that are interesting and challenging but not overly difficult. Another way of making learning enjoyable is by sharing it with a partner or partners who have similar goals, an arrangement that can have additional benefits as well. In Modular Online Growth and Use of Language (MOGUL) terms, these various strategies are about establishing and maintaining or strengthening connections between !val! in affective structures (AfS) and the goal representation in CS. Again, they are best handled with conscious planning, monitoring and troubleshooting.

Another interesting aspect of motivation, which has received little if any attention in this context, is the traditional idea of willpower, which is undergoing a rebirth in social psychology (Baumeister & Tierney, 2011). As briefly described in Chapter 2, there is considerable evidence that people can deliberately enhance their willpower and learn how to use it more effectively. A crucial aspect of this use is the automatization of will in particular applications, such as dieting or studying. Making decisions automatic reduces or removes the need for a constant conscious focus on what should be done. But this automatization is achieved through the use of deliberate, conscious processes.

Based on the view of language learning presented in this book, the primary focus of learning activities should be on getting extensive experience with the language, especially extensive input of a type and in a manner that allow a reasonable level of comprehension (cf. Krashen's comprehensible input). This experience should be acquired in realistic contexts that are reasonably well matched with contexts in which the person wants to use the language in the future. Additionally, it should be acquired in a manner that encourages positive affect (value) and engages SELF. Finding and identifying the materials and activities that are best suited for particular learners in particular contexts with particular goals is very much a conscious activity. This selection will inevitably involve a trade-off between comprehensibility and authenticity. Material that is completely natural is likely to be quite difficult for learners; material that is readily comprehensible may well have acquired its comprehensibility through sacrifices in authenticity. Finding an appropriate balance is, again, a conscious function.

Conclusion

While explicit knowledge of language form has a very secondary role in language learning, it can, at least in principle, have effects. Other types of awareness, particularly of perceptual input representations and of the representations involved in the planning and management of learning, are of much greater significance.

Some Final Thoughts

In this final section, I want to close with a few observations about the topics of this book and the state of the field.

On views of consciousness and human nature

We are simultaneously conscious creatures, using conscious processes to manage our lives in (relatively) rational, controlled ways, and unconscious creatures, necessarily relying on unconscious processes for most of what we do in our lives. Both these aspects of our nature must be given their due, the interesting questions being exactly how and to what extent each is relevant in particular types of cases. For language learning, first and second, the unconscious side takes centre stage, at least if the learning is to be successful.

On innateness and modularity

Any discussion of consciousness and learning must deal with the issue of modularity, and with the specific form that the modularity question takes in language learning. Is there a language module and/or a number of smaller linguistic modules? If so, to what extent and in what ways is it tied up with our genetic endowment? A problem I have with much of the SLA literature related to consciousness is that it tends to assume the 'nothing special' view of language, according to which language and its development can be understood without reference to specifically linguistic principles. Perhaps more disturbingly, this assumption tends to be made without any acknowledgement that it *is* a theoretical assumption, one that can be challenged.

The innateness issue is often presented in an exaggerated form, suggesting differences that are much more stark than is actually the case. Most importantly, there is no genuine issue of whether language learning is controlled by genes or by the environment. Everything we are and everything we do represents an interaction of the two. Those who emphasize the genetic aspects have to recognize that the role of genes in the brain's development is not nearly so straightforward as the popular 'blueprint' metaphor would suggest (see Chapter 2). For the case of language, it is very unlikely that our genes contain a precise specification of each feature of the language module. Those features develop as a complex interaction of the specifically linguistic influences with everything else that is going on as the brain develops, and much of the module's structure can no doubt be attributed to the same genes that underlie the development of other modules.

It should also be emphasized that universal grammar (UG) has never been claimed to cover more than a relatively small, 'core' part of the things we call 'language'. The essential point is that this core serves as the foundation for the successful acquisition of a language as a whole. In MOGUL terms, the function of UG is to ensure the existence of PS and SS, with the principles of combination and well-formedness that comprise the phonological and syntactic processors and the primitives with which the processors work. The set of representations established in SS and PS is necessarily quite rich, if the person is to be competent in the language, but the great majority of language-related representations are found elsewhere. Meanings and contexts reside in CS, associated emotions and values in AfS, sounds and written forms in POpS and motor representations in motor structures (MS), to say nothing of the potentially rich conceptual linguistic knowledge found in CS.

Establishing contents of PS and SS that respect the UG-based principles and account for the input received by the learner is a substantial task. The majority of language learning, however, consists of the development of connections between PS/SS and representations outside the core, and most of these representations are themselves shaped to varying degrees by their association with the language being acquired. This learning is not itself a UG matter, but it depends very much on the existence and proper development of PS and SS, which depend on UG. All of this learning is, once more, the interaction of genetic influences with experience.

If the blueprint metaphor and the equation of language and its development with UG are simplistic, no less simplistic is the idea that language can be explained as simply emerging from usage, without reference to the genetic factors that shape the brain. Language does not emerge in the societies of intelligent and highly interactive chimpanzees, or in chimpanzees that are raised in human society. In some form or other, the relatively small genetic differences between humans and chimps have to underlie the development of language. This could in principle mean either that those genetic differences include specifically linguistic features or that language is the product of more general capacities for which these differences are responsible. But there is no disputing the fact that language is based on an interaction of specifically human genetics and experience in the world, especially the social world.

That said, the actual differences in theoretical stances are substantial, and important. For the topic of language learning, first and second, the essential issue is whether the innate features guiding learning include features that are specifically linguistic in nature. Like many others, I believe that they do. Again, this is not to say that language learning is based entirely on linguistic constraints. The nature of perception, especially, must be considered crucial. The nature of our conceptual representations and the way they are constructed may be no less important. Nor can we afford to overlook the role of affect or that of the motor system. And of course, we have to take into account the influence of the world around us. The essential claim is that we cannot understand language and its development without recognizing that language is a part of human nature.

The contrasting views on innateness and modularity can be illustrated by a comparison of MOGUL with two prominent approaches that reject the modularity of language – the cognitive grammar of Ronald Langacker (2008) and William O'Grady's (2005) emergentist model. Both of these authors hold that language acquisition is to be explained in terms of the cognitive and social factors that also shape other learning, without reference to specifically linguistic principles, except as they arise as a result of these other factors. This idea is fundamentally at odds with MOGUL, and the conceptions of grammar that go with it. These theories, Langacker's especially, could not be incorporated into the framework without undergoing fundamental change. But important commonalities and shared goals can be identified.

First, MOGUL is similar to O'Grady's approach in its view of learning, specifically in its rejection of learning mechanisms as such in favour of processing and its lingering effects. The two theories also share the idea of competition as a central principle of processing and learning (see Sharwood Smith et al., 2013). More generally, MOGUL shares the interest of O'Grady, Langacker and others in connecting language to cognition in general and to the environmental contexts in which it is used. Generative linguistics, with its focus on the innate language module, might well be accused of distancing itself too much from these concerns (Jackendoff, 2003), but this problem is by no means inherent in the approach. Whatever the language faculty looks like, it must be connected to other aspects of cognition. The assumptions of innateness and modularity simply dictate different ways to investigate the connections, ways that I explored in Chapters 7 and 8.

A widely shared view among linguists is that language is about form-meaning mappings. As described in Chapter 2, language must connect ideas to sounds (written forms, gestures) if it is to express ideas and allow us to understand the ideas expressed by others. A fundamental divide among linguists is how direct these mappings are. The standard view among generative linguists is that they are mediated by a more or less autonomous, innately based grammatical component, which has its own principles and must be understood, to at least a large extent, on its own terms. In MOGUL, this is SS. Langacker rejects this component, seeking instead a very direct relation between sound and meaning.

This is a genuine and crucial difference between a cognitive linguistic approach like Langacker's and the generative approach we have adopted in MOGUL, though there is a danger that the contrast will be seen as greater than it actually is. PS–SS–CS connections involving individual representations at each level are of the essence in the Jackendovian account of language that MOGUL incorporates, as they are (in different terms) in cognitive grammar. The difference is that for Langacker there is nothing other than these direct connections; nothing exists specifically to make grammar as a system work. And of course in cognitive grammar the connections develop without any innate base that is specifically linguistic, a claim that seems to me unlikely, based on the discussion in Chapter 2.

A central theme for O'Grady and Langacker, and other cognitive linguists, is of course the commonalities between language processing and other cognition. The hypothesis of an innate language module is fully consistent with a significant degree of similarity across modules, between SS and CS in particular. I suggested above that the genes underlying the various modules probably have considerable overlap. Indeed, a plausible hypothesis is that SS began as a portion of CS, and as it became specialized for language processing, its resemblance to the conceptual system gradually declined; however, it would be quite surprising if no commonalities remained. Whether or not this hypothesis is accurate, SS presumably evolved in a manner that would allow it to interface well with CS, for the connection of syntactic forms to the conceptual meanings of those forms, and so a high degree of compatibility necessarily exists.

MOGUL thus shares much with these non-modular, 'nothing special' approaches, and much of what they are trying to do can be incorporated into the framework. But we must ultimately return to the fundamental issue: In order to explain language acquisition, do we have to give a prominent place to principles that are specifically linguistic? The MOGUL answer – unlike that of O'Grady and Langacker – is yes.

On the concepts of psychology

The central concepts used in scientific psychology came to us from folk psychology, perhaps the most interesting examples being learning, memory, perception and attention. These traditional concepts have defined the major branches of the field and framed the research questions that are pursued. We thus face, in normal practice, the very real danger of being caught in traditional ways of thinking, ways that could in the long term prove to be obstacles to the achievement of a genuine scientific understanding of ourselves. On the other hand, these concepts surely have value. They came to dominate folk psychology because they provide reasonably good descriptions of our normal experience with ourselves and others; it is useful in daily life to think in terms of such concepts as memory and attention. They can thus serve as reasonable starting points for the development of a more scientific understanding. So while we should not casually dismiss them, nor should we be wedded to them.

I have suggested that the mind is best seen in terms of a parsimonious architecture of processor–store pairs, all operating in accordance with general principles of processing but diverging greatly in their details as a result of their differing specializations. Within such a framework, the traditional concepts of folk psychology are abstractions from the workings of the system. Learning is the lingering effect of processing. Attention is a name for the complex processing activity that results in particular representations receiving especially extensive and intensive processing. Perception is the construction of a series of representations in specialized sensory modules, culminating (except in the case of subliminal perception) in a synchronized set of representations in POpS. Memory is the representations that comprise the contents of the stores, along with their patterns of connections across stores and their activation levels. These ideas do not neatly correspond to the things we refer to when we use the words *learning, attention, perception* and *memory* in ordinary life, but this is what should be expected as we move away from an adherence to traditional concepts and explore routes to a more profound understanding.

On research – past, present and future

In Chapters 7 and 8, I identified many open questions, sometimes explicitly, sometimes in terms such as 'we should expect…'. All of these constitute potential topics for empirical research. Particularly noteworthy is the need for greater concern with affective factors, especially value. I have also suggested that a serious exploration, theoretical or empirical, of consciousness and its place in L2 learning is only feasible within an established framework providing reasonable, if far from conclusive, positions on the nature of the mind and its workings. MOGUL is such a framework.

Regarding the development of the framework itself, with an eye to the place of consciousness, it is not difficult to find potentially worthwhile directions. The MOGUL project is extremely ambitious, and a great many areas could benefit from further development and probably revision. The reader may have noticed that in referring to the language module, I have typically focused on the morphosyntactic submodule, SS. A closer look is needed at the development of PS in the context of consciousness. The place of affect and value in learning is another topic that deserves more attention than it has so far received. I have been vague, for example, on exactly how affective representations are connected to representations in the language module. Similar comments apply to the SELF representation, regarding both its nature and the way it interacts with all the processes involved in L2 learning and use. A final example I will note is working memory. Its status in MOGUL has received substantial development, but important issues remain open.

The question of exactly how research on consciousness and L2 learning should be carried out within this theoretical framework is a large one, and as my focus is on developing the framework, I will be somewhat superficial here. The questions we are interested in involve awareness of L2 knowledge in its various forms, both in itself and as part of input processing, and the relations between such awareness and success in acquisition. For experimental research, this of course requires operationalization and measurement of awareness and of successful acquisition.

The standard way to operationalize awareness is verbal report: participants are asked what they are aware of. A look at the implicit learning literature in psychology (see references in Chapter 6) shows that this is by no means a trivial matter. Awareness can be probed in a variety of ways, and the choice of means can significantly affect the findings. Thus, some familiarity with that literature is of considerable value for designing research on consciousness and L2 learning. A variant of verbal report is think aloud. Participants are given a linguistic task and are asked to speak out their thoughts as they are carrying it out. Their recorded narrative then serves as another (imperfect) window on their awareness, or lack of it. In either form of verbal report, the awareness could be of linguistic features or of context or the feelings they are experiencing or of the task itself and how to execute it.

A more technically challenging way of operationalizing awareness is through eye movements made during a linguistic task (see Winke et al., 2013). With the proper equipment, researchers can determine the points in the text on which the eyes fix and the time of each fixation. These can then serve as a measure of what in the text gets processed most and what might not be processed at all. Awareness can be associated, imperfectly, with relatively sustained fixation. There is of course a substantial gap between the identification of significant points in the text and conclusions about the specific processing that is going on at those points, a gap that must be filled by theoretical inference.

Ultimately, neural research may provide the best operationalizations of awareness. The account of consciousness that I have proposed is based on activation level, in a cognitive sense. Activation in the neural sense is a standard part of neural research. So the concept of activation level has the potential to bridge the cognitive and the neural. If a solid bridge can be established, great opportunities will be opened for research. Unfortunately, a considerable gap remains between these possibilities and the ability to realize them in practice.

Empirical research on consciousness and learning also requires a way of operationalizing L2 knowledge and changes in it. In Chapter 6, I described some important features of good assessment, notably the type of test that is used. Tests that allow or encourage the use of explicit knowledge cannot be taken as legitimate indicators of the state of the language module or its external connections because conceptual linguistic knowledge is likely to play a prominent role, especially if the test is looking at knowledge of structures that were explicitly taught. Tests of spontaneous communicative use of the language, in the absence of any focus on the particular forms being studied, are the best candidates for genuine measures of modular knowledge, though the possible use of automatized conceptual linguistic knowledge must also be recognized. It is thus essential for researchers to be clear about the type of knowledge they are studying and make sure that the testing provides a legitimate measure of that type of knowledge.

Another issue for test type involves the distinction between using a form appropriately and simply using it. We cannot judge the success of learning, for modular or non-modular knowledge, by looking specifically at whether learners use a form when they are supposed to (e.g. Day & Shapson, 1991); a reasonable judgement requires an equal concern with whether they use it when they are *not* supposed to. Research and common experience have shown that learners tend to use forms that they are taught to use, even when they have little or no grasp of how to use those forms (see Lightbown, 1983, 1985, 1987; Lightbown *et al.*, 1980; Pica, 1983; Weinert, 1987). Therefore, showing that they do use an instructed form is not showing that any meaningful success has been achieved. We have to pay equal attention to *misuses*.

Research also needs to be concerned with long-term effects. One reason for this concern is that knowledge acquired during an instructional treatment, especially if it is explicit (conceptual) knowledge, is likely to be very active immediately after the treatment and could make a significant contribution to performance on the instructed forms simply for this reason, even with relatively communicative testing. Research has in fact found in a number of cases that significant results on immediate post-tests are no longer apparent on delayed post-tests (Harley, 1989; Lightbown *et al.*, 1980; Pienemann, 1989; White, 1991; for the results of follow-up testing for White's study, see Schwartz & Gubala-Ryzak, 1992; White, 1992). In Norris and Ortega's (2000) overall sample, they found that effect sizes declined substantially (0.22) from immediate to delayed post-test, and the delays in these studies were typically short. So follow-up testing is a necessity for measures of success in acquisition.

These are all points that must be considered in assessing success in acquisition. This of course includes an assessment of learning in research on its relation to consciousness. As I have discussed these points in various papers (e.g. Truscott, 1996, 1998, 2004, 2005, 2007a, 2007b), I will not pursue them further here.

One kind of topic that can be investigated using such operationalizations is awareness of a person's L2 knowledge at various stages of learning. This has traditionally been the focus of UG-based research. It means looking at the relation between knowledge, as revealed by testing of various sorts, and awareness of that knowledge. Targets can be both modular and conceptual linguistic knowledge, as well as their connections with affective and contextual representations and self.

Research aimed at the language module inevitably faces the limitation that we do not really know what the contents of the module look like. This is very much a theory-dependent question. In this sense it is easier to study conceptual linguistic knowledge, which is much closer to awareness and less specialized. To study the growth of the language module, we need to make theoretical assumptions. The natural source is the extensive UG-oriented research that has been carried out in SLA (see Herschensohn & Young-Scholten, 2013). Given the MOGUL framework, with its roots in Jackendoff's architecture, the *Simpler Syntax* of Culicover and Jackendoff (2005) is also relevant.

A broad issue that appears here and elsewhere, and applies to essentially any theoretical approach to L2 learning (see Chapter 6), is the problem of separating the two types of linguistic knowledge: the modular linguistic knowledge found in SS from the conceptual linguistic knowledge found in CS. One way to make this separation is, again, to provisionally adopt a specific theory. Another way is to distinguish types of testing, as described above and in Chapter 6. And of course the two can be and should be merged. Given the importance of consciousness for the distinction, we can reasonably hope that research along these lines will help to clarify the issue.

The focus of UG-based research has typically been on strictly linguistic knowledge, with little attention to affect or self. Connections between SS and CS (though generally not phrased in such terms) have, however, become a major topic of research in recent years (e.g. Sorace, 2011), and this work includes to a considerable extent the role of context in learning. It can be incorporated in the MOGUL framework, and research conducted within the framework can take it as a foundation.

As an example of relevant UG-based research, consider Lardiere's (2008, 2009) work on *feature assembly*, briefly described in Chapters 7 and 8. Again, the leading idea is that the central differences between languages are in the ways that functional categories are combined in the lexical items of each language and that the heart of L2 learning is therefore establishing the appropriate ways of bundling them in the L2. Within the framework developed in this book, we can ask about awareness of the functional category combinations themselves (SS representations), their meanings (CS representations), the forms associated with them (PS, AS and VS representations) and the affect associated with them (AfS representations).

In addition to studying the state of L2 knowledge as such, research can look at the contents of consciousness when the learner is processing input. Again, the targets can include both linguistic information and affect, context and self, as well as the relations among them. This sort of research is closely related to existing work on 'noticing' (see Chapter 6), which can, with theoretical reformulation, provide models for further research (see Truscott & Sharwood Smith, 2011, for related discussion).

Another direction of research looks more directly at the relation between awareness and learning. A model for this type of work is the rich body of research aimed at testing the effects of instruction, most often in grammar but also vocabulary and sometimes pragmatics. Much of the research on noticing has also been of this type.

This is by no means an exhaustive survey of potential research within the framework I have presented in this book. For example, many of the topics considered here, particularly the more social aspects of learning, also lend themselves to qualitative investigation. But I will not pursue this or the many other additional possibilities here.

And finally – on implicit learning inside and outside the language module

Development of the language module – the heart of language acquisition – is a form of implicit learning. I have criticized other approaches to consciousness in SLA for their assumption of a generic implicit learning process, which does not recognize distinctions based on the target of the learning. So some clarification is needed here regarding the nature of implicit learning in the MOGUL framework, particularly as it occurs within the language module.

Within this framework, implicit learning is simply any change that occurs on the basis of information that has not been consciously represented, except in the sense that it is implicitly present in the perceptual representation that constitutes the input. This definition does not require any reference to the target of the learning, so we might say that implicit learning in the module is essentially the same mechanism as implicit learning anywhere else, that it is simply generic implicit learning. But such a statement would require two very important clarifications.

First, within the MOGUL framework there are no learning mechanisms at all, implicit or explicit. There is only processing and its lingering effects. Second, the character of the implicit learning is determined to a very large extent by the fact that it is occurring within the language module. Implicit development of SS is the combining of existing syntactic representations, built from syntactic primitives, in accordance with the inherent principles of the syntax processor. So, while it will share features with the development of other modules, it will inevitably be dramatically different. One important implication of this analysis is that the products of this learning will not be the low-quality representations that likely characterize implicit learning as it is induced in laboratory experiments (except in regard to their activation level).

The characteristics of implicit learning outside the language module, like those of implicit learning within the module, depend on the target of the learning, i.e. on where the processing and the changes that result from it are taking place. If they are in a lower-level sensory module, they should involve the sort of fine-tuning of the module that characterizes development early in life. These are the kinds of changes, like those in the language module, that fall within a narrow range of possibilities for the particular module, changes that it is designed to undergo on the basis of specific, narrowly defined types of input. So as in the case of the language module, the resulting representations will not be of low quality.

Implicit processing at the higher level of the perceptual systems – POpS – is much less specialized and constrained, because these systems do not serve such narrow, specialized functions, and so its consequences are likely to be quite different. Because of these characteristics of the systems, the processor in each case will typically not be able to construct from implicit information a representation that is well suited for any particular purpose. The resulting implicit representations will therefore be low quality. The same description applies to processing in CS and the products of that processing. This is to say that implicit learning in these areas is the implicit learning which is the subject of almost all the research and theorizing that has been done on the subject.

And this brings out the essential point about implicit learning, i.e. learning that occurs without awareness of the information being learned. It has all the limitations that are commonly attributed to it – except when it occurs in an appropriate part of the system, namely one that is by nature specialized to use very specific kinds of information in very specific ways.

The language module is one such unit and so its development can occur without awareness of the information that is used in that development, i.e. implicitly. It *does* occur without such awareness because representations in this highly specialized and relatively isolated module cannot reach the activation levels that are necessary for awareness. Conscious processes certainly have their roles – essential roles – but language acquisition is at its heart an unconscious process.

References

Alanen, R. (1995) Input enhancement and rule presentation in second language acquisition. In R. Schmidt (ed.) *Attention and Awareness in Second Language Acquisition* (pp. 259–299). Honolulu, HI: University of Hawai'i Press.

Allport, A. (1993) Attention and control: Have we been asking the wrong questions? A critical review of twenty-five years. In D.E. Meyer and S. Kornblum (eds) *Attention and Performance XIV: Synergies in Experimental Psychology, Artificial Intelligence, and Cognitive Neuroscience* (pp. 182–218). Cambridge, MA: MIT Press.

Amaral, L. and Roeper, T. (2014) Multiple grammars and second language representation. *Second Language Research* 30, 3–36.

Anderson, A.K., Christoff, K., Stappen, I., Panitz, D., Ghahremani, D.G., Glover, G., Gabrieli, J.D.E. and Sobel, N. (2003) Dissociated neural representations of intensity and valence in human olfaction. *Nature Neuroscience* 6, 196–202.

Anderson, J.R. (1983a) *The Architecture of Cognition*. Cambridge, MA: Harvard University Press.

Anderson, J.R. (1983b) A spreading activation theory of memory. *Journal of Verbal Learning and Verbal Behavior* 22, 261–295.

Anderson, J.R. (1993) *Rules of the Mind*. Hillsdale, NJ: Erlbaum.

Anderson, J.R. (1995) *Cognitive Psychology and its Implications* (4th edn). New York: W.H. Freeman.

Andrade, J. (ed.) (2001) *Working Memory in Perspective*. Hove: Psychology Press.

Ariely, D. (2009) *Predictably Irrational: The Hidden Forces that Shape our Decisions* (revised and expanded edition). New York: Harper.

Aron, A.R. (2008) Progress in executive-function research: From tasks to functions to regions to networks. *Current Directions in Psychological Science* 17, 124–129.

Atkinson, R.C. and Shiffrin, R.M. (1968) Human memory: A proposed system and its control processes. In K.W. Spence and J.T. Spence (eds) *The Psychology of Learning and Motivation: Advances in Research and Theory* (pp. 89–195). New York: Academic Press.

Baars, B. (1988) *A Cognitive Theory of Consciousness*. New York: Cambridge University Press.

Baars, B. (1997a) *In the Theater of Consciousness: The Workspace of the Mind*. New York: Oxford University Press.

Baars, B.J. (1997b) Some essential differences between consciousness and attention, perception, and working memory. *Consciousness and Cognition* 6, 363–371.

Baars, B.J. (2007) The global workspace theory of consciousness. In M. Velmans and S. Schneider (eds) *The Blackwell Companion to Consciousness* (pp. 236–246). Malden, MA: Blackwell.

Baars, B.J., Ramsøy, T.Z. and Laureys, S. (2003) Brain, conscious experience and the observing self. *Trends in Neurosciences* 26, 671–675.

Baddeley, A. (1996b) Exploring the central executive. *Quarterly Journal of Experimental Psychology* 49A, 5–28.

Baddeley, A. (2000) Short-term and working memory. In E. Tulving and F.I.M. Craik (eds) *The Oxford Handbook of Memory* (pp. 77–92). Oxford: Oxford University Press.

Baddeley, A. (2007) *Working Memory, Thought, and Action*. Oxford: Oxford University Press.

Baddeley, A. (2012) Working memory: Theories, models, and controversies. *Annual Review of Psychology* 63, 1–29.
Baddeley, A.D. (1986) *Working Memory*. Oxford: Clarendon Press.
Baddeley, A.D. (1996a) The concept of working memory. In S.E. Gathercole (ed.) *Models of Short-term Memory* (pp. 1–27). Hove: Erlbaum.
Baddeley, A.D. and Hitch, G. (1974) Working memory. In G.H. Bower (ed.) *The Psychology of Learning and Motivation: Advances in Research and Theory* (pp. 47–89). New York: Academic Press.
Baddeley, A.D., Allen, R.J. and Hitch, G.J. (2011) Binding in visual working memory: The role of the episodic buffer. *Neuropsychologia* 49, 1393–1400.
Bargh, J.A. (1992) The ecology of automaticity: Toward establishing the conditions needed to produce automatic processing effects. *American Journal of Psychology* 105, 181–199.
Bargh, J.A. (1997) The automaticity of everyday life. In R.S. Wyer Jr. (ed.) *Advances in Social Cognition. Vol. 10. The Automaticity of Everyday Life* (pp. 1–61). Mahwah, NJ: Erlbaum.
Barrett, H.C. and Kurzban, R. (2006) Modularity in cognition: Framing the debate. *Psychological Review* 113, 628–647.
Barrett, L.F. (2005) Feeling is perceiving: Core affect and conceptualization in the experience of emotion. In L.F. Barrett, P.M. Niedenthal and P. Winkielman (eds) *Emotion and Consciousness* (pp. 255–284). New York: Guilford Press.
Barrett, L.F. and Russell, J.A. (1999) The structure of current affect: Controversies and emerging consensus. *Current Directions in Psychological Science* 8, 10–14.
Barrett, L.F., Niedenthal, P.M. and Winkielman, P. (eds) (2005) *Emotion and Consciousness*. New York: Guilford Press.
Barsalou, L.W. (1999) Perceptual symbol systems. *Behavioral and Brain Sciences* 22, 577–660.
Barsalou, L.W. (2008) Grounded cognition. *Annual Review of Psychology* 59, 617–645.
Batstone, R. (1994) *Grammar*. Oxford: Oxford University Press.
Baumeister, R.F., Bratslavsky, E., Muraven, M. and Tice, D.M. (1998) Ego depletion: Is the active self a limited resource? *Journal of Personality and Social Psychology* 74, 1252–1265.
Baumeister, R.F., Schmeichel, B.J. and Vohs, K.D. (2007) Self-regulation and the executive function: The self as controlling agent. In A.W. Kruglanski and E.T. Higgins (eds) *Social Psychology: Handbook of Basic Principles* (2nd edn) (pp. 516–539). New York: Guilford Press.
Baumeister, R.F. and Masicampo, E.J. (2010) Conscious thought is for facilitating social and cultural interactions: How mental simulations serve the animal-culture interface. *Psychological Review* 117, 945–971.
Baumeister, R.F., Masicampo, E.J. and Vohs, K.D. (2011) Do conscious thoughts cause behavior? *Annual Review of Psychology* 62, 331–361.
Baumeister, R.F. and Tierney, J. (2011) *Willpower: Rediscovering the Greatest Human Strength*. New York: Penguin Press.
Bechara, A. and Naqvi, N. (2004) Listening to your heart: Interoceptive awareness as a gateway to feeling. *Nature Neuroscience* 7, 102–103.
Bechara, A., Damasio, H., Tranel, D. and Damasio, A.R. (1997) Deciding advantageously before knowing the advantageous strategy. *Science* 275, 1293–1295.
Beebe, L.M. (1985) Input: Choosing the right stuff. In S.M. Gass and C.G. Madden (eds) *Input in Second Language Acquisition* (pp. 404–414). Rowley, MA: Newbury.
Behrmann, M. (2000) The mind's eye mapped onto the brain's matter. *Current Directions in Psychological Science* 9, 50–54.

Berent, G., Kelly, R., Schmitz, K. and Kenney, P. (2009) Visual input enhancement via essay coding results in deaf learners' long-term retention of improved English grammatical knowledge. *Journal of Deaf Studies and Deaf Education* 14, 190–204.
Berridge, K.C. and Winkielman, P. (2003) What is an unconscious emotion? (The case for unconscious "liking"). *Cognition and Emotion* 17, 181–211.
Berry, D.C. (1994) Implicit and explicit learning of complex tasks. In N.C. Ellis (ed.) *Implicit and Explicit Learning of Languages* (pp. 147–164). London: Academic Press.
Bialystok, E. (1979) Explicit and implicit judgements of L2 grammaticality. *Language Learning* 29, 81–103.
Bishop, D. (2006) What causes specific language impairment in children? *Current Directions in Psychological Science* 15, 217–221.
Bishop, D. and Mogford, K. (eds) (1988) *Language Development in Exceptional Circumstances*. Hove: Erlbaum.
Bock, K. and Griffin, Z.M. (2000) The persistence of structural priming: Transient activation or implicit learning? *Journal of Experimental Psychology: General* 129, 177–192.
Bock, K.J. (1986) Syntactic persistence in language production. *Cognitive Psychology* 18, 335–387.
Boitano, J.J. (1996) Edelman's biological theory of consciousness. In S.R. Hameroff, A.W. Kaszniak and A.C. Scott (eds) *Toward a Science of Consciousness: The First Tucson Discussions and Debates* (pp. 507–540). Cambridge, MA: MIT Press.
Bowers, J.S. and Marsolek, C.J. (eds) (2003) *Rethinking Implicit Memory*. Oxford: Oxford University Press.
Broadbent, D.E. (1958) *Perception and Communication*. New York: Pergamon Press.
Brown, R. and Kulik, J. (1977) Flashbulb memories. *Cognition* 5, 73–99.
Brunel, N. and Wang, X.-J. (2001) Effects of neuromodulation in a cortical network model of object working memory dominated by recurrent inhibition. *Journal of Computational Neuroscience* 11, 63–85.
Buchanan, T.W. (2007) Retrieval of emotional memories. *Psychological Bulletin* 133, 761–779.
Buchanan, T.W. and Adolphs, R. (2002) The role of the human amygdala in emotional modulation of long-term declarative memory. In S.C. Moore and M. Oaksford (eds) *Emotional Cognition: From Brain to Behaviour* (pp. 9–34). Amsterdam: Benjamins.
Calder, A.J., Lawrence, A.D. and Young, A.W. (2001) Neuropsychology of fear and loathing. *Nature Reviews Neuroscience* 2, 352–363.
Calvin, W.H. and Bickerton, D. (2000) *Lingua Ex Machina: Reconciling Darwin and Chomsky with the Human Brain*. Cambridge, MA: MIT Press.
Caplan, D. and Waters, G.S. (1999) Verbal working memory and sentence comprehension. *Brain and Behavioral Sciences* 22, 77–126.
Carr, T.H. and Curran, T. (1994) Cognitive factors in learning about structured sequences. *Studies in Second Language Acquisition* 16, 205–230.
Carroll, S. (2001) *Input and Evidence: The Raw Material of Second Language Acquisition*. Amsterdam: John Benjamins.
Carroll, S.E. (1999) Putting "input" in its proper place. *Second Language Research* 15, 337–388.
Carruthers, P. (1996) *Language, Thought and Consciousness*. Cambridge: Cambridge University Press.
Carruthers, P. (2006) *The Architecture of the Mind: Massive Modularity and the Flexibility of Thought*. Oxford: Clarendon.
Caston, V. (2002) Aristotle on consciousness. *Mind* 111, 751–815.
Chabris, C. and Simons, D. (2009) *The Invisible Gorilla: And Other Ways Our Intuitions Deceive Us*. New York: Broadway Paperbacks.

Chafe, W. (1996) Comments on Jackendoff, Nuyts, and Allwood. *Pragmatics & Cognition* 4, 181–196.

Chang, F., Bock, K. and Goldberg, A.E. (2003) Can thematic roles leave traces of their places? *Cognition* 90, 29–49.

Chang, F., Dell, G.S., Bock, K. and Griffin, Z.M. (2000) Structural priming as implicit learning: A comparison of models of sentence production. *Journal of Psycholinguistic Research* 29, 217–229.

Charland, L.C. (2005) Emotion experience and the indeterminacy of valence. In L.F. Barrett, P.M. Niedenthal and P. Winkielman (eds) *Emotion and Consciousness* (pp. 231–254). New York: Guilford Press.

Chomsky, N. (1965) *Aspects of the Theory of Syntax*. Cambridge, MA: MIT Press.

Chomsky, N. (1986) *Knowledge of Language: Its Nature, Origin, and Use*. New York: Praeger.

Chun, M.M. and Marois, R. (2002) The dark side of visual attention. *Current Opinion in Neurobiology* 12, 184–189.

Clark, H.H. and Clark, E.V. (1977) *Psychology and Language: An Introduction to Psycholinguistics*. New York: Harcourt Brace Jovanovich.

Cleeremans, A. (1993) *Mechanisms of Implicit Learning: Connectionist Models of Sequence Processing*. Cambridge, MA: MIT Press.

Cleeremans, A. (2006) Conscious and unconscious cognition: A graded, dynamic perspective. In Q. Jing, M.R. Rosenzweig, G. d'Ydewalle, H. Zhang, H.-C. Chen and K. Zhang (eds) *Progress in Psychological Science Around the World: Vol. 1 Neural, Cognitive and Developmental Issues* (pp. 401–418). Hove: Psychology Press.

Cleeremans, A. and Jiménez, L. (2002) Implicit learning and consciousness: A graded, dynamic perspective. In R.M. French and A. Cleeremans (eds) *Implicit Learning and Consciousness: An Empirical, Computational and Philosophical Consensus in the Making?* (pp. 1–40). Hove: Psychology Press.

Cleland, A.A. and Pickering, M.J. (2006) Do writing and speaking employ the same syntactic representations? *Journal of Memory and Language* 54, 185–198.

Cohen, J.D. (1997) Dimensions of consciousness: A commentary on Kinsbourne and Hobson. In J.D. Cohen and J.W. Schooler (eds) *Scientific Approaches to Consciousness* (pp. 397–402). Mahwah, NJ: Erlbaum.

Cohen, J.D. (2005) The vulcanization of the human brain: A neural perspective on interactions between cognition and emotion. *Journal of Economic Perspectives* 19 (4), 3–24.

Cohen, J.D., Braver, T.S. and Brown, J.W. (2002) Computational perspectives on dopamine function in prefrontal cortex. *Current Opinion in Neurobiology* 12, 223–229.

Collins, A.M. and Loftus, E.F. (1975) A spreading activation theory of semantic processing. *Psychological Review* 82, 407–428.

Conway, M.A. (2005) Memory and the self. *Journal of Memory and Language* 53, 594–628.

Conway, M.A., Singer, J.A. and Tagini, A. (2004) The self and autobiographical memory: Correspondence and coherence. *Social Cognition* 22, 495–537.

Cooney, J.W. and Gazzaniga, M.S. (2003) Neurological disorders and the structure of human consciousness. *Trends in Cognitive Sciences* 7, 161–165.

Corder, S.P. (1967) The significance of learners' errors. *IRAL* 5, 161–170.

Cosmides, L. and Tooby, J. (1992) Cognitive adaptations for social exchange. In J.H. Barkow, L. Cosmides and J. Tooby (eds) *The Adapted Mind: Evolutionary Psychology and the Generation of Culture* (pp. 163–122). New York: Oxford University Press.

Courchène, R., Glidden, J.I., St. John, J. and Thérien, C. (eds) (1992) *Comprehension-based Second Language Teaching/L'Enseignement des Langues Secondes axe sur la Comprehension*. Ottawa: University of Ottawa Press.

Courtney, S.M., Petit, L., Maisog, J.M., Ungerleider, L.G. and Haxby, J.V. (1998) An area specialized for spatial working memory in human frontal cortex. *Science* 279, 1347–1351.

Cowan, N. (1993) Activation, attention, and short-term memory. *Memory and Cognition* 21, 162–167.
Cowan, N. (2001) The magical number 4 in short-term memory: A reconsideration of mental storage capacity. *Behavioral and Brain Sciences* 24, 87–185.
Cowan, N. (2005) *Working Memory Capacity.* New York: Psychology Press.
Crick, F. (1994) *The Astonishing Hypothesis: The Scientific Search for the Soul.* New York: Charles Scribner's Sons.
Crick, F. and Koch, C. (1990) Some reflections on visual awareness. *Cold Spring Harbor Symposia on Quantitative Biology* 55, 953–962.
Crick, F. and Koch, C. (1998) Consciousness and neuroscience. *Cerebral Cortex* 8, 97–107.
Crick, F. and Koch, C. (2000) The unconscious homunculus. In T. Metzinger (ed.) *The Neuronal Correlates of Consciousness* (pp. 103–110). Cambridge, MA: MIT Press.
Crick, F. and Koch, C. (2003) A framework for consciousness. *Nature Neuroscience* 6, 119–126.
Crick, F. and Koch, C. (2007) A neurobiological framework for consciousness. In M. Velmans and S. Schneider (eds) *The Blackwell Companion to Consciousness* (pp. 567–579). Malden, MA: Blackwell.
Critchley, H.D., Wiens, S., Rotshtein, P., Öhman, A. and Dolan, R.J. (2004) Neural systems supporting interoceptive awareness. *Nature Neuroscience* 7, 190–195.
Csikszentmihaly, M. (1990) *Flow: The Psychology of Optimal Experience.* New York: HarperCollins.
Culicover, P. and Jackendoff, R. (2005) *Simpler Syntax.* Oxford: Oxford University Press.
Curran, T. and Keele, S.W. (1993) Attentional and nonattentional forms of sequence learning. *Journal of Experimental Psychology: Learning, Memory, and Cognition* 19, 189–202.
Dade, L.A., Zatorre, R.J., Evans, A.C. and Jones-Gotman, M. (2001) Working memory in another dimension: Functional imaging of human olfactory working memory. *NeuroImage* 14, 650–660.
Damasio, A. (2003) *Looking for Spinoza: Joy, Sorrow, and the Feeling Brain.* Orlando, FL: Harcourt.
Damasio, A. (2010) *Self Comes to Mind: Constructing the Conscious Mind.* New York: Pantheon Books.
Damasio, A.R. (1994) *Descartes' Error: Emotion, Reason and the Human Brain.* London: Papermac.
Damasio, A.R. (1999) *The Feeling of What Happens: Body and Emotion in the Making of Consciousness.* New York: Harcourt Brace.
Damasio, A.R., Tranel, D. and Damasio, H. (1998) Somatic markers and the guidance of behavior. In J.M. Jenkins, K. Oatley and N.L. Stein (eds) *Human Emotions: A Reader* (pp. 122–135). Malden, MA: Blackwell.
Davidson, R.J. and Irwin, W. (1999) The functional neuroanatomy of emotion and affective style. *Trends in Cognitive Sciences* 3, 11–21.
Day, E.M. and Shapson, S.M. (1991) Integrating formal and functional approaches to language teaching in French immersion: An experimental study. *Language Learning* 41, 25–58.
de Bot, K. (2008) Introduction: Second language development as a dynamic process. *Modern Language Journal* 92, 166–178.
Dehaene, S. and Changeux, J.-P. (1997) A hierarchical neuronal network for planning behavior. *Proceedings of the National Academy of Sciences of the United States of America* 94, 13293–13298.
Dehaene, S. and Changeux, J.-P. (2000) Reward-dependent learning in neuronal networks for planning and decision making. *Progress in Brain Research* 126, 217–229.

Dehaene, S. and Changeux, J.-P. (2005) Ongoing spontaneous activity controls access to consciousness: A neuronal model for inattentional blindness. *PLoS Biology* 5, 910–927.

Dehaene, S. and Changeux, J.-P. (2011) Experimental and theoretical approaches to conscious processing. *Neuron* 70, 200–227.

Dehaene, S. and Naccache, L. (2001) Towards a cognitive neuroscience of consciousness: Basic evidence and a workspace framework. *Cognition* 79, 1–37.

Dehaene, S., Kerszberg, M. and Changeux, J.-P. (1998) A neuronal model of a global workspace in effortful cognitive tasks. *Proceedings of the National Academy of Sciences USA* 95, 14529–14534.

Dehaene, S., Sergent, C. and Changeux, J.-P. (2003) A neuronal network model linking subjective reports and objective physiological data. *Proceedings of the National Academy of Sciences of the United States of America* 100, 8520–8525.

DeKeyser, R. (1994) Implicit and explicit learning of L2 grammar: A pilot study. *TESOL Quarterly* 28, 188–194.

DeKeyser, R. (2003) Implicit and explicit learning. In C. Doughty and M.H. Long (eds) *The Handbook of Second Language Acquisition* (pp. 313–348). Oxford: Blackwell.

DeKeyser, R.M. (1997) Beyond explicit rule learning: Automatizing second language morphosyntax. *Studies in Second Language Acquisition* 19, 195–221.

DeKeyser, R.M. and Sokalski, K.J. (1996) The differential role of comprehension and production practice. *Language Learning* 46, 613–642.

Dell, G.S. (1986) A spreading-activation theory of retrieval in sentence production. *Psychological Review* 93, 283–321.

Demoulin, S., Leyens, J.-P., Paladino, M.-P., Rodriguez-Torres, R., Rodriguez-Perez, A. and Dovidio, J.F. (2004) Dimensions of "uniquely" and "non-uniquely" human emotions. *Cognition and Emotion* 18, 71–96.

Denton, D.A., McKinley, M.J., Farrell, M. and Egan, G.F. (2009) The role of primordial emotions in the evolutionary origin of consciousness. *Consciousness and Cognition* 18, 500–514.

Destrebecqz, A. and Cleeremans, A. (2001) Can sequence learning be implicit? New evidence with the process dissociation procedure. *Psychonomic Bulletin and Review* 8, 343–350.

Destrebecqz, A. and Cleeremans, A. (2003) Temporal effects in sequence learning. In L. Jiménez (ed.) *Attention and Implicit Learning* (pp. 181–213). Amsterdam: Benjamins.

Dewaele, J.-M. (2005) Investigating the psychological and emotional dimensions in instructed language learning: Obstacles and possibilities. *Modern Language Journal* 89, 367–380.

Diekelmann, S. and Born, J. (2010) The memory function of sleep. *Nature Reviews Neuroscience* 11, 114–126.

Dienes, Z., Broadbent, D. and Berry, D. (1991) Implicit and explicit knowledge bases in artificial grammar learning. *Journal of Experimental Psychology: Learning, Memory, and Cognition* 17, 875–887.

Dijksterhuis, A. and Aarts, H. (2010) Goals, attention, and (un)consciousness. *Annual Review of Psychology* 61, 467–490.

Dijksterhuis, A., Bos, M.W., Nordgren, L.F. and van Baaren, R.B. (2006) On making the right choice: The deliberation-without-attention effect. *Science* 311, 1005–1007.

Dijkstra, T. and van Heuven, W.J.B. (1998) The BIA model and bilingual word recognition. In J. Grainger and A.M. Jacobs (eds) *Localist Connectionist Approaches to Human Cognition* (pp. 189–225). Mahwah, NJ: Erlbaum.

Dolan, R.J. (2002) Emotion, cognition, and behavior. *Science* 298, 1191–1194.

Doughty, C. and Varela, E. (1998) Communicative focus on form. In C. Doughty and J. Williams (eds) *Focus on Form in Classroom Second Language Acquisition* (pp. 114–138). Cambridge: Cambridge University Press.

Driver, J., Davis, G., Russell, C., Turatto, M. and Freeman, E. (2001) Segmentation, attention and phenomenal visual objects. *Cognition* 80, 61–95.

Du, S., Tao, Y. and Martinez, A.M. (2014) Compound facial expressions of emotion. *PNAS (Early Edition)* 111, E1454–E1462.

Dulany, D.E., Carlson, R.A. and Dewey, G.I. (1984) A case of syntactical learning and judgment: How conscious and how abstract? *Journal of Experimental Psychology: General* 113, 541–555.

Dulay, H., Burt, M. and Krashen, S. (1982) *Language Two.* New York: Oxford University Press.

Edelman, G. (1989) *The Remembered Present: A Biological Theory of Consciousness.* New York: Basic Books.

Edelman, G.M. (1987) *Neural Darwinism: The Theory of Neuronal Group Selection.* New York: Basic Books.

Edelman, G.M. (1992) *Bright Air, Brilliant Fire: On the Matter of the Mind.* London: Penguin.

Edelman, G.M. (2003) Naturalizing consciousness: A theoretical framework. *Proceedings of the National Academy of Sciences of the United States of America* 100, 5520–5524.

Edelman, G.M. (2004) *Wider Than the Sky: The Phenomenal Gift of Consciousness.* New Haven, CT: Yale University Press.

Edelman, G.M. (2006) *Second Nature: Brain Science and Human Knowledge.* New Haven, CT: Yale University Press.

Edelman, G.M. and Tononi, G. (2000). *A Universe of Consciousness: How Matter Becomes Imagination.* New York: Basic Books.

Edelman, G.M., Gally, J.A. and Baars, B.J. (2011) Biology of consciousness. *Frontiers in Psychology* 2 (4). doi: 10.3389/fpsyg.2011.00004 (accessed 11 July 2014).

Egi, T. (2004) Verbal reports, noticing, and SLA research. *Language Awareness* 13, 243–264.

Eichenbaum, H. and Cohen, N.J. (2001) *From Conditioning to Conscious Recollection: Memory Systems of the Brain.* New York: Oxford University Press.

Ellis, N. (1994b) Vocabulary acquisition: The implicit ins and outs of explicit cognitive mediation. In N.C. Ellis (ed.) *Implicit and Explicit Learning of Languages* (pp. 211–282). London: Academic Press.

Ellis, N.C. (ed.) (1994a) *Implicit and Explicit Learning of Languages.* London: Academic Press.

Ellis, N.C. (2002a) Frequency effects in language processing: A review with implications for theories of implicit and explicit language acquisition. *Studies in Second Language Acquisition* 24, 143–188.

Ellis, N.C. (2002b) Reflections on frequency effects in language processing. *Studies in Second Language Acquisition* 24, 297–339.

Ellis, N.C. (2005) At the interface: Dynamic interactions of explicit and implicit language knowledge. *Studies in Second Language Acquisition* 27, 305–352.

Ellis, N.C. (2006a) Language acquisition as rational contingency learning. *Applied Linguistics* 27, 1–24.

Ellis, N.C. (2006b) Selective attention and transfer phenomena in L2 acquisition: Contingency, cue competition, salience, interference, overshadowing, blocking, and perceptual learning. *Applied Linguistics* 27, 164–194.

Ellis, N.C. (2011) Implicit and explicit SLA and their interfaces. In C. Sanz and R.P. Leow (eds) *Implicit and Explicit Language Learning: Conditions, Processes, and Knowledge in SLA and Bilingualism* (pp. 35–48). Washington, DC: Georgetown University Press.

Ellis, N.C. and Larsen-Freeman, D. (2006) Language emergence: Implications for applied linguistics — Introduction to the special issue. *Applied Linguistics* 27, 558–589.

Ellis, R. (1988) *Classroom Second Language Development: A Study of Classroom Interaction and Language Acquisition.* New York: English Language Teaching.

Ellis, R. (1993) The structural syllabus and second language acquisition. *TESOL Quarterly* 27, 91–113.

Ellis, R. (1994) A theory of instructed second language acquisition. In N.C. Ellis (ed.) *Implicit and Explicit Learning of Languages* (pp. 79–114). London: Academic Press.

Ellis, R. (1995) Interpretation tasks for grammar teaching. *TESOL Quarterly* 29, 87–105.

Ellis, R. (2002) Does form-focussed instruction affect the acquisition of implicit knowledge? A review of the research. *Studies in Second Language Acquisition* 24, 223–236.

Ellis, R., Loewen, S., Elder, C., Erlam, R., Philp, J. and Reinders, H. (2009) *Implicit and Explicit Knowledge in Second Language Learning, Testing and Teaching*. Bristol: Multilingual Matters.

Engelien, A., Huber, W., Silbersweig, D., Stern, E., Frith, C.D., Döring, W., Thron, A. and Frackowiak, R.S.J (2000) The neural correlates of "deaf-hearing" in man: Conscious sensory awareness enabled by attentional modulation. *Brain* 123, 532–545.

Eraña, A. (2012) Dual process theories versus massive modularity hypotheses. *Philosophical Psychology* 25, 855–872.

Ericsson, K.A. and Simon, H.A. (1993) *Protocol Analysis: Verbal Reports as Data* (rev. edn). Cambridge, MA: MIT Press.

Evans, D. (2001) *Emotion: A Very Short Introduction*. Oxford: Oxford University Press.

Evans, D. (2004) The search hypothesis of emotion. In D. Evans and P. Cruse (eds) *Emotion, Evolution, and Rationality* (pp. 179–191). Oxford: Oxford University Press.

Evans, D. and Cruse, P. (eds) (2004) *Emotion, Evolution, and Rationality*. Oxford: Oxford University Press.

Evans, J.S.B.T. (2008) Dual-processing accounts of reasoning, judgment, and social cognition. *Annual Review of Psychology* 59, 255–278.

Evans, J.S.B.T. and Over, D.E. (2008) Whole mind theory: Massive modularity meets dual processes. *Thinking & Reasoning* 14, 200–208.

Feather, N.T. (1990) Bridging the gap between values and actions. In E.T. Higgins and R.M. Sorrentino (eds) *Handbook of Motivation and Cognition: Foundations of Social Behavior. Volume 2* (pp. 151–192). New York: Guilford Press.

Fedorenko, E., Gibson, E. and Rohde, D. (2006) The nature of working memory capacity in sentence comprehension: Evidence against domain-specific working memory resources. *Journal of Memory and Language* 54, 541–553.

Felix, S.W. (1987) *Cognition and Language Growth*. Dordrecht: Foris.

Five Graces Group (2009) Language is a complex adaptive system: Position paper. *Language Learning* 59, Suppl. 1, 1–26.

Flavell, J.H., Miller, P.H. and Miller, S.A. (1993) *Cognitive Development* (3rd edn). Englewood Cliffs, NJ: Prentice Hall.

Fodor, J.A. (1983) *The Modularity of Mind: An Essay on Faculty Psychology*. Cambridge, MA: MIT Press.

Fodor, J.A. (2000) *The Mind Doesn't Work That Way: The Scope and Limits of Computational Psychology*. Cambridge, MA: MIT Press.

Foster, J.K. (2009) *Memory: A Very Short Introduction*. Oxford: Oxford University Press.

Frantzen, D. (1995) The effects of grammar supplementation on written accuracy in an intermediate Spanish content course. *Modern Language Journal* 79, 329–344.

Fredrickson, B.L. (1998) What good are positive emotions? *Review of General Psychology* 2, 300–319.

Freeman, W.J. (2003) A neurobiological theory of meaning in perception. Part I: Information and meaning in nonconvergent and nonlocal brain dynamics. *International Journal of Bifurcation and Chaos* 13, 2493–2511.

Frenda, S.J., Nichols, R.M. and Loftus, E.F. (2011) Current issues and advances in misinformation research. *Current Directions in Psychological Science* 20, 20–23.

Frijda, N.H. (1986) *The Emotions*. Cambridge: Cambridge University Press.

Frijda, N.H. (1988/1998) The laws of emotion. In J.M. Jenkins, K. Oatley and N.L. Stein (eds) *Human Emotions: A Reader* (pp. 270–287). Malden, MA: Blackwell.

Fuster, J.M. (2008) *The Prefrontal Cortex* (4th edn). London: Academic Press.
Fuster, J.M. (2009) Cortex and memory: Emergence of a new paradigm. *Journal of Cognitive Neuroscience* 21, 2047–2072.
Gaillard, R., Dehaene, S., Adam, C., Clémenceau, S., Hasboun, D., Baulac, M., Cohen, L. and Naccache, L. (2009) Converging intracranial markers of conscious access. *PLoS Biology* 7(3): e1000061. doi:10.1371/journal.pbio.1000061
Gailliot, M.T. and Baumeister, R.F. (2007) The physiology of willpower: Linking blood glucose to self-control. *Personality and Social Psychology Review* 11, 303–327.
Gailliot, M.T., Baumeister, R.F., DeWall, C.N., Maner, J.K., Plant, E.A., Tice, D.M., Brewer, L.E. and Schmeichel, B.J. (2007) Self-control relies on glucose as a limited energy source: Willpower is more than a metaphor. *Journal of Personality and Social Psychology* 92, 325–336.
Gailliot, M.T., Peruche, B.M., Plant, E.A. and Baumeister, R.F. (2009) Stereotypes and prejudice in the blood: Sucrose drinks reduce prejudice and stereotyping. *Journal of Experimental Social Psychology* 45, 288–290.
Gallistel, C.R. and King, A.P. (2009) *Memory and the Computational Brain: Why Cognitive Science Will Transform Neuroscience*. Malden, MA: Wiley-Blackwell.
Garde, M.M. and Cowey, A. (2000) "Deaf hearing": Unacknowledged detection of auditory stimuli in a patient with cerebral deafness. *Cortex* 36, 71–80.
Gascoigne, C. (2006) Explicit input enhancement: Effects on target and non-target aspects of second language acquisition. *Foreign Language Annals* 39, 551–564.
Gass, S.M. (1988) Integrating research areas: A framework for second language studies. *Applied Linguistics* 9, 198–217.
Gass, S.M. (1997) *Input, Interaction, and the Second Language Learner*. Mahwah, NJ: Erlbaum.
Gazzaniga, M.S. (1985) *The Social Brain: Discovering the Networks of the Mind*. New York: Basic Books.
Gazzaniga, M.S. (1989) Organization of the human brain. *Science* 245, 947–952.
Gazzaniga, M.S. (1992) *Nature's Mind: The Biological Roots of Thinking, Emotions, Sexuality, Language, and Intelligence*. London: Penguin.
Gazzaniga, M.S. (1998) *The Mind's Past*. Berkeley, CA: University of California Press.
Gazzaniga, M.S. (2011) *Who's in Charge? Free Will and the Science of the Brain*. New York: HarperCollins.
Gigerenzer, G. (2007) *Gut Feelings: The Intelligence of the Unconscious*. New York: Penguin Books.
Gilbert, D. (2005) *Stumbling on Happiness*. New York: Vintage Books.
Glimcher, P.W., Camerer, C., Fehr, E. and Poldrack, R.A. (eds) (2009) *Neuroeconomics: Decision Making and the Brain*. London: Academic Press.
Goldberg, E. (2009) *The New Executive Brain: Frontal Lobes in a Complex World*. Oxford: Oxford University Press.
Goldin-Meadow, S. (2003) *The Resilience of Language: What Gesture Creation in Deaf Children Can Tell Us About How All Children Learn Language*. New York: Psychology Press.
Gottfried, J.A., Smith, A.P.R., Rugg, M.D. and Dolan, R.J. (2004) Remembrance of odors past: Human olfactory cortex in cross-modal recognition memory. *Neuron* 42, 687–695.
Gray, J., Schaefer, A., Braver, T.S. and Most, S.B. (2005) Affect and the resolution of cognitive control dilemmas. In L.F. Barrett, P.M. Niedenthal and P. Winkielman (eds) *Emotion and Consciousness* (pp. 51–66). New York: Guilford Press.
Green, P.S. and Hecht, K. (1992) Implicit and explicit grammar: An empirical study. *Applied Linguistics* 13, 168–184.
Greenfield, S. (2002) Mind, brain and consciousness. *British Journal of Psychiatry* 181, 91–93.

Greenfield, S.A. and Collins, T.F.T. (2005) A neuroscientific approach to consciousness. *Progress in Brain Research* 150, 11–23.

Greenwald, A.G. (1980) The totalitarian ego: Fabrication and revision of personal history. *American Psychologist* 35, 603–618.

Greenwald, A.G., Klinger, M.R. and Schuh, E.S. (1995) Activation by marginally perceptible ("subliminal") stimuli: Dissociation of unconscious from conscious cognition. *Journal of Experimental Psychology: General* 24, 22–42.

Gregg, K. (1984) Krashen's monitor and Occam's razor. *Applied Linguistics* 5, 79–100.

Gregg, K.R. (2003) The state of emergentism in second language acquisition. *Second Language Research* 19, 95–128.

Gregoric, P. (2007) *Aristotle on the Common Sense*. Oxford: Oxford University Press.

Grossberg, S. and Pearson, L.R. (2008) Laminar cortical dynamics of cognitive and motor working memory, sequence learning and performance: Toward a unified theory of how the cerebral cortex works. *Psychological Review* 115, 677–732.

Hadamard, J. (1954) *An Essay on the Psychology of Invention in the Mathematical Field*. New York: Dover.

Haegens, S., Osipova, D., Oostenveld, R. and Jensen, O. (2010) Somatosensory working memory performance in humans depends on both engagement and disengagement of regions in a distributed network. *Human Brain Mapping* 31, 26–35.

Hagger, M.S., Wood, C., Stiff, C. and Chatzisarantis, N.L.D. (2010) Ego depletion and the strength model of self-control: A meta-analysis. *Psychological Bulletin* 136, 495–525.

Haidt, J. (2001) The emotional dog and its rational tail: A social intuitionist approach to moral judgment. *Psychological Review* 108, 814–834.

Haidt, J. (2012) *The Righteous Mind: Why Good People Are Divided by Politics and Religion*. London: Penguin Books.

Hamann, S. (2003) Nosing in on the emotional brain. *Nature Neuroscience* 6, 106–108.

Hameroff, S.R. and Penrose, R. (1996) Orchestrated reduction of quantum coherence in brain microtubules: A model for consciousness. In S.R. Hameroff, A.W. Kaszniak and A.C. Scott (eds) *Toward a Science of Consciousness: The First Tucson Discussions and Debates* (pp. 507–540). Cambridge, MA: MIT Press.

Han, Z., Park, E.S. and Combs, C. (2008) Textual enhancement of input: Issues and possibilities. *Applied Linguistics* 29, 597–618.

Han, Z.-H. and Peverly, S. (2007) Input processing: A study of *ab initio* learners with multilingual backgrounds. *The International Journal of Multilingualism* 4, 17–37.

Hannula, H., Neuvonen, T., Savolainen, P., Hiltunen, J., Ma, Y.-Y., Antila, H., Salonen, O., Carlson, S. and Pertovaara, A. (2010) Increasing top-down suppression from prefrontal cortex facilitates tactile working memory. *NeuroImage* 49, 1091–1098.

Hardie, W.F.R. (1976) Concepts of consciousness in Aristotle. *Mind* 85, 388–411.

Hardt, O., Einarsson, E.Ö. and Nader, K. (2010) A bridge over troubled water: Reconsolidation as a link between cognitive and neuroscientific memory research traditions. *Annual Review of Psychology* 61, 141–167.

Harley, B. (1989) Functional grammar in French immersion: A classroom experiment. *Applied Linguistics* 10, 331–359.

Harris, J.A., Harris, I.M. and Diamond, M.E. (2001) The topography of tactile working memory. *Journal of Neuroscience* 21, 8262–8269.

Hayes, N.A. and Broadbent, D.E. (1988) Two modes of learning for interactive tasks. *Cognition* 28, 249–276.

Henkin, R.I. and Levy, L.M. (2002) Functional MRI of congenital hyposmia: Brain activation to odors and imagination of odors and tastes. *Journal of Computer Assisted Tomography* 26, 39–61.

Herschensohn, J. and Young-Scholten, M. (eds) (2013) *The Cambridge Handbook of Second Language Acquisition*. Cambridge: Cambridge University Press.

Hill, C. (2009) *Consciousness*. Cambridge: Cambridge University Press.

Howatt, A.P.R. (1984) *A History of English Language Teaching*. Oxford: Oxford University Press.
Hulstijn, J. (2005) Theoretical and empirical issues in the study of implicit and explicit second-language learning: Introduction. *Studies in Second Language Acquisition* 27, 129–140.
Hulstijn, J. and Hulstijn, W. (1984) Grammatical errors as a function of processing constraints and explicit knowledge. *Language Learning* 34, 23–43.
Hupbach, A., Gomez, R., Hardt, O. and Nadel, L. (2007) Reconsolidation of episodic memories: A subtle reminder triggers integration of new information. *Learning and Memory* 14, 47–53.
Hurlburt, R.T. and Akhter, S.A. (2008) Unsymbolized thinking. *Consciousness and Cognition* 17, 1364–1374.
Hyun, J.-S., Woodman, G.F., Vogel, E.K., Hollingworth, A. and Luck, S.J. (2009) The comparison of visual working memory representations with perceptual inputs. *Journal of Experimental Psychology: Human Perception and Performance* 35, 1140–1160.
Izard, C.E. (2009) Emotion theory and research: Highlights, unanswered questions, and emerging issues. *Annual Review of Psychology* 60, 1–25.
Jack, A.I. and Shallice, T. (2001) Introspective physicalism as an approach to the science of consciousness. *Cognition* 79, 161–196.
Jackendoff, R. (1987) *Consciousness and the Computational Mind*. Cambridge, MA: MIT Press.
Jackendoff, R. (1996) How language helps us think. *Pragmatics & Cognition* 4, 1–34.
Jackendoff, R. (1997) *The Architecture of the Language Faculty*. Cambridge, MA: MIT Press.
Jackendoff, R. (1999) The representational structures of the language faculty and their interactions. In C. Brown and P. Hagoort (eds) *The Neurocognition of Language* (pp. 37–70). Oxford: Oxford University Press.
Jackendoff, R. (2002) *Foundations of Language*. Oxford: Oxford University Press.
Jackendoff, R. (2003) Précis of *Foundations of Language: Brain, Meaning, Grammar, Evolution*. *Behavioral and Brain Sciences* 26, 651–707.
Jackendoff, R. (2007) *Language, Consciousness, Culture: Essays on Mental Structure*. Cambridge, MA: MIT Press.
James, W. (1890/1950) *The Principles of Psychology*. New York: Dover.
Jarrold, C. (2001) Applying the working memory model to the study of atypical development. In J. Andrade (ed.) *Working Memory in Perspective* (pp. 126–150). Hove: Psychology Press.
Jiménez, L., Vaquero, J.M.M. and Lupiáñez, J. (2006) Qualitative differences between implicit and explicit sequence learning. *Journal of Experimental Psychology: Learning, Memory, and Cognition* 32, 475–490.
Johnson, M.K. (1992) MEM: Mechanisms of recollection. *Journal of Cognitive Neuroscience* 4, 268–280.
Johnson, M.K. and Reeder, J.A. (1997) Consciousness as meta-processing. In J.D. Cohen and J.W. Schooler (eds) *Scientific Approaches to Consciousness* (pp. 261–293). Mahwah, NJ: Erlbaum.
Johnson-Laird, P.N. (1988) A computational analysis of consciousness. In A.J. Marcel and E. Bisiach (eds) *Consciousness in Contemporary Science* (pp. 357–368). Oxford: Oxford University Press.
Johnston, W.A. and Dark, V.J. (1986) Selective attention. *Annual Review of Psychology* 37, 43–75.
Joliot, M., Ribary, U. and Llinás, R. (1994) Human oscillatory brain activity near 40 Hz coexists with cognitive temporal binding. *Proceedings of the National Academy of Sciences USA* 91, 11748–11751.
Jonides, J., Lewis, R.L., Nee, D.E., Lustig, C.A., Berman, M.G. and Moore, K.S. (2008) The mind and brain of short-term memory. *Annual Review of Psychology* 59, 193–224.

Jung, J. (1971) *The Experimenter's Dilemma*. New York: Harper & Row.
Just, M.A., Cherkassky, V.L., Aryal, S. and Mitchell, T.M. (2010) A neurosemantic theory of concrete noun representation based on the underlying brain codes. *PLoS One* 5(1): e8622. doi:10.1371/journal.pone.0008622
Kadia, K. (1988) The effect of formal instruction on monitored and spontaneous naturalistic interlanguage performance: A case study. *TESOL Quarterly* 22, 509–515.
Kahneman, D. (2011) *Thinking, Fast and Slow*. London: Allen Lane.
Kahneman, D. and Treisman, A. (1984) Changing views of attention and automaticity. In R. Parasuraman and D.R. Davies (eds) *Varieties of Attention* (pp. 29–61). Orlando, FL: Academic Press.
Karmiloff-Smith, A. (1992) *Beyond Modularity: A Developmental Perspective on Cognitive Science*. Cambridge, MA: MIT Press.
Kihlstrom, J.F. (1987) The cognitive unconscious. *Science* 237, 1445–1452.
Kihlstrom, J.F. (1996) Perception without awareness of what is perceived, learning without awareness of what is learned. In M. Velmans (ed.) *The Science of Consciousness: Psychological, Neuropsychological and Clinical Reviews* (pp. 23–46). London: Routledge.
Kihlstrom, J.F. (1997) Consciousness and me-ness. In J.D. Cohen and J.W. Schooler (eds) *Scientific Approaches to Consciousness* (pp. 451–468). Mahwah, NJ: Erlbaum.
Kihlstrom, J.F. and Klein, S.B. (2006) Self-knowledge and self-awareness. *Annals of the New York Academy of Sciences* 818, 4–17.
Kihlstrom, J.F., Dorfman, J. and Park, L. (2007) Implicit and explicit memory and learning. In M. Velmans and S. Schneider (eds) *The Blackwell Companion to Consciousness* (pp. 525–539). Malden, MA: Blackwell.
Kinder, A. and Shanks, D.R. (2001) Amnesia and the declarative/nondeclarative distinction: A recurrent network model of classification, recognition, and repetition priming. *Journal of Cognitive Neuroscience* 13, 648–669.
Kinsbourne, M. (1988) Integrated field theory of consciousness. In A.J. Marcel and E. Bisiach (eds) *Consciousness in Contemporary Science* (pp. 239–256). Oxford: Clarendon Press.
Kinsbourne, M. (1997) What qualifies a representation for a role in consciousness? In J.D. Cohen and J.W. Schooler (eds) *Scientific Approaches to Consciousness* (pp. 335–355). Mahwah, NJ: Erlbaum.
Kinsbourne, M. (2006) From unilateral neglect to the brain basis of consciousness. *Cortex* 42, 869–874.
Knopman, D.S. and Nissen, M.J. (1987) Implicit learning in patients with probable Alzheimer's disease. *Neurology* 37, 784–788.
Koch, C. (2004) *The Quest for Consciousness: A Neurobiological Approach*. Englewood, CO: Roberts and Company.
Koch, C. (2012) *Consciousness: Confessions of a Romantic Reductionist*. Cambridge, MA: MIT Press.
Koch, C. and Greenfield, S. (2007) How does consciousness happen? *Scientific American* 297, 76–83.
Koch, C. and Tononi, G. (2008) Can machines be conscious? *IEEE Spectrum* 45, 54–59.
Koch, C. and Tononi, G. (2011) A test for consciousness. *Scientific American* 304 (6), 44–47.
Koch, C. and Tsuchiya, N. (2007) Attention and consciousness: Two distinct brain processes. *Trends in Cognitive Sciences* 11, 16–22.
Koch, C. and Tsuchiya, N. (2012) Attention and consciousness: Related yet different. *Trends in Cognitive Sciences* 16, 103–105.
Kosslyn, S.M., Ganis, G. and Thompson, W.L. (2001) Neural foundations of imagery. *Nature Reviews Neuroscience* 2, 635–642.
Kowal, M. and Swain, M. (1997) From semantic to syntactic processing: How can we promote it in the immersion classroom? In R.K. Johnson and M. Swain (eds)

Immersion Education: International Perspectives (pp. 284–309). New York: Cambridge University Press.

Krashen, S.D. (1979) A response to McLaughlin: The monitor model: Some methodological considerations. *Language Learning* 29, 151–167.

Krashen, S.D. (1981) *Second Language Acquisition and Second Language Learning.* Oxford: Pergamon.

Krashen, S.D. (1982) *Principles and Practice in Second Language Acquisition.* New York: Pergamon Press.

Krashen, S.D. (1983) Newmark's 'ignorance hypothesis' and current second language acquisition theory. In S. Gass and L. Selinker (eds) *Language Transfer in Language Learning* (pp. 135–153). Rowley, MA: Newbury.

Krashen, S.D. (1985) *The Input Hypothesis: Issues and Implications.* London: Longman.

Krashen, S.D. (1992) Formal grammar instruction...another educator comments... *TESOL Quarterly* 26, 409–411.

Krashen, S.D. (1993) The effect of formal grammar teaching: Still peripheral. *TESOL Quarterly* 27, 722–725.

Krashen, S.D. (2002) *Explorations in Language Acquisition and Use: The Taipei Lectures.* Taipei: Crane.

Krashen, S.D. and Terrell, T.D. (1988) *The Natural Approach: Language Acquisition in the Classroom.* New York: Prentice Hall.

Kuhl, J. (1986) Motivation and information processing: A new look at decision making, dynamic change, and action control. In R.M. Sorrentino and E.T. Higgins (eds) *Handbook of Motivation and Cognition: Foundations of Social Behavior* (pp. 404–434). New York: Guilford Press.

Kurzban, R. (2010) *Why Everyone (Else) Is a Hypocrite: Evolution and the Modular Mind.* Princeton, NJ: Princeton University Press.

Lambon Ralph, M.A., Sage, K., Jones, R.W. and Mayberry, E.J. (2010) Coherent concepts are computed in the anterior temporal lobes. *Proceedings of the National Academy of Sciences USA* 107, 2717–2722.

Lane, R.D. and Nadel, L. (2000) *Cognitive Neuroscience of Emotion.* Oxford: Oxford University Press.

Lang, P.J. (1995) The emotion probe: Studies of motivation and attention. *American Psychologist* 50, 372–385.

Langacker, R. (2008) *Cognitive Grammar: A Basic Introduction.* New York: Oxford University Press.

Lara, A.H., Kennerley, S.W. and Wallis, J.D. (2009) Encoding of gustatory working memory by orbitofrontal neurons. *Journal of Neuroscience* 29, 765–774.

Lardiere, D. (2008) Feature assembly in second language acquisition. In J. Liceras, H. Zobl and H. Goodluck (eds) *The Role of Features in Second Language Acquisition* (pp. 106–140). Mahwah, NJ: Erlbaum.

Lardiere, D. (2009) Some thoughts on the contrastive analysis of features in second language acquisition. *Second Language Research* 25, 173–227.

Lashley, K.S. (1923) The behavioristic interpretation of consciousness I. *Psychological Review* 30, 237–272.

Lawrence, A.D. and Calder, A.J. (2004) Homologizing human emotions. In D. Evans and P. Cruse (eds) *Emotion, Evolution, and Rationality* (pp. 15–47). Oxford: Oxford University Press.

Lazarus, R.S. (1991/1998) Emotion and adaptation. In J.M. Jenkins, K. Oatley and N.L. Stein (eds) *Human Emotions: A Reader* (pp. 38–44). Malden, MA: Blackwell.

Leary, M.R. (2007) Motivational and emotional aspects of the self. *Annual Review of Psychology* 58, 317–344.

LeDoux, J. (1996) *The Emotional Brain: The Mysterious Underpinnings of Emotional Life*. New York: Simon and Schuster.
LeDoux, J. (2002) *Synaptic Self: How Our Brains Become Who We Are*. New York: Viking.
Lee, S.-K. and Huang, H.-T. (2008) Visual input enhancement and grammar learning: A meta-analytic review. *Studies in Second Language Acquisition* 30, 307–331.
Lehrer, J. (2009) *How We Decide*. Boston, MA: Mariner Books.
Lehto, J. (1996) Are executive function tests dependent on working memory capacity? *Quarterly Journal of Experimental Psychology* 49A, 29–50.
Leow, R.P., Egi, T., Nuevo, A.M. and Tsai, Y.-C. (2003) The roles of textual enhancement and type of linguistic item in adult L2 learners' comprehension and intake. *Applied Language Learning* 13(2), 1–16.
Leung, J.H.C. and Williams, J.N. (2011) The implicit learning of mappings between forms and contextually derived meanings. *Studies in Second Language Acquisition* 33, 33–55.
Levelt, W.J.M. (1999) Producing spoken language: A blueprint of the speaker. In C.M. Brown and P. Hagoort (eds) *The Neurocognition of Language* (pp. 83–122). Oxford: Oxford University Press.
Levelt, W.J.M., Roelofs, A. and Meyer, A.S. (1999) A theory of lexical access in speech production. *Behavioral and Brain Sciences* 22, 1–75.
Lewicki, P. (1986) *Nonconscious Social Information Processing*. New York: Academic Press.
Libet, B. (1966) Brain stimulation and conscious experience. In J.C. Eccles (ed.) *Brain and Conscious Experience (Study week September 28 to October 4, 1964, of the Pontifica Academia Scientiarum)* (pp. 165–181). New York: Springer-Verlag.
Libet, B. (1982) Brain stimulation in the study of neuronal functions for conscious sensory experience. *Human Neurobiology* 1, 235–242.
Libet, B., Gleason, C.A., Wright, E.W. and Pearl, D.K. (1983) Time of conscious intention to act in relation to onset of cerebral activity (readiness potential): The unconscious initiation of a freely voluntary act. *Brain* 106, 623–642.
Libet, B., Pearl, D.K., Morledge, D.E., Gleason, C.A., Hosobuchi, Y. and Barbaro, N.M. (1991) Control of the transition from sensory detection to sensory awareness in man by the duration of a thalamic stimulus. *Brain* 114, 1731–1757.
Lightbown, P.M. (1983) Acquiring English L2 in Quebec classrooms. In S.W. Felix and H. Wode (eds) *Language Development at the Crossroads* (pp. 101–120). Tübingen: Gunter Narr.
Lightbown, P.M. (1985) Input and acquisition for second language learners in and out of classrooms. *Applied Linguistics* 6, 263–273.
Lightbown, P.M. (1987) Classroom language as input to second language acquisition. In C.W. Pfaff (ed.) *First and Second Language Acquisition Processes* (pp. 169–187). Cambridge: Newbury.
Lightbown, P.M., Spada, N. and Wallace, R. (1980) Some effects of instruction on child and adolescent ESL learners. In R.C. Scarcella and S.D. Krashen (eds) *Research in Second Language Acquisition: Selected Papers of the Los Angeles Second Language Acquisition Research Forum* (pp. 162–172). Rowley, MA: Newbury.
Linden, D.J. (2011) *Pleasure: How Our Brains Make Junk Food, Exercise, Marijuana, Generosity & Gambling Feel So Good*. Oxford: Oneworld.
Llinás, R. and Ribary, U. (1993) Coherent 40-Hz oscillation characterizes dream state in humans. *Proceedings of the National Academy of Sciences USA* 90, 2078–2081.
Llinás, R.R. and Paré, D. (1991) Of dreaming and wakefulness. *Neuroscience* 44, 521–535.
Llinás, R., Ribary, U., Contreras, D. and Pedroarena, C. (1998) The neuronal basis for consciousness. *Philosophical Transactions: Biological Sciences* 353, 1841–1849.
Lockwood, M. (1989) *Mind, Brain and Quantum: The Compound 'I'*. Oxford: Basil Blackwell.
Loftus, E. (1997) Creating false memories. *Scientific American* 277, 70–75.

Loftus, E.F. (2005) Planting misinformation in the human mind: A 30-year investigation of the malleability of memory. *Learning and Memory* 12, 361–366.

Logan, G.D. (1988) Toward an instance theory of automatization. *Psychological Review* 95, 492–527.

Long, M.H. (1977) Teacher feedback on learner error: Mapping cognitions. In H.D. Brown, C.A. Yorio and R.H. Crymes (eds) *On TESOL '77: Teaching and Learning English as a Second Language: Trends in Research and Practice* (pp. 278–293). Washington, DC: TESOL.

Long, M.H. and Robinson, P. (1998) Focus on form: Theory, research, and practice. In C. Doughty and J. Williams (eds) *Focus on Form in Classroom Second Language Acquisition* (pp. 15–41). New York: Cambridge University Press.

Long, M.H., Inagaki, S. and Ortega, L. (1998) The role of implicit negative feedback in SLA: Models and recasts in Japanese and Spanish. *Modern Language Journal* 82, 357–371.

Lundqvist, D. and Öhman, A. (2005) Caught by the evil eye: Nonconscious information processing, emotion, and attention to facial stimuli. In L.F. Barrett, P.M. Niedenthal and P. Winkielman (eds) *Emotion and Consciousness* (pp. 97–122). New York: Guilford Press.

Lust, B. (2006) *Child Language: Acquisition and Growth*. Cambridge: Cambridge University Press.

Lyster, R. (1994) The effect of functional-analytic teaching on aspects of French immersion students' sociolinguistic competence. *Applied Linguistics* 15, 263–287.

Mack, A. (2003) Inattentional blindness: Looking without seeing. *Current Directions in Psychological Science* 12, 180–184.

Mack, A. and Rock, I. (1998) *Inattentional Blindness*. Cambridge, MA: MIT Press.

Mackey, A. (1999) Input, interaction, and second language development: An empirical study of question formation in ESL. *Studies in Second Language Acquisition* 21, 557–587.

Mackey, A. (2006) Feedback, noticing and instructed second language learning. *Applied Linguistics* 27, 405–430.

Mackey, A. and Philp, J. (1998) Conversational interaction and second language development: Recasts, responses, and red herrings? *Modern Language Journal* 82, 338–356.

MacLean, P.D. (1949) Psychosomatic disease and the "visceral brain": Recent developments bearing on the Papez theory of emotion. *Psychosomatic Medicine: Experimental and Clinical Studies* 11, 338–353.

MacLean, P.D. (1952) Some psychiatric implications of physiological studies on frontotemporal portion of limbic system visceral brain. *Electroencephalography and Clinical Neurophysiology* 4, 407–418.

MacLean, P.D. (1990) *The Triune Brain in Evolution: Role in Paleocerebral Functions*. New York: Plenum Press.

Mager, R.F. (1961) On the sequencing of instructional content. *Psychological Reports* 9, 405–413.

Maia, T.V. and Cleeremans, A. (2005) Consciousness: Converging insights from connectionist modeling and neuroscience. *Trends in Cognitive Sciences* 9, 397–404.

Mameli, M. (2004) The role of emotions in ecological and practical rationality. In D. Evans and P. Cruse (eds) *Emotion, Evolution, and Rationality* (pp. 159–178). Oxford: Oxford University Press.

Mandler, G. (1975) Consciousness: Respectable, useful, and probably necessary. In R.L. Solso (ed.) *Information Processing and Cognition: The Loyola Symposium* (pp. 229–254). Hillsdale, NJ: Erlbaum.

Mandler, G. (1984) *Mind and Body: Psychology of Emotion and Stress*. New York: W.W. Norton.

Mandler, G. (1992) Toward a theory of consciousness. In H.-G. Geissler, S.W. Link and J.T. Townsend (eds) *Cognition, Information Processing, and Psychophysics: Basic Issues* (pp. 43–65). Hillsdale, NJ: Erlbaum.

Mandler, G. (1997) Consciousness redux. In J.D. Cohen and J.W. Schooler (eds) *Scientific Approaches to Consciousness* (pp. 479–498). Mahwah, NJ: Erlbaum.

Mandler, G. (2002) *Consciousness Recovered: Psychological Functions and Origins of Conscious Thought*. Amsterdam: John Benjamins.

Mangan, B. (1993) Taking phenomenology seriously: The "fringe" and its implications for cognitive research. *Consciousness and Cognition* 2, 89–108.

Mangan, B. (2007) Cognition, fringe consciousness, and the legacy of William James. In M. Velmans and S. Schneider (eds) *The Blackwell Companion to Consciousness* (pp. 673–685). Malden, MA: Blackwell.

Marcus, G. (2004) *The Birth of the Mind: How a Tiny Number of Genes Creates the Complexities of Human Thought*. New York: Basic Books.

Marcus, G. (2013) The problem with the neuroscience backlash. *The New Yorker*, 19 June. See http://www.newyorker.com/online/blogs/elements/2013/06/the-problem-with-the-neuroscience-backlash.html (accessed 11 July 2014).

Martin, A. (2007) The representation of object concepts in the brain. *Annual Review of Psychology* 58, 25–45.

Martin, A. and Chao, L.L. (2001) Semantic memory and the brain: Structure and processes. *Current Opinion in Neurobiology* 11, 194–201.

Martin, C.D., Dering, B., Thomas, E.M. and Thierry, G. (2009) Brain potentials reveal semantic priming in both the 'active' and the 'non-attended' language of early bilinguals. *NeuroImage* 47, 326–333.

Mather, G. (2011) *Essentials of Sensation and Perception*. London: Routledge.

Mathews, R.C., Buss, R.R., Stanley, W.B., Blanchard-Fields, F., Cho, J.R. and Druhan, B. (1989) Role of implicit and explicit processes in learning from examples: A synergistic effect. *Journal of Experimental Psychology: Learning, Memory and Cognition* 15, 1083–1100.

May, J. (2001) Specifying the central executive may require complexity. In J. Andrade (ed.) *Working Memory in Perspective* (pp. 261–277). Hove: Psychology Press.

McClelland, J.L. (1997) The neural basis of consciousness: Reflections on Kihlstrom, Mandler, and Rumelhart. In J.D. Cohen and J.W. Schooler (eds) *Scientific Approaches to Consciousness* (pp. 499–509). Mahwah, NJ: Erlbaum.

McClelland, J.L. and Rogers, T.T. (2003) The parallel distributed processing approach to semantic cognition. *Nature Reviews Neuroscience* 4, 310–322.

McClelland, J.L. and Rumelhart, D.E. (1981) An interactive activation model of context effects in letter perception: Part 1. An account of basic findings. *Psychological Review* 88, 375–407.

McGaugh, J.L. (2004) The amygdala modulates the consolidation of memories of emotionally arousing experiences. *Annual Review of Neurosciences* 27, 1–28.

McGaugh, J.L. (2006) Make mild moments memorable: Add a little arousal. *Trends in Cognitive Sciences* 10, 345–347.

McGovern, K. and Baars, B.J. (2007) Cognitive theories of consciousness. In P.D. Zelazo, M. Moscovitch and E. Thompson (eds) *The Cambridge Handbook of Consciousness* (pp. 177–205). Cambridge: Cambridge University Press.

McLaughlin, B. (1978) The Monitor Model: Some methodological considerations. *Language Learning* 28, 309–332.

McLaughlin, B. (1987) *Theories of Second-language Learning*. London: Edward Arnold.

McLaughlin, B. (1990) Restructuring. *Applied Linguistics* 11, 113–128.

Mennim, P. (2007) Long-term effects of noticing on oral output. *Language Teaching Research* 11, 265–280.

Merikle, P.M., Smilek, D. and Eastwood, J.D. (2001) Perception without awareness: Perspectives from cognitive psychology. *Cognition* 79, 115–134.

Meyer, D.E. and Kieras, D.E. (1997) A computational theory of executive cognitive processes and multiple-task performance: Part 1. Basic mechanisms. *Psychological Review* 104, 3–65.

Mikels, J.A., Reuter-Lorenz, P.A., Beyer, J.A. and Fredrickson, B.L. (2008) Emotion and working memory: Evidence for domain-specific processes for affective maintenance. *Emotion* 8, 256–266.

Minsky, M. (1988) *The Society of Mind*. New York: Simon and Schuster.

Mitchell, R. and Myles, F. (2004) *Second Language Learning Theories* (2nd edn). London: Arnold.

Mitchell, T.M., Shinkareva, S.V., Carlson, A., Chang, K.-M., Malave, V.L., Mason, R.A. and Just, M.A. (2008) Predicting human brain activity associated with the meanings of nouns. *Science* 320, 1191–1195.

Miyake, A. and Shah, P. (eds) (1999) *Models of Working Memory: Mechanisms of Active Maintenance and Executive Control*. Cambridge: Cambridge University Press.

Miyake, A., Friedman, N.P., Emerson, M.J., Witzki, A.H. and Howerter, A. (2000) The unity and diversity of executive functions and their contributions to complex "frontal lobe" tasks: A latent variable analysis. *Cognitive Psychology* 41, 49–100.

Montague, P.R., King-Casas, B. and Cohen, J.D. (2006) Imaging valuation models in human choice. *Annual Review of Neuroscience* 29, 417–448.

Montague, R. (2006) *Your Brain Is (Almost) Perfect: How We Make Decisions*. New York: Plume.

Moore, S.C. and Oaksford, M. (eds) (2002) *Emotional Cognition: From Brain to Behaviour*. Amsterdam: Benjamins.

Moors, A. and De Houwer, J. (2006) Automaticity: A theoretical and conceptual analysis. *Psychological Bulletin* 132, 297–326.

Moray, N. (1969) *Attention: Selective Processes in Vision and Hearing*. London: Hutchinson.

Morgan, G. (2005) Biology and behavior: Insights from the acquisition of sign language. In A. Cutler (ed.) *Twenty-First Century Psycholinguistics: Four Cornerstones* (pp. 191–206). Mahwah, NJ: Erlbaum.

Morrison, S.E. and Salzman, C.D. (2010) Re-valuing the amygdala. *Current Opinion in Neurobiology* 20, 221–230.

Morsella, E. (2005) The function of phenomenal states: Supramodular interaction theory. *Psychological Review* 112, 1000–1021.

Moscovitch, M., Vriezen, E. and Goshen-Gottstein, Y. (1993) Implicit tests of memory in patients with focal lesions or degenerative brain disorders. *Handbook of Neuropsychology* 8, 133–173.

Most, S.B., Scholl, B.J., Clifford, E.R. and Simons, D.J. (2005) What you see is what you set: Sustained inattentional blindness and the capture of awareness. *Psychological Review* 112, 217–242.

Mudrik, L., Breska, A., Lamy, D. and Deouell, L.Y. (2011) Integration without awareness: Expanding the limits of unconscious processing. *Psychological Science* 22, 764–770.

Muranoi, H. (2000) Focus on form through interaction enhancement: Integrating formal instruction into a communicative task in EFL classrooms. *Language Learning* 50, 617–673.

Muraven, M. and Baumeister, R.F. (2000) Self-regulation and depletion of limited resources: Does self-control resemble a muscle? *Psychological Bulletin* 126, 247–259.

Müller, V.C. (2005) There must be encapsulated nonconceptual content in vision. In A. Raftopoulos (ed.) *Cognitive Penetrability of Perception: Attention, Action, Strategies, and Bottom-up Constraints* (pp. 157–170). New York: Nova Science.

Myers, D.G. (2002) *Intuition: Its Powers and Perils*. New Haven, CT: Yale University Press.

Nairne, J.S. (2002) Remembering over the short term: The case against the standard model. *Annual Review of Psychology* 53, 53–81.
Nakayama, K. (2000) Modularity in perception, its relation to cognition and knowledge. In E.B. Goldstein (ed.) *Blackwell Handbook of Sensation and Perception* (pp. 736–759). Malden, MA: Blackwell.
Nassaji, H. and Fotos, S. (2004) Current developments in research on the teaching of grammar. *Annual Review of Applied Linguistics* 24, 126–145.
Neisser, U. and Jopling, D.A. (1997) *The Conceptual Self in Context: Culture, Experience, Self-understanding*. Cambridge: Cambridge University Press.
Nicholas, H., Lightbown, P.M. and Spada, N. (2001) Recasts as feedback to language learners. *Language Learning* 51, 719–758.
Nisbett, R.E. and Wilson, T.D. (1977) Telling more than we can know: Verbal reports on mental processes. *Psychological Review* 84, 231–259.
Nissen, M.J. and Bullemer, P. (1987) Attentional requirements of learning: Evidence from performance measures. *Cognitive Psychology* 19, 1–32.
Nissen, M.J., Knopman, D.S. and Schacter, D.L. (1987) Neurochemical dissociation of memory systems. *Neurology* 37, 789–794.
Norman, D.A. (1968) Toward a theory of memory and attention. *Psychological Review* 75, 522–536.
Norris, J.M. and Ortega, L. (2000) Effectiveness of L2 instruction: A research synthesis and quantitative meta-analysis. *Language Learning* 50, 417–528.
Nosofsky, R.N. and Zaki, S.R. (1998) Dissociations between categorization and recognition in amnesic and normal individuals: An exemplar-based interpretation. *Psychological Science* 9, 247–255.
Nørretranders, T. (1998) *The User Illusion: Cutting Consciousness Down To Size*. Trans. Jonathan Sydenham. New York: Penguin.
Oatley, K. (2004) *Emotions: A Brief History*. Malden, MA: Blackwell.
Ornstein, R. (1991) *The Evolution of Consciousness: Of Darwin, Freud, and Cranial Fire: The Origins of the Way We Think*. New York: Touchstone.
Ortony, A., Clore, G.L. and Collins, A. (1988) *The Cognitive Structure of Emotions*. Cambridge: Cambridge University Press.
Overstreet, M. (1998) Text enhancement and content familiarity: The focus of learner attention. *Spanish Applied Linguistics* 2, 229–258.
O'Grady, W. (2005) *Syntactic Carpentry: An Emergentist Approach to Syntax*. Mahwah, NJ: Erlbaum.
Panksepp, J. (1998) *Affective Neuroscience: The Foundations of Human and Animal Emotions*. Oxford: Oxford University Press.
Panksepp, J. (2003a) At the interface of the affective, behavioral, and cognitive neurosciences: Decoding the emotional feelings of the brain. *Brain and Cognition* 52, 4–14.
Panksepp, J. (2003b) Damasio's error? *Consciousness & Emotion* 4, 111–134.
Panksepp, J. (2005) Affective consciousness: Core emotional feelings in animals and humans. *Consciousness and Cognition* 14, 30–80.
Panksepp, J. (2007) Affective consciousness. In M. Velmans and S. Schneider (eds) *The Blackwell Companion to Consciousness* (pp. 114–129). Malden, MA: Blackwell.
Paradis, M. (2004) *A Neurolinguistic Theory of Bilingualism*. Amsterdam: Benjamins.
Paradis, M. (2009) *Declarative and Procedural Determinants of Second Languages*. Amsterdam: Benjamins.
Parasuraman, R. (1998) The attentive brain: Issues and prospects. In R. Parasuraman (ed.) *The Attentive Brain* (pp. 3–15). Cambridge, MA: MIT Press.
Park, E.S. and Han, Z.-H. (2008) Learner spontaneous attention in L2 input processing: An exploratory study. In Z.-H. Han (ed.) *Understanding Second Language Process* (pp. 106–132). Clevedon: Multilingual Matters.

Pashler, H. (1995) Attention and visual perception: Analyzing divided attention. In S.M. Kosslyn and D.N. Osherson (eds) *An Invitation to Cognitive Science, Vol. 2. Visual Cognition* (2nd edn) (pp. 71–100). Cambridge, MA: MIT Press.

Pasternak, T. and Greenlee, M.W. (2005) Working memory in primate sensory systems. *Nature Reviews Neuroscience* 6, 97–107.

Penrose, R. (1989) *The Emperor's New Mind: Concerning Computers, Minds, and the Laws of Physics.* London: Oxford University Press.

Penrose, R. (1994) *Shadows of the Mind: A Search for the Missing Science of Consciousness.* London: Oxford University Press.

Peretz, I. and Hyde, K. (2003) What is specific to music processing? Insights from congenital amusia. *Trends in Cognitive Sciences* 8, 362–367.

Peretz, I. and Zatorre, R.J. (2005) Brain organization for music processing. *Annual Review of Psychology* 56, 89–114.

Perruchet, P. and Pacteau, C. (1990) Synthetic grammar learning: Implicit rule abstraction or explicit fragmentary knowledge? *Journal of Experimental Psychology: General* 119, 264–275.

Perruchet, P. and Pacteau, C. (1991) Implicit acquisition of abstract knowledge about artificial grammars: Some methodological and conceptual issues. *Journal of Experimental Psychology: General* 120, 112–116.

Persaud, N. (2008) How can I tell how I think till I see what I say? *Consciousness and Cognition* 18, 1375.

Persaud, N., McLeod, P. and Cowey, A. (2007) Post-decision wagering objectively measures awareness. *Nature Neuroscience* 10, 257–261.

Phelps, E.A. (2006) Emotion and cognition: Insights from studies of the human amygdala. *Annual Review of Psychology* 57, 27–53.

Pica, T. (1983) Adult acquisition of English as a second language under different conditions of exposure. *Language Learning* 33, 465–497.

Pienemann, M. (1989) Is language teachable? Psycholinguistic experiments and hypotheses. *Applied Linguistics* 10, 52–79.

Pinker, S. (1994) *The Language Instinct: The New Science of Language and Mind.* London: Penguin.

Pinker, S. (1997) *How the Mind Works.* London: Penguin.

Plutchik, R. (1970) Emotions, evolution, and adaptive processes. In M.B. Arnold (ed.) *Feelings and Emotions: The Loyola Symposium* (pp. 3–24). New York: Academic Press.

Plutchik, R. (1980) *Emotion: A Psychoevolutionary Synthesis.* New York: Harper and Row.

Pobric, G., Jefferies, E. and Lambon Ralph, M.A. (2010) Amodal semantic representations depend on both anterior temporal lobes: Evidence from repetitive transcranial magnetic stimulation. *Neuropsychologia* 48, 1336–1342.

Posner, M.I. (1994) Attention: The mechanisms of consciousness. *Proceedings of the National Academy of Sciences USA* 91, 7398–7403.

Posner, M.I. and Boies, S.J. (1971) Components of attention. *Psychological Review* 78, 391–408.

Posner, M.I. and Fan, J. (2008) Attention as an organ system. In J.R. Pomerantz (ed.) *Topics in Integrative Neuroscience: From Cells to Cognition* (pp. 31–61). Cambridge: Cambridge University Press.

Pothos, E.M. (2007) Theories of artificial grammar learning. *Psychological Bulletin* 133, 227–244.

Power, M. and Dalgleish, T. (1997) *Cognition and Emotion: From Order to Disorder.* Hove: Psychology Press.

Prabhu, N.S. (1987) *Second Language Pedagogy.* Oxford: Oxford University Press.

Pribram, K.H. (1971) *Languages of the Brain: Experimental Paradoxes and Principles in Neuropsychology.* Englewood Cliffs, NJ: Prentice-Hall.

Pribram, K.H. and Meade, S.D. (1999) Conscious awareness: Processing in the synapto-dendritic web. *New Ideas in Psychology* 17, 205–214.

Prince, M. (1925) The problem of personality: How many selves have we? *Pedagogical Seminary and Journal of Genetic Psychology* 32, 266–292.

Prinz, J.J. (2007) The intermediate level theory of consciousness. In M. Velmans and S. Schneider (eds) *The Blackwell Companion to Consciousness* (pp. 247–260). Malden, MA: Blackwell.

Pylyshyn, Z. (1999) Is vision continuous with cognition? The case for cognitive impenetrability of visual perception. *Behavioral and Brain Sciences* 22, 341–423.

Pylyshyn, Z. (2003) *Seeing and Visualizing: It's Not What You Think*. Cambridge, MA: MIT Press.

Raftopoulos, A. (2005) Perceptual systems and a viable form of realism. In A. Raftopoulos (ed.) *Cognitive Penetrability of Perception: Attention, Action, Strategies, and Bottom-up Constraints* (pp. 73–106). New York: Nova Science.

Rawson, K.A. (2004) Exploring automaticity in text processing: Syntactic ambiguity as a test case. *Cognitive Psychology* 49, 333–369.

Raynor, J.O. and McFarlin, D.B. (1986) Motivation and the self-system. In R.M. Sorrentino and E.T. Higgins (eds) *Handbook of Motivation and Cognition: Foundations of Social Behavior* (pp. 315–349). New York: Guilford Press.

Reber, A.S. (1989) Implicit learning and tacit knowledge. *Journal of Experimental Psychology: General* 118, 219–235.

Reber, A.S. (1990) On the primacy of the implicit: Comments on Perruchet and Pacteau. *Journal of Experimental Psychology: General* 119, 340–342.

Reber, A.S. (1993) *Implicit Learning and Tacit Knowledge: An Essay on the Cognitive Unconscious*. Oxford: Oxford University Press.

Reiner, A. (1990) An explanation of behavior [Review of *The Triune Brain in Evolution. Role in Paleocerebral Functions* by Paul MacLean]. *Science* 250, 303–305.

Rensink, R.A. (2002) Change detection. *Annual Review of Psychology* 53, 245–277.

Ribary, U., Ioannides, A.A., Singh, K.D., Bolton, J.P.R., Lado, F., Mogilner, A. and Llinás, R. (1991) Magnetic field tomography of coherent thalamocortical 40 Hz oscillations in humans. *Proceedings of the National Academy of Sciences USA* 88, 11037–11041.

Ricciardi, E., Bonino, D., Gentili, C., Sani, L., Pietrinia, P. and Vecchi, T. (2006) Neural correlates of spatial working memory in humans: A functional magnetic resonance imaging study comparing visual and tactile processes. *Neuroscience* 139, 339–349.

Rissman, J. and Wagner, A.D. (2012) Distributed representations in memory: Insights from functional brain imaging. *Annual Review of Psychology* 63, 101–128.

Roberts, I. (1994) Universal Grammar and L1 acquisition. In N.C. Ellis (ed.) *Implicit and Explicit Learning of Languages* (pp. 455–475). London: Academic Press.

Robinson, P. (1995) Attention, memory, and the "noticing" hypothesis. *Language Learning* 45, 283–331.

Robinson, P. (1996a) *Consciousness, Rules, and Instructed Second Language Acquisition*. New York: Peter Lang.

Robinson, P. (1996b) Learning simple and complex second language rules under implicit, incidental, rule-search, and instructed conditions. *Studies in Second Language Acquisition* 18, 27–67.

Robinson, P. (1997) Generalizability and automaticity of second language learning under implicit, incidental, enhanced, and instructed conditions. *Studies in Second Language Acquisition* 19, 223–247.

Robinson, P.J. and Ha, M.A. (1993) Instance theory and second language rule learning under explicit conditions. *Studies in Second Language Acquisition* 15, 413–438.

Roediger, H.L. III. (2003) Reconsidering implicit memory. In J.S. Bowers and C.J. Marsolek (eds) *Rethinking Implicit Memory* (pp. 3–18). Oxford: Oxford University Press.

Roediger, H.L. III and McDermott, K.B. (1993) Implicit memory in normal human subjects. In H. Spinnler and F. Boller (eds) *Handbook of Neuropsychology, Vol. 8* (pp. 63–131). Amsterdam: Elsevier.

Roediger, H.L. III and McDermott, K.B. (1995) Creating false memories: Remembering words not presented in lists. *Journal of Experimental Psychology: Learning, Memory, and Cognition* 21, 803–814.

Roeper, T. (1999) Universal bilingualism. *Bilingualism: Language and Cognition* 2, 169–186.

Rosa, E.M. and Leow, R.P. (2004) Awareness, different learning conditions, and second language development. *Applied Psycholinguistics* 25, 269–292.

Ross, M. (1989) The relation of implicit theories to the construction of personal histories. *Psychological Review* 96, 341–357.

Rossetti, Y., Rode, G. and Boisson, D. (1995) Implicit processing of somaesthetic information: A dissociation between where and how? *NeuroReport* 6, 506–510.

Ruchkin, D.S., Grafman, J., Cameron, K. and Berndt, R.S. (2003) Working memory retention systems: A state of activated long-term memory. *Behavioral and Brain Sciences* 26, 709–777.

Sacks, J.S. (1967) Recognition memory for syntactic and semantic aspects of connected discourse. *Perception and Psychophysics* 2, 437–442.

Sacks, O. (2010) *The Mind's Eye*. New York: Picador.

Salaberry, M.R. (1997) The role of input and output practice in second language acquisition. *Canadian Modern Language Review* 53, 422–451.

Sanz, C. and Leow, R.P. (eds) (2011) *Implicit and Explicit Language Learning: Conditions, Processes, and Knowledge in SLA and Bilingualism*. Washington, DC: Georgetown University Press.

Sanz, C. and Morgan-Short, K. (2004) Positive evidence versus explicit rule presentation and explicit negative feedback: A computer-assisted study. *Language Learning* 54, 35–78.

Saunders, J. and MacLeod, M.D. (2006) Can inhibition resolve retrieval competition through the control of spreading activation? *Memory and Cognition* 34, 307–322.

Sauter, D. (2010) More than happy: The need for disentangling positive emotions. *Current Directions in Psychological Science* 19, 36–40.

Savignon, S.J. (1991) Communicative language teaching: State of the art. *TESOL Quarterly* 25, 261–277.

Savolainen, P., Carlson, S., Boldt, R., Neuvonen, T., Hannula, H., Hiltunen, J., Salonen, O., Ma, Y.-Y. and Pertovaara, A. (2011) Facilitation of tactile working memory by top-down suppression from prefrontal to primary somatosensory cortex during sensory interference. *Behavioural Brain Research* 219, 387–390.

Schachter, J. (1999) Review of *Consciousness, Rules, and Instructed Second Language Acquisition*, by Peter Robinson. *Studies in Second Language Acquisition* 21, 663–664.

Schachter, S. and Singer, J.E. (1962) Cognitive, social, and physiological determinants of emotional state. *Psychological Review* 69, 379–399.

Schacter, D.L. (1990) Toward a cognitive neuropsychology of awareness: Implicit knowledge and anosognosia. *Journal of Clinical and Experimental Neuropsychology* 12, 155–178.

Schacter, D.L. and Tulving, E. (1994) What are the memory systems of 1994? In D.L. Schacter and E. Tulving (eds) *Memory Systems 1994* (pp. 1–38). Cambridge, MA: MIT Press.

Scherer, K.R., Dan, E.S. and Flykt, A. (2006) What determines a feeling's position in affective space? A case for appraisal. *Cognition and Emotion* 20, 92–113.

Schmidt, R. (1993) Awareness and second language acquisition. *Annual Review of Applied Linguistics* 13, 206–226.

Schmidt, R. (1994) Implicit learning and the cognitive unconscious: Of artificial grammars and SLA. In N.C. Ellis (ed.) *Implicit and Explicit Learning of Languages* (pp. 165–209). London: Academic Press.

Schmidt, R. (2010) Attention, awareness, and individual differences in language learning. In W.M. Chan, S. Chi, K.N. Cin, J. Istanto, M. Nagami, J.W. Sew, T. Suthiwan and I. Walker (eds) *Proceedings of CLaSIC 2010*, Singapore, December 2–4 (pp. 721–737). Singapore: National University of Singapore, Centre for Language Studies.

Schmidt, R. and Frota, S.N. (1986) Developing basic conversational ability in a second language: A case study of an adult learner of Portuguese. In R.R. Day (ed.) *Talking to Learn: Conversation in Second Language Acquisition* (pp. 237–326). Rowley, MA: Newbury.

Schmidt, R.W. (1990) The role of consciousness in second language learning. *Applied Linguistics* 11, 129–158.

Schmidt, R.W. (1995) Consciousness and foreign language learning: A tutorial on the role of attention and awareness in learning. In R. Schmidt (ed.) *Attention and Awareness in Foreign Language Learning* (pp. 3–63). Honolulu, HI: Second Language Teaching and Curriculum Center, University of Hawai'i.

Schmidt, R.W. (2001) Attention. In P. Robinson (ed.) *Cognition and Second Language Instruction* (pp. 3–32). Cambridge: Cambridge University Press.

Schneider, W. and Pimm-Smith, M. (1997) Consciousness as a message aware control mechanism to modulate cognitive processing. In J.D. Cohen and J.W. Schooler (eds) *Scientific Approaches to Consciousness* (pp. 65–80). Mahwah, NJ: Erlbaum.

Schneider, W. and Shiffrin, R.M. (1977) Controlled and automatic human information processing: I. Detection, search, and attention. *Psychological Review* 84, 1–66.

Schuchert, S.A. (2004) The neurobiology of attention. In J.H. Schumann, S.E. Crowell, N.E. Jones, N. Lee, S.A. Schuchert and L.A. Wood (eds) *The Neurobiology of Learning: Perspectives from Second Language Acquisition* (pp. 129–158). Mahwah, NJ: Erlbaum.

Schultz, W. (1998) Predictive reward signal of dopamine neurons. *Journal of Neurophysiology* 80, 1–27.

Schumann, J.H. (1978a) *The Pidginization Process: A Model for Second Language Acquisition*. Rowley, MA: Newbury.

Schumann, J.H. (1978b) The acculturation model for second-language acquisition. In R.C. Gingras (ed.) *Second-Language Acquisition and Foreign Language Teaching* (pp. 27–50). Arlington, VA: Center for Applied Linguistics.

Schutter, D.J.L.G. and van Honk, J. (2004) Extending the global workspace theory to emotion: Phenomenality without access. *Consciousness and Cognition* 13, 539–549.

Schwartz, B.D. (1986) The epistemological status of second language acquisition. *Second Language Research* 2, 120–159.

Schwartz, B.D. (1993) On explicit and negative data effecting and affecting competence and linguistic behavior. *Studies in Second Language Acquisition* 15, 147–163.

Schwartz, B.D. and Gubala-Ryzak, M. (1992) Learnability and grammar reorganization in L2A: Against negative evidence causing the unlearning of verb movement. *Second Language Research* 8, 1–38.

Schwartz, B.D. and Sprouse, R.A. (1996) L2 cognitive states and the Full Transfer/Full Access model. *Second Language Research* 12, 40–72.

Schwartz, M.F., Dell, G.S., Martin, N., Gahl, S. and Sobel, P. (2006) A case-series test of the interactive two-step model of lexical access: Evidence from picture naming. *Journal of Memory and Language* 54, 228–264.

Seager, W. (2002) Emotional introspection. *Consciousness and Cognition* 11, 666–687.

Shah, P. and Miyake, A. (1996) The separability of working memory resources for spatial thinking and language processing: An individual differences approach. *Journal of Experimental Psychology: General* 125, 4–27.

Shallice, T. (1972) Dual functions of consciousness. *Psychological Review* 79, 383–393.

Shallice, T. (1988a) *From Neuropsychology to Mental Structure*. Cambridge: Cambridge University Press.
Shallice, T. (1988b) Information-processing models of consciousness: Possibilities and problems. In A.J. Marcel and E. Bisiach (eds) *Consciousness in Contemporary Science* (pp. 305–333). Oxford: Oxford University Press.
Shallice, T. and Cooper, R.P. (2011) *The Organisation of Mind*. Oxford: Oxford University Press.
Shanks, D.R. (2003) Attention and awareness in "implicit" sequence learning. In L. Jiménez (ed.) *Attention and Implicit Learning* (pp. 11–42). Amsterdam: Benjamins.
Shanks, D.R. and Berry, C.J. (2012) Are there multiple memory systems? Tests of models of implicit and explicit memory. *Quarterly Journal of Experimental Psychology* 65, 1449–1474.
Shanks, D.R., Johnstone, T. and Kinder, A. (2002) Modularity and artificial grammar learning. In R.M. French and A. Cleeremans (eds) *Implicit Learning and Consciousness: An Empirical, Philosophical and Computational Consensus in the Making* (pp. 93–120). New York: Psychology Press.
Shanks, D.R. and St. John, M.F. (1994) Characteristics of dissociable human learning systems. *Behavioral and Brain Sciences* 17, 367–447.
Shapiro, K.L., Caldwell, J. and Sorensen, R.E. (1997) Personal names and the attentional blink: A visual "cocktail party" effect. *Journal of Experimental Psychology: Human Perception and Performance* 23, 504–514.
Sharwood Smith, M. (1981) Consciousness-raising and the second language learner. *Applied Linguistics* 2, 159–168.
Sharwood Smith, M. (1991) Speaking to many minds: On the relevance of different types of language information for the L2 learner. *Second Language Research* 7, 118–132.
Sharwood Smith, M. (1993) Input enhancement in instructed SLA: Theoretical bases. *Studies in Second Language Acquisition* 15, 165–179.
Sharwood Smith, M. (2004) In two minds about grammar: On the interaction of linguistic and metalinguistic knowledge in performance. *Transactions of the Philological Society* 102, 255–280.
Sharwood Smith, M. (2007) Understanding attrition within a MOGUL framework. In B. Köpke, M.S. Schmid, M. Keijzer and S. Dostert (eds) *Language Attrition: Theoretical Perspectives* (pp. 39–51). Amsterdam: Benjamins.
Sharwood Smith, M. (2013) Possibilities and limitations of enhancing language input: A MOGUL perspective. In A.G. Benati, M.J. Arche and C. Laval (eds) *The Grammar Dimension in Instructed Second Language Learning* (pp. 36–57). London: Continuum.
Sharwood Smith, M. (2014) Can you learn to love grammar and so make it grow? On the role of affect in L2 development. In L. Aronin and M. Pawlak (eds) *Essential Topics in Applied Linguistics and Multilingualism: Studies in Honor of David Singleton* (pp. 3–20). Berlin: Springer Verlag.
Sharwood Smith, M. and Truscott, J. (2005) Stages or continua in second language acquisition: A MOGUL solution. *Applied Linguistics* 26, 219–240.
Sharwood Smith, M. and Truscott, J. (2006) Full Transfer Full Access: A processing-oriented interpretation. In S. Unsworth, T. Parodi, A. Sorace and M. Young-Scholten (eds) *Paths of Development in L1 and L2 Acquisition: In Honor of Bonnie D. Schwartz* (pp. 201–216). Amsterdam: Benjamins.
Sharwood Smith, M. and Truscott, J. (2008) MOGUL and crosslinguistic influence. In D. Gabryś-Barker (ed.) *Morphosyntactic Issues in Second Language Acquisition* (pp. 63–85). Clevedon: Multilingual Matters.
Sharwood Smith, M. and Truscott, J. (2010) Consciousness and language: A processing perspective. In E.K. Perry, D. Collerton, F.E.N. LeBeau and H. Ashton (eds) *New Horizons in the Neuroscience of Consciousness* (pp. 129–138). Amsterdam: Benjamins.

Sharwood Smith, M. and Truscott, J. (2014) *The Multilingual Mind: A Modular Processing Perspective.* Cambridge: Cambridge University Press.

Sharwood Smith, M. and Truscott, J. (in press) Explaining input enhancement: A MOGUL perspective. *IRAL.*

Sharwood Smith, M., Truscott, J. and Hawkins, R. (2013) Explaining change in transition grammars. In J. Herschensohn and M. Young-Scholten (eds) *The Cambridge Handbook of Second Language Acquisition* (pp. 560–580). Cambridge: Cambridge University Press.

Shepard, R.N. (1990) *Mind Sights: Original Visual Illusions, Ambiguities, and Other Anomalies, With a Commentary on the Play of Mind in Perception and Art.* San Francisco: W.H. Freeman.

Shiffrin, R.M. (1988) Attention. In R.C. Atkinson, R.J. Herrnstein, G. Lindzey and R.D. Luce (eds) *Stevens' Handbook of Experimental Psychology, Volume 2: Learning and Cognition* (2nd edn) (pp. 739–811). New York: Wiley.

Shiffrin, R.M. and Schneider, W. (1977) Controlled and automatic human information processing: II. Perceptual learning, automatic attending, and a general theory. *Psychological Review* 84, 127–190.

Sigman, M. and Dehaene, S. (2006) Dynamics of the central bottleneck: Dual-task and task uncertainty. *PLoS Biology* 4, 1227–1238.

Simard, D. (2009) Differential effects of textual enhancement formats on intake. *System* 37, 124–135.

Simons, D.J. (2000) Attentional capture and inattentional blindness. *Trends in Cognitive Sciences* 4, 147–155.

Simons, D.J. and Rensink, R.A. (2005) Change blindness: Past, present, and future. *Trends in Cognitive Sciences* 9, 16–20.

Smith, C.A. and Ellsworth, P.C. (1985) Patterns of cognitive appraisal in emotion. *Journal of Personality and Social Psychology* 48, 813–838.

Smith, L.B. (2009) Dynamic executives. *Developmental Science* 12, 22–23.

Smith, L.B. and Thelen, E. (2003) Development as a dynamic system. *Trends in Cognitive Sciences* 7, 343–348.

Smith, N. and Tsimpli, I.-M. (1995) *The Mind of a Savant: Language Learning and Modularity.* Oxford: Blackwell.

Snow, M.A., Met, M. and Genesee, F. (1989) A conceptual framework for the integration of language and content in second/foreign language instruction. *TESOL Quarterly* 23, 201–217.

Soon, C.S., Brass, M., Heinze, H.-J. and Haynes, J.-D. (2008) Unconscious determinants of free decisions in the human brain. *Nature Neuroscience* 11, 543–545.

Sorace, A. (2011) Pinning down the concept of "interface" in bilingualism. *Linguistic Approaches to Bilingualism* 1, 1–33.

Sperber, D. (1994) The modularity of thought and the epidemiology of representations. In L.A. Hirschfeld and S.A. Gelman (eds) *Mapping the Mind: Domain Specificity in Cognition and Culture* (pp. 39–67). Cambridge: Cambridge University Press.

Spivey, M.J. and Marian, V. (1999) Cross talk between native and second languages: Partial activation of an irrelevant lexicon. *Psychological Science* 10, 281–284.

Squire, L.R. (1992) Memory and the hippocampus: A synthesis from findings with rats, monkeys and humans. *Psychological Review* 99, 195–231.

Squire, L.R. and Kandel, E.R. (2000) *Memory: From Mind to Molecules.* New York: Scientific American.

Stapp, H. (2007) Quantum mechanical theories of consciousness. In M. Velmans and S. Schneider (eds) *The Blackwell Companion to Consciousness* (pp. 300–312). Malden, MA: Blackwell.

Stoerig, P. and Cowey, A. (1997) Blindsight in man and monkey. *Brain* 120, 535–559.

Storbeck, J. and Clore, G.L. (2007) On the interdependence of cognition and emotion. *Cognition and Emotion* 21, 1212–1237.

Swain, M. (1985) On communicative competence: Some roles for comprehensible input and comprehensible output in its development. In S.M. Gass and C.G. Madden (eds) *Input in Second Language Acquisition* (pp. 235–253). Rowley, MA: Newbury.

Terrell, T.D. (1991) The role of grammar instruction in a communicative approach. *Modern Language Journal* 75, 52–63.

Terrell, T.D., Baycroft, B. and Perrone, C. (1987) The subjunctive in Spanish interlanguage: Accuracy and comprehensibility. In B. VanPatten, T.R. Dvorak and J.F. Lee (eds) *Foreign Language Learning: A Research Perspective* (pp. 119–131). New York: Newbury.

Thagard, P. (2006) *Hot Thought: Mechanisms and Applications of Emotional Cognition*. Cambridge, MA: MIT Press.

Thierry, G. and Wu, Y.J. (2007) Brain potentials reveal unconscious translation during foreign-language comprehension. *Proceedings of the National Academy of Sciences USA* 104, 12530–12535.

Thompson, R.F. (2009) Habituation: A history. *Neurobiology of Learning and Memory* 92, 127–134.

Thompson, R.F. and Madigan, S.A. (2005) *Memory: The Key to Consciousness*. Princeton, NJ: Princeton University Press.

Tong, C., Wolpert, D.M. and Flanagan, J.R. (2002) Kinematics and dynamics are not represented independently in motor working memory: Evidence from an interference study. *Journal of Neuroscience* 22, 1108–1113.

Tononi, G. (2004) An information integration theory of consciousness. *BMC Neuroscience* 5 (42). See http://www.biomedcentral.com/1471-2202/5/42 (accessed 11 July 2014).

Tononi, G. (2007) The information integration theory of consciousness. In M. Velmans and S. Schneider (eds) *The Blackwell Companion to Consciousness* (pp. 287–299). Malden, MA: Blackwell.

Tononi, G. (2008) Consciousness as integrated information: A provisional manifesto. *Biological Bulletin* 215, 216–242.

Tononi, G. (2012) *PHI: A Voyage from the Brain to the Soul*. New York: Pantheon Books.

Tononi, G. and Edelman, G.M. (1998) Consciousness and complexity. *Science* 282, 1846–1851.

Tononi, G. and Koch, C. (2008) The neural correlates of consciousness: An update. *Annals of the New York Academy of Sciences* 1124, 239–261.

Tononi, G. and Sporns, O. (2003) Measuring information integration. *BMC Neuroscience* 4 (31). See http://www.biomedcentral.com/1471-2202/4/31 (accessed 11 July 2014).

Tooby, J. and Cosmides, L. (1992) The psychological foundations of culture. In J.H. Barkow, L. Cosmides and J. Tooby (eds) *The Adapted Mind: Evolutionary Psychology and the Generation of Culture* (pp. 19–136). New York: Oxford University Press.

Towell, R. and Hawkins, R. (1994) *Approaches to Second Language Acquisition*. Clevedon: Multilingual Matters.

Towse, J.N. and Houston-Price, C.M.T. (2001) Reflections on the concept of the central executive. In J. Andrade (ed.) *Working Memory in Perspective* (pp. 240–260). Hove: Psychology Press.

Trahey, M. and White, L. (1993) Positive evidence and preemption in the second language classroom. *Studies in Second Language Acquisition* 15, 181–204.

Truscott, J. (1996) The case against grammar correction in L2 writing classes. *Language Learning* 46, 327–369.

Truscott, J. (1998) Noticing in second language acquisition: A critical review. *Second Language Research* 14, 103–135.

Truscott, J. (2004) The effectiveness of grammar instruction: Analysis of a meta-analysis. *English Teaching & Learning* 28(3), 17–29.

Truscott, J. (2005) The continuing problems of oral grammar correction. *International Journal of Foreign Language Teaching* 1 (2), 17–22. See http://www.tprstories.com/ijflt/IJFLTSpring05.pdf (accessed 11 July 2014).

Truscott, J. (2006) Optionality in second language acquisition: A generative, processing-oriented account. *International Review of Applied Linguistics* 44, 311–330.

Truscott, J. (2007a) The effect of error correction on learners' ability to write accurately. *Journal of Second Language Writing* 16, 255–272.

Truscott, J. (2007b) Grammar teaching and the evidence: A response to Nassaji and Fotos (2004) *International Journal of Foreign Language Teaching*. See http://www.tprstories.com/ijflt/IJFLTJuly07.pdf (accessed 11 July 2014).

Truscott, J. (2013a) Modularity. In P. Robinson (ed.) *The Routledge Encyclopedia of Second Language Acquisition* (pp. 433–435). New York: Routledge.

Truscott, J. (2013b) The MOGUL framework for SLA. In P. Robinson (ed.) *The Routledge Encyclopedia of Second Language Acquisition* (pp. 435–436). New York: Routledge.

Truscott, J. (2014) Multiple grammars and MOGUL. *Second Language Research* 30, 75–78.

Truscott, J. and Sharwood Smith, M. (2004) Acquisition by processing: A modular approach to language development. *Bilingualism: Language and Cognition* 7, 1–20.

Truscott, J. and Sharwood Smith, M. (2011) Input, intake, and consciousness: The quest for a theoretical foundation. *Studies in Second Language Acquisition* 33, 497–528.

Turner, J.H. (2000) *On the Origins of Human Emotions: A Sociological Inquiry into the Evolution of Human Affect*. Stanford, CA: Stanford University Press.

Ullman, M.T. (2005) A cognitive neuroscience perspective on second language acquisition: The declarative/procedural model. In C. Sanz (ed.) *Mind and Context in Adult Second Language Acquisition: Methods, Theory, and Practice* (pp. 141–178). Washington, DC: Georgetown University Press.

Umiltà, C. (1988) The control operations of consciousness. In A.J. Marcel and E. Bisiach (eds) *Consciousness in Contemporary Science* (pp. 334–356). Oxford: Oxford University Press.

Uttl, B., Ohta, N. and Siegenthaler, A.L. (eds) (2006) *Memory and Emotion: Interdisciplinary Perspectives*. Malden, MA: Blackwell.

van Geert, P. (2008) The dynamic systems approach in the study of L1 and L2 acquisition: An introduction. *Modern Language Journal* 92, 179–199.

van Gelder, T. (1998) The dynamical hypothesis in cognitive science. *Behavioral and Brain Sciences* 21, 615–665.

VanPatten, B. (1994) Evaluating the role of consciousness in second language acquisition: Terms, linguistic features & research methodology. *AILA Review* 11, 27–36.

VanPatten, B. (1996) *Input Processing and Grammar Instruction in Second Language Acquisition*. Norwood, NJ: Ablex.

VanPatten, B. (2002) Processing instruction: An update. *Language Learning* 52, 755–803.

VanPatten, B. (2011) Stubborn syntax: How it resists explicit teaching and learning. In C. Sanz and R.P. Leow (eds) *Implicit and Explicit Language Learning: Conditions, Processes, and Knowledge in SLA and Bilingualism* (pp. 9–22). Washington, DC: Georgetown University Press.

VanPatten, B. and Sanz, C. (1995) From input to output: Processing instruction and communicative tasks. In F.R. Eckman, D. Highland, P.W. Lee, J. Mileham and R.R. Weber (eds) *Second Language Acquisition: Theory and Pedagogy* (pp. 169–185). Mahwah, NJ: Erlbaum.

Vogeley, K. and Fink, G.R. (2003) Neural correlates of the first-person perspective. *Trends in Cognitive Sciences* 7, 38–42.

Walker, M.P. and Stickgold, R. (2006) Sleep, memory, and plasticity. *Annual Review of Psychology* 57, 139–166.

Wallach, D. and Lebiere, C. (2003) Implicit and explicit learning in a unified architecture of cognition. In L. Jiménez (ed.) *Attention and Implicit Learning* (pp. 215–250). Amsterdam: Benjamins.

Wallis, J.D. (2007) Orbitofrontal cortex and its contribution to decision-making. *Annual Review of Neuroscience* 30, 31–56.

Wegner, D.M. (2002) *The Illusion of Conscious Will*. Cambridge, MA: MIT Press.

Weinert, R. (1987) Processes in classroom second language development: The acquisition of negation in German. In R. Ellis (ed.) *Second Language Acquisition in Context* (pp. 83–99). Englewood Cliffs, NJ: Prentice-Hall.

Weiskrantz, L. (1986) *Blindsight*. New York: Oxford University Press.

Weiskrantz, L. (2007) The case of blindsight. In M. Velmans and S. Schneider (eds) *The Blackwell Companion to Consciousness* (pp. 175–180). Malden, MA: Blackwell.

White, J. (1998) Getting the learners' attention. In C. Doughty and J. Williams (eds) *Focus on Form in Classroom Second Language Acquisition* (pp. 85–113). Cambridge: Cambridge University Press.

White, L. (1991) Adverb placement in second language acquisition: Some effects of positive and negative evidence in the classroom. *Second Language Research* 7, 133–161.

White, L. (1992) On triggering data in L2 acquisition: A reply to Schwartz and Gubala-Ryzak. *Second Language Research* 8, 120–137.

White, T.L. (1998) Olfactory memory: The long and short of it. *Chemical Senses* 23, 433–441.

Whong, M. (2007) Seeking consensus: Generative linguistics and language teaching. *Leeds Working Papers in Linguistics and Phonetics* 12, 143–155.

Whong, M. (2011) *Language Teaching: Linguistic Theory in Practice*. Edinburgh: Edinburgh University Press.

Wigmore, V., Tong, C. and Flanagan, J.R. (2002) Visuomotor rotations of varying size and direction compete for a single internal model in motor working memory. *Journal of Experimental Psychology: Human Perception and Performance* 28, 447–457.

Williams, J. and Evans, J. (1998) What kind of focus and on which forms? In C. Doughty and J. Williams (eds) *Focus on Form in Classroom Second Language Acquisition* (pp. 139–155). Cambridge: Cambridge University Press.

Williams, J.N. (2005) Learning without awareness. *Studies in Second Language Acquisition* 27, 269–304.

Wills, T.A. and Stoolmiller, M. (2002) The role of self-control in early escalation of substance use: A time-varying analysis. *Journal of Consulting and Clinical Psychology* 70, 986–997.

Winitz, H. (ed.) (1981) *The Comprehension Approach to Foreign Language Instruction*. Rowley, MA: Newbury.

Winke, P.M., Godfroid, A. and Gass, S.M. (2013) Introduction to the special issue: Eye-movement recordings in second language research. *Studies in Second Language Acquisition* 35, 205–212.

Winter, B. and Reber, A.S. (1994) Implicit learning and the acquisition of natural languages. In N. C. Ellis (ed.) *Implicit and Explicit Learning of Languages* (pp. 115–145). London: Academic Press.

Wu, Y.J. and Thierry, G. (2012) Unconscious translation during incidental foreign language processing. *NeuroImage* 59, 3468–3473.

Yasue, K. (1999) Quantum monadology. In S.R. Hameroff, A.W. Kaszniak and D.J. Chalmers (eds) *Toward a Science of Consciousness III: The Third Tucson Discussions and Debates* (pp. 317–327). Cambridge, MA: MIT Press.

Zobl, H. (1995) Converging evidence for the "acquisition-learning" distinction. *Applied Linguistics* 16, 35–56.

Author Index

Aarts, H., 6
Adolphs, R., 24
Akhter, S., 102
Alanen, R., 189
Allport, A., 29
Amaral, L., 92
Anderson, A., 23
Anderson, J., 40, 84, 146
Andrade, J., 58
Ariely, D., 7, 24
Aristotle, 76
Aron, A., 26
Atkinson, R., 42, 58, 65, 76

Baars, B., 4, 6, 25, 28, 29, 30, 31, 42–46,
    47, 48, 51, 58, 59, 61, 62, 64, 66, 67,
    68, 69, 73, 76, 85, 98, 101, 103, 104,
    106, 107, 111–113, 117, 118, 119,
    123, 124, 125, 126, 146
Baddeley, A., 17, 26, 29, 30, 42, 48,
    58–59, 65, 76, 77, 117
Bargh, J., 6, 106
Barrett, H., 30, 31
Barrett, L., 19, 23
Barsalou, L., 80
Batstone, R., 196
Baumeister, R., 6, 25, 237
Bechara, A., 6, 21
Beebe, L., 159, 199
Behrmann, M., 111
Berent, G., 189
Berridge, K., 21
Berry, D., 149
Bialystok, E., 151
Bickerton, D., 2
Bishop, D., 33, 34
Bock, K., 84
Boies, S., 42
Boitano, J., 51
Born, J., 230

Bowers, J., 149
Broadbent, D., 42, 65, 149
Brown, R., 212
Brunel, N., 59
Buchanan, T., 20, 24
Bullemer, P., 140, 149
Burt, M., 131

Calder, A., 20
Calvin, W., 2
Caplan, D., 77
Carr, T., 140, 149
Carroll, S., 157
Carruthers, P., 30, 31, 33, 37, 102
Caston, V., 76
Chabris, C., 109, 110
Chafe, W., 67
Chang, F., 84
Changeux, J.-P., 47
Chao, L., 17
Charland, L., 23
Chomsky, N., 2, 55, 73, 131, 132, 152
Chun, M., 110
Clark, E., 203
Clark, H., 203
Cleeremans, A., 63, 149, 184, 185
Cleland, A., 84
Clore, G., 19
Cohen, J., 94, 116
Cohen, N., 91
Collins, A., 84
Collins, T., 59, 63
Conway, M., 26
Cooney, J., 48–49, 63, 113
Cooper, R., 10, 39, 118
Corder, S., 158, 217
Cosmides, L., 19, 80
Courchène, R., 192
Courtney, S., 17
Cowan, N., 18, 65

Cowey, A., 109
Crick, F., 54–55, 63, 67
Critchley, H., 21
Cruse, P., 19
Csikszentmihaly, M., 120
Culicover, P., 245
Curran, T., 140, 149

Dade, L., 17
Dalgleish, T., 20
Damasio, A., 19, 20, 21, 22, 23, 24, 30, 49–51, 63, 66, 67, 68, 77, 78, 80, 85, 88, 97, 113–114
Dark, V., 29
Davidson, R., 17
Day, E., 139
de Bot, K., 91, 152
De Houwer, J., 106
Dehaene, S., 39, 47–48, 61, 66, 67, 113
DeKeyser, R., 40, 137, 151
Dell, G., 84
Demoulin, S., 20
Denton, D., 85
Destrebecqz, A., 149, 184
Dewaele, J.-M., 195
Diekelmann, S., 230
Dienes, Z., 140
Dijksterhuis, A., 6
Dijkstra, T., 84
Dolan, R., 23
Doughty, C., 139
Driver, J., 29
Du, S., 20
Dulany, D., 149
Dulay, H., 131, 159, 178, 198

Edelman, G., 22, 24, 47, 48, 51–53, 54, 55, 63, 64, 67, 68, 91, 97, 99, 114, 115
Egi, T., 144, 145
Eichenbaum, H., 91
Ellis, N., 42, 143, 151–155, 224, 234
Ellis, R., 133, 138, 139, 145, 151, 152
Ellsworth, P., 22
Engelien, A., 109
Eraña, A., 37
Ericsson, K., 149
Evans, D., 19, 20, 23, 24
Evans, J., 139
Evans, J.S.B.T., 36, 37

Fan, J., 29
Feather, N., 25

Fedorenko, E., 77
Felix, S., 133
Fink, G., 25
Five Graces Group, 152
Flavell, J., 33
Fodor, J., 30, 31, 61, 132
Foster, J., 58
Fotos, S., 145
Frantzen, D., 133, 135
Fredrickson, B., 19
Freeman, W., 15, 69
Frenda, S., 7, 18, 219
Frijda, N., 19, 20, 22
Frota, S., 142, 146, 196
Fuster, J., 17, 18, 59, 65

Gaillard, R., 47
Gailliot, M., 25
Gallistel, C., 10
Garde, M., 109
Gascoigne, C., 189
Gass, S., 161
Gazzaniga, M., 4, 32, 48–49, 63, 66, 113
Gigerenzer, G., 6
Gilbert, D., 6
Glimcher, P., 24
Goldberg, E., 32, 60, 103
Goldin-Meadow, S., 33
Gottfried, J., 17
Gray, J., 23, 24
Green, P., 151
Greenfield, S., 59, 60, 61, 62, 63, 66
Greenlee, M., 17
Greenwald, A., 5, 26, 63, 109
Gregg, K., 136, 137, 140, 152, 153
Gregoric, P., 76
Griffin, Z., 84
Grossberg, S., 17
Gubala-Ryzak, M., 245

Ha, M., 141
Hadamard, J., 5
Haegens, S., 17
Hagger, M., 25
Haidt, J., 36
Hamann, S., 23
Hameroff, S., 60
Han, Z., 189, 190, 191
Hannula, H., 17
Hardie, W., 76
Hardt, O., 18
Harley, B., 133, 139, 245

Harris, J., 17
Hawkins, R., 40
Hayes, N., 149
Hecht, K., 151
Henkin, R., 109
Herschensohn, J., 245
Hill, C., 9
Hitch, G., 17, 76
Houston-Price, C., 29
Howatt, A., 130
Huang, H., 190
Hulstijn, J., 151
Hulstijn, W., 151
Hupbach, A., 18, 229
Hurlburt, R., 102
Hyde, K., 77
Hyun, J.-S., 17

Irwin, W., 17
Izard, C., 19

Jack, A., 39
Jackendoff, R., 15, 30, 32, 55–58, 61, 64, 65, 66, 67, 70, 72, 73, 78, 84, 85, 90, 97, 101, 111, 116–117, 241, 245
James, W., 29, 40, 67
Jarrold, C., 29
Jiménez, L., 149, 184
Johnson, M., 68, 69
Johnson-Laird, P., 39, 42
Johnston, W., 29
Joliot, M., 63
Jonides, J., 17
Jopling, D., 25
Jung, J., 150
Just, M., 17

Kadia, K., 133, 135
Kahneman, D., 7, 24, 36, 106
Kandel, E., 148
Karmiloff-Smith, A., 30
Keele, S., 140
Kieras, D., 29
Kihlstrom, J., 5, 25, 30, 40, 42, 63, 64, 66, 81, 109, 149, 170
Kinder, A., 149
King, A., 10
Kinsbourne, M., 59, 63, 98, 108, 116
Klein, S., 25
Knopman, D., 149
Koch, C., 6, 54, 55, 59, 62, 63, 66, 67, 146
Kosslyn, S., 20, 111

Kowal, M., 145
Krashen, S., 129, 130–131, 132–142, 143, 146, 148, 152, 155, 176, 192, 231, 238
Kuhl, J., 25
Kulik, J., 212
Kurzban, R., 30, 31

Lambon Ralph, M., 80
Lane, R., 19
Lang, P., 23
Langacker, R., 240, 241, 242
Lara, A., 17
Lardiere, D., 172, 221, 246
Larsen-Freeman, D., 152
Lashley, K., 97
Lawrence, A., 20
Lazarus, R., 20
Leary, M., 25
Lebiere, C., 149
LeDoux, J., 17, 19, 20, 36, 85
Lee, S., 190
Lehrer, J., 6, 7
Lehto, J., 30
Leow, R., 152, 190
Leung, J., 151
Levelt, W., 84
Levy, L., 109
Lewicki, P., 6, 149
Libet, B., 6, 122
Lightbown, P., 133, 244, 245
Linden, D., 23, 24
Llinás, R., 63, 64
Lockwood, M., 60
Loftus, E., 7, 18, 26, 84, 219
Logan, G., 106
Long, M., 133, 139, 145
Lundqvist, D., 19, 24
Lust, B., 33
Lyster, R., 139

Mack, A., 29, 109, 110
Mackey, A., 139, 144, 155
MacLean, P., 19
MacLeod, M., 84
Madigan, S., 24
Mager, R., 217
Maia, T., 63
Mameli, M., 23
Mandler, G., 40, 41, 42, 67, 97
Mangan, B., 67, 124
Marcus, G., 10, 31
Marian, V., 207

Marois, R., 110
Marsolek, C., 149
Martin, A., 17, 91
Martin, C., 207
Masicampo, E., 6
Mather, G., 16
Mathews, R., 149
May, J., 29
McClelland, J., 17, 63, 80, 84
McDermott, K., 18, 149
McFarlin, D., 25
McGaugh, J., 24
McGovern, K., 29, 46, 58, 61, 67, 117
McLaughlin, B., 133, 134, 140
Meade, S., 60, 108
Mennim, P., 145
Merikle, P., 5, 63, 109, 170
Meyer, D., 29
Mikels, J., 17
Minsky, M., 4
Mitchell, R., 225
Mitchell, T., 17
Miyake, A., 18, 29, 65, 77
Mogford, K., 33
Montague, R., 22, 24, 94
Moore, S., 19
Moors, A., 106
Moray, N., 29, 110
Morgan, G., 33
Morgan-Short, K., 151
Morrison, S., 22, 24
Morsella, E., 63, 64
Moscovitch, M., 150
Most, S., 110
Mudrik, L., 54
Müller, V., 85
Muranoi, H., 139
Muraven, M., 26
Myers, D., 7
Myles, F., 225

Naccache, L., 47
Nadel, L., 19
Nairne, J., 18
Nakayama, K., 85
Naqvi, N., 21
Nassaji, H., 145
Neisser, U., 25, 109
Nicholas, H., 144
Nisbett, R., 6
Nissen, M., 140, 149
Norman, D., 18

Nørretranders, T., 6
Norris, J., 135, 153, 245
Nosofsky, R., 149

Oaksford, M., 19
Oatley, K., 20
O'Grady, W., 240, 241, 242
Öhman, A., 19, 24
Ornstein, R., 4
Ortega, L., 135, 153, 245
Ortony, A., 20, 22
Over, D., 37
Overstreet, M., 189

Pacteau, C., 149
Palmer, A., 130
Panksepp, J., 19, 68, 85
Paradis, M., 32, 138, 142, 148, 152
Parasuraman, R., 29
Paré, D., 63
Park, E., 189
Pashler, H., 29
Pasternak, T., 17
Pearson, L., 17
Penrose, R., 60
Peretz, I., 17, 77
Perruchet, P., 149
Persaud, N., 6, 102
Peverly, S., 190
Phelps, E., 19, 24
Philp, J., 139, 155
Pica, T., 244
Pickering, M., 84
Pienemann, M., 133, 245
Pimm-Smith, M., 65, 66, 69
Pinker, S., 30, 80, 111
Plutchik, R., 20
Pobric, G., 80
Posner, M., 29, 42, 48
Pothos, E., 149
Power, M., 20
Prabhu, N., 130
Pribram, K., 60, 68, 108
Prince, M., 4
Prinz, J., 55
Pylyshyn, Z., 85

Raftopoulos, A., 85
Rawson, K., 106
Raynor, J., 25
Reber, A., 140, 148, 149
Reeder, J., 68

Reiner, A., 20
Rensink, R., 110
Ribary, U., 63, 64
Ricciardi, E., 17
Rissman, J., 17
Roberts, I., 132
Robinson, P., 141, 145, 151
Rock, I., 29, 109, 110
Roediger, H., 18, 84, 149
Roeper, T., 92
Rogers, T., 17, 80
Rosa, E., 151
Ross, M., 26
Rossetti, Y., 109
Ruchkin, D., 18, 65
Rumelhart, D., 84
Russell, J., 23

Sacks, J., 203
Sacks, O., 35
Salaberry, M., 139
Salzman, C., 22, 24
Sanz, C., 139, 151
Saunders, J., 84
Sauter, D., 83
Savignon, S., 89
Savolainen, P., 17
Schachter, J., 141
Schachter, S., 20
Schacter, D., 40–41, 148
Scherer, K., 20
Schmidt, R., 42, 140, 141, 142, 143,
    144, 145, 146, 147, 150, 158, 160,
    165, 168, 169, 170, 175, 176, 188,
    196, 231
Schneider, W., 65, 66, 69, 106
Schuchert, S., 29
Schultz, W., 94
Schumann, J., 133, 135, 195
Schutter, D., 46
Schwartz, B., 132, 133, 208, 245
Schwartz, M., 84
Seager, W., 19
Shah, P., 18, 65, 77
Shallice, T., 10, 39, 41, 47, 48, 118
Shanks, D., 149
Shannon, C., 53, 69
Shapiro, K., 110
Shapson, S., 139, 244
Sharwood Smith, M., 30, 72, 90, 91,
    92, 95, 141, 142, 188, 189, 195, 196,
    208, 240, 246

Shepard, R., 34
Shiffrin, R., 42, 58, 65, 76, 106
Sigman, M., 48
Simard, D., 189
Simon, H., 149
Simons, D., 109, 110
Singer, J., 20
Smith, C., 22
Smith, L., 26, 91, 152
Smith, N., 33
Snow, M., 178
Sokalski, K., 40
Soon, C., 6
Sorace, A., 246
Sperber, D., 31
Spivey, M., 207
Sporns, O., 53
Sprouse, R., 208
Squire, L., 148
St. John, M., 149
Stapp, H., 60
Stickgold, R., 18, 230
Stoerig, P., 109
Stoolmiller, M., 25
Storbeck, J., 19
Swain, M., 145, 178

Terrell, T., 130, 133, 135, 192, 196
Thagard, P., 10, 23
Thelen, E., 91, 152
Thierry, G., 207
Thompson, R., 24, 104
Tierney, J., 25, 237
Tong, C., 17
Tononi, G., 47, 48, 51, 52, 53–54, 55, 63,
    64, 68, 69, 115
Tooby, J., 19, 80
Towell, R., 40
Towse, J., 29
Trahey, M., 191
Treisman, A., 106
Truscott, J., 30, 72, 90, 91, 92, 95, 135,
    139, 140, 142, 143, 177, 188, 207, 208,
    245, 246
Tsimpli, I., 33
Tsuchiya, N., 146
Tulving, E., 148
Turner, J., 19

Ullman, M., 148
Umiltà, C., 42
Uttl, B., 24

van Geert, P., 91
van Gelder, T., 152
van Heuven, W., 84
van Honk, J., 46
VanPatten, B., 132, 139, 142, 144
Varela, E., 139
Vogeley, K., 25

Wagner, A., 17
Walker, M., 18, 230
Wallach, D., 149
Wallis, J., 24
Wang, X., 59
Waters, G., 77
Wegner, D., 6
Weinert, R., 133, 244
Weiskrantz, L., 109
White, J., 189
White, L., 133, 191, 245
White, T., 17

Whong, M., 72
Wigmore, V., 17
Williams, J., 139
Williams, J.N., 151
Wills, T., 25
Wilson, T., 6
Winitz, H., 192
Winke, P., 243
Winkielman, P., 21
Winter, B., 140
Wu, Y., 207
Wundt, W., 23

Yasue, K., 60
Young-Scholten, M., 245

Zaki, S., 149
Zatorre, R., 17
Zobl, H., 133

Subject Index

acquisition, 1, 2, 16, 21, 25, 28, 32, 33, 34, 37, 71, 92, 95, 130, 131, 141, 142, 143, 144, 146, 148, 151, 152, 153, 155, 157, 158, 172, 176, 178, 193, 207, 208, 222, 225, 226, 231, 234, 235, 239, 240, 241, 243, 245, 246, 248
  See also acquisition by processing theory, acquisition-learning distinction, growth, learning, second language acquisition
acquisition by processing theory (APT), 89–91, 168, 171, 178, 201
acquisition-learning distinction, 130, 131, 132, 133–140, 141, 148, 231
activation, 18, 22, 41, 42, 44, 45, 47, 48, 50, 52, 54, 58, 59, 61–70, 75, 76, 80, 83, 84–86, 87, 88, 90, 92, 93, 94, 95, 96–125, 144, 153, 158, 160, 162, 163, 165, 166, 167, 168, 170, 171, 174, 175, 178, 179, 181, 183, 184, 187, 188, 194, 196, 197, 198, 201, 203, 204, 205, 210, 211, 212, 213, 214, 215, 216, 217, 219, 222, 223, 224, 226, 227, 229, 232, 233, 234, 236, 242, 244, 247, 248
  resting level of, 84, 85, 88, 93, 94, 100, 105, 107, 110, 119, 120, 184, 185, 202, 203, 204, 205, 207, 208, 209, 210, 211, 212, 213, 215, 216, 218, 219, 220, 222, 226
  current level of, 84, 88, 98, 102, 107, 108, 112, 114, 122, 160, 161, 203, 208, 212
  spreading, 40, 84, 163, 180, 206
Activation Hypothesis, 96–111, 120, 125, 183, 212
  statement of, 98
actual domain (of a module), 31

  See also proper domain
affect, 22, 50, 68, 74, 82, 95, 100–101, 157, 158, 166–167, 169, 189, 195–199, 211–212, 213, 216–217, 218, 226–227, 228, 229, 238, 240, 243, 245, 246
  See also emotion, affective structures
affective structures (AfS), 74, 76, 82–83, 85, 88, 93, 94, 100, 101, 102, 103, 118, 119, 122, 123, 125, 166, 169, 171, 177, 195, 198, 204, 210, 212, 216, 222, 226, 227, 228, 229, 237, 239, 246
AfS. *See* affective structures
alien (ALIEN), 82, 178, 179, 181, 200
amygdala, 20, 22, 36
anxiety, 121, 160, 167, 195, 196, 197, 198
apperception, 161, 165, 166
appraisal, 20, 21, 83, 85, 100
APT. *See* acquisition by processing theory
architecture. *See* cognitive architecture
AS. *See* auditory structures
attention, 8, 24, 28–30, 41, 42, 44, 47, 48, 50, 57, 58, 61, 62, 66–67, 69, 70, 85, 86, 97, 99, 106, 109, 110, 114, 116, 117, 138, 140, 142, 143, 145, 146, 156, 160, 161, 162, 176, 194, 231, 242
  in MOGUL, 85–86, 99
attention to the task, 140
auditory structures (AS), 75, 77, 79, 101, 105, 106, 117, 119, 123, 162, 163, 164, 165, 169, 174, 183, 191, 205, 213, 214, 222, 233, 235, 236, 246
automaticity/automatisation, 104, 106–107, 109, 136, 137, 142, 152, 153, 185–187, 188, 202, 209–210, 214–215, 237, 244
awareness. *See* consciousness

binding problem, 77
blindsight, 109
blueprint metaphor, 31, 239, 240
Braille, 26, 161
brain, 3, 5, 10, 11, 17, 18, 19, 20, 21, 22, 24, 27, 29, 32, 35, 38, 39, 41, 42, 47, 48, 49, 50, 51, 52, 55, 58, 59, 60, 61, 62, 63, 69, 77, 78, 79, 80, 83, 91, 103, 109, 111, 113, 114, 118, 120, 122, 123, 124, 125, 148, 153, 201, 239, 240
built-in syllabus, 217

Chinese, 191, 222, 223
coactivation, 18, 74, 77, 94, 114, 165, 173, 204, 211, 216
cognition, 1, 10, 15, 19, 22, 26, 36, 64, 68, 71, 82, 89, 99, 104, 126, 131, 219, 240, 241
cognitive, 1, 3, 6, 9, 10, 11, 15, 17, 18, 19, 20, 22, 24, 25, 26, 27, 28, 29, 30, 36, 37, 38, 40, 41, 42, 44, 46, 47, 50, 53, 55, 56, 60, 63, 65, 66, 68, 69, 70, 71, 72, 83, 84, 85, 91, 95, 97, 99, 100, 101, 103, 104, 108, 110, 111, 112, 114, 116, 121, 122, 124, 125, 142, 143, 147, 148, 153, 156, 158, 180, 187, 193, 195, 199, 204, 212, 240, 241, 244
cognitive architecture, 15, 37, 39, 40, 42, 56, 65, 68, 71, 72, 73, 74, 84, 85, 93, 97, 99, 120, 125, 153, 157, 199, 202, 242, 245
coherence (in processing/representation), 5, 39, 43, 44, 46, 47, 48, 50, 57, 63, 64, 77, 80, 82, 83, 86, 87, 88, 90, 111, 113, 120, 121, 122, 123
coindexing, 77, 84, 85, 87, 88, 89, 90, 94, 95, 100, 105, 107, 114, 123, 165, 167, 169, 171, 172, 173, 175, 177, 178, 179, 180, 181, 184, 194, 196, 204, 205, 207, 212, 214, 215, 216, 221, 222, 223, 224, 225, 226, 228, 230, 236
communicative competence, 89
competence vs. learned linguistic knowledge, 132
competition, 43, 44, 85, 86–88, 89, 105, 112, 122, 160, 162, 179, 190, 191, 202, 207–209, 210, 211, 219, 220, 221, 222, 224, 240
computational tractability, 33

conceptual structures (CS), 74, 75, 76, 78, 79, 80–81, 82, 83, 85, 86, 87, 88, 89, 90, 94, 95, 100, 101, 102, 103, 105, 106, 112, 117, 118, 123, 124, 140, 157, 158, 163, 164, 165, 167, 169, 170, 171, 172, 173, 174, 176, 177, 179, 180, 181, 183, 185, 186, 187, 192, 193, 194, 197, 198, 204, 205, 206, 207, 208, 209, 210, 211, 213, 214, 215, 216, 217, 218, 222, 223, 224, 225, 227, 228, 229, 230, 232, 233, 235, 236, 237, 239, 241, 245, 246, 247
connectionist, 63, 91
conscious awareness system (CAS), 41
consciousness (awareness)
  and learning (acquisition), 1, 2, 8, 9, 10, 11, 15, 37, 60, 71, 72, 76, 81, 95, 96, 106–107, 126, 129, 130, 132, 136, 137, 140, 141, 142, 143, 144, 146, 155, 168, 174–175, 176, 177, 181, 188, 189, 194, 195, 197, 198, 199–200, 202, 211, 224, 226, 228, 231, 232, 234, 235–238, 243, 244, 245, 246, 248
    See also acquisition-learning distinction, explicit learning, implicit learning, learning, subliminal learning
  definitions of, 3, 9–10
  in MOGUL, 96–126
    See also Activation Hypothesis
  in perception, 4–5, 45, 110, 120, 156, 158, 159–168, 169, 170, 171, 174–175, 176, 177, 178, 179, 183, 201, 202, 206, 210, 224, 235
    See also explicit perception, implicit perception, perception, subliminal perception
  indirect, 99, 120, 164, 165, 167, 171, 181, 183, 193, 194, 207, 211, 214, 215, 218, 224, 228, 230, 236
  objects of, 29, 57, 66, 153
  in MOGUL, 97, 98, 99, 101, 103, 115, 117, 206, 210–211, 214, 224
  of affect/emotion, 19, 20–21, 46, 68, 100–101, 120, 121–122, 166–167, 169, 178, 195, 197–198, 212, 216, 217, 227, 228, 246

Subject Index   285

of self/SELF, 4, 25, 44, 50, 51, 64, 66,
    99, 102, 103, 112, 115, 118, 120,
    122, 167, 211, 225, 246
of value, 40, 49, 57, 67, 100–101, 116,
    166–167, 177, 178, 195, 197–198
theories of, 1, 11, 25, 28, 29, 38–70,
    83, 96, 97, 98, 99, 103, 104, 108,
    110, 111–117, 118, 119, 122, 124,
    125, 126, 147
    major themes in, 38, 41–42, 43,
        50, 55, 59, 60–69, 70, 96, 97,
        98–99, 102, 103
consolidation. *See* memory consolidation
context
    cognitive, 11, 25, 30, 44, 47, 51, 66,
        158
    in MOGUL, 78, 80, 89, 94–95, 118,
        119, 160, 167, 169, 171, 174, 179,
        180, 181, 189, 190, 194, 195, 199,
        202, 204, 208, 210–211, 216, 218,
        223, 225–226, 228, 229, 239, 245
    internal, 158, 194, 208, 211, 217
    in perception, 156, 157, 158, 189
    of learning, 2, 9, 10, 178, 195, 199,
        213, 214, 217, 223, 225, 226,
        238, 246
    of research and testing, 141, 151, 232
core language faculty, 78, 79
cortex, 19, 20, 22, 36, 47, 48, 52, 60, 61,
    62, 63, 77, 78, 80, 83, 113
    See also prefrontal cortex
CS. *See* conceptual structures

declarative knowledge, 19, 41, 135, 148,
    153, 184
decision-making, 21, 23–24, 25, 49, 66,
    86–88, 89, 101
DICE model, 40–41
dishabituation, 106
dominant focus model, 59, 116
dominate (a store), 76, 82, 85, 86–88, 89,
    93, 105, 107, 109, 111, 113, 118, 122,
    123, 125, 160, 161, 162, 163, 164,
    167, 170, 171, 175, 177, 183, 184,
    205, 207, 209, 212
dopamine, 24, 55, 94
dual-process, 36
dynamic core, 47, 48, 51–53, 63,
    114–115

emergentism, 91, 152, 153, 240
emotion, 8, 17, 19–21, 22, 23, 24, 40, 46,
    49, 54, 57, 62, 67, 68, 82, 83, 85, 87,
    89, 100, 120, 121–122, 166, 171, 178,
    197, 204, 212, 239
    See also affect, affective structures
episodic buffer, 17, 58, 65, 77, 117
episodic memory, 19, 39, 41
evolution, 2, 21–22, 31, 33, 49, 50, 68, 80,
    81, 99, 120, 151, 180, 241
executive, 17, 25, 26, 29, 30, 39, 41, 42,
    47, 48, 52, 58, 61, 65–66, 70, 88, 97,
    99, 102, 113
experimenter's dilemma, 150
explicit knowledge, 129, 130, 133, 134,
    135, 137, 138, 139, 148, 149, 151,
    152, 153, 154, 155, 238, 244
explicit learning, 129, 130, 132, 133, 134,
    137, 138, 141, 148, 149, 150, 152,
    153, 155, 181, 182, 183, 184, 186,
    199, 224, 230, 231
explicit memory, 19
explicit perception, 181, 182, 183,
    184, 199
explicit processing, 153, 189, 190,
    192, 224
extramodular, 81, 155, 169, 177, 180, 181,
    188, 190, 191, 192, 194, 198, 199,
    200, 202, 209, 213, 214, 215, 216,
    217, 218, 227, 228, 229, 233, 234

face recognition, 31, 35, 219
Feature Assembly Hypothesis, 172
feature values, 92, 172, 206, 221
fire together, wire together, 204, 209
flashbulb memories, 212
flow, 120
follow-up representations, 160, 161–162,
    163, 164, 165, 166, 168, 170–171,
    174, 175, 176, 182, 183, 187, 192,
    235, 245
framework, 9, 11, 19, 28, 30, 37, 43, 46,
    54–55, 66, 68, 70, 71, 72, 73, 76, 77,
    78, 80, 81, 95, 96, 97, 98, 99, 103,
    104, 108, 110, 113, 114, 115, 122,
    125, 125, 126, 150, 155, 156, 168,
    169, 172, 176, 197, 199, 202, 218,
    219, 240, 241, 242, 243, 245,
    246, 247
frequency, 152, 203, 204, 222
    internal/external distinction, 204
fringe, 67
full transfer full access, 208
functional categories, 80, 171, 172–173,
    187, 204, 205–206, 207, 208–209,
    220, 221, 222, 224, 227, 246

286 Subject Index

functional specialization, 16, 28, 34–37, 41, 43, 61, 69, 72, 73, 74, 77, 81, 131, 148, 174, 177, 185–186, 215, 241, 242, 245, 247, 248

generalizations, 145, 214, 216
global broadcasting, 43–44, 45, 46, 63, 64, 111, 112, 126
global neuronal workspace, 39, 47–48, 113
global workspace (GW), 29, 31, 43, 44, 45, 46, 47, 53, 61, 63, 64, 67, 76, 85, 111, 112, 125
Global Workspace Theory (GW Theory), 42–46, 59, 98, 111–113, 115, 116, 119
goals, 10, 11, 19, 26, 28, 29, 30, 44, 45, 47, 49, 66, 67, 69, 75, 81, 86, 89, 94, 96, 99, 101, 157, 179, 193, 213, 217, 234, 237, 238
growth, 91, 93, 131, 132, 175, 191, 245
GW. *See* global workspace, Global Workspace Theory

habituation, 104–106, 108, 109, 110
holistic theories of consciousness, 38, 59–60, 61, 68, 108, 116
homunculus, 26, 29, 30

identity, 28, 225
image (Damasio's), 50, 51, 78, 97, 113, 114
immersion, 178, 179, 198
implicit knowledge, 19, 40, 129, 133, 134, 138, 143, 149, 152, 153, 154, 247
implicit learning, 1, 84, 129, 133, 140, 141, 144, 147–155, 181–188, 199, 231, 243, 246–248
implicit memory, 19, 40
implicit perception, 182, 183, 184–5, 199, 215
index, 74, 76, 82, 84, 88, 90, 93, 94, 95, 102, 107, 172, 173, 178, 194, 195, 203, 204, 205, 209, 210, 211, 212, 216, 218, 222, 223, 226, 228
inflection, 72, 161
information integration, 53–54, 55, 115
informativeness, 44, 46, 68, 69, 70, 96, 99, 103–111, 125, 126
innateness, 2, 22, 30, 33, 34, 73, 79, 81, 93, 94, 119, 131, 152, 153, 155, 187, 215, 238–242
inattentional blindness, 47, 109, 110

input, 2, 8, 10, 11, 16, 18, 31, 32, 32, 34, 40, 41, 44, 49, 51, 52, 60, 68, 72, 75, 77, 78, 79, 82, 83, 84, 86, 87, 90, 91, 92, 93, 95, 97, 99, 101, 106, 107, 108, 109, 129, 131, 136, 140, 141, 142, 143, 144, 145, 146, 149, 152, 153, 155, 156–200, 203, 204, 205, 206, 207, 208, 209, 210, 214, 215, 220, 221, 223, 224, 226, 227, 228, 229, 231, 233, 235, 236, 238, 239, 243, 246, 247
input enhancement, 72, 142, 188–199, 235
input flood, 189, 190–191
input preferences, 159, 178–179, 180, 181, 198–199
instruction. *See* teaching
intake, 142, 156, 158–159
integrated information. *See* information integration
interfaces, 73, 74, 75, 76, 78, 79, 84, 86, 89, 90, 105, 112, 113, 114, 125, 173, 174, 180, 193, 204, 206, 236, 241
intermediate levels theory, 55–58, 116–117
Irish, 172

Japanese, 136, 225

language comprehension, 84, 87, 92, 189, 192, 193, 196, 197, 198, 205, 206, 208, 222, 227, 232, 233, 235, 236, 238
language module, 32, 74, 78–80, 81, 132, 140, 148, 155, 157, 160, 164, 171, 174, 175, 176, 177, 180, 181, 186, 187, 188, 190, 192, 193, 194, 198, 200, 203, 204, 205, 206, 207, 210, 213, 214, 215, 217, 218, 220, 222, 224, 225, 227, 228, 229, 230, 232, 233, 234, 235, 236, 238, 239, 241, 243, 244, 245, 246, 247, 248
  looseness of the term, 78
  not equivalent to 'language', 78, 79
language production, 84, 87, 92, 134, 136, 141, 178, 179, 180, 196, 197, 198, 202, 205, 208, 212–213, 217–218, 223, 227, 228–229, 233, 234, 236
learned linguistic knowledge. *See* competence
learning, 1, 2, 3, 5, 6, 8, 9, 10, 11, 15, 16, 18, 19, 20, 21, 22, 23, 24, 26, 28, 33,

34, 37, 38, 46, 52, 60, 62, 71, 72, 73, 76, 79, 81, 82, 83, 84, 89, 90, 91, 92, 93, 94, 95, 96, 106, 126, 129, 130, 131, 132, 140, 141, 142, 143, 144, 146, 147, 148, 149, 150, 151, 152, 153, 154, 155, 156, 157, 160, 161, 168, 170, 172, 175, 176, 177, 178, 180, 181, 182, 183, 184, 186, 187, 189, 192, 193, 194, 195, 196, 197, 199, 201, 202, 203, 205, 206, 207, 208, 211, 213, 214, 218, 220, 221, 222, 223, 224, 225, 226, 227, 228, 230, 231, 232, 234, 235, 236, 237, 238, 239, 240, 242, 243, 244, 245, 246, 247
   associative, 93, 94
   See also acquisition, acquisition-learning distinction, growth, second language acquisition, acquisition by processing theory
learning mechanisms, rejection of, 148, 240, 247
levels of explanation, 10, 11, 63
limbic system, 19, 22, 54, 83, 94
limited capacity, 63, 123
local, 18, 47, 48, 52, 53, 54, 55, 61, 63, 64, 79, 115
long-term memory (LTM), 17, 18, 59, 65, 67, 73, 76, 98, 201
LTM. *See* long-term memory

memory consolidation, 18, 24, 152, 156, 174, 186, 193, 201, 202–218, 219, 222, 224, 225, 226, 227, 229, 230
   fast-track consolidation, 212
memory restructuring, 18, 52, 156, 174, 186, 201, 202, 214, 218–229, 230
memory store, 15, 18, 37, 42, 58, 64–65, 70, 97
   in MOGUL, 72, 73, 74, 75, 76, 77, 78, 79, 80, 81, 82, 83, 84, 85, 86, 87, 88, 89, 90, 94, 95, 97, 98, 109, 111, 112, 113, 114, 118, 125, 161, 162, 163, 169, 172, 173, 180
message aware control mechanism, 69
metalinguistic, 28, 72, 78, 80, 132, 157, 216
modularity, 30–37, 41, 60, 61–62, 70, 77, 79, 132, 136, 238–242
MOGUL, 11, 43, 71–95, 140, 144, 150, 155, 156, 157, 158, 159, 168, 169, 172, 176, 178, 183, 185, 189, 192, 194, 195, 196, 200, 202, 203, 204, 212, 218, 219, 237, 239, 240, 241, 242, 243, 245, 246, 247
   and consciousness, 96–126
Monitor Model, 129, 130–131
moral judgements, 36
morphology, 5, 28, 72, 78, 164
morphosyntax, 30, 78, 132, 164, 222, 234, 243
motivation, 2, 23, 25, 49, 225, 237
motor structures (MS), 78, 85, 86, 87, 88, 101, 106, 107, 118, 209, 210, 239
MS. *See* motor structures
Multiple-Entry, Modular Memory System (MEM), 68–69
multistore units, 171, 173–174, 204, 205

natural selection, 10, 21, 31, 73, 81
native speaker, 172, 178, 179, 195, 199
neural correlates of consciousness, 54, 55
neurobiological framework, 54–55
neuromodulators, 52, 55, 59, 61
neuron, 47, 52, 53, 55, 59, 60, 61, 62, 63, 91, 122
   See also global neuronal workspace
neuroscience, 1, 3, 10, 47, 77, 88, 155
NH. *See* Noticing Hypothesis
no-interface position, 138, 232
noise in the data, 92, 173
nothing special assumption, 2, 144, 148, 155, 176, 239, 241
noticing, 1, 129, 132, 142–147, 150, 152, 153, 155, 158, 182, 188, 246
   in MOGUL, 164–166, 168, 175–177
noticing the gap, 146–147, 166
Noticing Hypothesis (NH), 142–146, 175–177
Num(ber), 172, 174, 187, 205, 206, 207, 208, 209, 221, 222

optionality, 72, 92, 95, 207, 208
output, 2, 8, 10, 16, 35, 41, 56, 69, 75, 76, 116, 125, 187, 196, 212, 213, 217, 227, 229, 233, 234, 236
   practice, 130, 212, 213, 217, 227, 228, 229
   pushed, 229

pain, 22, 23, 49
parsimony, 2, 69, 96, 99, 103, 125, 183, 242
passive, 192, 193, 233
perception, 16, 20, 51, 58, 69, 87, 110, 120, 145, 155, 156–200, 201, 202,

205, 206, 210, 212, 220, 221, 224, 229, 235, 240, 242
  See also subliminal perception, implicit perception, explicit perception
perceptual bias of consciousness, 45, 46, 57, 98, 119, 125
perceptual output structures (POpS), 73, 74, 75, 76–78, 79, 80, 82, 83, 84, 85, 88, 89, 98, 101, 102, 103, 105, 106, 108, 109, 110, 111, 112, 113, 114, 115, 116, 117, 118, 120, 121, 122, 123, 124, 125, 156, 157, 159, 160, 161, 162, 163, 164, 165, 167, 169, 170, 171, 174, 175, 177, 181, 182, 183, 184, 185, 186, 191, 196, 206, 207, 214, 215, 216, 224, 228, 233, 239, 242, 247
phi, 53
phonetics, 27, 28
phonological structures (PS), 56, 74, 75, 78, 79, 85, 87, 89, 101, 117, 157, 171, 172, 173, 174, 180, 187, 191, 204, 205, 206, 208, 218, 221, 222, 223, 224, 225, 229, 230, 233, 239, 241, 243, 246
plasticity, 32
pleasure, 22, 24, 49, 83
POpS. *See* perceptual output structures
pragmatics, 27, 28, 78, 169, 246
prefrontal cortex, 22, 25, 35, 36, 47, 48, 66, 103
priming, 84, 86, 109, 184, 215
primitives, 32, 73, 75, 79, 81, 82, 239, 247
procedural knowledge, 19, 41, 148, 152, 153
processing, 2, 4, 5, 6, 8, 11, 15, 16, 17, 18, 20, 21, 29, 30, 31, 37, 38, 39, 40, 41, 42, 43, 44, 48, 50, 55, 56, 57, 60, 61, 64, 66, 67, 68, 69, 71, 72, 73, 74, 75, 76, 77, 80, 81, 83–89, 90, 91, 93, 94, 95, 97, 99, 100, 101, 102, 103, 104, 105, 107, 108, 109, 110, 111, 112, 113, 115, 116, 117, 118, 120, 121, 122, 123, 124, 125, 129, 149, 152, 153, 154, 156, 157, 158, 159, 160, 161, 162, 163, 164, 168, 169, 170, 171, 172, 173, 174, 176, 177, 180, 181, 182, 183, 184, 185, 186, 187, 188, 189, 190, 191, 192, 199, 201, 202, 203, 205, 206, 207, 209, 210, 211, 212, 213, 215, 216, 218, 220, 221, 222, 223, 224, 225, 226, 227, 228, 229, 233, 235, 240, 241, 242, 243, 244, 246, 247
processor, 15, 32, 37, 39, 41, 43, 44, 45, 46, 47, 57, 65, 69, 72, 73, 74, 75, 77, 78, 79, 80, 81, 82, 83, 85, 86, 87, 88, 89, 90, 91, 97, 105, 106, 107, 108, 109, 111, 112, 117, 124, 159, 168, 169, 170, 173, 174, 181, 182, 184, 185, 186, 187, 188, 203, 205, 206, 208, 210, 215, 219, 223, 227, 229, 233, 239, 242, 247
prodrop, 92
pronunciation, 161, 172, 204
proper domain (of a module), 31
  See also actual domain
PS. *See* phonological structures

quality of representations, 149, 184, 185, 187, 215, 247
quantum theories of consciousness, 38, 60, 61

reactivation, 95, 203, 204, 205, 207, 229
redundancy effects, 104, 108, 109, 110
re-entrant, 52, 55, 115, 122
reinforcement, 94
representation, 10, 11, 15, 16, 18, 22, 25, 26, 27, 28, 29, 30, 33, 37, 39, 40, 41, 42, 43, 44, 45, 46, 47, 48, 50, 55, 56, 57, 58, 59, 63, 64, 65, 66, 67, 68, 69, 72, 73, 74, 75, 76, 77, 78, 79, 80, 81, 82, 83, 84, 85, 86, 87, 88, 89, 90, 91, 92, 93, 94, 95, 97, 98, 99, 100, 101, 102, 103, 104, 105, 106, 107, 108, 109, 110, 111, 112, 113, 114, 115, 116, 117, 118, 119, 120, 121, 122, 123, 124, 125, 139, 149, 152, 153, 156, 157, 158, 159, 160, 161, 162, 163, 164, 165, 166, 167, 168, 169, 170, 171, 172, 173, 174, 175, 176, 177, 178, 179, 180, 181, 182, 183, 184, 185, 186, 187, 188, 189, 190, 191, 192, 193, 194, 195, 196, 197, 198, 199, 201, 202, 203, 204, 205, 206, 207, 208, 209, 210, 211, 212, 213, 214, 215, 216, 217, 218, 219, 220, 221, 222, 223, 224, 225, 226, 227, 228, 229, 230, 232, 233, 234, 235, 236, 237, 238, 239, 240, 241, 242, 243, 245, 246, 247, 248
representational Darwinism, 91, 203, 213, 220, 221
reproduction, 10, 22, 49

resting level. *See* activation
restructuring. *See* memory restructuring
rightness (feeling of), 67, 100, 101, 102, 124, 166, 177, 179, 181, 183, 193, 197
rules of language, 34, 134, 136, 137, 145, 169, 193, 214, 234

salience, 52, 53, 57, 91, 101, 189, 190, 191, 192, 194, 196, 235
scene (Edelman's), 51–52, 53, 97, 114, 115
second language acquisition (SLA), 1, 11, 29, 38, 40, 42, 96, 129, 131, 132, 133, 142, 143, 147, 148, 150, 151, 152, 153, 155, 157, 158, 176, 195, 231
self, 4, 10, 24–26, 28, 30, 39, 40, 48, 49, 50, 51, 64, 65, 66, 81–82, 88, 89, 94–95, 99, 102, 113, 114, 115, 120, 122, 181, 200, 211, 225, 245, 246
L2 self/SELF, 225
SELF representation, 81, 82, 85, 88, 89, 94, 99, 102, 103, 112, 118, 125, 158, 167, 200, 211, 225, 229, 238, 243
semantic hub, 80
semantics, 19, 27, 28, 40, 55, 80
sensation, 5, 8, 10, 16, 17, 32, 39, 40, 45, 50, 51, 52, 55, 64, 69, 74, 75, 76, 77, 78, 80, 82, 84, 85, 91, 98, 101, 106, 109, 111, 112, 113, 114, 115, 116, 117, 119, 124, 125, 150, 156, 157, 186, 192, 201, 204, 209, 242, 247
serial, 46, 86, 120–122, 123
short-term memory (STM), 17, 14, 42, 56, 57, 58, 61, 64–65, 70, 76, 77, 97, 98
sign language, 26, 33, 34, 79, 161
simple awareness of input, 145, 160, 161, 163, 168, 170, 175, 176, 177, 190, 192, 206, 207
SLA. *See* second language acquisition
SmS. *See* somatosensory structures
Somali, 172
somatic markers, 24, 88
somatosensory structures (SmS), 106, 209
Spanish, 135, 172, 180, 184, 208, 221
spatial, 17, 41, 58
speaker models, 159, 178
spelling, 161, 169, 172, 204, 213
SS. *See* syntactic structures
STM. *See* short-term memory
store. *See* memory store

subliminal learning, 62, 140, 160, 170, 181, 182, 183, 184, 185, 186, 188, 199, 206
subliminal perception, 5, 8, 62, 109, 160, 162, 167, 181, 182, 183, 184, 185, 199, 206, 242
supramodular interaction theory, 63
survival, 1, 10, 20, 21, 22, 23, 49, 50, 83, 84, 85, 125
synchronization, 39, 50, 52, 55, 61, 63, 64, 66, 67, 70, 76, 77, 85, 89, 97, 98, 100, 113, 114, 115, 120, 121, 122, 123, 242
syntactic structures (SS), 74, 78, 79, 85, 87, 89, 92, 101, 157, 164, 171, 172, 173, 174, 180, 181, 186, 187, 193, 204, 205, 206, 208, 209, 218, 221, 222, 223, 224, 225, 227, 229, 230, 233, 235, 236, 239, 241, 243, 245, 246, 247

teaching (instruction), 1, 9, 72, 129–130, 132, 133, 134, 135, 136, 138, 139, 140, 141, 145, 153, 154, 155, 159, 178, 179, 180, 193, 195, 196, 197, 198, 199, 214, 226, 228, 229, 231, 232, 234, 237, 244, 246
thalamocortical system, 47, 48, 52, 54, 55, 63, 64
threshold paradox, 112, 126
theory of mind, 35–36
thought, 58, 85, 102, 119, 124, 237

UG. *See* universal grammar
ultimate attainment, 72, 221
unconscious acquisition, 130, 131, 132, 133, 136, 138, 140, 141, 142, 143, 144, 148, 152, 154, 155, 176, 187, 231, 232, 234, 235, 236, 238
unconscious mind, 3, 4, 7
universal grammar (UG), 33, 34, 72, 78, 79, 93, 129, 130, 131–132, 172, 208, 227, 228, 239, 240, 245, 246
unsymbolized thinking, 102
usage-based, 152

value, 15, 21–24, 25, 40, 47, 49, 50, 52, 53, 54, 57, 61, 67–68, 69, 70, 82, 83, 87, 88, 89, 93–94, 97, 99, 100–101, 113, 114, 115, 116, 125, 156, 157, 158, 159, 160, 166–167, 169, 171, 172, 177–179, 189, 190, 193, 195, 196, 197,

198, 199, 204, 211–212, 216–217, 226–227, 228, 238, 242, 243
See also !val!, !harm!
views of consciousness and human nature, 4–9, 129, 231
visual illusions, 34–35, 36
visual structures (VS), 75, 79, 90, 101, 106, 107, 109, 123, 169, 189, 204, 209, 213, 222, 236, 246
voice in the head (inner speech), 45, 64, 75, 119, 123, 171, 183
VS. *See* visual structures

weak interface position, 138
willpower, 25, 26, 237
WM. *See* working memory
word order, 161, 162, 163, 164, 165, 170, 171, 172, 174, 184, 208, 209, 214, 215, 216, 234
words, 27, 28, 32, 45, 78, 80, 87, 94, 100, 101, 112, 119, 124, 136, 144, 145, 161, 162, 163, 165, 169, 171, 172, 173, 174, 186, 191, 195, 196, 197, 203, 204, 205, 206, 208, 209, 213, 214, 216, 219, 220, 222–224, 234, 235
working memory (WM), 17, 18, 39, 40, 42, 48, 58–59, 65, 76, 77, 95, 116, 117, 152, 154, 201, 243
wrongness (feeling of), 67, 100, 101, 102, 124, 156, 166, 177, 178, 179, 193, 197, 210

!harm!, 83, 88, 89, 93, 94, 100, 101, 124, 125, 166, 167, 177, 178, 179, 195, 196, 197, 210, 217, 226, 227
See also value
!val!, 82, 83, 87, 88, 89, 93, 94, 100, 101, 124, 125, 166, 167, 177, 178, 179, 195, 196, 197, 198, 211, 216, 226, 227, 237
See also value

For Product Safety Concerns and Information please contact our EU Authorised Representative:

Easy Access System Europe

Mustamäe tee 50

10621 Tallinn

Estonia

gpsr.requests@easproject.com

www.ingramcontent.com/pod-product-compliance
Lightning Source LLC
Chambersburg PA
CBHW071158300426
44113CB00009B/1244